Interwar Symphonies and the Imagination

The symphony has long been entangled with ideas of self and value. Though standard historical accounts suggest that composers' interest in the symphony was almost extinguished in the early 1930s, this book makes plain the genre's continued cultural dominance, and argues that the symphony can illuminate issues around space/geography, race, and postcolonialism in Germany, France, Mexico, and the United States. Focusing on a number of symphonies composed or premiered in 1933, this book recreates some of the cultural and political landscapes of an uncertain historical moment – a year when Hitler took power in Germany and the Great Depression reached its peak in the United States. *Interwar Symphonies and the Imagination* asks what North American and European symphonies from the early 1930s can tell us about how people imagined selfhood during a period of international insecurity and political upheaval, of expansionist and colonial fantasies, scientised racism, and emergent fascism.

EMILY MACGREGOR is a British Academy Postdoctoral Fellow in the Music Department, King's College London. She was awarded the 2019 Jerome Roche Prize of the Royal Musical Association for a distinguished article by a scholar at an early stage of their career, and previously held a Marie Curie Global Fellowship. Dr MacGregor appears regularly on BBC Radio 3.

MUSIC IN CONTEXT

Founding editor

Julian Rushton
University of Leeds

General editor

J. P. E. Harper-Scott
Royal Holloway, University of London

The aim of Music in Context is to illuminate specific musical works, repertoires, or practices in historical, critical, socio-economic, or other contexts; or to illuminate particular cultural and critical contexts in which music operates through the study of specific musical works, repertoires, or practices. A specific musical focus is essential, while avoiding the decontextualization of traditional aesthetics and music analysis. The series title invites engagement with both its main terms; the aim is to challenge notions of what contexts are appropriate or necessary in studies of music, and to extend the conceptual framework of musicology into other disciplines or into new theoretical directions.

Books in the series

Simon P. Keefe, *Mozart's Requiem: Reception, Work, Completion*
J. P. E. Harper-Scott, *The Quilting Points of Musical Modernism: Revolution, Reaction, and William Walton*
Nancy November, *Beethoven's Theatrical Quartets: Opp. 59, 74, and 95*
Rufus Hallmark, *'Frauenliebe und Leben': Chamisso's Poems and Schumann's Songs*
Anna Zayaruznaya, *The Monstrous New Art: Divided Forms in the Late Medieval Motet*
Helen Deeming and Elizabeth Eva Leach, *Manuscripts and Medieval Song: Inscription, Performance, Context*
Emily Kilpatrick, *The Operas of Maurice Ravel*
Roderick Chadwick and Peter Hill, *Olivier Messiaen's* Catalogue d'oiseaux: *From Conception to Performance*
Catherine A. Bradley, *Polyphony in Medieval Paris: The Art of Composing with Plainchant*
Daniel M. Grimley, *Delius and the Sound of Place*
Owen Rees, *The Requiem of Tomás Luis de Victoria (1603)*
Nicole Grimes, *Brahms's Elegies: The Poetics of Loss in Nineteenth-Century German Culture*
Jane D. Hatter, *Composing Community in Late Medieval Music: Self-Reference, Pedagogy, and Practice*
Daniel Elphick, *Music behind the Iron Curtain: Weinberg and His Polish Contemporaries*
Emily MacGregor, *Interwar Symphonies and the Imagination: Politics, Identity, and the Sound of 1933*

Interwar Symphonies and the Imagination

Politics, Identity, and the Sound of 1933

EMILY MACGREGOR

King's College London

CAMBRIDGE
UNIVERSITY PRESS

Shaftesbury Road, Cambridge CB2 8EA, United Kingdom

One Liberty Plaza, 20th Floor, New York, NY 10006, USA

477 Williamstown Road, Port Melbourne, VIC 3207, Australia

314–321, 3rd Floor, Plot 3, Splendor Forum, Jasola District Centre,
New Delhi – 110025, India

103 Penang Road, #05–06/07, Visioncrest Commercial, Singapore 238467

Cambridge University Press is part of Cambridge University Press & Assessment,
a department of the University of Cambridge.

We share the University's mission to contribute to society through the pursuit of
education, learning and research at the highest international levels of excellence.

www.cambridge.org
Information on this title: www.cambridge.org/9781009172783
DOI: 10.1017/9781009172776

First published 2023

A catalogue record for this publication is available from the British Library.

Library of Congress Cataloging-in-Publication Data
Names: MacGregor, Emily Jean, 1987– author.
Title: Interwar symphonies and the imagination : politics, identity, and the sound of 1933 /
Emily MacGregor.
Description: [1.] | Cambridge, United Kingdom ; New York : Cambridge University Press,
2023. | Series: Music in context | Includes bibliographical references and index.
Identifiers: LCCN 2022025597 (print) | LCCN 2022025598 (ebook) | ISBN 9781009172783
(hardback) | ISBN 9781009172776 (ebook)
Subjects: LCSH: Symphony – 20th century. | Music – Social aspects – History – 20th century.
| Music – Political aspects – History – 20th century. | Nineteen thirty-three, A.D.
Classification: LCC ML1255 .M17 2023 (print) | LCC ML1255 (ebook) | DDC 784.2/
18409043–dc23/eng/20220531
LC record available at https://lccn.loc.gov/2022025597
LC ebook record available at https://lccn.loc.gov/2022025598

ISBN 978-1-009-17278-3 Hardback

In memory of Philip MacGregor

Contents

Figures

Examples

Preface

Note on the Structure

By way of initial orientation, I offer the following overview of how the book is structured. Chapter 1 is both the introduction to the tight frame around 1933 and a case study, Kurt Weill's Symphony No. 2 (1933–4). Composed as Weill made his escape from Nazi Berlin to Paris and premiered in Amsterdam and New York, it sets up the transatlantic scope of the book. I return to Weill's symphony in light of where the book has been in Chapter 6. In the meantime, Chapter 2 takes us back to Berlin to examine the context for Weill's exile and the fast-changing political and musical terrain precipitated by Hitler's rise to power. Chapters 3 and 4 are primarily set on the other side of the Atlantic, dealing with the legacies of Germanic ideals associated with the symphony in the United States and Mexico. Coming full circle, Chapter 5 then returns to Europe to trace in reverse the journey of Weill's symphony, spotlighting a Parisian symphony premiered in Berlin. In Chapter 6, after, as promised at the outset, revisiting Weill's symphony at its New York premiere, the book arrives at the present day. It argues for the remarkable persistence of the symphonic genre in conferring cultural and political agency. Focusing on the contemporary revival of Florence Price's Symphony in E minor (1931–2), it also suggests the potential of symphonies from the turbulent years around 1933 to invigorate a differently dynamic symphonic landscape.

Translations

Unless otherwise noted, translations are my own.

Acknowledgements

This book could not have been completed without the support and expertise of many others; any errors or oversights, however, are mine. Several mentors shaped the work in fundamental ways. Daniel M. Grimley oversaw this project in its first incarnation, always asking the right, and most difficult, questions. Anne C. Shreffler then guided its remodelling into a book. Albrecht Riethmüller supported my research while I was based in Berlin, and Peter Franklin supervised the project's development in its earliest stages. At Cambridge University Press, I would like to thank Kate Brett and Benedict Taylor, as well as J. P. E. Harper-Scott and Julian Rushton, former editors of Music in Context, for their thoughts and guidance. Thank you, all.

My funding came from the Arts and Humanities Research Council (AHRC); the Deutsche Akademische Austausch Dienst (DAAD); Worcester College, University of Oxford; a Marie Skłodowska-Curie Global Fellowship; and the British Academy.

Many colleagues and friends read drafts of chapters at different stages of the book's development. I would like to mention in particular Harriet Boyd-Bennett, Edwina Christie, Jonathan Cross, Alexander W. Cowan, James Grande, Neil Gregor, George K. Haggett, Monica Hershberger, Lyndsey Hoh, Amanda Hsieh, Julian Johnson, Felipe Ledesma-Nuñez, Natasha Loges, Chris May, David H. Miller, Juliana M. Pistorius, Hannah Proctor, Jesús Ramos-Kittrell, Caitlin Schmid, Arman Schwartz, Anne Searcy, Douglas Shadle, Fiona Smyth, Christabel Stirling, Amy Tobin, Laura Tunbridge, Imaobong Umoren, Paul Watt, Rachel Wood, and Christopher Wiley, as well as the anonymous reviewers for Cambridge University Press.

Much of the research for this project was carried out in Germany and North America, and many research libraries, librarians, and archivists helped bring this book to fruition. In Berlin, I would like to thank Franziska Gulde-Druet at the Stiftung Berliner Philharmoniker and the staff at the Staatliches Institüt für Musikforschung and in the newspaper department of the Staatsbibliothek zu Berlin for their help and advice. In the United States, I am grateful in particular to Robin

Rausch and James Wintle at the Performing Arts Division of the Library of Congress, Washington, DC; to Dave Stein at the Weill-Lenya Research Center, New York; and to Suzanne Lovejoy and Richard Boursey at the Irving S. Gilmore Music Library at Yale University. Thanks also to staff at the New York Public Library, the New York Philharmonic Archives, and the Rosenthal Archives in Chicago. I would like to extend further thanks to the staff of the Oxford University Music Faculty Library, especially Jennifer Legg, and to Liz Berndt-Morris and Kerry Masteller at Harvard Music Library. Lastly, Matt Hill kindly undertook research on my behalf in the Archivo General de la Nación in Mexico City.

I am grateful for particular conversations and/or correspondence over the past few years with Sarah Able, Chelsea Burns, Lucy Caplan, Christopher Chowrimootoo, Suzannah Clark, Jacob Cohen, Sarah Collins, Timothy F. Coombes, Emily I. Dolan, Grace Edgar, Naomi Graber, David Grundy, Carol A. Hess, Jonathan Hicks, Benjamin Korstvedt, Kim H. Kowalke, Carol J. Oja, Roger Parker, Frankie Perry, Hannah Ryley, Leonora Saavedra, Jürgen Schebera, Kay Kaufman Shelemay, and Christina Taylor Gibson.

The book's core ideas were developed within a number of different intellectual communities: Oxford University Music Department; the Kluge Center at the Library of Congress, Washington, DC; the Fakultät für Musik- und Theaterwissenschaft at Freie Universität Berlin; and Harvard University Music Department. I revised the manuscript during postdocs at Royal Holloway, University of London, and King's College London. My thanks to colleagues and friends too numerous to mention by name in those places, whose thoughts and feedback contributed to the shape of my developing arguments. Likewise, I would like to thank intellectual communities meeting at the American Musicological Society, the Royal Musical Association, the Society for American Music, and those who were part of the Hearing Landscapes Critically Network that met in Oxford, Stellenbosch, and at Harvard between 2012 and 2016.

Two chapters of this book present revised versions of material first published elsewhere. A version of Chapter 2 was previously published as 'Listening for the *Intimsphäre*: Recovering Berlin 1933 through Hans Pfitzner's Symphony in C-sharp Minor', in *The Musical Quarterly* 101 (2018): 35–75. Material in Chapter 3 previously appeared in a different form as 'Roy Harris's *Symphony 1933*: Biographical Myth-making and Liberal Myth-building in the American West', in *Journal of*

Musicological Research 38 (2019): 266–284. My thanks to Oxford University Press and to Taylor and Francis.

I am indebted to Liv-Birte Buchmann, Rouven Kunstmann, Linus Schumacher, and Sebastian Wedler for consulting on my translations of German sources, and to Lola San Martín Arbide for advising on my translations from French. Spanish translations were provided by Sirio Canos Donnay and Lola San Martín Arbide, while David and Jonathan Sanchéz gave further Spanish language research support. Linda Bakkum, Anne Hillebrand, Josephine Kahn, Liselotte Snijders, and Juliana M. Pistorius tackled the Dutch materials. The musical examples that I did not put together myself were generously created by Chris May and Alexander Cowan.

Moral support and motivation came from many friends and several academic writing groups, including the online group set up by Sofie Narbed during the pandemic; the Oxford Writing Group, run by Alice Kelly; and an ad hoc group of graduate students, postdocs, and friends willing to join me in my favourite café to write together in the city in which I was based at the time. Thanks to Oliver Bennett for the many phone calls and for encouraging me to get a dog. Not that I needed much encouraging. Jakob Reckhenrich got me through the manuscript's final stages and made me believe it was worth doing.

Finally, and most importantly, I would like to thank my family – Heather, Frederick, and Rory – and my father, Phil, who died in 2019. 'Just finish the book', he would say. And also, 'Don't work too hard.' I hope I've managed to roughly find the balance. His absence is a huge gap.

Abbreviations

Berlin Philharmonic Archive	Stiftung Berliner Philharmoniker, Berlin
Chávez Correspondence	Correspondence and scores belonging to Carlos Chávez, JOB 93–4, New York Public Library Music Division, Astor, Lenox, and Tilden Foundations, New York
Coolidge Collection	Elizabeth Sprague Coolidge Foundation Collection, Music Division, Library of Congress, Washington, DC
Copland Collection	Aaron Copland Collection, Music Division, Library of Congress, Washington, DC
Harris Papers	Roy Harris Papers, Music Division, Library of Congress, Washington, DC
Slonimsky Collection	Nicolas Slonimsky Collection, Music Division, Library of Congress, Washington, DC
Weill-Lenya	Weill-Lenya Research Center, New York

1 | Between Europe and America: Kurt Weill's Symphony in a Suitcase

On 21 March 1933, Kurt Weill fled Berlin, having heard he was on a Nazi blacklist following a wave of arrests of prominent intellectuals that coincided with the Reichstag fire in late February. In his single suitcase was a completed draft of the opening movement of his Second Symphony (or *Symphonic Fantasy*), his first effort at large-scale instrumental composition in ten years, and what would prove to be his final symphonic composition.[1] A commission from the eminent Parisian music patron Princesse Edmond de Polignac in 1932 and originally destined to be premiered in her private salon, it represented the tentative promise of further work in France. Perhaps this was what in part determined his course to Paris. Visiting the previous year, he had been warmly received as the latest bright young thing from Germany. In Berlin he had been hiding out at the home of the couple Caspar and Erika Neher – the former Weill's colleague, the latter Weill's lover – since the beginning of March. Whether Caspar was aware of his wife's liaison with Weill is unclear. The couple drove him across the border; it is hard to imagine the emotional charge in the vehicle.

One of the many people to be tossed out of the political maelstrom of Berlin 1933, Weill then completed his symphony in exile on the outskirts of Paris in 1934, drawing on material from his stage works. According to conventional music-historical scripts, Weill, the socialist and populist theatre composer internationally famed for his works with Bertolt Brecht, should have been an unlikely contributor to this genre; he was negotiating territory historically considered the pinnacle of 'high art' music and home to Beethoven, Brahms, and Bruckner, a genre encumbered by specifically Germanic idealist nationalism, at least since its reception by nineteenth-century ideologues.[2] What is more, the work is challenging for Weill

---

[1] The history of the work's title – and associated questions about its genre status – will be discussed in more depth further on. Throughout this book, the work will be referred to as Symphony No. 2; however, note that the official title *Fantaisie symphonique* or Symphony No. 2 has recently been agreed in preparation for the forthcoming Kurt Weill Edition.

[2] For discussion of the nationalistic ideological colouring of the symphony in early nineteenth-century critical reception, see Sanna Pederson, 'A. B. Marx, Berlin Concert Life and German National Identity', *19th-Century Music* 18 (1994–5): 87–107; Celia Applegate, 'How German Is

biographers.[3] As a salon commission from a wealthy heiress, the symphony was written for a bourgeois world that Weill had previously critiqued.[4] The Symphony No. 2 provokes several questions: why, suddenly and seemingly uncharacteristically, write a *symphony* of all things?[5] And why, to put a finer point on it, at this precise moment turn to the symphonic genre as the darkening German political regime precipitated his escape?

From a broad perspective, this is a book concerned with symphonies in the interwar period. Its more specific concern, though, is how people imagined selfhood in and around a specific year. It argues that, given the symphony's lively intellectual history of entanglement with ideas of the self (or selves), it is a genre uniquely placed to illuminate what thinking about people's sense of self meant in 1933, at a moment of great international insecurity. By taking a number of symphonies composed or premiered in 1933 and applying a transnational lens, it is possible to reclaim some of the fine grain of the cultural and political landscapes of that incredible, uncertain historical moment. The book begins by tracing the international journey of Weill's symphony in exile from its conception to its transatlantic

---

It? Nationalism and the Idea of Serious Music in the Early Nineteenth Century', *19th-Century Music* 21 (1998): 274–96.

[3] Weill's Second Symphony has received only limited critical attention compared to much of his *oeuvre*, being the subject of only a handful of studies to date: Robert Bailey, 'Musical Language and Formal Design in Weill's Symphonies', in *A Stranger Here Myself: Kurt Weill-Studien*, ed. Kim H. Kowalke and Horst Edler (Hindelsheim: Georg Olms Verlag, 1993), 207–15; Christian Kuhnt, '"Das Gegenteil von Pastorale": Anmerkungen zu Kurt Weills 2. Sinfonie', in *Exilmusik: Komposition während der NS-Zeit*, ed. Frederich Geiger and Thomas Schäfer (Hamburg: von Bockel, 1999), 315–32; Jürgen Schebera, 'Amsterdam, 11. Oktober 1934: Einiges zur Uraufführung von Weills *Sinfonie Nr.2*', in *Kurt Weill-Studien*, ed. Nils Grosch, Joachim Lucchesi, and Jürgen Schebera (Stuttgart: M & P Verlag für Wissenschaft und Forschung, 1996), 109–18; Misako Ohta, 'Kurt Weill und Gustav Mahler: Der Komponist Weill als Nachfolger Mahlers', *Gakushūin Daigaku kenkyū ronshū* 2 (1998): 39–58.

[4] See Ronald Taylor, *Kurt Weill: Composer in a Divided World* (London: Simon & Schuster, 1991), 203.

[5] As far as it is possible to infer from the available primary sources, it seems Polignac only commissioned a work for orchestra, and that it was Weill's decision to write a symphony. Sylvia Kahan supplies the most authoritative range of primary sources illuminating this issue. She cites a letter from Weill to his publisher of 7 November 1932 (emphasis added): 'I have . . . received from the Princess Polignac a commission to write her *an orchestra work* to be premiered at her house and to be dedicated to her.' See Sylvia Kahan, *Music's Modern Muse: A Life of Winnaretta Singer Princesse de Polignac* (Rochester: University of Rochester Press, 2003), 292. In her footnotes she mentions a letter from Weill to Lotte Lenya of 29 November 1932 in which Weill writes (emphasis added): '*The symphony* is coming along. La Polignac has already paid me 5,000 francs.' Cited in *Speak Low (When You Speak Love): The Letters of Kurt Weill and Lotte Lenya*, trans. and ed. Kim H. Kowalke and Lys Symonnette (London: Hamish Hamilton, 1996), 105. Kahan, *Music's Modern Muse*, 489.

premieres. The present chapter thus serves two functions: it is both the book's initial case study and its introduction, weaving in and out of the two registers. Then, via a series of five other main symphonic case studies, the book will revisit the Symphony No. 2's international settings to build a sense of the stakes for the genre in those places. The chapters traverse Berlin, Paris, and a slightly more fluid US East Coast nexus centring on New York and Boston, with pit stops in Mexico City and Chicago, to consider some music that today is hardly known, whether by concert-goers or the bulk of musicologists: Hans Pfitzner's Symphony in C♯ minor, Roy Harris's *Symphony 1933*, Florence Price's Symphony in E minor, Aaron Copland's *Short Symphony*, and Arthur Honegger's *Mouvement symphonique n° 3*.

Subjectivity will be a recurrent term in this volume. It is taken to mean a sense of selfhood or consciousness that operates at both individual and collective levels – something that symphonies and symphonic discourse (here meaning written commentary responding to symphonic music) grappled with throughout the nineteenth century and beyond. Alongside illuminating subjectivity in 1933, a central claim is that these largely forgotten symphonies and the specific cultural anxieties they produce offer insights into how people thought about an area with close ideological links to subjectivity – namely, political and aesthetic notions of space.

The nation-state, itself a particular kind of imagined space, has strongly orientated much existing scholarship on symphonies.[6] Symphonies are taught as German or Russian, or American or French, for example. Weill's symphony forms the starting point for this volume because the nation-state so evidently fails it as a hermeneutic frame. A work that reveals the symphony circa 1933 as swept up in political events which had a global reach, Weill's symphony demonstrates clearly that the genre at this time was an international phenomenon. Yet, while looking globally, the composers I consider simultaneously held a critical mirror to their local contexts. Furthermore, Weill's symphony puts a focus on the Germanic aesthetic and philosophical heritage that was the genre's ideological centre of gravity – and, in so doing, on how that heritage policed contemporary

---

[6] For some, it has acted as a hermeneutic limit; for more recent work, it has been a more porous and flexible construct. See, for instance, Andrew Deruchie, *The French Symphony at the Fin de Siècle: Style, Culture, and the Symphonic Tradition* (Rochester: University of Rochester Press, 2013). Although centred on the United States, Douglas W. Shadle's exploration of the nineteenth-century American symphony has an explicit transnational dimension, however; see Shadle, *Orchestrating the Nation: The Nineteenth-Century American Symphonic Enterprise* (New York: Oxford University Press, 2016).

ideas about symphonies, particularly about who was allowed to compose them. I suggest that only if we widen our viewfinder beyond the nation-state and bring these works from 1933 into contact with one another can we understand the deep anxieties they reveal about the genre, and what its instability at this time tells us about corresponding ideas of selfhood and space. After all, this was an era characterised by international mobility and displacement, exchange of ideas and cultures across borders, globalised uncertainty, and international antagonism, when politics brimmed with anxieties about space, personal freedom, and international boundaries. Just what was the symphony in 1933? And what do we think it is today?

When Weill used material from his own expressly political stage works in his symphony, he underlined the genre's status in the early twentieth century as something far beyond a purely musical object. The symphonic genre was a tool of political critique, both embedded within and sceptical of social discourses about exile, high art, internationalism, political reform, and popular culture. These social discourses were transformative for modern notions of subjectivity. In some ways, Weill's work foregrounds the genre's typically modern self-awareness. The symphonic genre itself had become a vehicle by which to reflect at a distance on both the suffocating geographical determinism and the nationalist self-aggrandising that had come to plague it, as well as to lampoon symphonic monumentalism's role in establishing political hegemonies.

Since the genre was no longer one that could sustain the nineteenth century's unabashed idealism, to decide to write a symphony in 1933 was necessarily to negotiate social discourses about mass tastes and markets. Previous scholars have suggested that Weill's work was simply a swiftly turned-out money-maker at a time of dire financial need.[7] His assets in Germany, of course, had been frozen, so the economic case must have been intense. But there is also a sense in which the work seems profoundly sincere. The symphonic genre retained much of its allure and prestige as the litmus test of a composer's capabilities: to what extent, then, was the

---

[7] See Ronald Sanders, *The Days Grow Short: The Life and Music of Kurt Weill* (New York: Limelight Editions, 1985), 203; Kahan, *Music's Modern Muse*, 309, 311; Schebera, 'Amsterdam', 109. Sanders suggests money was a major motivating factor for the symphony. Kahan highlights Weill's letters to Lenya in which he refers to the money he was being paid for the symphony (or waiting to be paid: Weill wrote, 'That beast [Polignac] hasn't given me my money' and 'I'm ready to string her up on one of the pipes of her organ if she doesn't give me my money'), citing Kowalke and Symonnette, *Speak Low*, 104–7 and 111–14. Kahan does not overtly suggest it was a major drive, however. Schebera positions money as important for Weill in this period, but he does not suggest that any financial motivations implied the work's superficiality.

work a conscious transition of musical register and a bid for elevated respect and recognition? Having studied with Ferruccio Busoni, Weill had credentials that rivalled those of any of his more 'serious' orchestral composer contemporaries, and, as he confided cryptically to Lotte Lenya the day after he finished the sketch, he was confident about the work: 'I'm very happy that I can also do something like this better than the others.'[8] Considering the fraught political context and the work's lengthy gestation – uncharacteristically protracted for Weill – some commentators have suggested that his self-quotation from stage works with an overt socialist agenda points towards a reading of the symphony as a powerful social commentary on changing relations between citizens and the State.[9] Why shouldn't this be commensurate with the genre's historically lofty ideals? It is hardly incompatible with financial motivation. Yet, if secondary literature on Weill's work at large has resisted such an interpretation, then this is revealing about the remarkable persistence of twentieth-century perceptions of true symphonic idealism as decontextualised, universal, and, above all, divorced from quotidian economic imperatives.

In the work's programme note, Weill took a playful and non-committal position on the musical content of his symphony, despite its flagrant borrowing from the stage. Perhaps this was a knowing gesture towards just some of these problematics of absolute music – after all, absolute music has always been a category steeped in ideology.[10] As Weill explained:

It is not possible for me to comment on the content of the work since it was conceived as pure musical form. But perhaps a Parisian friend of mine was right when she suggested that an appropriate title would be a word that expressed the opposite of 'pastoral', should such a word exist. I do not know.[11]

Weill's remarks, particularly the reference to 'pastoral', also hint at the work's clear dialogue with the Germanic symphonic tradition. Following

---

[8] Letter from Weill to Lotte Lenya, 16 December 1933, in Kowalke and Symonnette, *Speak Low*, 107.

[9] The following sources endorse a political reading of the symphony, challenging pervasive characterisations of the work that suggest it was simply a popular crowd-pleaser or a superficial sideline contribution to Weill's theatrically orientated *oeuvre* and ideology. See Kuhnt, 'Das Gegenteil von Pastorale'; Schebera, 'Amsterdam'; Stephen Johnson, 'After Mahler: The Central European Symphony in the Twentieth Century', in *A Guide to the Symphony*, ed. Robert Layton (Oxford: Oxford University Press, 1995), 382–401.

[10] Mark Evan Bonds, *Music as Thought: Listening to the Symphony in the Age of Beethoven* (Princeton: Princeton University Press, 2006); Laurenz Lütteken, *Sinfonie als Bekenntnis: Zürcher Festspiel-Symposium 2010* (Kassel: Baerenreiter, 2011), 8–9.

[11] Kurt Weill, programme note in Programme of the Subscription Concert (Bruno Walter/ Concertgebouw Orchestra), 11 October 1934 (hereafter Concertgebouw Programme Note).

eighteenth-century classical symphonic models, the symphony is in three movements – Sonata (*Sostenuto – Allegro molto*), Largo (titled 'Cortège', referencing the funereal slow movement of Beethoven's *Eroica*), and Rondo (*Allegro vivace*) – and is unified by motivic interactions (described by one commentator as 'Lisztian thematic transformations'[12]). These, however, are disguised on the surface level by a sense of disjunction (bear in mind the theatrical *Verfremdungseffekt* developed with Brecht) resulting from the abrupt succession of orchestral gestures and almost cinematic cuts between diverse musical materials that reference multiple historical and contemporary forms. Indeed, Weill's integration of dance structures, march, sonata form, Cortège, and lyrical song invites comparison with Mahler's famed all-embracing attitude to the symphony.[13] Adorno's commentary on Mahler could equally apply to Weill: 'All categories are eroded . . . none are established within unproblematic limits. Their dissolution does not arise from a lack of articulation but revises it: neither the distinct nor the blurred is defined conclusively; both are in suspension.'[14] Also noteworthy – and again referencing the Mahlerian model – is the bittersweet humour with which the work is invested (Adorno calls its Mahlerian instantiation 'gallows humour'):[15] the grotesquerie of the trombone and woodwind glissandos; the faux-militant trumpet fanfares; the impossibly quick triplet motif of the closing bars.[16] The bald repetition of the march for winds in the final movement creates a particular moment of generic fluidity, manipulating the forces present in the orchestra to create a popular-sounding marching band. Given that commentators have hypothesised that the march alludes to the paradox of the menacing yet ludicrous appearance of 'goosestepping Nazis', does the repetition critique the mindlessness of political complicity and critique popular forms as

---

[12] Douglas Jarman, *Kurt Weill: An Illustrated Biography* (London: Orbis, 1982), 94. See also Bailey, 'Musical Language'. Bailey provides an analysis of the symphony's first movement, examining its motivic unity.

[13] Plenty of commentators have done the same, or drawn up other seemingly Mahlerian influences on the work: see, for example, Antony Beaumont, booklet accompanying Kurt Weill, Die Deutsche Kammerphilharmonie Bremen, cond. Antony Beaumont, *Symphony No. 1, Quodlibet, Symphony No. 2*, CD, Chandos Records Ltd, 2006, CHSA 5046, 12; Ohta, 'Kurt Weill und Gustav Mahler'; Jarman, *Kurt Weill*, 95; Jürgen Schebera, *Kurt Weill: An Illustrated Life*, trans. Caroline Murphy (New Haven, CT: Yale University Press, 1995), 223.

[14] Theodor W. Adorno, *Mahler: A Musical Physiognomy*, trans. Edmund Jephcott (Chicago: University of Chicago Press, 1992), 23.

[15] Ibid.

[16] As Stephen Johnson writes in reference to Weill's Second Symphony, 'we should not forget we are dealing with an accomplished ironist here: one who, no less than Mahler, could use popular styles to poignant, disturbing or even downright brutal effect'. Johnson, 'After Mahler', 391.

channels of mass propaganda?[17] A question mark similarly hangs over the C major ending. To tack on a gesture towards notions of purity and simplicity is farcical, and seems to function in the same way as Igor Stravinsky's critique of C major and the assumptions it carries in *Symphony in C* (1938–40). Sibelius's Symphony No. 7 of 1924 notwithstanding, that no symphony could really end in C major with a straight face by 1934 confirms the self-consciousness that haunted the genre.

Initially, a premiere for the symphony was not forthcoming. It was not until August 1934 that Bruno Walter, exiled from Berlin in the same week as Weill, agreed to take up the symphony for performance (under pressure from Weill's advocate and pupil from Berlin Maurice Abravanel).[18] (The events surrounding Walter's exile from Berlin are given further attention in Chapter 2.) Walter was quick to get the ball rolling; the inaugural performance took place in Amsterdam on 11 October 1934, with immediate subsequent performances in The Hague and Rotterdam.[19] A few weeks later, Walter took the work to the United States, presenting it at Carnegie Hall in New York on 13 and 14 December. Weill could not have hoped for a more prestigious opening for his first piece of absolute music in ten years; as he wrote to Lenya, 'I'm afraid the gods will be envious' (the 'envy of the gods' being a jinx).[20] Early insecurities about his ability to develop the right style ('den richtigen Stil') for an orchestral work were long forgotten.[21] After attending the rehearsal for the performance at Amsterdam's Concertgebouw, he appeared to have every reason to remain buoyant, reporting to Lenya: 'Just a quick note. The rehearsal [of the Second Symphony] was wonderful. Walter does it marvellously and everyone is really enthusiastic, especially the *entire orchestra*! It's a good piece and sounds fantastic.'[22]

[17] For example, Beaumont, booklet accompanying Kurt Weill, *Symphony No. 1, Quodlibet, Symphony No. 2*, CD, 12.

[18] See Schebera, 'Amsterdam', 110–11. On 7 June 1934, Walter wrote to Abravanel that he of course had enormous interest in listening to Weill's symphony. Weill-Lenya, series 47.

[19] Atypically for a Polignac commission, the promised private salon performance did not take place until after the premiere. The work was finally performed in the large music room, avenue Henri-Martin, on 24 June 1935. See Kahan, *Music's Modern Muse*, 328.

[20] Schebera, 'Amsterdam', 111.

[21] Kuhnt, 'Das Gegenteil von Pastorale', 318. Kuhnt quotes a letter from Weill to Universal Edition, found photocopied at Weill-Lenya.

[22] Letter from Weill to Lenya, 10 October 1934, in Kowalke and Symonette, *Speak Low*, 145. This letter is frequently cited to confirm Weill's positive attitude to the symphony. See, for example, Kowalke, *Kurt Weill in Europe* (Michigan: Ann Arbor, 1979), 86; Schebera, *Kurt Weill*, 223; Schebera, 'Amsterdam', 114; Bailey, 'Musical Language', 207; Taylor, *Kurt Weill*, 203.

'I Had Prepared Myself for Much Worse Things!'

Weill's optimism, however, was misplaced. He misjudged the complex and restrictive discourses used to police the symphonic genre. The work animated and agitated reviewers, provoking divisive and inconsistent responses, and, if anything, it seemed his *Dreigroschenoper* success stacked the odds against his symphony's chances.[23] Juxtaposed in the programme with Brahms's Fourth Symphony, a mainstay of the repertory, the yardstick against which Weill's symphony was to be measured was especially diminishing. The reviewer for *Eemlanden* reported snidely: 'That was not so bad! I had prepared myself for much worse things! ... Modern, very modern, but funny and fluent, and without sentimentality.'[24] For the most part, however, critics came down even harder on Weill, and a Maastricht newspaper spelled out some major and recurrent qualms:

Kurt Weill is the composer of the *Dreigroschenoper*, and I fear that will remain his fate for years to come. It is no disgrace, of course, though it would be better for him to accept it, rather than attempting to force his talent in this pretty hopeless direction. Because, to be honest, Weill's *Symphonische Symphonie* is not much more than a number of expanded songs. The result? Rather ridiculous. And not only is the song style ill-fitted to symphonic forms; the nature of Weill's music is little suited to absolute music. Weill is a man of the theatre ....[25]

As many questions as the reception raises about the nature of Weill's music, it raises still more about the nature of 'absolute' music. Ultimately, these questions about nature or character seem to point to insidious underlying questions and assumptions about Weill himself – and to judgements about the kinds of people who listened to his music. When, as we will see towards the end of this chapter, the reviewers gendered his 'popular' music as feminine to argue it did not belong in the concert hall, when they criticised his supposedly superficial thematic development, and when they questioned his motivations for writing a symphony, these critics were not reacting solely to aspects of 'pure' music; rather, they were responding to social discourses relating to Weill's popular status and fame, political discourses linked to the socialist message of *Die Dreigroschenoper*, racial

---

[23] The only existing research that has been done on this body of reviews is in a German-language article by Schebera. See Schebera, 'Amsterdam', especially 116.

[24] H. F. K., 'Belangrijke nieuwe muziek in het Concertgebouw: Serge Prokofieff en Kurt Weill', *Eemlanden*, 12 October 1934 (trans. Liselotte Snijders).

[25] 'Weill en Prokofieff – Symphonie in Songs – Prokofieffs derde pianoconcert', *Maast.* (Maastricht newspaper?), 12 October 1934 (trans. Josephine Kahn).

discourses bound up with his Jewish heritage, and to the perceived internationalism of Weill's musical voice (at odds with symphonic, and specifically Germanic, nationalism). What is more, the reviewers did so while communicating their unease about Amsterdam's fringe relationship to Germanic symphonic culture: cultural anxiety about being on the margins.

Crucially, as will be shown by the critical reception of Weill's symphony in Amsterdam, the story of the Weill premiere indicates how symphonies and their discursive contexts blur the borders of those aesthetic, subjective-interior, and political spaces where subjectivity plays out and in relation to which it is reflexively assembled. Yet, since existing literature on symphonies and their discursive contexts in this period lacks a comparative perspective, we begin on the back foot, ill-equipped to approach the Amsterdam reviews, and still less able to compare their subtleties with the reception of Weill's work in New York a few weeks later, where a whole raft of different localised histories and concerns – not to mention attitudes towards Germany – were at play. As the reception begins to disrupt inherited conceits about the symphonic genre's universality, it reveals that serious foundational work piecing together a fuller, more globalised picture of symphonic discourse is still required.

The Symphony in 1933

Weill's Symphony No. 2, Pfitzner's Symphony in C♯ minor, Harris's *Symphony 1933*, Copland's *Short Symphony*, Honegger's *Mouvement symphonique n° 3*, and Price's Symphony in E minor make up a constellation of works that complement one another aesthetically, ideologically, and biographically, overlapping and contrasting in complex and unexpected ways. Together, they hatch more finely a sense of what it is that we are dealing with when we talk about 'the symphony' in the interwar period, and specifically in the pivotal year 1933, when Germany pulled the trigger on a political upheaval whose shockwaves would be felt globally through the twentieth century and beyond. They capture a keener sense of the era and communicate a more capacious vision for the symphonic genre than previous studies. Steering away from the mode of aesthetic survey, as this volume explores how the genre uncovers localised ideas about subjectivity, space, and exclusion, it pursues connections with diverse cultural and political areas: fascism, liberal ideologies, exile, gender, race, imagined geographies, post-colonial anxieties, as well as recording technology, ballet, Classical Greek sculpture, Weimar dialectics, Pan-Americanism.

The kaleidoscopic scope of the symphony's cultural history becomes a way of illuminating the book's central themes.

The transnational dimension here is vital. This book spotlights how fundamentally a transnational perspective is needed fully to understand both the symphonic genre and the localised political and social issues shaping the written discourse emerging in response to symphonies in the years around 1933. Far from a hermetically sealed, purely musical topic, as many previous studies have characterised the genre, in 1933 the symphony was clearly an interdisciplinary phenomenon and a window onto the cultural and political contours of the moment.[26] The focus, therefore, is at times less on the musical works themselves than it is on what the *idea* of the symphony and people's responses to it tell us about the works' settings. I am interested in the symphony as a locus around which a set of critical rhetorics and discourses continually re-emerge and are reconstructed.

Utopian Enlightenment (and typically Germanic) philosophical narratives about sovereignty and space have long been wedded to the symphonic genre. In 1933, political developments applied particular pressure to them, often taking them to breaking point. The year in which Hitler took power and the Great Depression reached its peak, 1933 was a fraught one for politics and economics, concentrating far-reaching social questions that intersect with 'symphonic' issues about selfhood, society, power, and spatial expansionism. This points to the symphony's darker, authoritarian side: to think of the symphony is often to conjure connotations of nationalistic power display or monumentality. Indeed, symphonic ideals have proved flexible allies for both free will and totalitarianism at different times and in

---

[26] The literature concerning symphonies, frequently in the mode of aesthetic survey, is very large, but for a selection of relevant studies see, for instance, Christopher Ballantine, *Twentieth Century Symphony* (London: Dobson, 1983); A. Peter Brown, *The Symphonic Repertoire*, vol. 3A *The European Symphony ca. 1800–ca. 1930: Germany and the Nordic Countries*, vol. 3B *The European Symphony ca. 1800–ca. 1930: Great Britain, Russia, and France*, vol. 4 *The Second Golden Age of the Viennese Symphony: Brahms, Bruckner, Dvořák, Mahler, and Selected Contemporaries* (Bloomington: Indiana University Press, 2002–7); Louise Cuyler, *The Symphony* (New York: Harcourt Brace Jovanovich, 1973); Manuel Gervink, *Die Symphonie in Deutschland und Österreich in der Zeit zwischen den beiden Weltkriegen* (Regensburg: G. Bosse, 1984); Layton, *Guide to the Symphony*; Lütteken, *Sinfonie als Bekenntnis*; Wolfgang Osthoff and Giselher Schubert, *Symphonik 1930–1950: Gattungsgeschichtliche und analytische Beiträge* (Mainz: Schott, 2003); Robert Simpson, *The Symphony: Elgar to the Present Day* (Aylesbury: Penguin Books, 1967); Wolfram Steinbeck and Christoph von Blumröder, *Die Sinfonie im 19. und 20. Jahrhundert* (Laaber: Laaber-Verlag, 2002); Richard Taruskin, *The Oxford History of Western Music*, vol. 3 *The Nineteenth Century*, vol. 4 *The Early Twentieth Century* (Oxford: Oxford University Press, 2005) (hereafter *OHWM*); Arnold Whittall, *Music Since the First World War* (London: Dent, 1977); Arnold Whittall, *Musical Composition in the Twentieth Century* (Oxford: Oxford University Press, 1999).

different places. The spectre of Germany and Austria and the genre's liberal-ist-idealist Germanic heritage looms large throughout this volume. To spot-light the year fascism took hold in Germany brings those Germanic social and political discourses historically associated with the genre to the fore – after all, to quote Karen Painter, 'the symphony was the most German of musical genres'.[27] And yet symphonic monumentalism is only a small part of the story. Spotlighting 1933 is also to spotlight a key moment of contingency, to allow us, if we look closely, paradoxically to see alternative possibilities and critical potentials in this music and in the discussions it generated. This is music that, even if it cannot exceed or overpower some political shifts taking place, may also dissent, music that can communicate visions for alternative realities. Investigating the legacies of Germanic liberalist-idealist discourses in different sociocultural contexts, each chapter investigates how different local political ideologies produce different visions of space and subjectivity, and how the case study symphonies allow us to explore them, along with their contradictions.

By 1933, political news travelled fast through vast cross-continental communications networks, shaping an increasingly globalised cultural consciousness. This generation of composers often seemed just as mobile: US composers Harris and Copland both studied – although they did not overlap – in Paris in the 1920s with Nadia Boulanger; Copland spent 1931–3 hopping between Germany, Morocco, the United States, and Mexico; Mexican composer and conductor Carlos Chávez, a prominent figure in Chapter 4, divided his formative years between New York, Paris, and Mexico City; Price had planned trips to France and England in the early 1950s to hear her works performed and meet with publishers, although ill heath, and then her untimely death, meant neither went ahead; Honegger was a Swiss-German working in Paris; even arch-German Pfitzner fre-quently conducted abroad (although the Nazi government put limits on his travel from 1933). But for the symphony, things were perhaps moving too fast, and too far. It was a genre that had lost confidence in its ideals; for many, symphonies seemed culturally out of time – a closed chapter, locked to cultural worlds and values that had died as the nineteenth century rolled into the twentieth. Other symphonic composers expressed this distance with self-reflective critique. The year 1933 thus seems a particularly problematic and unstable moment for a genre so insistent on its absolute, self-contained status, and for pervasive narratives about the symphony as

---

[27] Karen Painter, *Symphonic Aspirations: German Music and Politics, 1900–1945* (Cambridge, MA: Harvard University Press: 2007), 3.

nationally particularised and geographically deterministic. Yet that sense of instability is also invigorating, giving us pause to look anew at how the symphony can be unfolded into transnational, cross-disciplinary spheres, inviting corresponding methodological approaches. By reframing the symphony, scholars can mine the genre and its discursive contexts for the social information they reveal. A methodology that opens up a contact point with 1933, moreover, lights up how this historical-ideological crossroads has legacies that shape the twenty-first century, too.

1933 as Epicentre

Viewed from a historical distance, the year 1933, where the symphonies in this book coalesce, was remarkable. The totalising Nazi political apparatus jerked into motion, tightening legal control over the German state as much as it did over spurious biological definitions of the German race.[28] Creative talent drained from Germany. Albert Einstein moved permanently to the United States after his university position in Berlin evaporated. German universities terminated the employment of Jewish academics. Aside from Weill and Bruno Walter, further musical figures to leave Germany in 1933 included Arnold Schoenberg, Erich Wolfgang Korngold, Egon Wellesz, and (although not Jewish) Ernst Krenek, whom the Nazis had decried as a cultural bolshevist. Likewise, 1933 saw the emigration of writers and cultural theorists such as Brecht, Thomas Mann, Alfred Döblin, Hannah Arendt, and Siegfried Kracauer. Many German exiles, like Walter Benjamin, spent 1933 in Paris, the French economy having largely withstood the 1929 economic crash.

Across the Atlantic in the Depression-struck United States, however, quite a different mood prevailed. As Franklin Delano Roosevelt took office as the 32nd president of the United States, the country began its most intimate flirtation with socialism. It was a rocky time. The Midwest saw the first storms preceding the dust-bowl crisis. Prohibition ended (although not until December). In Chicago, wealthy spectators from around the globe marvelled at the Century of Progress International Exposition. And 1933 was a fulcrum moment for Pan-American relations (at least from a US perspective): Roosevelt launched the Good Neighbor Policy, and it was the year that saw the term 'Mexican Vogue' coined in the *New York Times*

---

[28] In 1933, the Nazis outlawed the existence of other political parties and began their eugenics programme through compulsory sterilisation of citizens with supposedly hereditary diseases.

Figure 1.1 Diego Rivera at work on his mural *Man at the Crossroads* at the Rockefeller Center, New York, 24 April 1933. Library of Congress, Prints and Photographs Division, NYWT&S Collection LC-DIG-ds-08080 (digital file from original item).

for the growing attraction of everything south of the border.[29] John Rockefeller commissioned a mural from Diego Rivera for the foyer of the Rockefeller Center in Manhattan; Rivera tested the boundaries of US socialist inclinations when he insisted on including an image of Lenin and it all ended in scandal (see Figure 1.1). The destroyed work was recreated in the newly opened Palacio de Bellas Artes concert hall in Mexico City in 1934 with the revised title *Man, Controller of the Universe*.

But a year cannot be remarkable all the time. For many, despite shifting political sands and economic hardships, things went on as normal. Cinema-goers would see Ginger Rogers get her silver screen break in *42nd Street* and King Kong scale the newly completed Empire State Building, advertising a modernist emblem in the New York skyline. Arguably the most iconic film from 1933 today, *King Kong* was not among the ten top-grossing films in the United States that year; the

[29] 'Noted Woman Archaeologist', *New York Times*, 15 April 1933, cited by Helen Delpar, 'Carlos Chávez and the Mexican "Vogue", 1925–1940', in *Carlos Chávez and His World*, ed. Leonora Saavedra (Princeton: Princeton University Press, 2015), 204.

homoerotic German import *Mädchen in Uniform* was, however. This was Hollywood's swansong period of forthright woman, sexual innuendo, and semi-nudity before stricter enforcement of the Hays code stopped all the fun and 1934 ushered in a more conservative cinema.[30] All-star musical comedy *Gold Diggers of 1933* took not only full advantage of the latitude, but also box offices by storm.[31] It featured hit song 'We're in the Money'; less well remembered, though, is the risqué duet 'Petting in the Park'. *Gold Diggers of 1933* also had a clear political subtext, and made 1933 synonymous with Depression hardship. It staged the class warfare characterising the early 1930s, ennobling the 'forgotten' workless common folk – his dole queues, her empty days staying warm in bed – and endorsing their mistrust of academic and economic elites.[32] It is a telling portrait of US social tensions and aspirations.

In this 'Century of Progress', people chipped away at the limits of human endeavour. The Nobel prize in physics went to Erwin Schrödinger for breakthroughs in quantum mechanics – his cat-in-a-box thought experiment came two years later. The first man to fly solo around the world achieved the feat in seven days, eighteen hours, and forty-nine minutes.[33] An aesthetic revolution in day-to-day transit took place when the London underground launched Harry Beck's redesigned tube maps, still iconic today, replacing scaled distances with bald, digestible angles in a modern colour scheme (see Figure 1.2). This design became the global prototype for city transport mapping. Elsewhere, US board game pioneers were busy developing Monopoly, which would reach stores in 1935. And while things went on relatively undisturbed for some, for others things ended: notable deaths included ex-US president Calvin Coolidge and Austrian architect Adolf Loos.

[30] The production code (known as the Hays code, after Will H. Hays, who led its development) was a Hollywood censorship code introduced in 1930 in response to the influence of a religious pressure group. They were alarmed at the commercial popularity of scintillating cinema with salacious themes, and foresaw morally degrading effects, especially on the psychological development of children. The Hays code was not fully enforced until 1934; the years 1930–4 are known as the pre-code era. See, for instance, Thomas Patrick Doherty, *Pre-Code Hollywood: Sex Immorality, and Insurrection in American Cinema, 1930–1934* (New York: Columbia University Press, 1999).

[31] It was the joint second-highest grossing film that year, tying with *Cavalcade*, behind Paramount's *I'm No Angel*. 'Actual Receipts at the Wickets Now Decide "Box-Office Champions of 1933"', *Washington Post*, 6 February 1934, 14.

[32] The real forgotten in this film were people of colour: the uncredited singer of the film's closing number, 'My Forgotten Man', was Etta Moten Barnett (1901–2004), best known for playing Bess in George Gershwin's *Porgy and Bess*.

[33] See Bryan B. Sterling, *Forgotten Eagle: Wiley Post, America's Heroic Aviation Pioneer* (New York: Carrol and Graf, 2001), 133.

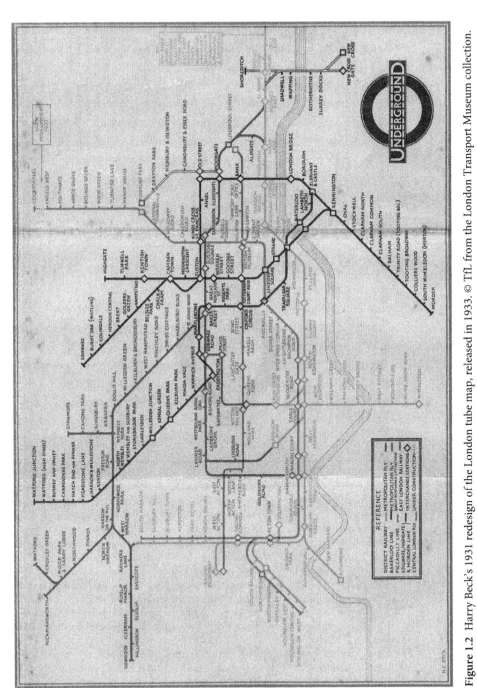

Figure 1.2 Harry Beck's 1931 redesign of the London tube map, released in 1933. © TfL from the London Transport Museum collection.

The year 1933 is the epicentre of this book, but not its hard limit. It is the historical trigger point – the year whose political events set in motion the course of Weill's Symphony No. 2, inextricably entwined with his life in exile – and this book spills beyond it in both directions. It is the synchronic point of overlap for all the case studies, featuring prominently in the genesis of each. All were either composed or premiered in that year, but their stories exceed it, too. Therefore, as in the opening vignette that outlined Weill's escape to Paris and work on his symphony in 1933, and its 1934 premiere, the book's discussion will often move from 1933 to the months on either side. Furthermore, in opening up a series of windows onto this moment, sometimes we find they cast new light on even less obviously proximate histories. The book will use the events of 1933 to catch other historical threads, which lead us further back, or to uncover and recombine historical snapshots of preceding eras.

To explore a tightly focused time period is to emulate a historical approach that in recent years has captured the imaginations of scholars and the public alike. Although as early as 1955 Raymond Postgate presented a single year as the focus for a historical study, chronicling month by month the politically momentous year 1848, it is only in the last decade or so that the 'year study' approach has really taken off, around ten years after Hans Ulrich Gumbrecht's 1997 study *1926: Ein Jahr am Rand der Zeit*.[34] The approach has been having its moment in popular non-fiction and documentary broadcasting, too: take BBC Four's *Bright Lights, Brilliant Minds: A Tale of Three Cities* (2014), which lit up three cities in three 'exceptional' years – Vienna in 1908, Paris in 1928, and New York in 1951[35] – or art historian Florian Illies's international bestseller *1913: The Year before the Storm*

---

[34] Hans Ulrich Gumbrecht, *In 1926: Living at the Edge of Time* (Cambridge, MA: Harvard University Press, 1997); Raymond Postgate, *Story of a Year: 1848* (London: J. Cape, 1955). Further examples include: Felipe Fernández-Armesto, *1492: The Year Our World Began* (London: Bloomsbury, 2010); Kevin Jackson, *Constellations of Genius: 1922: Modernism Year One* (London: Hutchinson, 2012); James Shapiro, *A Year in the Life of William Shakespeare: 1599* (London: Faber and Faber, 2005). Within musicology, Benjamin Piekut has more recently examined the New York experimental scene in 1964. See Benjamin Piekut, *Experimentalism Otherwise: The New York Avant-Garde and Its Limits* (Berkeley: University of California Press, 2011); Hugh MacDonald, *Music in 1853* (Woodbridge: Boydell Press, 2012); Beate Kutschke and Barley Norton, *Music and Protest in 1968* (Cambridge: Cambridge University Press, 2013). Taking an adjacent approach, Tamara Levitz's *Modernist Mysteries: Perséphone* (New York: Oxford University Press, 2012) is a micro-historical analysis of the premiere of Stravinsky's ballet in 1934.

[35] *Bright Lights, Brilliant Minds: A Tale of Three Cities*, BBC4, written by James Fox, produced by Julian Birkett and Helen Shariatmadari, three episodes, www.bbc.co.uk/programmes/b04fh387 (accessed 1 August 2016), first broadcast 20 August 2014.

(2013).[36] More recently Sam Mendes's Hollywood blockbuster thriller *1917* (2019) immersed audiences in the messiness and futility of the First World War, using the technical cinematic means of what seemed like two unbroken takes.[37] A common trope within year studies is to focus on a year that demarcates some kind of shift.[38] The year 1933 falls squarely within this category. Such studies, however, are at their most successful where they resist writing as if change already hung in the air, emphasising instead the contingency of historical events and the provisional status of human experience. Given what we know now, it is easy to filter our responses to 1933 through a sense of grim inevitability, forgetting that at the time the future was uncertain. This book thinks about the year's cultural landscape as one shaped most strongly by memory and other processes of weaving the past into the present.

If there is a genre that cannot help but look back, it is the symphony. Indeed, the symphony has often been about the social mechanisms of memory, about commemorating. The years after the Great War, therefore, presented a problem for composers seeking to grapple with the genre's blend of large-scale thematic integration and populism. After Europe had witnessed tragedy of unprecedented proportions, the symphonic genre's pre-war expansionist ideals, spearheaded by those like Mahler or Scriabin, or its earlier heroic narratives rang hollow against the senselessness of mechanised destruction. Even its tumultuous stories of Romantic introspection seemed out of place in the face of post-war nihilism. What was left to celebrate? Could either the symphony's nationalism or its opulent universalism be rescued? The symphonic dream as it had once been conceived seemed in tatters.

In 1933, looking back was in the foreground in other ways. A great number of composers died around this time: Alban Berg, Edward Elgar, Gustav Holst, and Franz Schreker. The passing of these composers who had bridged the late Romanticism of the twentieth century with interwar Europe – another figure was Frederick Delius, whose death fell in 1934 – perhaps contributed to the feeling of the curtain falling on the symphonic tradition, particularly in Austria and Germany. The anxieties that caused such cultural nostalgia were indeed especially acute in Germany – a reaction,

[36] Florian Illies, *1913: Der Sommer des Jahrhunderts* (Frankfurt am Main: S. Fischer, 2012); published in English as Illies, *1913: The Year before the Storm*, trans. Shaun Whiteside and Jamie Lee Searle (Brooklyn: Melville House, 2013).
[37] *1917*, film, directed by Sam Mendes, Hollywood: Universal Pictures, 2019.
[38] See, for instance, Fernández-Armesto, *1492*; Jackson, *Constellations of Genius*; Kutschke and Norton, *Music and Protest in 1968*.

as Pamela Potter puts it, to a 'fear that Germany's musical strength was about to fade into oblivion'.[39] On top of the symphonic silence from Sibelius and Nielsen from the mid-1920s, the ideological torch many still wanted to hold for a certain pre-modernist utopian conservatism was being gradually starved of fuel. The male lead in *Gold Diggers of 1933* was an unlikely figure to have hit the nail on the head: symphonies had become something that in many people's eyes – as the Boston heir turned Broadway songwriter Brad (Dick Powell) put it – 'you have to be half-dead to compose'.

Others struggled to escape the symphony's aesthetic history. Those serialist composers seeking symphonic relevance went inwards, attempting to rationalise and compress the genre. Indeed, for some historians the 'pointillistic canons' of Webern's 1928 two-movement Op. 21 mark the nihilist self-erasure of the nineteenth-century Austro-Germanic symphonic tradition and even went so far as to 'obliterate the nineteenth-century concept of the word "symphony"'.[40] Reinhold Brinkmann makes a similar point about how Schoenberg's Chamber Symphony Op. 9 solved the nineteenth century's problem of symphonic form, integrating the genre's traditional four movements into one tightly wrought, compressed structure.[41]

So far, we have a clear sense of an ending. Or, at least, this is what conventional historical narratives tell us. Symphonic surveys suggest a period of lull and stagnation had set in right around 1933. It is understandable but misleading: the tacit assumption is that not only was the genre dwindling after its nineteenth-century heyday[42] but that it had become something of a poisoned chalice, given the marked anti-German political sentiment following the Great War. In that climate, the genre's public muscle-flexing was in dubious taste. Many contemporaries were afraid sonata form had had its day. For instance, a historical touchstone such as the 1928 international Columbia Gramophone competition for a new lyric symphony – a commercial attempt to re-energise a flagging field – does

---

[39] Pamela Potter, *Most German of the Arts: Musicology and Society from the Weimar Republic to the End of Hitler's Reich* (New Haven, CT: Yale University Press, 1998). See, in particular, 'Attempts to Define "Germanness" in Music', 200–34.

[40] Brown, *Symphonic Repertoire*, vol. 4, 892.

[41] See Reinhold Brinkmann, 'The Compressed Symphony: On the Historical Content of Schoenberg's Op. 9', trans. Irene Zedlacher, in *Schoenberg and His World*, ed. Walter Frisch (Princeton: Princeton University Press, 2012), 141–61, especially 149–53.

[42] This narrative is outlined by Brown, *Symphonic Repertoire*, in particular vol. 4; also by Painter, *Symphonic Aspirations* (on page 3 she writes that the genre 'dwindled into irrelevance' after Mahler's death, despite its continuing prominence in music criticism). The decline narrative is challenged, however, by studies such as Ballantine, *Twentieth Century Symphony*.

nothing to dispel a narrative of crisis (and simultaneously indicates the stakes for the genre – namely, that it was still worth cultivating). It is true that 1933 was a moment when many of those twentieth-century composers whose work in the genre is best documented turned their attention away from the symphony. Symphonies by Sergei Prokofiev, Dmitri Shostakovich, Kurt Atterberg, Howard Hanson, Roger Sessions, Stravinsky, and Ernst Krenek, to name a few such composers, are conspicuously absent in this year. And if, as symphonic surveys also have it, from the early 1930s a new symphonic current influenced by the Nordic frugality of Sibelian tonal logic began to stimulate symphonic production in the United States and the United Kingdom, 1933 arrived just at the tipping point, before that counter-narrative of re-emergence really gained momentum.

Despite falling in the no-man's land between two monolithic symphonic narratives – one of decline, the other of regrowth – this aesthetic climate was nonetheless enormously productive for symphonic composition. In 1933 and the years immediately either side of it, works emerged across Europe and in the United States from seasoned symphonic composers as well as from more unlikely quarters, focusing tensions between the genre's nineteenth-century ideological legacies and wide-ranging, but typically modernist anxieties. The selective list in Figure 1.3 illustrates the magnitude of this body of works, as well as their geographical distribution. And that is not to mention unfinished works (for instance, Kaikhosru Shapurji Sorabji's Choral Symphony, begun in 1931) or planned symphonies from composers who died before their works could be completed (Edward Elgar's Symphony No. 3 and Alban Berg's *Symphonic Pieces from Lulu*).

The table demonstrates that a number of women were writing symphonies in the years either side of 1933: apart from Price, to whom we will turn in Chapter 6, listed here are Frida Kern and Johanna Senfter. Taking a feminist perspective on symphonic contribution in the period likewise makes it difficult to argue that in 1933 the symphony was a genre past its sell-by date. Austrian composer and conductor Kern, who composed *Symphonische Musik* Op. 20 (1934), began her training at the Musikakademie in Vienna at the fairly late age of 32; after finishing her studies in 1927, she established a women's orchestra, which toured Europe and North Africa. Senfter is another largely forgotten composer, and the symphony she wrote in 1933 has a significant part to play in her historiography. Her Symphony No. 6 quoted the National Socialist hymn 'Horst-Wessel-Lied' as a counterpoint to 'Wachet auf ruft uns die Stimme'. Following the end of the Second World War, this symphonic quotation

Argentina	Juan José Castro, Symphony No. 2 (*Sinfonía Bíblica*) (1932), Symphony No. 3 (*Sinfonía Argentina*) (1934)
Austria	Hanns Eisler, *Kleine Sinfonie* (1932)
	Frida Kern, *Symphonische Musik* Op. 20 (1934)
	Franz Schmidt, Symphony No. 4 in C major (1932–3)
	Alexander Zemlinsky, *Sinfonietta* Op. 23 (1934)
Estonia	Eduard Tubin, Symphony No. 1 in C minor (1931–4)
France	Arthur Honegger, *Mouvement symphonique n° 3* (1932–3)
	Albert Roussel, Symphony No. 4 in A major (1934)
	Kurt Weill, Symphony No. 2 (1932–4) (begun in Berlin)
Germany	Paul Dessau, Symphony No. 2 (1934; reworking and premiere 1962)[43]
	Karl Amadeus Hartmann, *Miserae* (or Symphony No. 1, withdrawn in 1950) (1933–4)
	Paul Hindemith, *Mathis der Maler* Symphony (1933–4)
	Hans Pfitzner, Symphony in C♯ minor Op. 36a (1932)
	Johanna Senfter, Symphony No. 6 (1933)
Hungary	Ernő Dohnányi, *Szimfónikus percek* (*Symphonic Minutes*) (1933)
Italy	Gian Francesco Malipiero, Symphony No. 1 *(in quattro tempi come le quattro stagioni)* (1933)
Mexico	Carlos Chávez, *Sinfonía de Antígona* (1933), *Llamadas, Sinfonía proletaria* (1934)
Poland	Józef Koffler, Symphony No. 2 (1933)
	Karol Szymanowski, Symphony No. 4 (*Symphonie concertante*) Op. 60 (1932)
Soviet Union	Dmitry Kabalevsky, Symphony No. 2 (1934), Symphony No. 3 (*Requiem*) (1933)
	Aram Khachaturian, Symphony No. 1 (1934)
	Nikolai Myaskovsky, Symphony No. 13 (1933), Symphony No. 14 (1933), Symphony No. 15 (1934)
United Kingdom	Arnold Bax, Symphony No. 5 (1932), Symphony No. 6 (1934–5)
	Havergal Brian, Symphony No. 4 (*Das Siegeslied*) (1932–3)
	Benjamin Britten, *Sinfonietta* Op. 1 (1932), *Simple Symphony* Op. 4 (for string orchestra) (1933–4)
	Ralph Vaughan Williams, Symphony No. 4 (1934)
	William Walton, Symphony No. 1 (1932–5)
United States	Aaron Copland, *Short Symphony* (Symphony No. 2) (1931–3)
	William Dawson, *Negro Folk Symphony* (1934)
	Duke Ellington, *Symphony in Black* (1934) (musical short released in 1935, integrating film with Ellington's extended composition *A Rhapsody of Negro Life*)
	Roy Harris, *Symphony 1933* (1933)
	Florence Price, Symphony No. 1 in E minor (1931–2)

Figure 1.3 Selective list of symphonic works composed c. 1933.

made Senfter's music ineligible for public performance, and Senfter herself politically toxic. A pupil of Max Reger, Senfter wrote music of the later Romantic tradition, strongly influenced by the vocal polyphony of Bach and Brahms, and in some ways her story parallels Pfitzner's, a composer

---

[43] Gervink, *Die Symphonie in Deutschland und Österreich*, 244.

who similarly ingratiated himself with the Nazis and whose Symphony in C♯ minor is the subject of Chapter 2.

Casting the net more broadly over the early 1930s, we also find symphonic works by Ethel Smyth, Elsa Barraine, Ina Boyle, and Elizabeth Maconchy. Smyth's choral symphony *The Prison* (1930) was premiered in 1931 in Edinburgh.[44] Barraine, who had won the Prix de Rome in 1929, wrote her first symphony, twenty-five minutes long, in 1931, and in 1933 came her six-minute orchestral work *Illustration symphonique pour 'Pogromes' d'André Spire*.[45] Irish composer Boyle's Symphony No. 2, *The Dream of the Rood* (named after the famous early medieval poem found in the Vercelli Book tenth-century manuscript), in three movements, dates from 1929 to 1930.[46] Vaughan Williams had examined the whole score during the composition lessons she took with him and liked it.[47] Only the first of her three symphonies, *Glencree* (1924–7), ever received a performance, however; it was another three-movement work ending, unusually, with a meditative slow movement.[48] Boyle sent out the manuscript of *The Dream of the Rood* to many conductors – Adrian Boult, Henry Wood, and Ernest Ansermet among those who received it – but none showed interest in performing it.[49] Maconchy wrote her first symphony in 1929–30; although it was later withdrawn, it received a play-through by the BBC Symphony Orchestra in 1932, conducted by Aylmer Buesst. In 1933, Constant Lambert considered her, alongside Britten, one to watch on the British music scene. 'There are regrettably few young composers of any personality in England today', he wrote, 'but in Miss Elizabeth Maconchy and Mr. Benjamin Britten we have two whose future development should be of the greatest interest'.[50]

---

[44] See Jürgen Schaarwächter, *Die britische Sinfonie 1914–1945* (Cologne: Dohr, 1995), 388–9.

[45] See Odile Bourin, Pierrette Germain-David, Catherine Massip, and Raffi Ourgandjian, eds., *Elsa Barraine, une compositrice au XXème siècle* (Sampzon: Éditions Delatour, 2010).

[46] See Séamas de Barra, *An Essay on the Music*, in Ita Beausang, *Ina Boyle (1889–1967): A Composer's Life, with an Essay on the Music by Séamas de Barra* (Cork: Cork University Press, 2018), 61–128, 82–3.

[47] Ita Beausang, *Ina Boyle (1889–1967): A Composer's Life, with an Essay on the Music by Séamas de Barra* (Cork: Cork University Press, 2018), 23.

[48] Elizabeth Maconchy, *Ina Boyle: An Appreciation with a Select List of Her Music* (Dublin: Dolmen Press, 1974).

[49] Beausang, *Ina Boyle*, 23.

[50] Constant Lambert, 'Matters Musical', *Sunday Referee*, 12 November 1933, found in Christa Brüstle, 'Elizabeth Maconchy and Béla Bartók: "Ultra-Modernity" in British Music', in *Elizabeth Maconchy: Music as Impassioned Argument*, ed. Christa Brüstle and Danielle Sofer (Vienna: Universal Editions, 2018), 124–49, 142. Annika Forkert has explored Maconchy's biography and reception history in relation to her colleagues William Walton, Britten, and Michael Tippett to come to a greater understanding of what 'did so much damage to Elizabeth

These many, varied symphonic works from the years around 1933 channel a range of sociopolitical concerns that are differently amplified in different contexts: about the twentieth-century bourgeois subject, about dislocation, about institutionalised and politicised forms of violence, about the lines of power along which art is divided and articulated as low or high, about mass production and expanding international markets. Like Weill's symphony, many of these works evince an ambivalent stance towards the genre and towards the idealist and nationalist discourses with which it was caught up: no longer playing by nineteenth-century rules, they manipulate or critique the form. If it has been argued that the twin starting points for the twentieth century's symphonic production are the aesthetic dualities of Mahlerian world-building and Sibelian logic, then, aesthetically, this body of works suggests the need to expand such a model.[51] Diverse further influences include *Neue Sachlichkeit* and *Zeitoper*, theatre, ballet, cinema, jazz, African-American musical traditions, and spare South American modernisms. An abundance of archival sources, moreover, make it clear that the symphony and its supporting institutions in the period were a thriving, if contested, international phenomenon. Considered as a body, these symphonies undoubtedly demonstrate the currency and immediacy of the form, in spite of the continuing dialogue they evince with its classical and Romantic heritage and ideals. But the ways in which they respond to the aesthetic and political climate are far from straightforward.

Amidst the Black literary, artistic, and musical innovation spurred by the Harlem Renaissance,[52] African-American intellectuals took on the symphonic genre in the years around 1933 as part of the movement's call to invest existing artistic forms with new, consciously racial meaning.[53] William Grant Still's *Afro-American Symphony* (completed in 1930), whose primary theme derives from a twelve-bar blues, was premiered in

---

Maconchy's reputation, compared to Britten'. See Annika Forkert, 'Beauty among Beasts? Maconchy, Walton, Tippett, and Britten', in Brüstle and Sofer, *Elizabeth Maconchy*, 63–85.

[51] David Fanning, 'The Symphony since Mahler: National and International Trends', in *The Cambridge Companion to the Symphony*, ed. Julian Horton (Cambridge: Cambridge University Press, 2013), 96–130.

[52] The Harlem Renaissance was a centre of gravity among the many Black Renaissances taking place around the same time in the first half of the twentieth century in Northern cities like Chicago, Washington, DC, and Philadelphia.

[53] See, for instance, Geneviève Fabre and Michel Feith, eds., *Temples for Tomorrow: Looking Back at the Harlem Renaissance* (Bloomington: Indiana University Press, 2001); Samuel A. Floyd, ed., *Black Music in the Harlem Renaissance: A Collection of Essays* (New York: Greenwood, 1990); Alain LeRoy Locke, *The Negro and His Music* (Port Washington, NY: Kennikat Press, 1968).

1931 by the Rochester Philharmonic Orchestra under Howard Hanson. Price's Symphony No. 1 in E minor, a work she had begun in 1931, was finally premiered in 1933 by the Chicago Symphony Orchestra. This was the first symphony by an African-American woman to be performed by a major US orchestra. It was well received, but was not published during her lifetime. William Dawson's *Negro Folk Symphony* (1934) was heard over the radio in a National Broadcasting Company production performed by the Philadelphia Orchestra in 1935; by contrast, at his own graduation ceremony, as the music school's orchestra played music Dawson himself had written, he had only been allowed to sit in the gallery, and a white proxy had received his diploma certificate.[54] What connected Still, Price, and Dawson was a project that aimed first and foremost at 'the elevation of the Negro Folk idiom – that is spirituals, blues, and characteristic dance music – to symphonic form'.[55]

As with the other works in Figure 1.3, these works evidence a careful weighing-up of both the symphonic genre's historical baggage and its scope for critique and renewal. Yet the symphony might seem an unlikely vessel for the United States' Black Renaissance, given the bare realities of racial segregation, which affected US concert halls and orchestras in ways that varied between cities and states: in the South it was enshrined bluntly in law through Jim Crowism, while no less powerfully determining the psyche – and, importantly, infrastructure and public spaces – of Northern cities.[56] It was not just about what had been put into law; there were also many documented instances of extra-legal racial policing of concert halls through day-to-day individual behaviours – for instance, ushers seating Black audience members only in the balcony or ticket collectors refusing Black patrons entry despite having a ticket.[57] The importance of African-American symphonic accomplishment and propagation was overstrained, carrying the weight of the hope for a basic universal human dignity that did not yet exist (and that it would take far more than aesthetics to achieve).

[54] See Rae Linda Brown, 'Selected Orchestral Music of Florence B. Price (1888–1953) in the Context of Her Life and Work' (PhD thesis, Yale University, 1987), 67–8.

[55] Brown, 'Florence B. Price's "Negro Symphony"', in Fabre and Feith, *Temples for Tomorrow*, 84–98, 91.

[56] See, for instance, Amy Absher, *The Black Musician and the White City: Race and Music in Chicago, 1900–1967* (Ann Arbor: University of Michigan Press, 2014), especially 'Musicians in the Segregated City: Chicago in the Early 1900s to 1930s', 16–47. For wider conceptual consideration of early twentieth-century Black audiences in the United States, see also Jacqueline Stewart, *Migrating to the Movies: Cinema and Black Urban Modernity* (Berkeley: University of California Press, 2005). At the time of writing, there is no overarching resource dealing with US segregation in the spaces of classical musical performance in the first half of the twentieth century. Variation from state to state and city to city makes the topic an unwieldy one.

[57] See Absher, *Black Musician*, 25.

Harlem Renaissance thinkers sought racial justice by demonstrating the equal nature of Black intellectual achievement within 'respected' cultural forms like the novel. As such, symphonic composition became a form of resistance to the status quo that nonetheless held Black artists in the binds of acquiescence, appeasing cultural institutions and value structures from which they had been systematically excluded. Necessarily, the trajectories of these symphonies were negatively impacted by the racist landscape onto which this music initially emerged, as well as – perhaps also playing some part in the Jewish Weill's symphonic reception – the racialised (white) subjectivities concert-goers and critics implicitly associated with absolute music and had in mind as they policed the genre. Additionally, symphonies by African-American composers are harder to recover from history than those by their white contemporaries. For example, on 7 January 1933, just three weeks before Hitler seized power, Hanson performed the third movement of Still's *Afro-American Symphony* in his Berlin Philharmonic concert of new American music. However, it was not listed on the concert programme; only favourable reviews in the German music journal *Die Allgemeine Musikzeitung* and in some US press coverage indicate that it was played and heard.[58] Not only did African-American composers face exceptional challenges in achieving performances, but, even when performances did take place, there is no guarantee today of straightforwardly finding a material trace.

Why have the works in Figure 1.3 dropped through the cracks of standard symphonic periodisation?[59] Sometimes they have been historicised (or even missed out on being historicised in the first place) in ways that excise them

---

[58] When consulting the Berlin Philharmonic's catalogue of concerts in 2013, I found the programme for Hanson's 7 January 1933 concert listed as follows: 'Griffes: Das Lustschloß von Kubla Khan, Mason: Ouvertüre Canticleer, Bennet: Concerto grosso, Sowerby: Mooney Music, Hanson: Pan und der Priester'. Heinz Pringsheimer, however, noted that 'most successful was the scherzo in the *Afro-American Symphony* by the Negro composer William Grant Still, which has jazz-style spiritedness and is not without refinement'. Likewise, the reviewer for the *New York Times* wrote that the audience 'demanded a repetition of Still's scherzo.' See 'Berlin Hails Hanson Offering Our Music', *New York Times*, 9 January 1933, 22, found in Judith Anne Still, *William Grant Still: A Bio-Bibliography* (Westport, CT: Greenwood, 1996), 170. Pringsheimer, 'Aus dem Berliner Musikleben', *Die Allgemeine Musikzeitung*, 13 January 1933, 17–28, 23. By contrast, the write-up of the concert in the conservative *Zeitschrift für Musik* made no mention of Still's scherzo. The listing in the Berlin Philharmonic's digital catalogue has since been amended in light of these reviews. See 'Konzerte der Berliner Philharmoniker 1932–1934 (In- und Ausland)', in Peter Muck, *100 Jahre Berliner Philharmonisches Orchester* (Schneider: Tutzing, 1982), as digitised and revised for the Berlin Philharmonic Archive, March 2013.

[59] German-language scholarship has fared somewhat better than that of the Anglosphere in beginning to deal with the symphonic tradition in the 1930s. See Gervink, *Die Symphonie in Deutschland und Österreich*; Schaarwächter, *Die britische Sinfonie*; Osthoff and Schubert, *Symphonik 1930–1950*, 310.

from the canon and from standard definitions of the symphony. The impulse retroactively to define the symphony, alongside twentieth-century commercial impulses to create a core concert repertory, has had a negative impact on this period and has led to it rarely figuring in history books or on concert programmes.[60] The fact that many of these works were antagonistic to the idea of the symphony or were testing its limits has been damaging for how the period has been remembered. It has remained a way of policing musical value ever since. Yet, social and aesthetic value judgements are hard to disentangle. As my primary interest is in the ideological legacy of discourse around symphonies, in this volume I am not preoccupied with the aesthetic question of what makes a symphony a symphony. For a musical work to be included in Figure 1.3, it is enough that the composer called it a symphony or symphonic. Neither is the primary aim of this book to show that a more diverse range of people than previously assumed or accounted for in terms of, for instance, gender or racial identity were writing symphonies in the early 1930s; that important research is work for a different project. More interesting to me is why a particular composer might choose to use such a freighted title, and what this might uncover about the status of the symphony by 1933.

Freighted it was. Beethoven proved a tough act to follow after the German idealist critical turn raised the experience his symphonies offered to listeners to the plane of the infinite. Coupled with preoccupations about looking back, then, was the idea of the symphony as a vehicle for expressing or exploring subjectivity. After all, in 1933 both the Depression and German fascism's reformulation of selfhood in relation to the collective put questions of modern subjectivity in the political foreground. Definitions and the drive to categorise cannot shoulder the blame alone. Interrogating the general absence of this body of works isolates some fault lines and pervasive intellectual frames that have grown up within the symphony's post-war intellectual history – in both scholarly networks and geographical asymmetries. Largely, these have responded to or aligned with contemporary intellectual currents and value systems. Disciplinary insistence on the autonomy of music from sociopolitical concerns has hit studies of the symphony particularly hard, and is partly responsible. So, too, is a cultural mainstream that sidelines geographies and national traditions outside hegemonic and political power centres.

---

[60] A number of unsuccessful attempts to define the symphony characterise scholarship from the 1960s and 1970s, which betrayed both individual compositional agendas and the kind of positivism shaping musicology in this period. See, for instance, Robert Simpson, *The Symphony: Haydn to Dvořák* (Aylesbury: Penguin Books, 1966), 9. Christopher Ballantine, in 1983, searched for a single 'symphonic essence'. He defined such a 'symphonic essence' as 'the musical preoccupation with dualism'. Ballantine, *Twentieth Century Symphony*, 13.

Symphonies have always been about space; indeed, space and subjectivity come hand in hand. The concert hall, as an archetype of the so-called public sphere, seems a good place to start thinking about these relationships. But alongside their performance spaces, the works considered in this book bring a host of other kinds of spaces with them, both physical and imagined: interior subjective space, the often politically charged cities outside, intimate aural worlds of chamber music, the nostalgic agrarian spaces on which collective national or even transnational identities imaginatively coalesce; the industrial spaces over which Romantic and coherent senses of selfhood seem to fracture; the colonial fantasies of simplicity and possibility to which those anxious about modernity turn. These spaces may seem disparate. Nonetheless, they are all focused by the symphony and the messy, shifting configuration of ideas and tropes with which it has become imbricated in the course of its intellectual history. Whether, at one extreme, the intangible internal spaces where we imagine selfhood resides or, at the other, those that charge entry and have cloak-rooms, all these spaces are ideologically constructed. All, from acoustically designed concert hall to pastoral idyll, capture aspects of the universal; the quasi-Platonic, abstract idea-form that leaves its shadows on the cave wall; the reproducible. Ideologies associated with symphonies can deepen the conceptual furrows engraving these universalised spaces in our collective imaginations.[61] Here, I investigate how symphonies conspire in these fantasies that orient us within the world, and particularly those spatial fantasies that collectivise selfhood.

Symphonies, Subjectivity, and Space: E. T. A. Hoffmann to Paul Bekker

By exploring the nexus of subjectivity and space in the symphonies of 1933, this book is part of a project to cultivate a more advanced understanding of the genre's deep entanglement with nineteenth-century Germanic philosophies of subjectivity, as well as its sociopolitical stakes.[62] On the one hand, the symphony is an idealist, expansionist project – starting around the beginning of the nineteenth century, aestheticians and musicians alike reconceived it as a 'manifestation of the infinite'.[63] On the other hand, it

---

[61] See Bonds, *Music as Thought*, in particular chapter 1, 'Listening with Imagination', 5–28, especially 22–8.

[62] On the former, see, for instance, Lütteken, *Sinfonie als Bekenntnis*, 138.

[63] Bonds, *Music as Thought*, 28.

directs its lens inwards onto subjective interiority, familiarising the listener with a universalised notion of selfhood.[64] E. T. A. Hoffmann's 1810 review of Beethoven's Fifth Symphony is a famous initial landmark in this trajectory of symphonic aesthetics. As Mark Evan Bonds demonstrates, however, Hoffmann's review was only made possible by a generational shift in how instrumental music was conceived around the turn of the nineteenth century. Suddenly, influenced by the ideas of those like Wilhelm Heinrich Wackenroder and Johann Gottfried Herder, critics' perceptions of instrumental music changed, with it coming to be seen as a uniquely sublime and elevated art form rather than merely sensually pleasing. Beethoven's contemporary reception has intimately linked the symphonic genre as a whole to the Romantic subjective turn. Hoffmann argued that Beethoven's Fifth Symphony opened up a transcendent 'unknown realm' quite apart from the physical world of the senses, allowing listeners to access that yearning for the 'infinite' that went far beyond conventional expression and signalled the dissolution of bounded selfhood.[65] Margaret Notley and others have shown how, as the nineteenth century went on, symphonic discourse struggled with questions about the relationship between individual sovereignty and mass publics, and about community-formation and the national imaginary.[66] Other scholars have made similar observations, while turning the spotlight on the genre's ethical ambivalence. As Daniel M. Grimley emphasises, 'simply "sounding together" has not always been an easy or politically straightforward task, and the idea of community that the symphony has often seemed to elevate can swiftly become more exclusive than inclusive'[67] For instance, the Germanic intellectual heritage of the idea of subjectivity bound up with the symphony is one that in 1933 was most straightforwardly available to communities who saw that philosophical tradition as theirs.

People thinking critically about music around the early nineteen thirties did so in a climate in which ideas simmered about the symphony as a phenomenon integrally linked to both society and to space. The notion of an infinite realm achieved through Romantic introspection was still

---

[64] Holly Watkins, *Metaphors of Depth in German Musical Thought: From E. T. A. Hoffmann to Arnold Schoenberg* (Cambridge: Cambridge University Press, 2011).

[65] E. T. A. Hoffmann, *E. T. A. Hoffmann's Musical Writings*: Kreisleriana, The Poet and the Composer, *Music Criticism*, ed. David Charlton and Martyn Clarke (Cambridge: Cambridge University Press, 1989), 238.

[66] See, for instance, Bonds, *Music as Thought*; Margaret Notley, *Lateness and Brahms: Music and Culture in the Twilight of Viennese Liberalism* (Oxford: Oxford University Press, 2007).

[67] Daniel M. Grimley, 'Symphony/Antiphony: Formal Strategies in the Twentieth-Century Symphony', in Horton, *Cambridge Companion to the Symphony*, 285–310, 285.

a pervasive current of thought. But in 1918 a new perspective entered the fray when Berlin music critic Paul Bekker theorised the symphony from a sociological angle. Written as the German imperial government began to crumble after the First World War, his treatise *Die Sinfonie von Beethoven bis Mahler* represents a useful starting point for unravelling the most salient conceptual areas for the case studies considered in this book.[68] Situating the genre within libertarian discourses, Bekker's optimistic vision of the symphony's intended audience – the *Hörerschaft*, or utopian assembly of listeners who come together for the duration of the work and, in so doing, reflect a perfect democratic social body – can be traced back to the genre's Enlightenment origins. The idealised public of listeners is quite literally composed by the music, and Bekker thus made the case for an intimate and reflexive connection between music, space, and listening community.[69] This seemed a radical departure from the kind of heroic symphonic narratives and Beethoven idolatry evinced in, for example, Felix Weingartner's roughly contemporary and enduringly successful *Die Sinfonie nach Beethoven*, first published in 1898 and revised for a fourth edition in 1926.[70]

Indeed, the fraught relationship between the individual and the collective in democratic thought has always been central to symphonic discourse. Writers in the early nineteenth century drew parallels between the composite, yet multi-voiced functioning of the orchestra and the idealised mechanisms of democratic social orders governed by ethical values of individual freedom and autonomy. They pointed to how the orchestra was a harmonious (understood literally) analogue to the needs of the autonomous individual and the collective requirements of the social order.[71] Bekker's text shows that the positive moral value invested in the symphonic genre in the nineteenth century seemed to have lost none of its potency by 1918, or if it had, then post-war republican optimism was the climate in which it could be resurrected. But the symphony has not always channelled egalitarian impulses. Frequently, the symphony and the orchestra have been put to politically dystopic use: in fascist Germany, for instance, the

---

[68] Paul Bekker, *Die Sinfonie von Beethoven bis Mahler* (Berlin: Schuster & Loeffler, 1918).

[69] Ibid., 15–16.

[70] Felix Weingartner, *Die Sinfonie nach Beethoven*, 4th ed. (Leipzig: Breitkopf & Härtel, 1926).

[71] See Bonds, *Music as Thought*, in particular 'Listening to the Aesthetic State: Cosmopolitanism', 63–78; see also Emily I. Dolan, *The Orchestral Revolution: Haydn and the Technologies of Timbre* (Cambridge: Cambridge University Press, 2013), in particular 'The Republic of Sound', 136–79. Dolan has argued for how the different instruments and instrumental characters in the orchestra represent autonomous individuals within a synthesised semi-utopian collective, reflecting late eighteenth- and early nineteenth-century contemporary philosophical discussions of the self and society.

stratified organisation of the symphony orchestra modelled the *Führerprinzip* (leader principle): gathered around the central authoritarian figure of the conductor, the large ensemble needed to perform a symphony as one body mirrored Nazi ideology.[72] Or, as Jacques Attali noted in 1977 in his critique of the capitalist ideological function of the orchestra as 'total spectacle', its hierarchically ranked, anonymous musicians fulfil 'the image of programmed labour in our society'.[73] The conductor, 'simultaneously entrepreneur and State', models the invisible, necessary power of the economic order. As Attali put it: 'Power is; it has no need to impose itself and the technique of conducting evolves from authority to discretion.'[74] Either way, whether utopian or dystopian, or something more ambivalent, the symphony simulates – or even stimulates – the political imagination.

Alongside politics, the symphonic genre came with an expansionist spatial impulse. For Bekker, the articulation of musical ideas that embraced all layers of society required a vast unfolding of energy, which in turn demanded a correspondingly vast physical space.[75] Put less prosaically, what he meant is that symphonies can be loud, and volume travels. Bekker wedded the symphonic genre to an idealisation of public space as a site for rational consensus, similar to the liberal coffee-house culture Jürgen Habermas later theorised in *The Structural Transformation of the Bourgeois Public Sphere*.[76] Notley and Benjamin Korstvedt have worked on the liberalist underpinnings of symphonic space, and signalled the value of more thorough critical attention to Habermas's social theory in relation to the symphony.[77] Yet Bekker's ideal symphony, epitomised – in one of the more pedestrian aspects of the treatise – by Beethoven's works, represents a direct, one-way conduit from the composer to the mass listening public, and such rhetoric perhaps uncovers an anti-democratic and coercive aspect to the symphony's power over the community it creates, which Bekker does not adequately reconcile. Indeed, symphonic space has been inflected differently in different ideological contexts. For instance, Alexander Rehding has excavated the strong fascist ideological charge to

---

[72] For discussion of the orchestra's symbolic role in Nazi Germany, see Painter, *Symphonic Aspirations*, in particular 214–15.

[73] Jacques Attali, *Noise: The Political Economy of Music*, trans. Brian Massumi (Minneapolis: University of Minnesota Press, 2006), 65–6.

[74] Ibid., 67.   [75] Bekker, *Die Sinfonie*, 11.

[76] See Jürgen Habermas, *The Structural Transformation of the Public Sphere: An Inquiry into a Category of Bourgeois Society*, trans. Thomas Burger and Frederick Lawrence (Cambridge, MA: MIT Press, 1989).

[77] Notley, *Lateness and Brahms*, 156–60; Benjamin M. Korstvedt, 'Reading Music Criticism beyond the Fin-de-Siècle Vienna Paradigm', *Musical Quarterly* 94 (2011): 156–210, 172.

the massive imagined spaces conjured up by the symphonic genre for 1930s German musicologists.[78] In line with totalitarian ideologies that renounced selfhood, these were expansive virtual arenas in relation to which the individual disintegrated.

Nations, Geographies, and Absolute Music

Since the Second World War, it has been common for many strands of scholarship on the symphony to reflect the qualities historically ascribed to symphonies themselves. If symphonies are monumental, so too have been the ways we have historicised them. Vast, grand, expansive, transcendent: symphonies, and their development and decline, have often been awkwardly wedded to other grand narratives, particularly political ones, or to privileged geographic regions. Indeed, until recently, much writing on the symphonic genre has been survey-type work, delimited by country and carefully periodised.[79] Through the twentieth century, the tendency of those general English- and German-language surveys of the symphony was towards the strongly uncritical and canonising, made all the more troubling by highly selective historical and geographical coverage.[80] Particularly in anglophone scholarship, the foundations of these approaches can be traced back to the post-war period: the legacy of the canon-forming, class-building music-appreciation guide is keenly felt, and the chronological life-and-works or nationally determined organisational principles of these guides have proved tough to shift. In addition, the genre's popularity meant the potential for a broader market appeal was prioritised over academic rigour in the mid-twentieth-century popular press. Of course, it is worth noting that studies and surveys of the symphony are not the only areas of scholarship in which works dealing with the genre can be found.[81] But as the place where the most explicit curation of

---

[78] See Alexander Rehding, *Music and Monumentality: Commemoration and Wonderment in Nineteenth-Century Germany* (Oxford; New York: Oxford University Press, 2009), especially 172–80.

[79] For an example of survey-type work organised around national narratives, see Brown, *Symphonic Repertoire*; Layton, *Guide to the Symphony*; Hartmut Krones, *Die österreichische Symphonie im 20. Jahrhundert* (Vienna: Böhlau, 2005).

[80] For examples of a particularly canonising genre, the chronological life-and-works-style study, see Ralph Hill, *The Symphony* (Harmondsworth: Penguin Books, 1949); Simpson, *The Symphony: Haydn to Dvořák*; Simpson, *The Symphony: Elgar to the Present Day*; H. H. Stuckenschmidt, *Twentieth Century Composers*, vol. 2 *Germany and Central Europe* (London: Weidenfeld & Nicolson, 1970).

[81] See, for instance, Rehding, *Music and Monumentality*.

the genre itself takes place, they shape many structures in our thinking and expectations about how information is located.

The nation, underlying the discursive field of much symphonic commentary, has profoundly determined much writing and thinking about symphonies. Since the nineteenth century, the symphonic genre has been intimately packaged up with nationalism and nationalising impulses and agendas. Creating a unique national symphonic style carried high stakes for the identity of many nation-states.[82] Like the geographical landscape, this is a terrain that has never been neutral or evenly weighted. Broadly put, the symphonic landscape and its scholarly representation crystallise around Austria and Germany: in the nineteenth century, around their political hegemony; in the twentieth century, around their decline. The hybrid Austro-Germany is a particularly problematic imagined space – one that only really existed, under the darkest possible conditions, for a brief while after the *Anschluss*. Douglas Shadle elucidates this centre of gravity in his book on the nineteenth-century symphony in the United States.[83] It is hardly surprising, then, that in twentieth-century symphony scholarship these national discourses (orientated by German-speaking nations) continued keenly to influence the territorialisation of discussions about the symphony.[84]

Related to the problem of geographical organisation, examining 1933 and the years immediately adjacent points to the politicised periodisation that plays out in how we narrativise the symphony, and how its close associations with Germany have been disruptive. If many studies match this narrative of symphonic decline, particularised to Austria and Germany,[85] with an emphasis on symphonic rejuvenation in anglophone countries especially[86] 'as the Roaring Twenties gave way to the more sober-minded thirties',[87] it is troubling how neatly this opposition mirrors the lines along which early

---

[82] See, for example, Pederson, 'A. B. Marx'; Jim Samson, 'Nations and Nationalism', in *The Cambridge History of Nineteenth-Century Music*, ed. Samson (Cambridge: Cambridge University Press, 2001), 568–600; Shadle, *Orchestrating the Nation*, 1–14, 'Introduction'.

[83] Shadle, *Orchestrating the Nation*, especially 'Introduction'.

[84] See, for instance, Krones, *Die österreichische Symphonie*.

[85] See Painter, *Symphonic Aspirations*, in which she traces a trajectory from 'Symphonic Idealism in Crisis' to 'Symphonic Defeat' in Germany. See also Cuyler, *The Symphony*. Cuyler heavily weights discussion towards symphonic development in the United States in the chapter 'The Symphony in the Twentieth Century'.

[86] See Taruskin, 'The Symphony Goes (Inter)National', in *OHWM*, vol. 3, 745–802, and 'In Search of the "Real" America', in *OHWM*, vol. 4, 559–674. See also Cuyler, *The Symphony*; Stedman, *The Symphony*.

[87] David Fanning, 'Symphonik 1930–1950: Gattungsgeschichtliche und analytische Beiträge' (book review), *Music and Letters* 85 (2004): 498–9, 498.

twentieth-century global conflicts were drawn.[88] How impartial were our historian-narrators? The era suffers from being framed as a bookend moment in standard symphonic narratives. Additionally, Nazi cultural policy was directly or indirectly responsible for the critical silence surrounding some works composed around 1933. Some were too closely affiliated with the new regime for comfort. Others either were never rehabilitated after a poor initial reception in Nazi Germany or never fully recovered from being identified with *entartete Kunst* (degenerate art).

There are broader issues, too, with more immediate stakes. Strongly influenced by the thought of another central figure in the symphony's intellectual history – namely, Eduard Hanslick – symphonies have been a key historical archetype of 'absolute' music, considered adrift from localised political and social concerns.[89] Perhaps more so than other genres, they have invited decontextualised analyses that focus on the hermetic world of musical construction.[90] As symphonic reception and criticism veered towards ideals

---

[88] Wolfgang Osthoff and Giselher Schubert have begun to interrogate this narrative by giving a more balanced account of the post-1930s symphonic revival beyond the United Kingdom and the United States. Osthoff and Schubert, *Symphonik 1930–1950*, 310.

[89] See, for instance, Arnold Whittall's 'Millennial Prelude' to his *Musical Composition in the Twentieth Century*, which was a 1999 rewrite of his 1977 textbook work *Music Since the First World War*. Both versions contain two chapters on symphonies. In its first few pages Whittall defended the continued relevance of his 1975 approach for the millennial reader:

> [M]uch of my own text may appear to subscribe to the outmoded heresy of autonomy . . . . It is the composition as music which dominates, even so, for there is always a sense in which the work of art, with the inevitable element of consolation in face of an alarming world which it brings with it, represents a triumph over the world and not a mere reflection of it. It is a product of the world that transcends its context. When [Roger] Scruton writes that 'music inspires and consoles us partly because it is unencumbered by the debris that drifts through the world of life' [Scruton, *Aesthetics*, 122] this is not just a pious poetic fantasy.

> Arnold Whittall, *Musical Composition in the Twentieth Century* (Oxford: Oxford University Press, 1999), 2–3. For further discussion of this position, see Whittall, 'Autonomy/Heteronomy: The Contexts of Musicology', in *Rethinking Music*, ed. Nicholas Cook and Mark Everist (Oxford: Oxford University Press, 1999), 73–101.

[90] For discussion on music analysis post-new musicology, particularly concerning using unity as the governing principle, see the dialogue in *Music Analysis* sparked by Robert P. Morgan, 'The Concept of Unity and Musical Analysis', *Music Analysis* 22 (2003): 7–50, with a whole section in *Music Analysis* 23 (2004): 333–85 devoted to responses from Kevin Korsyn, Daniel K. L. Chua, Jonathan D. Kramer, and Joseph Dubiel (with an introduction by Jonathan Cross). Also in the latter issue is Kofi Agawu's reflection on the state of music analysis at the time, 'How We Got Out of Analysis, and How to Get Back in Again', *Music Analysis* 23 (2004): 267–86. See also Ian Biddle on music analysis as textual activity in 'The Gendered Eye: Music Analysis and the Scientific Outlook in German Early Romantic Music Theory', in *Music Theory and Natural Order from the Renaissance to the Early Twentieth Century*, ed. Suzanne Clark and Alexander Rehding (Cambridge: Cambridge University Press, 2001), 183–96. Critical discussion of separatist impulses in music analysis and of critiques of formalism can be found in Jim Samson, 'Analysis in Context', in Cook and Everist, *Rethinking Music*, 35–54.

of 'absolute' musical autonomy, the symphony's connection with privileged subjects became troublingly implicit, integrally embedded within the autonomous musical work, such that to elevate autonomous music as 'universal' became insidiously to elevate a certain kind of personhood as 'universal'. The musical information such approaches yield is rich; the scope of the social information symphonies could yield, however, has not yet been adequately explored. Such work betrays a persistent assumption that has changed little over the past several decades: that engagement with the symphony requires no social or political context.[91]

Such emphasis on musical autonomy does not bode well for the symphony's resilience as new curricula are developed. Since the symphony, with its origins in sonata form, was claimed to be the most abstract of orchestral genres, it has remained one of the genres most impervious to the radically changing intellectual currents of the twentieth- and twenty-first-century humanities, and to altering priorities of musicology as a whole. Despite the revisionary efforts of those like Susan McClary and Rose Rosengard Subotnik,[92] or by James Hepokoski,[93] some major subsequent scholarship on the symphony has continued to be haunted by past disciplinary insistence on music's special autonomous aesthetic status, reifying 'music' into its 'value-free object of study'.[94] Studies such as A. Peter Brown's from the

---

[91] Such decontextualisation appears frequently in symphony scholarship. It characterises studies from Ballantine's 1983 self-proclaimed 'first intensive published investigation' of the genre in this period (Ballantine, *Twentieth Century Symphony*, 11) to Brown's colossal study of 2002, which barely concedes any lines of influence extending beyond the musical establishment (Brown, *Symphonic Repertoire*). Karen Painter's 2008 work to demonstrate the contested political ground supplied by the symphony by focusing on the genre in Germany in the early twentieth century was thus long overdue. See Painter, *Symphonic Aspirations*, 6.

[92] See Susan McClary, *Feminine Endings* (Minneapolis: University of Minnesota Press, 1991), in particular chapter 3, 'Sexual Politics in Classical Music', 53–79 and 127–30. See also Susan McClary, 'Constructions of Subjectivity in Schubert's Music', in *Queering the Pitch: The New Gay and Lesbian Musicology*, ed. Philip Brett, Elizabeth Wood, and Gary C. Thomas (New York: Routledge, 2006), 205–33; Rose Rosengard Subotnik, *Developing Variations: Style and Ideology in Western Music* (Minneapolis: University of Minnesota Press, 1991).

[93] For example, see James Hepokoski, 'Masculine. Feminine. Are Current Readings of Sonata Form in Terms of a "Masculine" and "Feminine" Dichotomy Exaggerated? James Hepokoski Argues for a More Subtle Approach to the Politics of Musical Form', *Musical Times* 135 (1994): 494–9, and his later work, such as Hepokoski, 'Back and Forth from Egmont: Beethoven, Mozart, and the Nonresolving Recapitulation', *19th-Century Music* 25 (2001–2): 127–54; Hepokoski, 'Beyond the Sonata Principle', *Journal of the American Musicological Society* 55 (2002): 91–154.

[94] See Philip V. Bohlman, 'Musicology as a Political Act', *Journal of Musicology* 11 (1993): 411–36, especially 422–4. The controversy and resistance triggered by McClary's analysis of Beethoven's Ninth Symphony in relation to – potentially violent – masculine sexuality is illuminating. See Susan McClary, 'Getting Down Off the Beanstalk', in *Feminine Endings*, 112–31, 129–30, and reactions such as Pieter van den Toorn, 'Politics, Feminism, and Contemporary Music Theory', *Journal of Musicology* 9 (1991): 275–99.

early to mid 2000s, for instance, seemed immune to (new) musicology's incorporation of post-colonial, post-structural, queer, and feminist perspectives, which have enriched opera studies in particular over the last three decades.[95] New musicology's strong bias towards opera suggests the diagnosis that opera is just more obviously interdisciplinary and hard to contain than so-called 'absolute' music, and also that the kinds of professional networks shared by scholars working towards the new musicological project had little in common with those working on the symphony. In addition, it is interesting – or telling – that, in the main, the symphonic genre continues to attract interest from only a limited scholarly demographic, with few people of colour or women.[96] The symphony continues, perhaps, to be revealing about particular kinds of subjectivities.

Confronted with the changing emphases of modern musicology, this has left the symphony particularly vulnerable. Opera studies and film music studies, for example, had to fight the essentialising impulses that have historically structured the discipline. To assure a place in academia, they developed bold critical frameworks around the 1990s.[97] However, the merits and

---

[95] See Brown, *Symphonic Repertoire*. There is a large literature on opera from feminist and queer perspectives. Some examples include: Carolyn Abbate, *Unsung Voices* (Princeton: Princeton University Press, 1991); Corinne E. Blackmer and Patricia Juliana Smith, eds., *En Travesti: Women, Gender Subversion, Opera* (New York: Columbia University Press, 1995). Post-colonial perspectives have also recently begun to influence the direction of opera studies. See, for example, Mary Ingraham, Joseph So, and Roy Moodley, *Opera in a Multicultural World: Coloniality, Culture, Performance* (New York: Routledge, 2016); Ralph P. Locke, *Musical Exoticism: Images and Reflections* (Cambridge: Cambridge University Press, 2009). Latterly, more scholarship has been preoccupied with understanding opera through critical race theory. See, for instance, Nina Eidsheim, 'Marian Anderson and "Sonic Blackness" in American Opera', *American Quarterly* 63 (2011): 641–71; Juliana M. Pistorius, 'Inhabiting Whiteness: The Eoan Group *La Traviata*, 1956', *Cambridge Opera Journal* 31 (2019): 63–84. In 2018, Naomi André published *Black Opera: History, Power, Engagement* (Urbana: University of Illinois Press, 2018). Both André and Pistorius were involved in founding the Black Opera Research Network (BORN) in 2020 'to serve as a platform for conversations on the history, experiences, politics, and practices of Black opera'. See https://blackoperaresearch.net/about/ (accessed 18 August 2022).

[96] When *A Guide to the Symphony*, edited by Robert Layton, was published in 1993 (with a later edition in 1995), of the eleven 'music experts' chosen as contributors, not one was female. Set against the frenetic revisionist disciplinary activity of the 1990s, this seemed revealing, if not wholly unexpected, and the 2013 *Cambridge Companion to the Symphony*, edited by Julian Horton, unfortunately merely confirmed that scholarship was not yet in a position where it could redress the balance – only two of its sixteen contributors were female. Although gender alone tells us nothing about the lenses through which writers approach the genre, such disproportional gender representation appears nonetheless indicative of the kind of conservative forces shaping this area of scholarship.

[97] Film music research has taken off since the mid 1980s. Since then, some studies definitional for the field have included: Claudia Gorbman, *Unheard Melodies: Narrative Film Music* (Bloomington, Indiana University Press, 1987); Kathryn Kalinak, *Settling the Score: Music and the Classical Hollywood Film* (Madison: University of Wisconsin Press, 1992); Caryl Flinn,

significance of the symphony as the pinnacle of Western art music and its work concept may have been assumed a priori. Now the tides have turned; what once seemed self-evident appears weak in current scholarly contexts, particularly in light of the shift of emphasis in the discipline towards addressing overdue ethical questions about colonial legacies, and towards popular musicology.[98] In this revised context, scholarship on symphonies now needs to prove just why we should devote our energy to what might be perceived as a privileged relic of the nineteenth century.[99] Perhaps its ongoing absence from the (post)-new musicological project, for instance, derives from its image as comparatively conservative, anachronistic, and also oppressively masculine in relation to other twentieth-century genres. Unfortunately, the cultural norms and assumptions that ensured the symphony's place on the scholarly agenda have ultimately proved an obstacle to producing a legacy of work that stands up to intellectual and methodological scrutiny by contemporary academia. For instance, there has been little activity in uncovering and collating sources and critical writing that build a sense of the ideological implications for the symphony in the early twentieth century.[100] If the current musicological climate is still highly receptive to the collaborative energy and interdisciplinary messiness that opera stages, perhaps scholars are overlooking possibilities for applying similar approaches to other genres and areas.

An Alternative History

This book begins that project. Those ways of engaging with the genre that became entrenched throughout the twentieth century have allowed particular periods, repertoires, and (national) voices to slip from history. The

Strains of Utopia: Gender, Nostalgia, and Hollywood Film Music (Princeton; Princeton University Press, 1992). Roughly concurrent disciplinary innovations in opera studies have been outlined under note 95: opera's emphasis on musical bodies challenged musicology's fetishist essentialism of the musical object.

[98] For more detailed discussion of the interdisciplinary tension this has engendered, see John Covach, 'Popular Music, Unpopular Musicology', in Cook and Everist, *Rethinking Music*, 452–70.

[99] Samantha Ege's research on Florence Price's Symphony in E minor is a good example of such work. Through detailed archival work alongside methods drawn from Black feminist biography, she shows how Price's symphony was the result of grassroots political activism and the collective agency and network-building of Black women in Chicago of the 1930s. See Ege, 'Composing a Symphonist: Florence Price and the Hand of Black Women's Fellowship', *Women and Music: A Journal of Gender and Culture* 24 (2020): 7–27.

[100] Painter's book is the exception. See Painter, *Symphonic Aspirations*. See also Nicholas E. Tawa, *The Great American Symphony* (Bloomington: Indiana University Press, 2009), which gives some sense of the ideological stakes for the American symphony.

early 1930s is just one of them. Framing the neglected and politically tumultuous year 1933 gives us access to a more finely calibrated plane on which to reformulate our understanding of the genre: one that invites interdisciplinary perspectives; one that disrupts linear narratives of individual composers and national traditions, setting the symphony in negotiation with contextual networks; one that tackles the important legacies of the idea of Germany and Austria for the genre head-on. As far as symphonies are concerned, it seems many new musicological agendas, in particular, have lost none of their urgency. Perspectives inspired by that movement still offer productive starting points for scholarship on the twentieth-century symphony, particularly since this body of music largely missed out on treatment in the first place. Issues like (post-colonial) power, gender, and race deserve to be put front and centre more often when we approach the symphony; their cross-disciplinary literatures offer ample theoretical underpinning.[101]

A key motivation for refocusing the lens on the genre is to come back to those core symphonic reception issues of subjectivity and space that many have observed are in need of more sophisticated analysis, and which were pressing issues in the cultural ferment of 1933. By this means, we can generate a higher resolution image of the genre's social and political role in different but coexistent sociocultural arenas. Building on established scholarship that considers how social practices at the symphony concert perpetuate hegemonic identities and value systems, I examine the symphony as a mechanism by which particular kinds of subjectivities asserted their status and maintained their power.[102] This is partly about how social, community-forming, and spatial rhetorics associated with the genre have aligned with particular political movements or ideologies – for example, fascism in Germany, US liberalism and Pan-Americanism across the Americas. In addition, however, this volume has a musical focus, examining how sound can play an active part in sustaining or undermining political impulses.

With these broad aims in mind, the six case studies serve the book's narrative and thematic coherence first and foremost. Although this is an overlooked repertoire, my curation of the 1933 symphonies does not

---

[101] Feminist disciplinary critique and potential models are offered by Suzanne Cusick. See Cusick, 'Gender, Musicology, and Feminism', in Cook and Everist, *Rethinking Music*, 471–98.

[102] See, for example, Christopher Small, *Musicking: The Meanings of Performing and Listening* (Hanover, NH: University Press of New England, 1998); Sven Oliver Müller, 'Political Pleasures with Old Emotions? Performances of the Berlin Philharmonic in the Second World War', *International Review of the Aesthetics and Sociology of Music* 43 (2012): 35–52.

attempt to represent every musical language and aesthetic theory of the moment. Nor does it attempt to demonstrate the diversity of contributors to the symphonic genre in 1933. For the most part, I am more interested in shining a light on where power is structurally located and exploring how the symphony might be an aesthetic and political mechanism deeply embedded in upholding the status quo. As such, a range of works have been selected for what they reveal about particular coexistent places, framed by the transatlantic story of Weill's Symphony No. 2. The approach fosters biographical, musical, and other kinds of connections between composers, the works, and the surrounding commentary that are contingent and unexpected – Pfitzner brushes shoulders with Copland and Price with Weill – and that traverse national boundaries – Copland goes to Mexico and Honegger is premiered in Berlin. More than a project of rehabilitation, it takes these neglected works and configures them differently in relation to one another, to see what kinds of knowledge are yielded.

Casting the geographical net across oceans is a rarer approach to one year than, say, concentrating on one, more focused, sense of place, but it suits the comparative history of a concept like the *idea* of the symphony. Detailed historical work on one particular place and period has been pervasive in much recent music scholarship.[103] This book adopts an alternative, but complementary transnational methodology. It seeks to tell a different historical narrative, but one that is clearly necessary if we are to understand a complex international phenomenon like the symphony. In common with those recent place-centred approaches, the scope of this volume is concerned with challenging musicology's inherited value systems and historical orthodoxies, as well as its geographical delineations entrenched by political asymmetries that have shaped the discipline. Likewise, it responds to some contemporary anxieties in music scholarship that have prompted renewed interest in actor-network theory (ANT);[104] methodologically, however, it aligns itself more closely, not with such object-oriented approaches, but with transnational historical ones like *histoire croisée* (or entangled history): the symphonies considered here – those of Weill, Price, Copland, Pfitzner, Honegger, and Harris – present

---

[103] For instance, a five-year European Research Council-funded project titled 'Music in London 1800–1851' at the music department of King's College London ended in 2018. By contrast, and perhaps exemplifying a disciplinary shift of emphasis that aligns more closely with my own approach, in 2023 another five-year European Research Council project will begin in the same department titled 'Beyond 1932: Rethinking Musical Modernity in the Middle East and North Africa'.

[104] See Benjamin Piekut, 'Actor-Networks in Music History: Clarifications and Critiques', *Twentieth-Century Music* 11 (2014): 191–215. See also Bruno Latour, *Reassembling the Social: An Introduction to Actor Network-Theory* (Oxford: Oxford University Press, 2005).

a clear opportunity to 'follow topics beyond national boundaries'.[105] This shadows a move in the last fifteen years or so in historical disciplines to emphasise 'the cultural and social connections between nation-states'. For historians Deborah Cohen and Maura O'Connor, 'methodological approaches, historical evidence, and categories of analysis inherited from the past need to be historicized. Rather than proceeding on the basis of established categories of "nation", "state", or "society", *histoire croisée* orientates itself around problems.'[106] Musicology has been diagnosed as needing this kind of perspective with real urgency; according to the authors of a 2014 volume on transatlantic music culture, it is a discipline which 'has traditionally been approached from within the category of the nation, often centring on composers and their works as representative of national achievements'.[107] If studies of the symphony have internalised these structures particularly rigidly, transnational approaches create opportunities to dismantle the category of 'nation' and geographical determinism so enmeshed in symphonic histories, while acknowledging their historical significance.

What the symphony in 1933, at this uncertain moment for the genre, precisely was is just the kind of 'problem' a transnational methodology can tackle. It is helpful, therefore, to re-imagine symphonies using ideas inspired by transnational thinking: as '"entangled" products of national crossings' and systems of aesthetic or cultural-political relations.[108] Unlike many place-centred or ANT-influenced studies, however, this book does not reject the work concept as a methodological starting point, but it does come at it critically. To understand the power structures in which the symphony, as an archetype of the work concept, is complicit, it helps to begin with the work concept in clear view.

'[Weill] Doesn't Give the Impression That a Symphony Was Burning inside Him'

Jinx or no jinx, at the Amsterdam premiere of his symphony in 1934 (see Figure 1.4), Weill came up against an inflexible set of beliefs about symphonies. His initial excitement about the excellent rehearsal had been

---

[105] Deborah Cohen and Maura O'Connor, *Comparison and History: Europe in Cross-National Perspective* (New York: Routledge, 2004), xii.

[106] Ibid., xiii.

[107] Felix Meyer *et al.*, eds., *Crosscurrents: American and European Music in Interaction, 1900–2000* (Woodbridge: Boydell Press, 2014), 12.

[108] Cohen and O'Connor, *Comparison and History*, xiii.

PROGRAMMA

VAN HET

ABONNEMENTS-CONCERT

(SERIE B)

DONDERDAG 11 OCTOBER 1934, 's avonds 8¼ uur

DIRIGENT

BRUNO WALTER

SYMPHONISCHE FANTASIE (SYMPHONIE No. I).......... KURT WEILL
    Sonate   (GEB. 1900)
    Largo
    Rondo
               Allereerste uitvoering

DERDE CONCERT (C GR. T., OP. 26) voor piano en
  orkest .... SERGE PROKOFIEFF
    Andante — Allegro   (GEB. 1891)
    Andantino — Variaties
    Allegro, ma non troppo

          Solist: de componist

— PAUZE —

VIERDE SYMPHONIE (E KL. T., OP. 98) .... JOHANNES BRAHMS
    Allegro non troppo   (1833—1897)
    Andante moderato
    Allegro giocoso
    Allegro energico e passionato

Steinway & Sons' Concertvleugel

Begin tweede deel ± 9.45, einde ± 10.30 uur

Figure 1.4 Front cover of the original programme for the world premiere of Kurt Weill's Second Symphony by the Concertgebouw Orchestra in Amsterdam. Note that the work is introduced as 'Symphony No. 1'; the symphony was retrospectively renumbered No. 2 to acknowledge Weill's one-movement student symphony (1921). The title *Fantaisie symphonique* or Symphony No. 2 has been agreed ahead of its appearance in the Kurt Weill Edition. Courtesy of the Weill-Lenya Research Center, Kurt Weill Foundation for Music, New York. Reproduced with the permission of the Royal Concertgebouw Orchestra Concert Archive.

short-sighted. Before we depart from the Netherlands, let us first delve further into the specifics of Weill's exclusion from the reception to gain a more concrete initial sense of how space and subjectivity were entwined in symphonic reception at this time. What critics had to say about the 'nature' of Weill's ostensibly theatrical music, alongside the way the reviews foregrounded the aesthetic legacies of ideals associated with nineteenth-century absolute music, is revealing for how this book's major themes are coupled. Unpacking it uncovers that critics' problems with the work had less to do with 'purely' musical aspects, and more to do with Weill and whether he, as a Jewish, socialist, supposedly popular theatre composer belonged in the reified space of the concert hall.

Several writers commented on the 'banality' or 'emptiness' of Weill's music, implicitly contrasting it with the depth of true symphonic language.[109] L. M. G. Arntzenius, writing in the Telegraaf, addressed this directly: '[O]ne could not trace any symphonic art in the normal sense of the word. Symphonic art requires an orchestra that has been more deeply touched and worked on.'[110] Such aesthetic legacies had clear nationalist-ideological correlates. Alongside metaphors of depth came those of organicism, another key Germanic symphonic ideology that embedded music in other social, scientific, and aesthetic discourses of the nineteenth century. Together, depth and organicism helped make music about subjective interiority and encumber it with the burden of national identity construction.[111] The reviewer in the socialist paper Het Volk, initialled P. F. S., suggested that 'all the "songs" that are interweaved in the piece display the same kind of primitive melody, which does not lend itself to the distinctive character of symphonic style: the development'.[112] Likewise, far from finding it to be a paragon of organic unity, the reviewer for the Dames Kroniek wrote uncharitably of Weill's thematic development that 'it all sticks together like dry sand', acidly describing the themes as simply 'appearing' rather than the more symphonic or organic 'developing'.[113] In a similar rhetorical vein, but with a more contemporary geneticist bent,

---

[109] See, for instance, H. R., 'Donderdagavondconcert Concertgebouw', Handelsblad, 12 October 1934 (trans. Linda Bakkum); Theo v. d. Bijl, 'Concertgebouw: Een nieuw werk van Kurt Weill', Jüd. (a Jewish periodical?), 12 October 1934 (trans. Snijders); L, 'Muziek: Concertgebouw', Dames Kroniek, 13 October 1934 (trans. Anne Hillebrand).

[110] L. M. G. Arntzenius, 'Walter's Tweede Avond – Première van Kurt Weill's "Symphonische Fantasie" – Prokofieff Oogst Succes', Telegraaf, 12 October 1934 (trans. Kahn).

[111] Watkins, Metaphors of Depth.

[112] P. F. S., 'Weill en Prokofieff – Première der symphonische fantasie bereidt een teleurstelling – Voortreffelijke uitvoering', Het Volk(?), 12 October 1934 (trans. Kahn).

[113] L., 'Muziek: Concertgebouw'.

another reviewer indicated that the music 'all remained in an embryonic state'.[114] Arntzenius summed up the supposed problem with the musical themes: 'Sometimes they have a song-like character, sometimes they appear to be a bit heavier, yet they never swell to become an actual piece, to become the foundation for, indeed, a symphonic sound. No, never will they reach the level of a true symphony.'[115]

If Weill's work was not a 'true symphony', how, then, should reviewers account for the obvious delight of the listening public in the wake of Weill's *Dreigroschenoper* fame: the fact that Weill bridged so-called 'high' and 'low' art forms and audiences? 'On the slippery floors [of the concert hall] he made the occasional clumsy gambol and he winked amicably and jovially at the distinguished ladies Rhythm and Melody, something which does not belong in a dignified symphonic milieu!'[116] Note the gendering of popular theatrical music's 'Rhythm and Melody' as feminine, reiterated in the gendering of a star-struck audience: 'There was a lot of applause for the piece by Kurt Weill (the young ladies in particular were very enthusiastic – of course because of the *Dreigroschenoper!*).'[117] Here, the symphony's community-forming impulse – a legacy of its Enlightenment origins – was inflected by specifically twentieth-century concerns.

Weill's exclusion shows how powerfully the idea of the symphony had been shaped by Romantic conceptions of creative authorship. As one anonymous reviewer observed, Weill 'doesn't give the impression that he *had* to write a symphony because it was burning inside him'.[118] But it is uncertain whether those inherited narratives about the feverish symphonic generative process still fully convinced. Equally uncertain is the status of the antisemitic stereotypes that peppered the reviews without ever quite rearing their heads explicitly. This suggests how notions of symphonic authenticity continued to be congruous with ideas of racial purity. After describing Weill's melodies as 'primitive', the reviewer for *Het Volk* went on:

Initially, coming from the schooling of Busoni, [Weill's] work displayed great seriousness. Abruptly this changed. Instead of increased intensification, stagnation set in. The composer had found a genre which promised him comfortable

---

[114] 'Concertgebouw: Wereldpremière van de Eerste Symphonie van Kurt Weill', n.d. (trans. Snijders).

[115] Arntzenius, 'Walter's Tweede Avond'.

[116] V. d. Bijl, 'Concertgebouw: Een nieuw werk van Kurt Weill'.

[117] H. F. K., 'Belangrijke nieuwe muziek in het Concertgebouw'.

[118] 'Concertgebouw: Wereldpremière'.

success. . . . Only those of a strong nature know how to avoid the dangers that the flush of victory brings along.[119]

The writer hints at weakness of character, popularism, and commercial success: this may have been how they felt about Weill's development as a composer, but note how this trio of tropes used to distance Weill from the supposedly pure and cerebral world of Germanic symphonic idealism (a world for 'those of a strong nature') converge with antisemitic ones. Such ambiguity characterised much of the language used by reviewers. It suggests the presence of insidious underlying ideas about how evolutionary theories determined racial hierarchies (e.g. 'intensification' versus 'primitive' 'stagnation'). There is a parallel with racialised responses to Mahler's supposedly song-like, theatrical symphonies twenty years earlier.

Just one reviewer briefly mooted – and discarded – the idea that the work might be a conscious critique. ('Is this a deliberate revolution? Difficult to believe: the unity seems too weak to destroy the fundaments of the existing literature.'[120]) Thus, the notion of symphonic critique was completely overlooked by most. It would seem that Weill had overestimated the reviewers' readiness to hear his work as positioned critically within the problematics of absolute music when remarking in the programme note that:

It is not possible for me to comment on the content of the work since it was conceived as pure musical form. But perhaps a Parisian friend of mine was right when she suggested that an appropriate title would be a word that expressed the opposite of 'pastoral', should such a word exist. I do not know.[121]

It is hard to say whether Weill's tongue was in his cheek or not. Weill suggests that it is impossible for a symphonic composer to engage discursively with the meaning of a 'pure musical form'. But by introducing the voice of a – clearly modern – Parisian 'Freundin' (the Princesse de Polignac perhaps?), he immediately undercuts that absolute position. It seems that ventriloquising thoughts about content through a feminine alter ego avoids threatening absolute music's (or his) masculinity. Weill reiterates that he himself did not know, hardening up his masculine, absolute stance. Furthermore, with a nod to 'the opposite of "pastoral"', Weill satirises the Beethovenian idea of the symphony and its nostalgic agrarian spaces, where people fantasise fully coherent versions of themselves, supposedly realised through authentic modes of being and quiet contemplation in

---

[119] P. F. S., 'Weill en Prokofieff.'   [120] Arntzenius, 'Walter's Tweede Avond'.
[121] Concertgebouw Programme Note.

nature. Instead, primed by the reference to Paris, city-dwelling readers were reminded of some home truths. Those modern subjects did not enjoy boundless fields and fresh air, but cramped urban living, micro-managed production lines, and neon-lit nights. Weill's (or his urban Parisian friend's) comment disrupts a long trajectory of German idealist thought about symphonies, coherent subjectivities, and infinite, universalised spaces. Christian Kuhnt locates this reading of 'the opposite of "pastoral"' more specifically within the political context. While thoroughly non-programmatic, via self-quotation and corruption of themes from Weill's existing works that bring the anxiety, poverty, and political perils of the late-Weimar era into the symphony's atmosphere, the work transports the listener to an anti-idyll.[122]

Either way, Dutch reviewers did not respond to any of Weill's knowing reflections on the fraught discourses of absolute music. It was as simple as this; Weill and his music, Dutch reviewers concluded, did not belong within the concert hall's reified walls. Race, political inclination, how popular aesthetics were gendered: these all seemed to play a part in his exclusion. So, too, did the *idea* of the symphony, which became an agent in policing those norms. But would this reception have differed elsewhere? Different contexts channel different cultural ideas about subjectivity and space. It follows that what we learn from Weill's exclusion is in some ways specific to Amsterdam. The reception pivoted on localised concerns, but was still shaped by an imagined sense of a symphonic ideal – the Weill criticism was shot through with a sense of deference to Germanic *symphonische* values. Were symphonic anxieties more pronounced in Amsterdam than they might have been in a more culturally assured city like Berlin or Vienna? Seductively fine-grained but, lacking comparative context that accounts for the symphony's internationalism, frustratingly hard to parse, this Amsterdam concert isolates and clarifies one of the key problems inherited from existing thought on the symphony. It is time some of those blanks were filled, creating a more robust sense of the social stakes for the genre. That is the task of the rest of the book, in which the chapters elucidate how particular symphonies focus ideas of subjectivity and space in a network of transnational contexts animated by the stories of particular musical works, which roughly overlap with those highlighted in the story of Weill's symphony: Berlin, Paris, Boston, New York, Mexico City, Chicago. Only then will some context be provided for the reactions to Weill's symphony two months later when Walter took the baton once again, this

---

[122] Kuhnt, 'Das Gegenteil von Pastorale', 329.

time in Carnegie Hall, New York, a concert that we will visit at the beginning of Chapter 6, before exploring the legacies of works from 1933 across the twentieth century and for the present day.

Ultimately, approaching the symphony in 1933 seems to be a matter of refining a critical framework capable of mediating the multiple and freighted historical layers that the discourse collapses together, and of dealing in a sophisticated way with the localised conditions for, and implications of, so-called universal values. Evidently a site at which cultural exchange takes place, the symphony in this period discloses anxieties about intercultural relations, but is also a vehicle for engaging imaginatively with other nations and identities and for formulating a sense of selfhood and community. Offering a glimpse into people's sense of their place in the world, symphonic discourse was a means of defining who they were, but equally, and often more revealingly, who they were not. The symphony may be a genre of privilege, but that is exactly the point. Attending critically to symphonies and their social discourses, a genre with high status despite its acute ethical ambivalence, remains a vital project.

2 | Listening for the *Intimsphäre* in Hans Pfitzner's Symphony in C♯ Minor

Berlin

In the same week that Weill fled Berlin for Paris, Hans Pfitzner's Symphony in C♯ minor Op. 36a, an orchestral transcription of his String Quartet Op. 36 (1925), was premiered in Munich. The concert coincided with the date the Enabling Act was passed – 23 March 1933 – when Adolf Hitler's political powers became total. A week later, on 30 March, it was played again by the Philharmonic Orchestra in Berlin. This chapter focuses on that second performance in the Philharmonie, a concert at which the effects of new Nazi policy and persecution could be felt in an immediate way. According to a witness account of events, ten days prior to the Pfitzner concert the Nazi authorities had threatened violence at the concert hall if Bruno Walter's regular concert with the Berlin Philharmonic – part of the 'Bruno Walter Series' – were to proceed as usual, which triggered Walter's immediate political exile.[1] His replacement by Richard Strauss, who donated his fee to the hard-up orchestra, has been well rehearsed in the secondary literature,[2] but it was certainly not the only concert affected by Walter's exit. Due to conductor 'reshuffles' ('*Umbesetzungen*', as they were described in one review)[3] between many of north Germany's major concert venues in the wake of Walter's departure, it was Pfitzner himself who unexpectedly took to the podium at short notice to conduct his new symphony at the 30 March concert of the composer's music. Although he

---

[1] This account of the events surrounding Walter's exile comes from the memoirs of Edith Stargardt-Wolff, who at the time had been due to inherit the concert agency responsible for the Berlin Philharmonic's engagements. Edith Stargardt-Wolff, *Wegbereiter grosser Musiker* (Berlin: Bote & G. Bock, 1954), 276–7; cited in Erik S. Ryding and Rebecca Pechefsky, *Bruno Walter: A World Elsewhere* (New Haven, CT: Yale University Press, 2001), 220.

[2] Coverage of Strauss's 20 March concert at the Berlin Philharmonic is extensive. See, for example, Michael Walter, *Richard Strauss und seine Zeit* (Laaber: Laaber-Verlag, 2000), 360–2; Raymond Holden, *Richard Strauss: A Musical Life* (New Haven, CT: Yale University Press, 2011), 152; Michael Kennedy, 'Taking Walter's Place' in *Richard Strauss: Man, Musician, Enigma* (Cambridge: Cambridge University Press, 1999), 269–79; Pamela M. Potter, 'Richard Strauss and the National Socialists: The Debate and Its Relevance', in *Richard Strauss: New Perspectives on the Composer and His Work*, ed. Bryan Gilliam (Durham, NC: Duke University Press, 1992), 93–113, 94–5; Michael Meyer, *The Politics of Music in the Third Reich* (New York: Peter Lang, 1993), 23–4; Erik Levi, *Music in the Third Reich* (Basingstoke: Macmillan, 1994), 42–3.

[3] Otto Steinhagen, 'Das Musikleben der Gegenwart: Berlin', *Die Musik* 25 (1933): 619–21, 619.

was not directly stepping in to cover Walter – Eugen Jochum had been on the original billing but was needed at Leipzig's Gewandhaus to cover the position Walter's exile now left unfilled – this last-minute switch made Walter's absence from the concert circuit plainly apparent.

Hitler's appointment as chancellor of Germany is one of the most infamous historical junctures in twentieth-century history, yet we still do not understand those chaotic, unco-ordinated first weeks following his seizure of power on 30 January as well as we should. The 30 March Pfitzner concert was clearly a major German cultural event, led by a major conservative cultural icon, but it has completely slipped from our historical consciousness. Through the prism of this concert and through close attention to the musical work at the heart of it – Pfitzner's thoroughly neglected C♯ Minor Symphony – this chapter aims to retrieve some of the fine grain of that incredible, uncertain political moment, when nothing was inevitable. In so doing, it brings into sharp relief the ideological stakes in 1933 for the symphonic genre in Germany's capital city, one of the twin cultural capitals (the other being Vienna) within the central European terrain inhabited by the German-speaking peoples that was the symphony's imagined ideological homeland.

Pfitzner's C♯ Minor Symphony raised musical questions that mirrored vital political ones about how Nazi ideology sought to change the relationship between a subjective interiority inherited from liberal nineteenth-century idealism and the collectivised political sphere. It tells us about how critics responded to those questions and how, in March 1933, the reformulation of space enacted by the new regime was still contingent and contested. Reviews of the concert, which received significant exposure in all the major Berlin newspapers and national music journals, uncover shifting currents in music criticism, which recursively fed back into the shifts playing out in the political landscape.[4] Figures like Pfitzner, who might today seem marginal to National Socialist history, are precisely those currently in most need of sustained critical attention, because their often bewildering political ambivalences help to sharpen the realities and contradictions of living in the Third Reich.[5] History, after all, reveals itself through the micro-historical, the peripheral, and the disregarded.

---

[4] After all, as contended by Benjamin Korstvedt, pointing to a sea-change in disciplinary methodology in recent decades, '[t]here is now little danger of supposing, let alone seriously arguing, that music criticism expressed little more than matters of musical taste and objective artistic judgment'. Korstvedt, 'Reading Music Criticism beyond the Fin-de-Siècle Vienna Paradigm', *Musical Quarterly* 94 (2011): 156–210, 166.

[5] For a discussion of Pfitzner's ambivalent politics and his divisiveness, see Jens Malte Fischer, 'The Very German Fate of a Composer: Hans Pfitzner', in *Music and Nazism: Art under Tyranny,*

As might be expected, praise flowed freely for a new symphonic work by a major conservative figure, with the *Berliner Lokal-Anzeiger* hailing it as 'a new masterpiece' and *Melos* as 'without doubt one of Pfitzner's strongest compositions'.[6] But such critical acclaim is not what offers unique insights into the historical texture of this time and place. They are instead to be found in something more easily overlooked – namely, critics' anxieties about genre.

A symphonic reworking of a string quartet presents a remarkable opportunity to investigate language relating to public and private spheres and spaces within a society in transition to fascism. Particular kinds of discussion are initiated by its position as a 'boundary-work'[7] between chamber music and symphony, and between private and public space. The concert and its reception can be read as a tipping point, at which nineteenth-century symphonic idealism and twentieth-century totalitarianism become visible as intimately entwined. As Karen Painter has noted, nothing altered identifiably in symphonic musical language or style when Hitler seized power; instead, it was the 'ideological valence' that changed.[8] March 1933 precedes any sedimentation of Nazi symphonic values – Painter has described the first two years of the Nazi government as an uncertain period of 'inconsistent scrambling' in cultural life[9] – but the symphony's reception anticipates their discourses. This points to a slippery slope between the aesthetics of absolute music and its artistic imperatives, and the collusive anonymisation and determinism of totalitarian regimes.

'The era of individualism died once and for all on 30 January', propaganda minister Joseph Goebbels stated in an address the weekend before Pfitzner's Berlin concert. 'The individual is being supplanted by the collective of the *Volk*.'[10] Yet, undercutting Goebbels's assertion, contemporary appraisals of Pfitzner's symphony suggest strongly that listeners 'heard' the intimate, subjective space of the string quartet as if preserved within the orchestral rendering. In this chapter, I consider the reshaping of political

---

1933–1945, ed. Michael H. Kater and Albrecht Riethmüller (Laaber: Laaber-Verlag, 2003), 75–89, 88.

[6] Walter Abendroth, 'Pfitzner-Abend der Philharmoniker', *Berliner Lokal-Anzeiger*, 31 March 1933; Karl Wörner, 'Hans Pfitzners Sinfonie in cis', *Melos* 12 (1933): 133.

[7] See *Allgemeine Musikzeitung*, 16 June 1933, 335.

[8] Karen Painter, *Symphonic Aspirations: German Music and Politics, 1900–1945* (Cambridge, MA: Harvard University Press, 2007), 217.

[9] Ibid., 219.

[10] Address given at the Berlin Haus des Rundfunks ('Die zukünftige Arbeit und Gestaltung des deutschen Rundfunks'), in Helmut Heiber, ed., *Goebbels Reden 1932–1945* (Düsseldorf: Gondrom, 1991), 82–107, 82.

and aesthetic notions of space in the context of the political transition, mining the reception of Pfitzner's symphonic re-orchestration for what it can reveal about how those two kinds of space are intertwined. A critical tenet of fascist ideology,[11] closely associated with what Michael Meyer has called 'the collectivisation of the individual',[12] is the reformulation of the relationship between subjectivity[13] and public space. Music can participate forcefully in this process. As Margaret Notley has observed, opposing the symphony and public space to chamber music and the subjective associations of the private sphere was a well-established critical tendency. In the Berlin reception, the respective spatial analogues for the two genres were likewise strongly implied through metaphors of force, space, and containment.[14] Against this specific political background, the work provokes a set of questions about the monumentalisation of the string quartet's

[11] While the definition and methodological viability of a congruous fascist ideology is the subject of ongoing debate, fascism scholarship from the 1990s onwards has seen the emergence of a so-called New Consensus. This intersection of perspectives, first identified by Roger Griffin, crystallises around the idea of 'interpreting fascism as a unique ideological articulation of radical revolutionary nationalism, "third way" politics, and holistic social organization'. See Aristotle A. Kallis, 'Fascist Ideology: The Quest for the "Fascist Minimum"', in *The Fascism Reader*, ed. Kallis (London: Routledge, 2003), 145–7.

[12] Meyer, *Politics of Music in the Third Reich*, 8.

[13] The problem of subjectivity was a prevalent theme in the work of many Weimar writers, philosophers, and social critics. In particular, they reflected on the unity and coherence of the modern subject, its moral structures, its autonomy, and its relationship to the mass or collective, or to the state. See, for example, Siegfried Kracauer, *The Mass Ornament: Weimar Essays*, trans. and ed. Thomas Y. Levin (Cambridge, MA: Harvard University Press, 1995). Martin Heidegger's holistic ontology of *Dasein* proposed an alternative to the Cartesian conception of the self. See Heidegger, *Being and Time*, trans. John Macquarrie and Edward Robinson (Oxford: Blackwell, 1967). For a meditation on state violence, law, freedom, and agency, see Walter Benjamin, 'Critique of Violence', in *Selected Writings*, ed. Marcus Bullock and Michael W. Jennings, vol. 1, *1913–1928* (Cambridge, MA: Belknap Press, 1996), 236–52, especially 241–2. Benjamin's critical reflections seem particularly salient in the context of an increasingly violent state and police force. Other Weimar essays addressing these themes include Hans Zehrer, 'The Revolution of the Intelligentsia', in *The Weimar Republic Sourcebook*, ed. Anton Kaes, Martin Jay, and Edward Dimendberg, 295–7, originally published as 'Die Revolution der Intelligenz', *Die Tat* 21 (1929): 486–507; Karl Mannheim, 'Ideology and Utopia', in *Weimar Republic Sourcebook*, 297–300, originally published as *Ideologie und Utopie* (Bonn: Cohen, 1929).

[14] Margaret Notley, *Lateness and Brahms: Music and Culture in the Twilight of Viennese Liberalism* (Oxford: Oxford University Press, 2007), 156–60. Notley notes that 'the metaphor of symphony as public oration (versus string quartet as conversation) was already current during Beethoven's lifetime' (159), citing Ludwig Finscher, 'Symphonie', in *Die Musik in Geschichte und Gegenwart*, 2nd ed., ed. Finscher (Kassel: Bärenreiter, 1998), vol. 9, columns 56–8. Also incisive for this discussion is Theodor W. Adorno's sociological analysis of the public and private distinctions between chamber and symphonic music in 'Chamber Music' and 'Conductor and Orchestra', in *Introduction to the Sociology of Music*, trans. E. B. Ashton [Ernst Basch] (New York: Continuum, 1989), 85–103, 104–17.

forces and about transgressing the corresponding real and imagined public and private spaces associated with each genre. Pfitzner's symphony simultaneously contributes to and contests fascism's ideological remodelling of space, both performing and defying an assimilation of the private to the public. The sense of autonomous subjectivity that fascist ideology seeks to erase is immanently connected with the essential core of the private sphere – or, to borrow a term from Thomas Burger, the *Intimsphäre*.[15] If the symphony, as the reviews begin to indicate, succeeds in preserving a sense of a private sphere beyond the reaches of political intrusion, then what are the implications for subjective autonomy and agency?

Pfitzner's symphony has only rarely been performed in the years since 1933,[16] and the project here is one without interest in its rehabilitation. Instead, it is to add to a broader theoretical investigation into how the symphonic genre is involved in fascism's reformulation of the relationship between space and subjectivity, building on work by Reinhold Brinkmann and Alexander Rehding. These scholars have compellingly examined National Socialist constructions of two interlinked aesthetic categories: respectively, the 'sublime' and the 'monumental'.[17] My methodology allies in part with Rehding's directive for understanding the 'machinations of monumentalization'. He proposes that examining arrangements – that is, musical material that has undergone some transformative process, as here the symphonic rescoring of a string quartet – might yield 'instructive insights on the workings of monumentality'.[18] Rehding underlines the stakes for the monumental in National Socialist Germany by paraphrasing Thomas Mann's shrewd observation on the dangers of monumental music – namely, that 'monumental music seems to exude moral authority without specifying the carrier of the authority, or indeed the nature of such morality'.[19] In relation to a large body of sociocultural literature on musical and cultural life in Germany in the late 1920s and early 1930s, scholars such as Painter and Bryan Gilliam have explored how far symphonic and Nazi

---

[15] Thomas Burger's definition of an *Intimsphäre* as 'the core of a person's private sphere which by law, tact, and convention is shielded from intrusion' illuminates the way in which these ideas are enmeshed. See Burger, translator's note, in Jürgen Habermas, *The Structural Transformation of the Public Sphere: An Inquiry into a Category of Bourgeois Society*, trans. Thomas Burger and Frederick Lawrence (Cambridge, MA: MIT Press, 1989), xvi.

[16] See Fischer, 'Very German Fate', 76.

[17] See Reinhold Brinkmann, 'The Distorted Sublime: Music and National Socialist Ideology: A Sketch', in *Music and Nazism: Art under Tyranny, 1933–1945*, ed. Michael Kater and Albrecht Riethmüller (Laaber: Laaber-Verlag, 2003), 43–63; Rehding, *Music and Monumentality*, 8.

[18] Rehding, *Music and Monumentality*, 15–16.   [19] Ibid., 8.

ideals converged.[20] Likewise, Sven Oliver Müller has used the Berlin Philharmonic as a case study to establish how the National Socialists used musical culture as 'a powerful instrument in consensus politics'.[21]

Excavating a single concert, this chapter's scope is more confined. Through the Pfitzner reception, it explores how established critical rhetorics had begun to take on new dimensions, shedding light on some of the inconsistencies of fascism and its roots in existing intellectual trends. The C♯ Minor Symphony's uncertain genre status, suspended between chamber music and symphony, was a central source of critical tension. Contemporary listeners couched their descriptions of the work in competing terms. They evoked monumentality and the sublime, but also celebrated the symphony's austerity and rejection of decadent orchestral colour. Whereas most reviewers applauded the symphony's success, there was nonetheless discomfort about how the work negotiated public and private space. Those musical moments at which contemporary reviewers argued that the work failed to convince as a symphony are analytically examined here in relation to conventional symphonic models, with particular consideration being given to the public and private sphere discourses closely associated with chamber and symphonic music. Two problematic symphonic-generic junctures, in particular, caught music critics' attention: the structure and thematic work of the first movement, and the close of the final movement. Then, in light of this discussion, some language in the reviews warrant broader examination, framed theoretically by Bekker's idealist Weimar symphonic aesthetics, on the one hand, and Brinkmann's and Rehding's work on the Nazi 'sublime' and 'monumental', on the other. The criticism arguably isolates this concert as a historical moment during which the sands began to shift more decisively between

---

[20] See, for example, Meyer, *Politics of Music in the Third Reich*; Levi, *Music in the Third Reich*; Erik Levi, *Mozart and the Nazis: How the Third Reich Abused a Cultural Icon* (New Haven, CT: Yale University Press, 2010); Michael H. Kater, *Composers of the Nazi Era: Eight Portraits* (New York: Oxford University Press, 2000); Pamela M. Potter, *Most German of the Arts: Musicology and Society from the Weimar Republic to the End of Hitler's Reich* (New Haven, CT: Yale University Press, 1998); Stephen Hinton, The Idea of Gebrauchsmusik: A Study of Musical Aesthetics in the Weimar Republic (1919–1933), with Particular Reference to the Works of Paul Hindemith (New York: Garland, 1989); Hinton, *Weill's Musical Theater: Stages of Reform* (Berkeley: University of California Press, 2012); Painter, *Symphonic Aspirations*; Bryan Gilliam, 'The Annexation of Anton Bruckner: Nazi Revisionism and the Politics of Appropriation', *Musical Quarterly* 78 (1994): 584–604.

[21] See Sven Oliver Müller, 'Political Pleasures with Old Emotions? Performances of the Berlin Philharmonic in the Second World War', *International Review of the Aesthetics and Sociology of Music* 43 (2012): 35–52, 38.

two value systems. It reveals that principles that had once seemed libertarian and utopian all too readily prepared the ground for totalitarian thought.

The Berlin Premiere of Pfitzner's Symphony at the Philharmonie

For Pfitzner, the 30 March concert at the Philharmonie had added significance as the Berlin premiere of his first-ever symphony. His reputation in contemporary circles as 'the last of the Romantics' was chiefly built on his works for stage, cantatas, and songs.[22] Composed during the latter part of 1932 when Pfitzner was sixty-three, such a late first foray into the genre may point to self-fashioning after Brahms, a central figure in the German symphonic canon. Brahms turned to symphonies later in life, after making his name in vocal, piano, and chamber music. In any case, this concert would have presented a crucial opportunity for Pfitzner to display his work in the sightlines of the new government, channelling the genre's status as a serious test of a composer's capabilities. From the moment he first imagined making a symphony out of his string quartet, he envisaged Berlin as the ideal location for the premiere, pointing to the cultural kudos the *Hauptstadt* could give the work.[23] His concession that it be premiered in Munich a week earlier came only after a generous offer from the mayor to put on an extra, 'appropriately "sensational"' concert for the new symphony, which overrode the composer's reservations about the city in which he lived – presumably related to 'wasting' a premiere where his celebrity was already assured.[24] After these initial Munich and Berlin concerts, numerous additional performances of the symphony in several German and Austrian cities followed throughout 1933.[25]

---

[22] E. d. W., 'Lettre de Berlin', *Revue Musicale* 14 (1933): 378.

[23] In correspondence with his publisher, initially Pfitzner indicated that he wanted to conduct the premiere himself, but not in Munich – 'perhaps in Berlin'. Letter to Otto Fürstner, 7 July 1932, in Hans Erich Pfitzner, *Briefe*, ed. Bernhard Adamy (Tutzing: Hans Schneider, 1991), 599.

[24] Letter to Fürstner, 8 September 1932, in Pfitzner, *Briefe*, 608–9.

[25] Other performances during 1933 took place in Dortmund (as part of the 1933 Tonkünstlerfest), Darmstadt, Düsseldorf, Wiesbaden, Bonn, Dessau, and Vienna. Pfitzner cancelled the performance that had been planned for the summer Salzburger Festspiele, in line with National Socialist policy in relation to Austria. How far Pfitzner was politically pressured into doing so is unclear, however. See further discussion in Birgit Jürgens, 'Pfitzners Wirken und seine Position im Nationalsozialismus: Ambivalenzen, Worte, Taten', in *'Deutsche Musik': Das Verhältnis von Ästhetik und Politik bei Hans Pfitzner* (Hildesheim: George Olms Verlag, 2009), 163–273, especially 229–51.

Pfitzner's letters to friends and colleagues from 1933 reveal his concern about his perceived peripheral standing in the Third Reich's artistic hierarchy, particularly in relation to those he saw as in the inner circle such as composer Richard Strauss and conductor Wilhelm Furtwängler, and his hope that the new nationalist government would elevate his reputation.[26] Indeed, Pfitzner sent Hitler numerous invitations to performances of his works in Berlin during this year, but to no avail, leaving Pfitzner disillusioned.[27] Just two weeks before the Berlin concert, on 15 March, Pfitzner wrote to Hitler reminding him of their single meeting in 1923 and asking for Hitler's support in his artistic endeavours.[28] Unknown to the composer, Hitler's 1923 visit to Pfitzner in hospital had ignited a loathing for Pfitzner that proved long-lasting: Goebbels remarked in a 1943 diary entry that 'the Führer really is very much against Pfitzner since, contrary to all evidence, he thinks him to be a half-Jew'.[29] Thus, Hitler would have nothing to do with Pfitzner, despite the composer's best efforts. Pfitzner's ambivalent relationship to the incumbent regime has been extensively documented elsewhere; like the timing of his letter to Hitler, much of Pfitzner's behaviour in the early months of 1933 seems self-interestedly opportunist.[30]

---

[26] Evidence of Pfitzner's hopes for the improvement of his situation under the National Socialists and the sense of injustice he subsequently felt upon being marginalised can be found in several of his letters. Pfitzner's letter of 15 March 1933 to Hitler immediately after the latter came to power is telling: 'I needn't ask whether you remember who I am; rather, I assume that you recall that hour – unforgettable to me – when you visited me in hospital in Schwabing. Whoever is, as you are, serious about art will understand me and fight, as I do, against injustice, endorse my work, and use the power that lies in your hands to support me in my ambitions'. Pfitzner, *Briefe*, 621–2. A letter to Viktor Junk, 5 December 1933, reveals Strauss and Furtwängler as the obvious figures of comparison: 'Of all the great names in music I am the only one . . . who has not been given a worthy position, let alone received higher honours, such as have been conferred upon Richard Strauss and Wilhelm Furtwängler.' Ibid., 643. See also letter to Margaritta Jüttner-Fischer, 5 October 1933, in which he writes about his disappointment and frustration with his position in the new Reich: 'I have received only ingratitude for the great sacrifice I made by cancelling my appearance in Salzburg. That is my position in the Third Reich where, were it all based on merit, I should be a kind of musical emperor.' Ibid., 639–40.

[27] See, for example, letter to Felix Wolfes, 5 December 1933: 'Hitler has not attended a single of my events, despite repeated invitations, but can be found every night at another concert or opera, as during this period at Das Rheingold, Die Walküre, Arabella, Butterfly, the Backhaus piano recital, Maria Müller's song recital, the aria concert by the world-famous tenor Gigli, etc.' Ibid., 645.

[28] Ibid., 621–2.

[29] Much more can be found on the relationship of Pfitzner to Hitler in Kater, *Composers of the Nazi Era*, 218–19.

[30] For a thorough discussion of Pfitzner's complex relationship with the National Socialist authorities, see, for example, Kater, *Composers of the Nazi Era*; John Williamson, *The Music of Hans Pfitzner* (Oxford: Clarendon Press, 1992), especially 'An Inner Emigration?', 301–48; Sabine Busch, *Hans Pfitzner und der Nationalsozialismus* (Stuttgart: J. B. Metzler, 2001); Jürgens, *'Deutsche Musik'*; Fischer, 'Very German Fate'.

Writing to his publisher in 1932 about his intentions to rework the string quartet for symphony orchestra, Pfitzner claimed that it was the structure and sound-world of the string quartet that artistically demanded its re-orchestration as a symphony.[31] The four-movement string quartet meanders between fluid chromatic work, with an emphasis on the tritone, and a more diatonic modality. In the resulting symphony, the string quartet is re-orchestrated in a literal sense – the two works are formally and harmonically identical. The string quartet's lines are given over to different instrumental groups, by which means the terse aural world of the string quartet is dissected and then muscled up with aural weight and power for a much larger spatial and acoustic platform.[32] As in the string quartet, the first and second movements of the symphony are paired, as are the third and fourth movements, and should be performed *attacca* 'to underline motivic relationships'.[33] C♯ minor appears too rarely in Pfitzner's compositional output for its use to be merely coincidental, as Johann Peter Vogel remarked in his 1991 analysis of the string quartet. He discerned musical references to Beethoven's late String Quartet Op. 131, but not to Mahler's Symphony No. 5, the other obviously canonical work in C♯ minor.[34] At the very end of the string quartet/ symphony, harmonic material from the opening four bars of the first movement returns, a unifying gesture in the string quartet that, as we will see, functions differently in the symphony.

Expectations for the symphony on the night of the Berlin concert would have been high, following the success of the official premiere in Munich the week before. Concluding the concert, Pfitzner's symphony was heard after Schubert's Symphony No. 8 in B Minor and two of Pfitzner's orchestral songs, 'Zorn' (1904) and 'Klage' (1915), sung by Hans Reinmar.[35] 'Klage'

---

[31] Letter to Fürstner, 17 June 1932, in Pfitzner, *Briefe*, 595. In a later letter he reiterated this argument: the re-orchestration was necessary because both harmony and form – indeed, the whole structure of the quartet – invited the shaping ('Gestaltung') as symphony. Letter to Fürstner, 29 June 1932, in Pfitzner, *Briefe*, 597.

[32] Readers unfamiliar with Pfitzner's C♯ Minor String Quartet Op. 36 and Symphony Op. 36a might find Johann Peter Vogel's detailed formal and harmonic analysis of the string quartet useful, given the formal identity between the two pieces. His work has provided an important point of reference for the overview of the symphony here. See Vogel, *Hans Pfitzner: Streichquartett Cis-Moll Op. 36* (Munich: Fink Verlag, 1991).

[33] See Pfitzner's remark at the end of the first movement in the string quartet score: Hans Pfitzner, *Quartett in cis-moll für 2 Violinen, Viola und Violoncello, opus 36* (Berlin: Adolph Fürstner Verlag, 1925), 18; see also Vogel, *Hans Pfitzner: Streichquartett Cis-Moll Op. 36*, 13.

[34] Ibid., 10–12.

[35] 'Konzerte der Berliner Philharmoniker 1932–1934 (In- und Ausland)', in Peter Muck, *100 Jahre Berliner Philharmonisches Orchester* (Schneider: Tutzing, 1982), digitised and revised for the Berlin Philharmonic Archive, March 2013. Unfortunately, there are no programmes for this

was so warmly received it had to be repeated – perhaps, as one reviewer suggested, it timely amplified nationalist sentiments.[36] In view of the last-minute switch in conductor from Jochum to Pfitzner, the atmosphere in the hall seems to have been something other than simply anticipatory. All the reviews by the major music journals led with the unexpected conductor swap, suggesting that Walter's continued absence upstaged the new symphony to some degree. Several journal critics also reported the evening of Walter's exile, when Strauss had stepped in for Walter at the eleventh hour, replacing the expected programme with Strauss's own works. Only the phrase 'anstelle von Bruno Walter' (instead of Bruno Walter) on the concert programme indicated Walter's unexplained absence from his series.[37] What is more, Walter's removal from the billing had met with resistance, requiring Goebbels's personal intervention for its implementation, and after the Strauss concert Hans Hinkel, leader of the Fighting League for German Culture (Kampfbund für deutsche Kultur, or KfdK)[38] and commissioner in the ministry of education, had to justify the events leading to Walter's exile, claiming, 'We never prevented this concert, nor did we forbid Bruno Walter, whose real name is Schlesinger, to conduct. However, it was impossible to offer the necessary protection.'[39]

It is not difficult to imagine, then, that at the Pfitzner concert the Walter affair was still prominent in audience discussions. So too, perhaps, were political developments vis-à-vis racial policy more generally, if the political topics that sat side by side with music commentary in newspaper coverage accurately reflect the thoughts of the concert-going public. In the 31 March issue of the *Berliner Börsen-Courier*, for example, the review of the Pfitzner concert was located on the second page of an issue headlined with news of the organised national boycott of Jewish businesses that was to begin the following day.[40] This commentary and rhetoric has to be read in dialogue with the political changes and conductor dismissals that flanked it in material documentation of the concert. A similar fate befell several

---

concert in the Berlin Philharmonic Archive; much pre-1944 material was lost after the Philharmonie – at its former site on Bernburgerstraße – was destroyed by Allied bombing.

[36] See Abendroth, 'Pfitzner-Abend'.

[37] Berlin Philharmonic Archive, P 1933 20.3, concert programme.

[38] An organisation aiming to protect German cultural values and challenge modernist art, founded by Alfred Rosenberg in 1929.

[39] *Berliner Lokal-Anzeiger*, 5 April 1933, quoted in Joseph Wulf, *Musik im Dritten Reich: Eine Dokumentation* (Gütersloh: Rowohlt, 1966), 23. This translation is Meyer's; he discusses the cancellation of Walter's March Philharmonie appearance with reference to Wulf's work in *Politics of Music in the Third Reich*, 43.

[40] Heinrich Strobel, 'Pfitzner dirigiert', *Berliner Börsen-Courier*, 31 March 1933.

prominent conductors by April 1933: Hermann Scherchen, Heinz Unger, and Joseph Rosenstock all lost their positions around the same time.[41]

Still, the differing ways in which the respective reviewers framed the situation suggest that attitudes towards Walter's exile among members of the audience were far from monochrome. Though not one of the critics for the major Berlin newspapers and national music journals clarified the reasons for Walter's departure, and none openly condemned the situation, it seems that the tone was not one of general assent, but rather one of studied neutrality. Representative was the report by editor Paul Schwers (1874–1939) in the conservative journal *Die Allgemeine Musikzeitung*, which explained simply that one of Jochum's Philharmonic concerts 'was conducted as a special concert by Hans Pfitzner, since Jochum had to conduct the Gewandhaus orchestra in Leipzig in place of Bruno Walter, following his departure for Amsterdam. By this means, Pfitzner got the opportunity to showcase in person his new C♯ Minor Symphony.'[42] The neutral stances may reflect increasing political pressure and scrutiny of the written word. *Gleichschaltung* (co-ordination) began to be applied to the press almost immediately after the Nazis took power, with the intention of centralising, standardising, and unifying printed publications. In February, the day following the Reichstag fire, a presidential decree had mandated the closure of newspapers deemed 'politically dangerous'.[43] It was not until 1936, however, that art criticism – legally termed *Kunstbetrachtung* – officially became little more than token praise for works that had already been passed by the censors.[44] Although in March 1933 no laws had yet been passed controlling

---

[41] All of these dismissals were reported in the April issue of *Die Musik*. See Meyer, *Politics of Music in the Third Reich*, 32.

[42] Schwers, 'Aus dem Berliner Musikleben', *Allgemeine Musikzeitung*, 7 April 1933, 207. Some commentators, reviewing several concerts in one report, commented on both high-profile changes of conductor in the preceding weeks at the same time. *Die Musik* cited a broader reshuffle of conductors as having affected this concert, emphasising Strauss's and Pfitzner's appearances over Walter's and Jochum's absences from Berlin. The way in which the conductor swaps were paired suggests that the circumstances of both absences were routine and comparable. The neutrality of tone is insidious, recasting events positively. Steinhagen, 'Musikleben der Gegenwart', 619. Less neutral was the report in the *Berliner Lokal-Anzeiger* by Nazi composer, music critic, musicologist, and author Walter Abendroth (1896–1973). He noted that, because of the re-organisation, Berliners had the opportunity to see 'the two greatest living representatives of German music' take the baton at the Philharmonie within a few days of each other. Abendroth, 'Pfitzner-Abend'.

[43] See Painter, *Symphonic Aspirations*, 209.

[44] Even then, scholars have debated the degree to which music criticism was affected in practical terms by the new decree. Fabian R. Lovisa, for example, has suggested that the impact of the *Kritikverbot* on music criticism has largely been overestimated. See Lovisa, *Musikkritik im Nationalsozialismus: Die Rolle deutschsprachiger Musikzeitschriften 1920–1945* (Laaber: Laaber-Verlag, 1993), 18, 197–208.

aesthetic criticism, and the *Schriftleitergesetz*, which prevented all writers of non-Aryan descent from writing professionally, would not be passed until October of the same year, Nazi policy and the public hounding of prominent intellectuals and musicians like Walter must have had an impact on what music critics deemed wise to put in print.

There were, however, exceptions to the neutral language used by most reviewers. Conservative nationalist critic and composer Fritz Stege (1896–1967) provides a case in point, writing for the Nazi-allied *Zeitschrift für Musik* and commending Strauss and Pfitzner for their short-notice appearances. Strauss, in particular, was hailed as a hero:

> Instead of Bruno Walter, it was Richard Strauss who appeared before the Berlin public, met with great enthusiasm and undeterred by threatening letters from a hate-filled America under the spell of Jewish influence. Then the conductors were changed again: Hans Pfitzner appeared, to help deliver the Berlin premiere of his C♯ Minor Symphony.[45]

If this portrayal was unsurprising, it still disturbs. Yes, Stege was also music critic for the main Nazi mouthpiece the *Völkische Beobachter*, had belonged to the KfdK since 1929, and was reporting in a journal that explicitly opposed 'modern' music. But up to this point, Stege had always written approvingly of Walter's Berlin concerts, and *Zeitschrift für Musik* had previously regarded Walter as a great 'German' conductor.[46]

Although publicly the journals seemed unable to acknowledge the circumstances surrounding Walter's exit, many prominent members of the musical community sympathised with Walter privately, as expressed in letters after his exile.[47] Pfitzner, too, certainly would have supported his friend and colleague,[48] an example of a Jewish artist who, in his opinion, was thoroughly 'German', as 'the nature of his disposition and thought throughout his entire life' apparently proved.[49] Had the symphony been simultaneously premiered in Munich and another German city, which Pfitzner initially suggested to his publisher, Walter would have been the

---

[45] Fritz Stege, 'Berliner Musik', *Zeitschrift für Musik* 5 (1933): 458. Abendroth, unsurprisingly, depicted the switch in conductors in a similarly jubilant tone: 'Extensive applause accompanied the master's descent from the podium, a conductor of such professionalism and inspiration that we would be delighted to welcome him here more often.' Abendroth, 'Pfitzner-Abend'.

[46] Ryding and Pechefsky, *Bruno Walter*, 223.   [47] For further discussion, see ibid., 224.

[48] For a detailed exploration of the relationship between Pfitzner and Walter, particularly after 1933, see Hans Rudolf Vaget, '"Der gute, alte Antisemitismus": Hans Pfitzner, Bruno Walter und der Holocaust', in *Bruckner-Probleme: Internationales Kolloquium 7–9 Oktober 1996 in Berlin*, ed. Albrecht Riethmüller (Stuttgart: Franz Steiner, 1999), 215–32.

[49] Letter to Carl-Friedrich Goerdeler, 10 September 1932, in Pfitzner, *Briefe*, 611.

only conductor Pfitzner would have considered to lead the other performance.[50] In his own antisemitism, Pfitzner appears to have believed that racial heritage could be neutralised or realigned by cultural assimilation.[51] Artistic triumph, moreover, proved this assimilation, and for Pfitzner Walter was a case in point.[52] Yet, even if Pfitzner thought that his idea of race was less absolute than it was for Nazi policy, and even though choosing a path of low resistance and acting to protect his own interests does not indicate wholehearted advocacy of the regime,[53] it ultimately made little difference: his antisemitism, as Joseph Wulf notes, allied '*weltanschaulich*' with the antisemitism of the National Socialists.[54]

Symphonic Problems: Exploring the Mechanisms of Monumentality

The review in the *Deutsche Allgemeine Zeitung*, by a critic who published simply under the name 'Runge',[55] was representative of the terms in which many journalists and music critics framed the work, conceptualising the genre transition spatially, evoking both force and excess, and affording the music a sense of agency: 'If one asks oneself why Pfitzner might have undertaken [the re-orchestration], the intensifying development of the

---

[50] Letter to Fürstner, 8 September 1932, in Pfitzner, *Briefe*, 609.

[51] See, for example, Vaget, 'Der gute, alte Antisemitismus'; Jürgens, '*Deutsche Musik*'; Williamson, *Music of Hans Pfitzner* ('An Inner Emigration?'); Kater, *Composers of the Nazi Era*; Busch, *Hans Pfitzner und der Nationalsozialismus*; Fischer, 'Very German Fate'.

[52] Indeed, Pfitzner's assessment of Walter as 'ein Deutscher' originates from a letter he wrote to the mayor of Leipzig, Carl-Friedrich Goerdeler, in September 1932, strongly recommending that the Jewish heritage of the opera director Otto Erhardt should not stand in the way of his appointment at the Leipzig Stadttheater, which he described as a 'socio-ethical' issue. In the letter, Pfitzner emphasised Erhardt's identity as a '*Künstler*' (artist). Pfitzner, *Briefe*, 609–11. In addition, Pfitzner petitioned in this year for the release of his Jewish friend and mentor Paul Nikolaus Cossman from Stadelheim prison, at not inconsiderable risk to himself, as Williamson notes in *Music of Hans Pfitzner*, 322–3. Busch, in *Hans Pfitzner und der Nationalsozialismus*, 123–30, furnishes more detailed commentary on the relationship between Pfitzner and Cossman and on Pfitzner's petitioning on Cossman's behalf from his initial arrest in 1933 to his death in hospital in Theresienstadt concentration camp in 1942.

[53] For a general reflection on the treatment and development of notions of consent and coercion in fascism scholarship, particularly in relation to choice and constraint, see Roberta Pergher and Guilia Albanese, 'Historians, Fascism, and Italian Society: Mapping the Limits of Consent', in *In the Society of Fascists: Acclamation, Acquiescence, and Agency in Mussolini's Italy*, ed. Pergher and Albanese (New York: Palgrave Macmillan, 2012), 1–28.

[54] Wulf, *Musik im Dritten Reich*, 334.

[55] It is likely that this was Otto Runge, former editor of the *Deutsche Allgemeine Zeitung* under its previous name *Norddeutsche Allgemeine Zeitung* from 1902 to 1917.

first movement springs to mind. Here the invention does indeed burst the frame of the string quartet, and demands the sound-world of the orchestra to build up.' But by contrast, Runge conceded: 'Other parts resist such a superficial, externalised effect; their historically informed use of techniques, pervaded by notions of the sublime, resist the shimmering colours of the orchestra.'[56] Reviewing the concert for the *Berliner Börsen-Courier*, Heinrich Strobel (1898–1970) observed that 'despite the great apparatus being used, the symphony has a sound that is austere, cold, in part even unsentimental'. According to these reviews, other musical passages oppose the shallow monumentalising effects of the orchestra; they recede inwards instead, and these writers imply the moral elevation of immanence over external appearance. Strobel went on to note that 'the four voices that constitute the specific sonority of the quartet are preserved'.[57]

Runge and Strobel point us towards the key tension in the reviews: the question of how (and how successfully) the work negotiates the relationship between the two genres, between the external and the immanent, and thus between public and intimate space. Which musical junctures presented a problem to reviewers, it may be asked? At what points did they hear echoes of the string quartet, the pull of the subjective domain, and query the work's symphonic achievements? Writing in the *Allgemeine Musikzeitung*, Schwers highlights two musical areas highly saturated with symphonic expectations as problematic: 'Much of the musical material, particularly in the first movement and the finale, strives against the orchestral guise . . . requiring brute force to be squeezed into a new sonic form.'[58]

---

[56] 'Fragt man sich, warum Pfitzner sie vorgenommen haben mag, so drängt sich zuerst der Gedanke an die großartig aufwachsende Durchführung des ersten Satzes auf. Hier sprengt die Erfindung tatsächlich den Rahmen des Streichquartetts und verlangt nach dem Wuchs des Orchesters. . . . Andere Partien wieder sträuben sich gerade gegen solche äußere Wirkung. Ihre In-sich-Gelehrtheit und Unsinnlichkeit scheut vor dem Farbenglanz des Orchesters zurück.' Runge, 'Pfitzner dirigiert seine neue Symphonie', *Deutsche Allgemeine Zeitung*, 31 March 1933. The multifaceted word *unsinnlich* and its nominal form *Unsinnlichkeit* present an interesting problem for the translator, which I have dealt with differently depending on the context. *Unsinnlich*, derived from *Sinn*, meaning sense, variously suggests something being unsensuous, but also ungraspable or 'intangible'. In addition, though less commonly, it can imply *Unsinn* (nonsense). It also evokes the sublime, that which is beyond logic, not tangible or knowable, and this has informed how I have translated *Unsinnlichkeit* here: 'pervaded by notions of the sublime'.

[57] 'Trotz des großen Apparats, der aufgewendet wird, hat die Sinfonie eine herbe, unsinnliche, nicht selten sogar harte Klanglichkeit. . . . Das vierstimmige Klangbild des Quartetts bleibt durchweg gewahrt.' Strobel, 'Pfitzner dirigiert', 2.

[58] The original reads: 'Breite Teile, vor allem im Anfangssatz und auch im Finale, widerstreben durchaus der orchestralen Einkleidung; sie sind rein quartettmäßig erfunden und durchgeführt und lassen sich nur mit Zwang in eine andere Klangform pressen.' Schwers, 'Aus dem Berliner Musikleben'.

Analysing those points – the first movement and the end of the last movement – might help to disclose how, to use a formulation of Rehding's, the 'mechanisms' of monumentality operate in the transition from string quartet to symphony, before the theoretical implications of monumental symphonic aesthetics are explored further on.[59]

The most useful analytical source for considering the shift from the aural space of the string quartet to that of a symphony is an essay in the April issue of the progressive journal *Melos* by the young Heidelberg music researcher Karl Wörner (1910–69). Founded in 1920 to champion new music, *Melos* would be renamed *Neues Musikblatt* in 1934 under the National Socialist government to distance the publication from its avant-gardist past. The April issue appeared just before major upheavals at the journal began: in May its politics were reformed, as part of which the progressive – and thus 'politically unreliable' – chief editor Hans Mersmann was replaced by the *Berliner Börsen-Courier*'s Strobel.[60] Prior to the change in editors, Wörner had written critically about reactionary and nationalist political action.[61]

Echoing Schwers's assessment, Wörner immediately spotted weaknesses in the symphonic facade:

Least satisfying orchestrally is the fervent gloom of the first movement. For one thing, it does not correspond to what one traditionally expects of the first movement as the principal movement in a symphony. It is built from four themes, and the sonata form is merely implied.[62]

First movements constitute the symphonic region in which a number of key generic expectations are set up: note Wörner's reflections on the importance of contrasting themes and sonata form. Marked moderato ('ziemlich ruhig'), Pfitzner's first movement opens in C♯ minor with – to adopt the thematic labelling in Vogel's analysis of the string quartet – a sinuously chromatic

---

[59] Rehding, *Music and Monumentality*, 9.

[60] Strobel's Jewish wife, Hilde Betty Levy, perhaps made Strobel a surprising choice for replacement editor. Indeed, his advocacy of the avant-garde had by 1938 earned him the contempt of the National Socialists, reflected in a humiliating caricature of him as a 'Vorkämpfer der Musikbolschewismus' in the publication accompanying the infamous Düsseldorf *Entartete Musik* exhibition. *Entartete Musik: Eine Abrechnung von Staatsrat Dr. H. S. Ziegler* (Düsseldorf: Völkischer Verlag, 1939), 9. Bertolt Brecht Archiv, Berlin, C3267.

[61] For instance, in the December 1932 issues of *Melos* he had spoken out against the increasingly pervasive reactionary 'modern political and cultural campaigns and slogans' that had led to the closure of the world-renowned Dessau Bauhaus. See Meyer, *Politics of Music in the Third Reich*, 29. Later, after serving in the *Wehrdienst* and imprisonment by US forces during the war, Wörner became head editor at Schott's journal department, a post he held from 1955 to 1959.

[62] Wörner, 'Hans Pfitzners Sinfonie in cis', 133.

four-bar polyphonic motto theme for solo woodwinds. Three additional themes are set out in the first movement's exposition (bars 5 to 84), only one of which – the song theme ('*Gesangsthema*') from bars 31 to 75 – is in the relative major key of E, playing the role of the second subject. Though a loose sonata structure can be traced, with the song theme (bars 140 to 175) reprised in the tonic major, C♯, in the recapitulation (bars 126 to 183), Vogel demonstrates how it is overlaid with a symmetrical Bartókian bridge structure bookended by the motto theme – ABCDCBA – with the two simultaneous forms in tension with each other.[63] However, as Wörner continues:

The themes in themselves contrast too little with one another to have an oppositional effect in the orchestral reworking; their inner complexity is much more clearly perceivable when played together by a chamber ensemble.[64]

For Wörner, the movement 'does not meet one's traditional expectations': he implies that it is compromised by the lingering trace of the string quartet's presence within. The oppositions musically immanent within and internal to the string quartet's arching, striving themes do not translate well into the symphonic form, which seems to need more pronounced kinds of musical oppositions between, not within, themes. Even more interesting are the conclusions Wörner draws about what is lost in the transition between the two mediums – namely, the subtlety of the 'delicate chamber quality' in the 'rhapsodic' motivic shapes of the second and fourth themes. Presumably he means the main theme – Vogel's '*Kopfthema*', bars 5 to 12, and the song theme, bars 31 to 75. 'Likewise,' he writes, 'the themes are stripped of their passionate, urging drive. In the symphony the whole movement appears somewhat uniform and cumbersome.' The brass make an easy target for the blame.[65]

Wörner suggests that the intrinsic delicacy of the themes and the subtlety of their differentiation is swamped by the heavy orchestral setting. Other listeners heard the internal complexity of the movement's thematic work as strain. Composer Hans Sachße (1891–1960) had first heard the work at the Munich premiere and wrote a piece in the *Zeitschrift für Musik* preparing readers for the symphony's upcoming performance at the June 1933 Dortmund Tonkünstlerfest. As he put it there, 'an extreme

---

[63] Vogel, *Hans Pfitzner: Streichquartett Cis-Moll Op. 36*, 15–16.

[64] 'Die Themen sind in sich zu wenig kontrastierend, um in der Orchesterbearbeitung gegensätzlich zu wirken, während ihre innere Differenziertheit beim kammermusikalischen Zusammenspiel viel stärker empfunden wird.' Wörner, 'Hans Pfitzners Sinfonie in cis', 133.

[65] Ibid.

Example 2.1 The opening bars of the first movement of Pfitzner's Symphony in C♯ minor, as quoted in Hans Sachße, 'Hans Pfitzner: Symphonie in cis-moll', *Zeitschrift für Musik* 6 (1933): 559–61, 560.

inner tension emanates right from the first melodic line, which, in wide leaps and with poignant exuberance, strives for the summit, only to sink back in resignation' (see Example 2.1).[66]

Sachße implies that the opening melody thematises the futile, powerless struggle of subjective being, centring the movement within the private sphere. It is worth taking a closer look at this opening passage, since its four solo contrapuntal lines make it such an obvious allusion to chamber musical space. Yet at the same time, by employing two bassoons and two clarinets, it sets up an aural world with a distinctly orchestral acoustic signature, hinting at the scope of the symphonic space that will unfold. Nonetheless, it presents a problem area within the symphonic form since, as a curiously circular and static gesture, it resists goal-directed development. The gestural arcs traced within the theme compress a sequence of key structural tones for the string quartet/symphony overall, inviting a reading of the work as a whole as the unfolding of chamber space into public, symphonic space (see Example 2.2).[67]

---

[66] 'Eine ungeheure innere Spannung geht gleich von der ersten Melodielinien aus, die in weiten Sprüngen mit schmerzlichem Überschwang dem Höhepunkt zustrebt, um resigniert zurückzusinken.' Hans Sachße, 'Hans Pfitzner: Symphonie in cis-moll', *Zeitschrift für Musik* 6 (1933): 559–61, 560. It is also worth mentioning that the ebb and flow of energy implied here strikingly recalls Ernst Kurth's symphonic wave discourse in his two-volume *Bruckner* of 1925, influenced by scientific-technological thought. See Ernst Kurth, *Selected Writings*, ed. and trans. Lee A. Rothfarb (Cambridge: Cambridge University Press, 1991).

[67] I have presented the string quartet scoring here to make reading the harmonic relationships more straightforward: in the symphonic rendering, the violin lines are taken by two clarinets in A, and the viola and cello lines are given to two bassoons. Pfitzner, *Quartett in cis-moll für 2 Violinen, Viola und Violoncello, opus 36*, 1.

Example 2.2 The motto theme: the opening four bars of the first movement of Pfitzner's String Quartet in C♯ minor Op. 36. Hans Pfitzner, *Quartett in cis-moll für 2 Violinen, Viola und Violoncello, opus 36* (Berlin: Adolph Fürstner Verlag, 1925), 1. All examples from Pfitzner's scores are reproduced by permission of Ernst Eulenburg Ltd.

Falling chromatically by a semitone from G♯ to G♮, the bass line in the first bar articulates a harmonic motion from i in second inversion to ♮V♮7 and foreshadows the importance of the tritone, G♮, to the work's harmonic and motivic development. Further semitone descending movement from E♮ to D♯ in the second half of the same bar anticipates the importance for the work of the second scale degree, D♯: D♯ is also the lowest note of the motto theme's arching gesture. At the beginning of the main theme, in bar 5, the second scale degree is stressed once more, this time in the upper line, falling on the downbeat as a suspension over a melodically elaborated i before resolving to C♯.

The upper range of the first violin line in the motto theme stresses an F♯ (although it is decorated by creeping up to G♯). This prefigures the subdominant tonal area of the scherzo second movement, which begins in F♯ minor, as well as the ambiguous status of G♯ as a tonal pivot for the third movement. The scherzo was a movement that critics suggested gained particularly from the orchestra's rich colour palate.[68] Marked 'sehr schnell', the string quartet's first violin lines are energised in the symphony by a solo clarinet, an effect described by a contemporary critic as 'ironic and

---

[68] 'Der scherzoartige zweite Satz … gewinn[t] überzeugend durch die reiche Farbenpalette des Orchesters'. Schwers, 'Aus dem Berliner Musikleben'. See also comments by Runge in *Deutsche Allgemeine Zeitung*: 'Auch dem Scherzo ist die Umarbeitung gut bekommen: es hat an äußere Wirkung sehr gewonnen.' As discussed above, this was probably Otto Runge. Runge, 'Pfitzner dirigiert seine neue Symphonie', *Deutsche Allgemeine Zeitung*, 31 March 1933.

grotesque'.[69] At the end of the movement a momentous climax is scored for full orchestra with crashing cymbals (bar 389), before ebbing away to almost nothing, at which point the solo clarinet takes the stage again for a whimsical afterword over a perfect cadence (bars 408 to 412). The third movement (*'langsam, ausdrucksvoll'*) hints at the dominant by beginning on a G♯, the same first note as in the motto theme's two outer parts. However, the initially chromatic melodic material makes this centre less conclusive. An arching, 'strikingly abstract' arpeggiated semiquaver gesture is heard unaccompanied in the first violins in 6/8 and opens by articulating a tritone before then being quasi-canonically passed between the other string voices (bars 1 to 10) – a somewhat inconclusive moment in terms of genre, too, where listeners are reminded of the quartet origins.[70] The movement oscillates abruptly between diatonic passages and meandering atonality. Thinking about the generative relationship between the motto theme and the rest of the symphonic work demands that we ask about the wider social ramifications of collapsing self-contained chamber space, and the solo string lines in the string quartet that one reviewer described as musical 'thoughts' ('*Gedanken*'),[71] out into a public symphonic acoustic world.

These subjective metaphors used to describe the motto theme and string quartet lines more generally suggest that the transition from string quartet to symphony can be expressed in terms that parallel the public rendering or 'collectivisation' of the individual critical within fascist ideology.[72] Yet, if the movement's musical effect is 'cumbersome',[73] then reading between the lines of the criticism reveals that the symphony does not successfully sublate the subject's inner world within the mass.

Equally freighted with genre convention are symphonic finales. How they discharge the energy accumulated throughout the symphony's duration back into the silence that borders the work is a major generic

---

[69] Wörner, 'Hans Pfitzners Sinfonie in cis', 133.   [70] Ibid., 134.

[71] 'Im allgemeinen übernehmen geschlossene Instrumentalgruppen die ursprünglich von Solostreichern vorgetragenen Gedanken.' Oscar von Pander, 'München', *Die Musik* 25 (1933): 628. It suggests an identity between sound and thought that recalls Schoenberg's use of the word in his 1931 manuscript *Zu: Darstellung des musikalischen Gedankens*, meaning something between a thought and an idea. Schoenberg's opening gambit refers to composing as '*thinking in tones and rhythms. Every piece of music is the presentation of a musical idea*' (emphasis in original). See Arnold Schoenberg, *The Musical Idea and the Logic, Technique, and Art of Its Presentation*, trans. and ed. Patricia Carpenter and Severine Neff (New York: Columbia University Press, 1995), 15. For a list of Schoenberg's various *Gedanke* manuscripts, written between 1923 and 1936, see ibid., xv–xvi.

[72] Meyer, *Politics of Music in the Third Reich*, 8.

[73] Wörner, 'Hans Pfitzners Sinfonie in cis', 133.

issue.[74] Pfitzner's fourth movement was no exception. In five sections, with the performance direction 'ziemlich schnell', the finale begins in C♯ minor and concludes in D♭ major, the enharmonic major equivalent. By contrast, the string quartet does not make the enharmonic switch, ending instead in the tonic major, C♯. Although, in general terms, this movement was singled out for praise, critics struggled to make sense of the final bars, where material from the motto theme that opened the first movement is echoed (bars 316 to 331). They seemed unable to square the quasi-cyclical return to the motto theme and its associated chamber space with what had come before. Wörner, for example, suggested that in this movement the symphonic effect was at its most immediate and thrilling, but stumbled in the final moments.[75] He was not alone in thinking this. For Sachße, too, writing in the *Zeitschrift für Musik*, a degree of discomfort was aroused by the final passage of the work.[76] Rather than evincing a seamless assimilation of the musical lines into an 'outsized' form,[77] the final passage, particularly from rehearsal number 65, seemed to render the otherwise obscured, naturalised monumental scaffolding encasing the string quartet partially visible.

Sachße noted the contrast between symphonic and chamber spheres in the final movement as a whole, describing the finale as 'a great symphonic closing movement', whose primary theme (Example 2.3) 'is whipped up into a mood of demonic wildness before returning to spheres of chamber music intimacy', as at the very beginning of the symphony.[78]

The movement's opening theme begins with a major second suspension of a D♯ over the C♯ in the bass, once again emphasising the structural

Example 2.3 Main theme of the fourth movement, as printed in Sachße, 'Symphonie in cis-moll', 561.

[74] Michael Talbot, *The Finale in Western Instrumental Music* (Oxford: Oxford University Press, 2001), 6.

[75] 'Der zweite und der letzte Satz des Streichquartettes kommt von sich aus einer Instrumentierung am meisten entgegen. Und hier ist auch der Eindruck der Sinfonie am unmittelbarsten und packendsten.' Wörner, 'Hans Pfitzners Sinfonie in cis', 132.

[76] Sachße, 'Symphonie in cis-moll', 561.   [77] See Rehding, *Music and Monumentality*, 5.

[78] 'Das Finale ist ein großer symphonischer Schlußsatz, dessen Hauptthema . . . in eine Stimmung dämonischer Wildheit gesteigert wird, um dann wieder am Schluß Sphären von kammermusikalischer Intimität aufzusuchen.' Sachße, 'Symphonie in cis-moll', 561.

importance of the D♯ first stressed in the motto theme at the very beginning of the first movement. In the final bars of the symphony, from 316 to 331, that motto theme returns once again. Sachße suggests that genre-space is being manipulated to cyclically unify the end of the finale with the beginning of the first movement. For Wörner, however, Pfitzner's negotiation of the distinction between intimate and public space at the close of the finale was unconvincing. 'The close of the finale has, in contrast [to the development of the first subject in the rest of the movement], the intimate quality of chamber music', he wrote. But he added that 'in the instrumentation it loses its contemplative, introspectively lyrical character'.[79] In light of both reviews, it seems that the critics could not listen to the symphony without also hearing the string quartet behind the symphonic bluster. And Pfitzner's re-orchestration fails, as Wörner implies, in that it renders the familiarity of the symphonic form strange. By reminding listeners of the chamber music space, Pfitzner exposes the symphonic monumentality as an unwieldy construction imposed upon the musical material.

But what is it that is unconvincing here? How is this passage corrupted by the added weight and the public exposure effected by the new genre? Given Wörner's critique of the ending, it seems likely that the problem is the juxtaposition between monumental musical forces and the intimacy of the original string quartet passage, perhaps as well as the inability of that passage to persuasively release the force and energy the movement has gained. In the string quartet, the final C♯ major passage at rehearsal number 65 with the key signature of C♯ minor (Example 2.4) is presented in the symphony in the enharmonically equivalent key of D♭ major (Example 2.5), but without the performance directions 'wieder zurück' (as at the beginning) or 'sehr ruhig' (very still).

In this version Pfitzner calls on far more expanded forces, using complete orchestral strings, soft woodwind and horn interjections, full-sounding trombone chords held pianissimo, strummed harp gestures, and pianissimo timpani that reiterate the plucked offbeat quavers in the harps and double basses. Some altered articulations and dynamic markings presumably respond to the increase in instruments. At a superficial level, D♭ major is simply a more straightforward key for woodwind and brass and therefore more suited to

---

[79] 'Der Schluß des Finales ist dagegen kammermusikalisch intim. Er verliert durch die Instrumentierung seinen nachdenklichen, beschaulich lyrischen Charakter.' Wörner, 'Hans Pfitzners Sinfonie in cis', 133.

Example 2.4 Fourth movement of Pfitzner's String Quartet in C♯ minor Op. 36, figure 65 to end. Pfitzner, *Quartett in cis-moll*, 63.

symphonic forces. But D♭ major and C♯ major are not the same thing, and any alteration, even seemingly for convenience, comes with an affective transformation. Historically, C♯ major had been considered a brighter, harder, more brilliant and remote tonality; in contrast, D♭'s affective associations were less tense, wistful, nostalgic, and introspective.[80] In Pfitzner's songs, C♯ minor

---

[80] Rita Steblin elucidates the mid-nineteenth-century 'psychological association of ever-increasing strength and brightness (or, conversely, weakness and sombreness) with the number of sharps

Example 2.4 (Cont.)

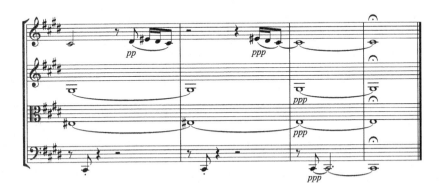

is the key associated with death, or with an unfulfilled wish for death, as in 'Der Kühne' (1988–9), 'Stimme der Sehnsucht' (1905), and 'Auf die

and flats'. See Steblin, *A History of Key Characteristics in the Eighteenth and Early Nineteenth Centuries* (Rochester: University of Rochester Press, 1996), especially 103–33.

Example 2.5 Fourth movement of Pfitzner's Symphony in C♯ minor, figure 65 to end. Hans Pfitzner, *Symphony cis-moll Op. 36a* (London: Eulenburg, 1987), 90–1.

Example 2.5 (Cont.)

Morgenröte' (1931), among others.[81] The change in key untethers the end
of Pfitzner's symphony from his string quartet's Beethovenian reference
point, as well as from Pfitzner's expressive connection of the tonal centre
to death, at least in the minor. Nevertheless, the historical associations of
the new tonality tie it to another equally ambivalent kind of annihilation.
Wagner's *Götterdämmerung* ends in Db major; it is the tonal area associated with the new world order as the gods are engulfed by flames and the
curtain falls.

At the very end of the movement, the fragmented echoes of the tritonal
harmonic tension in the first movement's motto theme are heard in the
woodwind at bars 316 and 317 (I in second inversion with the Ab in the
bass descending to G♮ for ♮IV[7], followed by V[7]) and again in bars 318 and
319 in the horns (iv in second inversion followed by VII[7], then I). In the
trombone and string parts, the symphony's structural emphasis on
the second scale degree – now Eb rather than D♯ – persists from bar
321, when the last fragmentary rendition of the movement's main theme
is heard, right up until the final two measures, where the suspension
finally resolves. These musical gestures – embodying different levels of
harmonic dissent, and recalling the compressed harmonic potentiality of
the first movement – are in turn, instrumental group by instrumental
group, assimilated into what is only ostensibly the tonic major, the tonal
world of Db. The enharmonicism disrupts the conventional circular unity
of the symphony's tonal space. To repurpose a point Thomas Bauman
made about the 'recapitulation' in the finale of Mahler's 'Resurrection'
Symphony, the 'new order' represented by this unexpected tonal domain
does not allow tonality to play its restorative symphonic role.[82] Rather,
the restorative function is fulfilled by the symphony's genre-spatial circularity, as noted by Sachße, suggesting that Pfitzner's symphony takes the
interplay between genre, subjectivity, and space as its subject matter. But
even so, the end of the work does not return to quite the same 'spheres of
chamber music intimacy' with which the first movement opened. This,
the contemporary music criticism makes clear, is an uneasy symphonic
conclusion, and such unease strongly indicates the music's critical
potential.

---

[81] Richard Mercier has explored the association of specific keys with ideas or emotions in
Pfitzner's songs. As he shows, all six of Pfitzner's songs that begin in C♯ minor are thematically
concerned with death. See Mercier, *The Songs of Hans Pfitzner: A Guide and Study* (Westport:
Greenwood Press, 1998), 1–3. See also Vogel, *Hans Pfitzner: Streichquartett Cis-Moll Op. 36*, 12.

[82] Thomas Bauman, 'Mahler in a New Key: Genre and the "Resurrection" Finale', *Journal of
Musicology* 23 (2006): 468–85, 479–80.

Transforming German Symphonic Aesthetics

As music journalists discussed the musical corners where Pfitzner's work 'failed' as a symphony, it became a valuable historical lightning rod for discourses surrounding the external and the immanent, and public and intimate space. Yet, asking questions of success or failure may have been to miss the point. For instance, when Sachße talked about the work's genre-spatial circularity, what he failed to articulate explicitly was something more radical: that Pfitzner's symphony – whether Pfitzner meant it to or not – called into question relationships between genre and space, and how subjectivity might be re-oriented or even re-composed within them. By insisting on those tensions between musical materials and orchestration, Pfitzner's symphony itself musically articulated anxieties about the exposition of intimate worlds within the public symphonic form.

But critics will be critics, and question success they of course did. Nonetheless, it is important to stress that any glimmers of uncertainty Pfitzner's symphony raised about genre, genre-space, and even the work's critical potential had little bearing on overall evaluations of the symphony, which, by almost all accounts, was a triumph. Like the bulk of the critical responses, Stege – in the same *Zeitschrift für Musik* review in which he had shown such obvious delight when Richard Strauss had appeared in Walter's place, 'undeterred by threatening letters from a hate-filled America under the spell of Jewish influence' – waxed rhapsodically about the symphony and the accomplishment of the transition between genres:

The development of the orchestral sound-world out of the string quartet is very interesting; the intended deepening and intensification of expression is fully achieved by the composer. The deeply profound work ... left a long-lasting impression.[83]

It is difficult, however, to read 'the intended deepening and intensification of expression' and the penetration it implies as innocuous, taking into account its overlap with Nazi revolutionary rhetoric, not to mention the pleasure Stege took in Walter's ousting. Threats of public violence are another kind of 'intensification of expression'. Goebbels used a similar kind of spatial-depth metaphor a few months later in a speech at the Philharmonie marking the 15 November opening of the *Reichskulturkammer*. He applauded the

---

[83] 'Die Entwicklung des orchestralen Klangbildes aus dem Streichquartettsatz ist hochinteressant, die beabsichtigte Vertiefung des Ausdrucks ist dem Komponist voll und ganz gelungen, das tief schürfende Werk ... hinterließ einen nachhaltigen Eindruck.' Stege, 'Berliner Musik', 458.

National Socialist revolution that was all-encompassing, and that 'took hold of all areas of public life and transformed them fundamentally.'[84] Stege was not the only writer to deploy this sort of metaphor to express the transformative effect of the shift in genre. The reviewer for the *Berliner Tageblatt* declared that the symphony 'reveals the work's ethos in its full scope and profundity'.[85] Although metaphors of depth have a rich history in German philosophical and aesthetic thought, as Holly Watkins has shown,[86] in the context of the evident Nazi sympathies of Stege's review the phrase points to a discomfort pervasive in the criticism about the wider and potentially transformative social implications of the act of re-inscribing the string quartet as a symphony. As Goebbels's Philharmonie speech went on: '[The revolution] has completely changed and formed anew the relationship of the people with each other, the relationship of the people to the state, and to the question of being.'[87] The genre discourses between the two musical forms were distinct, particularly in terms of the kind of implied voice, listeners, and space associated with each. What, then, exactly is the 'deepening' process taking place in the transition from string quartet to symphony?

Having looked at how critics at the Berlin concert heard subjective chamber space in the symphony, and how that identifies the music as a politically critical domain, the focus now shifts to the question of where and how the process of collusion between fascist and symphonic values began to take place. The same body of reviews and commentary is illuminating. As was the case, to a greater or lesser extent, with all symphonies from the nineteenth and early twentieth centuries, Pfitzner's symphony was caught between two competing ideological poles. On one side, reflecting themes woven into critical writing on the genre throughout the

---

[84] 'Die Revolution, die wir gemacht haben, ist eine totale. Sie hat alle Gebiete des öffentlichen Lebens erfaßt und von Grund auf umgestaltet.' Heiber, *Goebbels Reden*, 131.

[85] 'Ein sehr seltener Fall, dass die Thematik stark und tragend genug ist, die Erweiterung der Form, die Bereicherung des klanglichen Ausdrucks nicht nur zuzulassen, sondern damit das Ethos erst in seinem ganzen Ernst und seiner Tiefe offenbar zu machen.' L. Bd, 'Im Rundfunk: Hans Pfitzners Sinfonie Cis-moll', *Berliner Tageblatt*, 1 April 1933.

[86] Holly Watkins, *Metaphors of Depth in German Musical Thought from E. T. A. Hoffmann to Arnold Schoenberg* (Cambridge: Cambridge University Press, 2011).

[87] 'Sie hat die Beziehungen der Menschen untereinander, die Beziehungen der Menschen zum Staat und zu den Fragen des Daseins vollkommen geändert und neu geformt.' Heiber, *Goebbels Reden*, 131. Here, Goebbels gestures at Heidegger's ontology of *Dasein*. The mode of being represented by *Dasein* is by definition interconnected with other selves, and indeed modes of relating to the self are profoundly determined by going through 'Others'. See Heidegger, *Being and Time*, especially 'Being-in-the-World as Being-With and Being-One's-Self: The "They"', 149–68.

nineteenth century, is the symphony as a product of the Enlightenment: an idealist vehicle for a multivoiced, yet cohesive, utopian social order governed by ethical values of individual freedom and autonomy.[88] On the other is the symphony's monumental ability to overwhelm and absorb the listening subject within the collective – an ability linked to the aesthetic of the sublime, but repurposed by National Socialist aesthetics.[89] The music reviews raise several themes marked by both of these symphonic ideologies. In March 1933, so soon after the Nazi takeover, the symphony's reception made clear that the way in which subjectivity, space, and force were articulated was still contested and plural. Because of its specific historical positioning and how it negotiates the divide between public and private spheres, Pfitzner's symphony and the commentary surrounding it can shed light on tensions between the transcendental symphonic idealism that continued to inflect the genre, on the one hand, and, on the other, the ideology and rhetoric of the totalitarian National Socialist aesthetic imperatives, which would crystallise in the coming months.

Enlightenment idealist values remained decisive for German symphonic aesthetics even towards the end of the First World War, channelling widespread optimism on the political left as the Weimar Republic was established. Exemplary was Bekker's 1918 treatise *Die Sinfonie von Beethoven bis Mahler*, introduced in Chapter 1.[90] (Pfitzner's and Bekker's intellectual positions were in many ways opposed: the composer had lambasted Bekker's writings in a well-known public spat, which reinforced Pfitzner's status as an archetypical anti-modernist.)[91] Bekker's concise monograph offers an important perspective that helps reconstruct a wider historical and ideological framework for reading the concert reviews. First and foremost, he claimed that 'the motivation for composing

---

[88] See, for example, Mark Evan Bonds, *Music as Thought: Listening to the Symphony in the Age of Beethoven* (Princeton: Princeton University Press, 2006). In particular, chapter 4 ('Listening to the Aesthetic State: Cosmopolitanism') deals with the symphony's role in philosophical representation of the relationship between the individual and society. Ibid., 63–78.

[89] See ibid., 44–62 (chapter 3, 'Listening to Truth: Beethoven's Fifth Symphony').

[90] However, Bekker was not necessarily arguing for these as eternal values invoked by the symphony. Rather, his historically situated analysis also argued that the close association of the symphony with these values was contingent upon the genre's maturity coinciding with the intellectual climate and democratic ideals of the period spanning from the French Revolution through to the end of the Napoleonic Wars. See Bekker, *Die Sinfonie*, 16.

[91] Pfitzner publicly attacked Bekker's 1911 book on Beethoven in his acerbic 1920 essay, *Die neue Aesthetik der musikalischen Impotenz* (Munich: Verlag der Süddeutschen Monatshefte, 1920). See also Paul Bekker, *Beethoven*, 2nd ed. (Berlin: Schuster & Loeffler, 1912). For further discussion, see, for example, Jürgens, 'Die Politisierung der "Einfallsästhetik": Erster Weltkrieg und Weimarer Republik', in '*Deutsche Musik*', 72–162.

a symphony is grounded … in the artist's wish to speak to a mass public'.[92] As previously discussed, Bekker's ideas about the symphonic genre as composing an idealised democratic space align with Habermas's later theorisation of the liberal public sphere.[93] He argued that the ideal symphony, achieved by Beethoven, opens a direct channel between the composer and the mass listening public, conveying musical ideas whose character requires a vast unfolding of energy ('*Kraftentfaltung*') into a correspondingly vast physical space.[94] More than this, the performance of such a symphony is equivalent to 'a musical assembly of the people, an assembly in which a shared sentiment, whose expression is reached through the music, is activated and comes alive'.[95] The symphony and its associated symphonic-generic space are thus unique in their potential to form universal communities, composed of all social levels. By contrast, for Bekker the string quartet or piano sonata are suited to very different kinds of musical and tonal ideas, which require far less force of sound and are correspondingly suited to smaller, more intimate, exclusive spaces.[96]

In 1933, only fifteen years after Bekker wrote *Die Sinfonie von Beethoven bis Mahler*, the symphonic ideals expressed there could barely have seemed more out of place. In principle, Bekker's formulation of symphonic space was in the spirit of creating an egalitarian symphonic listening community comprising all layers of society, unified by faith in principles of ethical freedom. But it is not at all difficult to anticipate how the National Socialist political backdrop, together with its totalitarian nation-forming imperatives – the 'Daseinskampf eines Volkes', as Goebbels put it, in loaded Heideggerian language[97] – began to corrupt and co-opt this community-forming impulse and rhetoric, anticipating the National Socialist vision of individual subjectivity dissolving within the collective consciousness of the masses and the vast imagined public spaces of the monumental.[98] For the degree to which it was informed by Enlightenment values, Bekker's symphonic theory did surprisingly little to preserve the sense of the individual listening subject and their autonomy, influenced, perhaps, by ideas prevalent in nineteenth-century philosophies of listening. Nietzsche famously diagnosed the decadence of Wagnerian music culture, claiming that the listening practices it commanded were fundamentally bound up with listeners' desires to submit to

---

[92] Bekker, *Die Sinfonie*, 12–13.   [93] See ibid., 16.   [94] Ibid., 11.   [95] Ibid., 15.
[96] See ibid., 8–11.   [97] Heiber, *Goebbels Reden*, 131.
[98] See Rehding's discussion of Albert Speer's monumental 'light cathedrals' in Rehding, *Music and Monumentality*, 173.

'the sublime, the profound, the overwhelming'.[99] And at this Pfitzner concert in particular, political circumstances put an insidious gloss on Bekker's conjectures about the appropriate amount of force required by symphonic ideas. Furthermore, Walter's underscored absence darkly recalled Bekker's proposition that such musical ideas command a particular imagined space and that they are generated from the conception of a particular kind of community. In March 1933, the limits of that community had been suddenly and strikingly redefined against constructions of racial purity.

The idea that in the string quartet some kind of surplus in the musical material was poised to 'burst' the frame, structure, or fabric of the chamber form recurred throughout the reception – the phrase most frequently used by critics (for instance, Runge, the *Berliner Lokal-Anzeiger*'s Walter Abendroth (1896–1973), and *Die Musik*'s Oscar von Pander (1883–1968)) was 'den Rahmen sprengen' (burst the frame).[100] For many listeners, the musical content embodied a sense of pent-up, even violent excess, barely contained by the conceptual space of the string quartet medium. In this light, the shift across the genre divide seems brutal – the wrenching apart of a terse and self-contained chamber form into another, unfamiliar sound-world. Implied in the bursting of the string quartet's frame is Bekker's idea of the symphonic compulsion to speak to the masses, because ideas generated by an idealised image of a symphonic space and symphonic community would exceed a chamber form. These modes of thinking governing symphonic space are aligned, to some extent, with Bekker's theorisation of the symphony as an agent capable of determining a specific space, and with this, an idealised image of a particular listening public. Yet Bekker's *Kraftentfaltung* suggests an uncomfortable parallel with what Goebbels called *die Volkwerdung* in his November 1933 Philharmonie address – that is, the Hegelian coming-into-being of the German people – and its *Lebensraum* (living space) corollary adopted by the Nazis as a fundamental justification

---

[99] See Friedrich Nietzsche, *The Case of Wagner, Nietzsche Contra Wagner, and Selected Aphorisms*, 3rd ed., trans. Anthony M. Ludovici (Gloucester: Dodo Press, 2008), 10.

[100] This imagery can be found in the *Deutsche Allgemeine Zeitung, Allgemeine Musikzeitung, Berliner Lokal-Anzeiger*, and *Die Musik* reviews: 'Hier sprengt die Erfindung tatsächlich den Rahmen des Streichquartetts und verlangt nach der Wuchs des Orchesters' (Runge, 'Pfitzner dirigiert seine neue Symphonie'); 'Sie birgt in der kammermusikalischen Gestalt Ausdruckswerte, die das gegebene Klanggefüge sprengen möchten' (*Allgemeine Musikzeitung*, 16 June 1933, 335); 'Jeder Musikalische aber wird jetzt hören, wie vieles, was in der Urfassung den Rahmen des Kammermusikalischen zu sprengen drohte, im Orchestersatz erst seine Erfüllung findet' (Abendroth, 'Pfitzner-Abend'); 'Es [droht] in der Intensität und Wucht seines Ausdrucks inhaltlich den Rahmen eines Streichquartetts zu sprengen' (Von Pander, 'München', 628).

for their geographical expansionism.[101] Influenced by Social Darwinism, *Lebensraum* doctrine asserted the natural rights of the Aryan race to prosper by settling in new territories.[102] Symphonies, as these writers seem to claim, have their own proper domain; according to the expansionist ideology of *Lebensraum*, so too do the German people.

For a totalitarian ideology that elevated the state above all else, the construction of a unified national imaginary was vital. The symphonic genre occupied a privileged place in such Nazi myth-making. Throughout the Third Reich, the Nazis exploited the symphony as a genre for ceremonial purposes at large concerts and over the radio. As Meyer observes, the 'collectivisation of the individual', essential to National Socialist ideology, was symbolised 'by the decline of the lied and the rise of the large orchestra'.[103] The dominant aesthetic for National Socialist Germany was the lofty transcendentalism of the monumental, 'with its grandiosity, lavishness, and spirituality'.[104] One aspect of the symphony's importance to the National Socialists, then, relates to the hierarchical social and spatial organisation of the symphony orchestra. The large collective of musicians needed to perform a symphony functioned as one musical body under a single conductor, reproducing Nazi ideology and the paternal authority of the *Führerprinzip* (leader principle) in particular.[105] The other aspect was the symphony's monumental aesthetic and had to do with the supposed overwhelming effect of the music on the listener.

The symphonic genre's status historically as an archetype 'for the experience of the sublime' points to a further theoretical perspective to inform our reading of the reviews, because shifting discourses relating to the sublime shed light on the changing status of the listening subject in totalitarian ideology.[106] The sublime, Brinkmann argues, 'categorises

---

[101] 'The meaning of *the* revolution, that *we* have created, is the coming into being of the German people as a nation. This, indeed, has been the yearning of all good Germans for two thousand years.' Heiber, *Goebbels Reden*, 133 (emphasis in the German original). See also Rehding's discussion of the political resonances of *Lebensraum*, a term that was used by musicologist Heinrich Besseler to evoke a musical monumentality determined by the expansive physical spaces it filled. Rehding, *Music and Monumentality*, 174–5.

[102] A more detailed exploration of *Lebensraum* ideology is provided as part of Paolo Giaccaria and Claudio Minca's discussion of the 'bio-geo-political nature of Hitler's geographies'. See 'For a Tentative Spatial Theory of the Third Reich', in *Hitler's Geographies: The Spatialities of the Third Reich*, ed. Giaccaria and Minca (Chicago: The University of Chicago Press, 2016), 19–44.

[103] Meyer, *Politics of Music in the Third Reich*, 9.

[104] Gilliam, 'Annexation of Anton Bruckner', 591.

[105] For discussion of the orchestra's symbolic role in Nazi Germany, see Painter, *Symphonic Aspirations*, esp. 214–15.

[106] Brinkmann, 'Distorted Sublime', 49.

the experience of vast, monumental, overpowering objects'.[107] Kant's *Critique of Judgment* proposed that the ability to experience the sublime was a property of the subject, asserting the individual's ability to 'exert self-determination and a state of autonomy, that is, to control the sublime'.[108] Yet, as Brinkmann explains, the sublime was ideologically recast under the National Socialists, being relocated within the monumental object itself. In this way, National Socialist aesthetic thought removed the aspect of the sublime that affirms the sovereignty of human subjectivity; the individual is radically reformulated in relation to the sublime, and in relationship to the collective, 'the *Gemeinschaft*, the *Volk*'.[109] Brinkmann puts it elegantly: 'What remains is the overwhelming power of the great or monumental, of the collective will, to which the subject must submit.'[110] Rehding expounds the spatial dimension of the sublime or monumental, drawing on Heinrich Besseler's and Arnold Schering's aesthetic theories of the mid-to-late 1930s: the monumental in Nazi Germany is embroiled with the creation of expansive virtual spaces in relation to which the individual disintegrates.[111] As he explains, '[t]he central concern of [monumental] musical space is not with meaning but with presence', the experience of which 'remains a void to be filled with political content'.[112] Thus, Rehding identifies the theatrical appearance of agency as one of monumentality's central trappings.[113] In effect, and as Painter similarly notes, National Socialist ideologues imbued the sublime musical object with 'a kind of subjectivity'; critically, this included the agency to wield force over the listening subject.[114] As we saw earlier, Pfitzner himself invoked an aligned narrative, which positioned the musical work as an agent driving the re-orchestration independently of its composer-creator, when he claimed that the string quartet musically 'demanded' a symphonic manifestation.[115]

Reviewers went further. In *Die Musik*, Otto Steinhagen endowed the C♯ Minor Symphony with the power to overwhelm the listening subject. 'Those who do not back away from immersing themselves in the exhausting tension of such a demanding musical experience will not be blinded by

---

[107] Ibid., 44.   [108] Ibid., 47.   [109] Ibid., 48.   [110] Ibid., 47.

[111] See Rehding, 'Faustian Descents', in *Music and Monumentality*, 169–96, especially 173–80. He cites Arnold Schering, 'Über den Begriff des Monumentalen in der Musik', in *Von großen Meistern in der Musik* (Leipzig: Breitkopf und Härtel, 1935), 7–44; Heinrich Besseler, 'Musik und Raum', in *Musik und Bild: Festschrift Max Seiffert*, ed. Besseler (Kassel: Bärenreiter, 1938), 151–60.

[112] Rehding, *Music and Monumentality*, 180.   [113] Ibid., 9.

[114] Painter, *Symphonic Aspirations*, 240.   [115] See Pfitzner, *Briefe*, 595, 597.

it, but in fact enlightened.'[116] *Die Musik*, one of the most influential journals on the German market, was well respected for its balanced political spectrum of opinion pieces from distinguished members of the musical establishment, but degenerated into a vehicle for official propaganda starting with the June 1933 issue, which led with an address from Goebbels.[117] 'Enlightened' does not quite capture the German imagery, however; those who submit to the musical experience are literally 'made seeing for the world of the Self'.[118] Although 'immersion' in the symphony is presented as emancipatory, listeners' autonomy is actually being restricted. Steinhagen spells out the mechanism of the sublime as reconceived by National Socialist ideologues. To disguise the sleight of hand he uses flattery: the listener is courageous. This plays into a strategy in emerging National Socialist discourses that appealed to notions of strength, duty, and freedom to collectivise the private sphere – that is, 'the world of the Self'. For instance, in an article titled 'Was ist Kultur' in the July 1933 issue of *Neue Literatur,* Fritz Rotosky wrote: 'The individual must be absorbed by the community with his soul in order to fulfil his innermost calling ... to do what is in his power ... makes a man free, in spite of having taken orders. He is free because he wants to obey.'[119]

The shared interiority Steinhagen evokes is Meyer's 'collectivisation of the individual': the eradication of the private subject and, alongside it, subjective agency, autonomy, and freedom of thought. So, too, is Walter's absence, which signals how the private sphere is wrenched out into the public context of the concert hall, and suggests the violent public disciplining of those individuals considered deviant – recall Goebbels's revolution that took hold of 'all areas of public life and transformed them fundamentally'. How we saw Stege frame the genre transition earlier – 'the intended deepening and intensification of expression' – takes on further grim significance. Racist violence was beginning to be embedded as a mechanism structuring the public sphere. And, alongside allied issues like family and religion, the private sphere was beginning to be forcibly pulled out into the public. Set against such brutalising discipline of spaces both real and imagined, the material resistance

---

[116] 'Wer die bis zur Erschöpfung reichende Anspannung des Mitgehens nicht scheut, den blendet sie nicht, macht ihn aber sehend für die Welt eines Eigenen.' Steinhagen, 'Musikleben der Gegenwart', 619.

[117] See Meyer, *Politics of Music in the Third Reich*, 34. For a more detailed analysis of *Die Musik* as a publication complicit in the *Gleichschaltung* in National Socialist Germany, see Lovisa, *Musikkritik im Nationalsozialismus*, 21–39.

[118] Steinhagen, 'Musikleben der Gegenwart', 619.

[119] Fritz Rotosky, 'Was ist Kultur', *Neue Literatur* (July 1933): 380, in Meyer, *Politics of Music in the Third Reich*, 25–26.

against this genre shift implied by Stege's phrase – a resistance that it nevertheless overcomes – sounds especially loaded. Through that phrase, any sense of boundary between symphony and string quartet is physically overpowered, co-opting the private sphere to make it assume a public character. As the studied neutrality of most of the responses to Walter's exile in the symphony's reception seems to show, language that publicly affirmed the private, and the autonomy of the individual subject, was losing traction.

Symphonic Aesthetics on the Threshold

Although the first few months after the fascist takeover were chaotic for music and musical institutions, and although the emergence of a National Socialist discourse on music was 'piecemeal' at best,[120] the reception of Pfitzner's symphony over the numerous additional performances throughout 1933 nonetheless offers a view of how symphonic aesthetics increasingly fostered National Socialist values. In March, the *Zeitschrift für Musik*'s review of the premiere in Munich by Wilhelm Zentner (1893–1982) deployed rhetoric connotative of Germanic ethnic superiority: 'The work is pervaded right into its very last fibres with Pfitzner's blood and spirit.'[121] At the Berlin premiere the following week, the *Berliner Börsen-Courier* echoed such sentiment, hailing the work as 'filled with a deep and authentic Romantic sensibility; it is the expression of a personality in which contemplative, brooding, and sensitive qualities synthesise uniquely'.[122] As the year progressed, the alignment with nationalist ideologies that linked idealist traditions of interiority and spirituality to ethnic purity became increasingly explicit. In the August edition of *Zeitschrift für Musik*, its former editor-in-chief and influential anti-modernist Alfred Heuß (1877–1934) described the performance at the Dortmund Tonkünstlerfest as the festival's high point, 'about which nothing further need be said, other than that it allowed us fleetingly to feel the breath of the beyond and recognise music once more as an art of metaphysics'.[123] And by October,

---

[120] Meyer, *Politics of Music in the Third Reich*, 209.

[121] 'Das Werk, bis in die letzte Faser vom Blut und Geiste Pfitzners durchwallt.' Wilhelm Zentner, 'Konzert und Oper: München', *Zeitschrift für Musik* 5 (1933): 503–4.

[122] '[Das Werk] ist erfüllt von einer tiefen und echten romantischen Gesinnung, es ist Ausdruck einer Persönlichkeit, in der sich Besinnliches, Grüblerisches und Empfindung eigenartig mischen.' Strobel, 'Pfitzner dirigiert'.

[123] The original reads: 'Über die weiter nichts gesagt sein soll, als daß sie wieder einmal den Atem einer Kunst des Metaphysischen verspüren ließ.' Alfred Heuß, 'Vom Tonkünstlerfest in Dortmund und noch wichtigeren Dingen', *Zeitschrift für Musik* 8 (1933): 808.

reviewing a concert in Dessau, the *Zeitschrift für Musik* claimed the C♯ Minor Symphony 'reflected all depths of the German soul'.[124] All these excerpts indicate the heritage of Nazi symphonic aesthetics in Romantic *völkisch* discourses, and evince a sense of a collectivised interiority that is closely linked to (or perhaps subordinated under) Pfitzner's paternal authorial subjectivity.

But the question of genre persisted for some. When the *Allgemeine Musikzeitung* wrote its programme notes for the performance at the Dortmund Tonkünstlerfest, it characterised the work as an intersection between two genres, exemplifying a new kind of 'boundary-work' ('*Grenzwerk*'): 'its substance is situated on a threshold, accommodating creativity in both chamber and symphonic music'. The idea of occupying the boundary allows seepage between, and the blurring of, the two spaces. Rather than reinforcing the spatial distinction between symphonic and chamber music spheres, the 'boundary-work' serves instead as a gateway that enables the erosion of that distinction and the collectivisation of the private sphere. The tension between string quartet and symphony and their different associated spaces is cast as a source of dynamic energy for the work, suggesting that the rhetoric that blurred public and private space was becoming increasingly normalised and familiar. In both incarnations the work is volatile, using language connoting strength and vigour that chimes with emerging Nazi discourses. As string quartet, the expressive material is poised ready to burst; as symphony, the harmonic colouring fails to corrupt the pure, clear strength of the four-voiced quartet ('*Vierstimmigkeit*'):

In the chamber music form [the work] contains latent values of expression that burst the limitations of the pre-given sound-world. In the symphonic [form] it actually preserves with clarity the strict character of the four instruments that – in terms of sound – only appears to be enhanced in the shading of intensity. Almost nowhere is the pure, clear energy diminished by mere harmonic padding. Music history certainly offers enough examples of such boundary-works, whose essence perhaps comes closest to the ideal of 'absolute' music.[125]

---

[124] Hans-Georg Bonte, 'Dessau', *Zeitschrift für Musik* 10 (October 1933): 1054.

[125] '[I]hre Substanz [liegt] auf der Grenzlinie zwischen kammermusikalischer und sinfonischer Erfindung . . . . Sie birgt in der kammermusikalischen Gestalt Ausdruckswerte, die das gegebene Klanggefüge sprengen möchten und wahrt in der sinfonischen den strengen Grundcharakter der realen Vierstimmigkeit, der nur in der Schattierung der Intensitätsgrade klanglich gesteigert erscheint, aber fast nirgends durch bloßes harmonisches Füllsel in seiner reinen, klaren Kraft gebrochen. Beispiele solcher Grenzwerke, deren Wesen vielleicht dem Ideal "absoluter" Musik am allernächsten kommt, bietet die Musikgeschichte ja genug.' 'Festprogramm der 63. Tonkünstler-Versammlung', *Allgemeine Musikzeitung*, 16 June 1933, 335.

Intimately entangled with German identity politics, of course, is 'the ideal of "absolute" music', a nexus at which the author of the programme note implies public and private space now elide without any conceptual friction. It is a deeply troubling elision, and of all the reviews, it is this one that most closely recalls the attitude Pfitzner himself expressed towards the musical material. Although recovering Pfitzner's intentions for the re-orchestration is frustrating, he certainly did not seem to feel 'the need to speak to a mass public', which Bekker posited as being fundamental to symphonic creativity.[126] That liberal-idealism seemed dead. Rather, depending on his audience, he variously suggested the work was a tragic manifestation of his creative impotence, or a bid for increased recognition for his string quartet.[127] But, referring to the music, he suggested that the content of his string quartet was equally suited to both symphonic and chamber space – in effect, a 'boundary-work'.

In Berlin in March 1933, however, critics did not hear it that way, and things looked less deterministic. Regardless of what their creators say or do, musical works have an independent socio-critical function. They initiate reactions and discussions that recursively loop back into the networks of values that constitute their social worlds. Though an appreciation of what it meant to participate in the concert and listen to Pfitzner's new symphony cannot of course be fully reconstructed here, the initial reviews convey a keen sense of how contemporary listeners experienced the simultaneous presence of both genres and the musical tension this caused. Critics largely staked out clear distinctions between chamber and symphonic worlds, between public and private space, just as Bekker had in *Die Sinfonie von Beethoven bis Mahler* at the liberal-idealist dawn of the Weimar Republic. Finally, Pfitzner's construction as an ethnically pure German did not yet guarantee the success of his symphony. These misgivings about genre show that no matter how decisively a particular element, like notions of racial authenticity, correlated with the value system of the emerging political regime, symphonic discourse remained unpredictably mutable.

Music, and the symphonic genre in particular, as these reviews show, can be a persuasive tool in the fascist reformulation of the relationship between subjectivity and space. But it can also oppose it. And, as these reviews also show, the music of Pfitzner's symphony seemed politically

---

[126] Bekker, *Die Sinfonie*, 12–13.

[127] See Pfitzner, *Briefe*, 619. See also ibid., 595, letter to Fürstner, 17 June 1932: 'das Erklingen als Sinfonie in einem größeren Kreis wird vielleicht beitragen zur sozusagen Popularisierung des Werkes als Streichquartett; denn eine Sinfonie hat immer ein größeres Publikum'.

elusive. By resisting the re-orchestration and conventional symphonic-generic markers, particularly in the first and fourth movements, Pfitzner's work also foregrounded an *Intimsphäre* that countered totalitarianism's goal of rendering the subject fully public.[128] The tension critics noted between an internalised musical idea and the physical symphonic manifestation meant that, ultimately, this symphonic work was unable to subsume the subjects and delicate voices of the string quartet within the monumental mass, demonstrating discomfort about the co-existence and manipulation of public and private space. In a sense, the C♯ Minor Symphony retained what Adorno later called chamber music's 'critical' function, driven by the 'premises of autonomy and independence extending all the way into the compositional ramifications of chamber music'.[129] To argue along similarly Adornian lines, how this work frustrated critics' expectations of symphonic 'expansiveness' and 'décor' indicated a political dimension that opposed fascist erasure of the subjective element.[130] In revealing to some listeners, if only briefly, the monumental scaffolding that jarred with the musical material, the symphony staked out a point of ideological conflict and uncertainty within the first few haphazard weeks of fascist Germany. Even symphonic discourse associated with a strongly nationalist figure like Pfitzner turns out to have the potential to be unexpectedly polyvalent.

---

[128] As noted above, Burger defines an *Intimsphäre* as 'the core of a person's private sphere which by law, tact, and convention is shielded from intrusion'. See Burger, translator's note, in Habermas, *Structural Transformation*, xvi.
[129] Adorno, *Introduction to the Sociology of Music*, 100.   [130] Ibid., 96.

Liberalism, Race, and the American West in Roy Harris's *Symphony 1933*

Boston – New York

First, to Chicago. As 1933 dawned, despite the success of William Grant Still's *Afro-American Symphony* of 1931, still no symphony by an African-American woman had ever been publicly performed. On 15 June, therefore, when Florence Price (1887–1953) had her Symphony in E minor premiered by the Chicago Symphony Orchestra at the city's most important concert venue, the 4,237-seat Chicago Auditorium, history was made – although with little fanfare.[1] The concert, conducted by Frederick Stock, was linked to the 1933 Chicago World's Fair and formed part of the 'Century of Progress Series' under the auspices of the Friends of Music. Price's work was performed in a concert devoted to prominent Black performers and composers, which fell on the second night of the four-day series. The concert had been financially underwritten by the Chicago Music Association, the local chapter of the National Association of Negro Musicians (NANM), although their contribution went unpublicised.[2] Music by Samuel Coleridge-Taylor was also on the programme, and the soloists were famed tenor Roland Hayes and up-and-coming pianist-composer Margaret Bonds.

Price's four-movement work musically responds to a dialogue about the symphony and American musical identity initiated by Dvořák with his 'New World' Symphony. It received glowing reviews in both the Black and the white press.[3] This was hardly surprising, for Price's Symphony in

---

[1] For a history of some of the conditions in Chicago that set the stage for the success of Price's symphony, particularly the networks of Black women and their institutions that elevated her, see Samantha Ege, 'Composing a Symphonist: Florence Price and the Hand of Black Women's Fellowship', *Women and Music: A Journal of Gender and Culture* 24 (2020): 7–27.

[2] Ibid., 25, citing Barbara Wright-Pryor, 'Maude Roberts George ... President of CMA of which Price was a member, underwrote the cost of the June 15, 1933 concert', *Africlassical*, 7 April 2014, https://africlassical.blogspot.com/2014/04/barbara-wright-pryor-maude-roberts.html.

[3] The write-up in the *Afro-American*, for instance, described how it showcased Price's 'panoramic' emergence as a composer, while the *Winnetka Talk*'s reviewer called it 'an unusually beautiful composition with great depth', concluding that 'an outstanding composer has been discovered'. 'Woman's Symphony Heard at Fair', *Afro-American*, 1 July 1933, 8; 'Symphony by Colored Woman Highly Praised', *Winnetka Talk*, 22 June 1933. See also E. S., '"Friends" Series to Close', *Musical Leader* 64 (25): 22 June 1933, 9; E. H. B. 'Second and Third Weeks of Symphony Concerts at Auditorium', *Music News*, 25 (25): 7 July 1933; Eugene Stinson, 'Music Views',

E minor had won first prize in the symphonic category in a prestigious competition sponsored by the Rodman Wanamaker Foundation the previous year.[4] But the 15 June premiere was not only the first public performance of Price's symphony; it was also the last in her lifetime. Howard Hanson rehearsed – but did not perform – it with the Eastman Orchestra. Its moment in the spotlight could not have been briefer.[5] Naïve calls for it to be given a 'place on the regular symphonic repertory' seemed hopelessly ill-attuned to the reactionary politics of concert programming.[6]

In 1935 Price first approached renowned supporter of new American music and conductor of the Boston Symphony Orchestra Serge Koussevitzky, hoping for his consideration of her music. It would not be Price's only such appeal to the conductor. 'My dear Dr Koussevitzky', she wrote in a later letter of 1943,

> To begin with I have two handicaps – those of sex and race. I am a woman; and I have some Negro blood in my veins. Knowing the worst, then, would you be good enough to hold in check the possible inclination to regard a woman's composition as long on emotionalism but short on virility and thought content – until you shall have examined some of my work?
>
> As to the handicap of race, may I relieve you by saying that I neither expect nor ask any concession on that score. I should like to be judged on merit alone – the great trouble having been to get conductors, who know nothing of my work . . . to even consent to examine a score.[7]

Chicago Daily News, 16 June 1933, 41. More lukewarm was Glenn Dillard Gunn writing for the *Chicago Herald and Examiner*, although he still conceded that 'it is a first effort in the larger forms worthy of respect'. Gunn, 'Roland Hayes is Soloist at Auditorium', *Chicago Herald and Examiner*, 16 June 1933, 13.

[4] She also won first prize for her Sonata in E minor for piano, meaning she won two out of the competition's three categories. For a detailed account of the Wanamaker contests, see Ege, 'Composing a Symphonist', 20–1.

[5] Some white reporters politicised how they reported the size of the audience. One account in the white press drew attention to the audience downstairs in the stalls, apparently 'pitifully small'. However, in the Black newspaper *The Chicago Defender* it was reported that upstairs, 'boxes, the balcony, and numerous galleries were filled with our own music lovers', from whom came 'unstinted and unending applause'. Bonds was summoned back to the stage six times, a feat that would have been difficult to achieve without significant audience energy. E. S., 'Local Pianist Plays Carpenter Work', *Musical Leader* 64 (25): 22 June 1933, 9; Nahum Daniel Brascher, 'Roland Hayes Concert Shows Progress of the Race in Music', *Chicago Defender*, 24 June 1933, 11.

[6] Stinson, 'Music Views'.

[7] Letter from Florence Price to Serge Koussevitzky, 5 July 1943, Schmitt Collection, Music Division, Library of Congress, found in Rae Linda Brown, 'Selected Orchestral Music of Florence B. Price (1888–1953) in the Context of Her Life and Work' (PhD thesis, Yale University, 1987), 8–9. See also Scott David Farrah, 'Signifyin(g): A Semiotic Analysis of Symphonic Works by

Although a performance by Koussevitzky was hardly the only measure of musical success in the United States, it would nonetheless have provided a significant platform for her work, bringing new audiences and a seal of approval from an establishment East Coast orchestra and conferring a certain kind of deeply ambivalent prestige upon someone to whom so many doors were closed. Closed those particular doors remained, however. Koussevitzky left the job of replying to his secretary and never performed her music.[8]

* * *

In April 1933, Koussevitzky commissioned the first symphony from budding American composer of 'Scotch-Irish' heritage Roy Harris (1898–1979).[9] Harris's friend Aaron Copland had engineered the introduction between the influential conductor and the still rather green composer – Harris was not long returned from Nadia Boulanger's composition school in Paris, although, like Copland, he was fast becoming considered one of the leading emergent young voices in US music. He was part of a generation that aimed to forge a sound-world listeners would recognise as 'American'.[10] Tapping into a nostalgic mythology prevalent in Depression-era Americana film and fiction, Harris, and others like him, responded to the anxieties about European cultural and political dominance that contributed to the era's isolationist politics. Anecdotally – if Harris's own account of events is to be believed – Koussevitzky specifically asked for 'a big symphony from the West'. In so doing, Koussevitzky mined the latent cultural capital in Harris's upbringing in Oklahoma and California, imagining the West as a composite territory. Koussevitzky's

---

William Grant Still, William Levi Dawson, and Florence B. Price' (PhD thesis, Florida State University, 2007), 13.

[8] According to Brown, Price wrote seven letters to Koussevitzky (8 August 1935, 18 September 1941, 5 July 1943, 6 November 1943, 22 May 1944, 7 June 1944, and 23 October 1944). The two responses from Koussevitzky's secretary were dated 17 November 1943 and 31 October 1944. Koussevitzky Collection, Music Division, Library of Congress, Washington, DC. See Rae Linda Brown, 'Lifting the Veil: The Symphonies of Florence B. Price', in *Florence Price: Symphonies Nos. 1 and 3*, ed. Rae Linda Brown and Wayne Shirley (Middleton: AR Editions, 2008), xv–lii, xxxvi.

[9] 'Scotch-Irish' comes from Nicolas Slonimsky, 'From the West: Composer New to Bostonians – Background for Roy Harris About to Be Heard at Symphony Hall', *Boston Evening Transcript*, 24 January 1934; Harris Papers, box 42. It means Protestant Irish, rather than Catholic Irish, not a mix of Scottish and Irish backgrounds.

[10] See, for instance, Aaron Copland, 'The Composer in America, 1923–1933', *Modern Music* 10 (1933): 90. Throughout this chapter, 'American' is used to refer to US identity, reflecting its use in the source material. Yet I do this with qualification: it is a reminder of the United States' historical success in colonising a word that in many contexts refers to the Americas as a whole.

commission implied a universalised American biographical authenticity that was closely tied to the rugged American pastoral landscape.[11]

The result was *Symphony 1933*. It is a boisterous work in three movements, although, given its excesses, Harris often loses a sense of control, and the formal construction could be tighter. Koussevitzky commemorated its Boston Symphony Hall premiere on 26 January 1934 as 'the first performance of a great American Symphony' in a signed note inside the cover of the manuscript score. The performance was also broadcast over the radio. Shortly afterwards, on 2 and 3 February, Koussevitzky performed Harris's symphony in Carnegie Hall in New York, where it was recorded, making it the first symphony by an American composer ever to be reproduced for the phonograph. Harris went on to become a figurehead for an American identity that reified the sovereignty of the individualist frontiersman alongside the American West. With Koussevitzky's support, enabling broad public exposure through multiple media channels, it seems that the status of *Symphony 1933* in a project of modern myth-building specifically tied to hegemonic visions of American national identity was more or less assured from the outset, capitalising on narratives vital to a country that prided itself on exceptionalism, firsts, and a romanticised vision of the American landscape.

This chapter is about whiteness, liberalism, and the West. It examines Harris's *Symphony 1933* and its reception, a historical moment that illuminates how white identity in the United States was constructed. In 1933, amidst the Depression and its economic hardships, anxieties about white working-class masculinity, the bedrock of America's self-image, were

---

[11] On Harris's unreliability, see Beth E. Levy, '"The White Hope of American Music"; or, How Roy Harris Became Western', *American Music* 19 (2001): 131–67, 132–3. See also ibid., 145, where Levy quotes what she believes to be the most detailed record of the circumstances of the commission, an excerpt from a 1966 oral history review:

Koussevitzky said, 'Copland has told me about you (I know about you already from Nadia Boulanger), but Copland says you are the American Mussorgsky.'
You see? And we had a laugh about it.
He said, 'You must write me a symphony.'
So I said, 'What kind of symphony?'
And he said, 'Oh, I want a big symphony from the West.'

There is some reason to doubt this version of events: Levy's observation that the 'big symphony from the West' anecdote only appears in sources from 1951 onwards is telling, although she also points to evidence that supports its credibility, such as Copland's anecdote about Koussevitzky telling his orchestra, 'the next Beethoven will from Colorado come!' See ibid., 163; Aaron Copland and Vivian Perlis, *Copland: 1900–1942* (New York: St Martin's Press, 1984), 109.

particularly acute.[12] The era's progressive politics and union activities
disturbed traditional gender roles in the family, which, as Elaine Tyler
May explains, 'created longing for a mythic past in which male breadwin-
ners provided a decent living, and homemakers were freed from outside
employment'.[13] The symphonic work that launched Harris's career provides a lens through which to examine discourses that, together, produce
and powerfully sustain white masculinity as the United States' dominant
form of identity, even as economic and ecological crises, as well as social
reform, threatened the status of white working-class men as productive
labourers. Depression-struck America had seen the mass dispossession and
westward exodus of agricultural workers, set against the backdrop of the
transition into a wage economy, the division of labour, and the alienation
of workers from the land.

Harris, his music, and the imagined Western landscapes of his child-
hood negotiate the gap between individual and collective identities in the
American national imagination. This chapter contributes to a broader
disciplinary discussion about the profound role of ideas of landscape in
conditioning notions of national 'authenticity' as part of nation-building
narratives and cultural nostalgia in North America and elsewhere, while
emphasising the conceptual role of the symphonic genre in that process.[14]
My discussion takes up a dialogue with existing work on *Symphony 1933* by
Beth E. Levy. She has thoroughly excavated the myth-making around the
premiere of his *Symphony 1933* as part of her investigation into how what
she calls Harris's 'Western mythology' first crystallised. The reviewers
embedded the symphony and its white composer in a collectively
imagined, idealised Western landscape, biographically linking Harris's

---

[12] For discussion of the crisis in masculinity, see, for instance, Michael Denning, *The Cultural Front: The Laboring of American Culture in the Twentieth Century* (London: Verso, 2010), 29–32.

[13] Elaine Tyler May, *Homeward Bound: American Families in the Cold War* (New York: Basic Books, 1988), 40.

[14] See, for instance, Denise Von Glahn, *The Sounds of Place: Music and the American Cultural Landscape* (Boston: Northeastern University Press, 2003); Von Glahn, *Music and the Skillful Listener: American Women Compose the Natural World* (Bloomington: Indiana University Press, 2013); Stephen Daniels, *Fields of Vision: Landscape Imagery and National Identity in England and the United States* (Cambridge: Polity Press, 1993). Beyond the American context, see, for example, Daniel M. Grimley, *Grieg: Music, Landscape, and Norwegian Identity* (Woodbridge: Boydell, 2006); Grimley, 'Landscape and Distance: Vaughan Williams and the Modernist Pastoral', in *Music and British Modernism, 1890–1930*, ed. Matthew Riley and Paul Rodmell (Aldershot: Ashgate, 2010), 147–74; Julian Johnson, *Webern and the Transformation of Nature* (Cambridge: Cambridge University Press, 1999).

romanticised 'Scotch-Irish' American subjectivity and the landscape falsely to imply that their relationship was immanent and organic. Using the reviews of *Symphony 1933*, Levy explains how Harris and the contemporary commentators blended fact and fiction, invested in collectivising Harris's biography as symbolic of a recognisably American heroic identity and uniquely American experience, distinct from those of Europe.[15]

The first part of this chapter examines the documentation surrounding the work's first performances, cutting a different path over the historical ground covered extensively by Levy. Levy's discussion prompts my exploration, which analyses correspondence, programmes, and reviews of how Harris's biographical connection with the Western landscape ties in to deeply embedded liberal discourses about ownership that intertwine sovereignty and property, with a view to illuminating some of the ideological means by which settler colonial connections with the landscape were legitimised as part of a broad colonial project of westward expansionism and appropriation.[16] In this context, liberalism refers to the political ideology whose central precept is that enshrining the autonomy of the individual benefits society as a whole and whose beginnings roughly coincide with the Enlightenment. Indeed, the colonised West has always been a contradictory and highly ideological imagined space, on the one hand promising the seemingly empty coordinates of which the pioneering individual is master, affording free motion and infinite geographical expansion beyond the limits of vision, but on the other being mapped, measured, and dissected into discrete units of property. The chapter traces some of the historical foundations for these tensions in the notions of space and American identity at the centre of the Harris 'myth' back to late eighteenth-century landscape politics, which coincide with a decisive era for the symphonic genre and its ideological inflections.

Harris and his symphony, I suggest, have far greater critical potential than what they tell us about 'Americanness'. Moving beyond the scope of Levy's arguments, then, the primary analytical focus of my chapter concerns the liberal ideological underpinnings of the Harris 'myth' and its contradictions. This reveals musical discourse as one of the means by

---

[15]   See Levy, 'The White Hope of American Music'; Levy, *Frontier Figures: American Music and the Mythology of the American West* (Berkeley: University of California Press, 2012).

[16]   The sources I have examined are from the Roy Harris Papers and related collections at the Music Division of the Library of Congress, Washington, DC. Levy's work draws largely on archival material from the Roy Harris Archive at California State University, Los Angeles.

which conflicts inherent within liberalism, which undergirded the imagined space of the West, were occluded and sustained. I align the tensions in the construction of the West vis-à-vis Harris with a core tension in the spatial narrative of American liberalism. Martin Bruckner and Hsuan L. Hsu, following Philip Fisher, have articulated this as 'an abstract, infinitely expandable, and easily damaged "democratic social space"'.[17]

Harris and his symphony are integrally situated in Fisher's liberal spatial narrative. Reception rhetorics inspired by the contradictory imagined Western landscapes central to Harris's biography converge with existing critical rhetoric associated with the symphonic genre. These include expansionist discourses – that is, the late nineteenth- and early twentieth-century drive to create ever larger symphonic structures, reflecting maximalist agendas in Germanic philosophy – and how the genre historically has been aligned with the liberal philosophy of the bourgeois public sphere.[18] I suggest that all these elements mutually reinforce one another. These overlapping critical discourses strengthen the hold and power of settler colonial visions of the West in the historical imagination. Playing out in a specifically US context, the conflicts deep within bourgeois symphonic liberalism and symphonic expansionism bolster the white communal national identity for which the Harris 'myth' stands.[19]

Symphony 1933 **and the Harris 'Myth'**

Harris's first major commission was secured when Copland and Harris attended one of music patron Elizabeth Sprague Coolidge's festival chamber concerts at the Library of Congress in Washington, DC in April 1933. It

---

[17] Martin Brückner and Hsuan L. Hsu, *American Literary Geographies: Spatial Practice and Cultural Production, 1500–1900* (Newark, DE: University of Delaware Press, 2007), 20.

[18] See Margaret Notley, *Lateness and Brahms: Music and Culture in the Twilight of Viennese Liberalism* (Oxford: Oxford University Press, 2007), 156–60; Benjamin M. Korstvedt, 'Reading Music Criticism beyond the Fin-de-Siècle Vienna Paradigm', *Musical Quarterly* 94 (2011): 156–210, 172. See also Jürgen Habermas, *The Structural Transformation of the Public Sphere: An Inquiry into a Category of Bourgeois Society*, trans. Thomas Burger and Frederick Lawrence (Cambridge, MA: MIT Press, 1989).

[19] Levy, 'The White Hope of American Music', 131. My argument responds to historical literature on the relationship between white identity and the American West. See, for example, Frank Van Nuys, *Americanizing the West: Race, Immigrants, and Citizenship, 1890–1930* (Lawrence: University Press of Kansas, 2002); Dan Moos, *Outside America: Race, Ethnicity, and the Role of the American West in National Belonging* (Hanover, NH: University Press of New England, 2005); Jason E. Pierce, *Making the White Man's West: Whiteness and the Creation of the American West* (Boulder: University Press of Colorado, 2016).

was there that Copland introduced Harris to Koussevitzky. Harris's claim that Koussevitzky had asked for 'a big symphony from the West', if true, set up the metaphorical terrain of its reception from the outset.[20] Harris began work on the symphony immediately, completing the first two movements in Coolidge's Washington apartment, which Coolidge had generously allowed Harris and his wife at the time, Hilda, to occupy free of charge in her absence.[21] At the end of May, Harris quipped in a letter to Copland: 'Koussevitzky piece is fulminating. It will have lots of surge in it. Quel Pun.'[22] Ready for Koussevitzky in late December,[23] *Symphony 1933* was premiered on 26 and 27 January 1934. Judging from Harris's letter to Coolidge after the Boston performances, the concerts were a resounding triumph, although the professional and diplomatic nature of Harris's relationship with Coolidge makes description in any other terms unlikely: 'The Symphony sounded and was received with a success beyond my wildest hopes. Dr. Koussevitzky gave me a wonderful performance – with insight and technical precision – and deep conviction.'[24] The symphony was then repeated and recorded live for the Columbia Masterworks label at Carnegie Hall in New York one week later, on 2 and 3 February. In spite of its frostier reception in New York, Harris's enthusiasm for the recording project was clear. As he reported to Slonimsky in February 1934: 'The Symphony was recorded and we believe [it] will be a knockout. The head engineer said he had never officiated over a clearer score – and that the balance was very even.'[25]

[20] Levy, 'The White Hope of American Music', 145.
[21] See letter from Hilda Harris to Elizabeth Sprague Coolidge, 11 November 1933, Coolidge Collection, box 38.
[22] Letter from Harris to Copland, 31 May 1933, Copland Collection, box 256.
[23] There is some uncertainty in the literature about precisely when Harris completed the symphony. Levy notes that 'Harris began work sometime between March and June 1933 and finished the scoring sometime between September and December of that year'. See Levy, 'The White Hope of American Music', 163. I have focused the timeline of completion more precisely by examining some ancillary correspondence. Harris was at Yaddo in Saratoga Springs in October with the purpose of finishing his symphony, as he telegrammed Coolidge. See telegram from Harris to Coolidge, 3 October 1933, Coolidge Collection, box 38. In November, Hilda wrote to Coolidge that Harris was working hard on the third movement of the symphony and that the completed work, including parts, would be finished by Christmas. See letter from Hilda Harris to Coolidge, 16 November 1933, Coolidge Collection, box 38. The following month, Harris wrote to Slonimsky: 'Koussevitzky told me he will not program the work until the *parts are in his hands*. And as the programs are made up in advance + publicity etc – I am determined to have it ready for him by New Years. So I can send him a telegram with a flourish. I want him to feel confident in my integrity.' Letter from Harris to Slonimsky, December 1933, Slonimsky Collection, box 143 (emphasis in original).
[24] Letter from Harris to Coolidge, n.d., Coolidge Collection, box 38.
[25] Letter from Harris to Slonimsky (February 1934?), Slonimsky Collection, box 143.

Harris's biographical connection with an idealised sense of the American West was strongly evoked in reviews of the symphony, yielding important consequences for the construction of an American identity that, despite its pretensions to hold for all Americans, was specifically racialised as white. The West's nostalgic spaces soothed modernist anxieties about urban living and were vital, as Levy has observed,[26] to the nurturing of the Harris 'myth', which entwined a kind of essentialised American subjectivity characterised by its pragmatism with an idealised notion of Western landscapes. The West has long held a mythological, utopian status as 'a wild, untouched land of terrain laden with golden opportunities', as Jennifer L. McMahon and B. Steve Csaki have noted.[27] Reviews of the premiere of Harris's symphony drew on the key tropes corresponding to the mythic West, being heavily strewn with metaphors associating landscape, masculinity, and organicism.[28] Henry Taylor Parker, in the *Boston Evening Transcript*, characterised what he heard as sounding 'American, first, in a pervading directness, in a recurring and unaffected roughness of musical speech – an outspoken symphony'.

Musically, too, the symphony was complicit in American myth-building, even if reviewers' explanations of precisely how the symphony musically represented the West were unspecific. To quote Parker again, the 'propulsive force' of the uneven rhythms and melodic scope 'seem to derive ... from the West that bred Mr Harris and in which he works most eagerly – from its air, its life, its impulses, even its gaits'.[29] Harris's symphony thrust forward, in language suggesting both masculine sexuality and the propulsive modern mechanised transportation that facilitated free passage through the West. Moses Smith's review in the *Boston Evening American* conflated the same assemblage of ideas: 'This music is virile. It has a destination.'[30] Similarly, in the *Boston Herald* George S. McManus described the work's 'rugged, driving sincerity', eliding masculinity and the landscape with the word 'rugged'.[31] In somewhat more oblique references

[26] Levy, 'The White Hope of American Music'.

[27] Jennifer L. McMahon and B. Steve Csaki, eds., *The Philosophy of the Western* (Lexington: University Press of Kentucky, 2010).

[28] Extracts from selected reviews of these concerts and the associated recording are published in Dan Stehman, *Roy Harris: A Bio-Bibliography* (New York: Greenwood Press, 1991). Other reviews are to be found in scrapbooks in the Harris Papers, and via ProQuest Historical Newspapers. I have noted the location of the source where clarity is required.

[29] Henry Taylor Parker, 'Manifold, Abundant, Individual', *Boston Evening Transcript*, 27 January 1934.

[30] Moses Smith, 'Stravinsky's Ballet Feature of Program at Symphony', *Boston Evening American*, 27 January 1934; found in Harris Papers, box 42.

[31] George S. McManus, 'Music', *Boston Herald*, 27 January 1934, 4. This review is cited in Stehman, *Roy Harris: A Bio-Bibliography*, 377.

to motion and propulsion invested with potent sexual energy, 'vigor' was a word that frequently recurred in the criticism: Francis D. Perkins described the 'vigor of the work';[32] Moses Smith complimented the 'breadth and vigor of many of its melodies';[33] W. J. Henderson observed 'vigor in all the score'.[34] There is more than a hint here at the American technological sublime, and some writers like Theodore Chanler for *Modern Music* evoked more specific forms of transportation in their allusions: there is 'a nervous vigor of pace that is as exhilarating as a dash of salt spray in the face'.[35] Perhaps Chanler heard those perilous ocean crossings that led settler colonialists to the New World.

Organicist imagery, a mainstay of symphonic criticism in the nineteenth century, linked music and music-developmental processes metaphorically to the natural order, using language that blended connotations of sex, science, and botany.[36] Later in his review Parker went on to state that '[n]ext to never does [Harris's melody] proceed in measured sequences. From a germ his themes broaden and lengthen in a fashion strange to the short-breathed musical hour', ultimately rendering 'an instinctive American quality to which we respond [just] as instinctively'.[37] Byron Adams has incisively contextualised the 'germ' metaphor in early twentieth-century Sibelius reception as a potent metaphor of virility.[38] It alluded to 'germ plasm', which, following German biologist August Weissman's influential theorisation of the 1880s, was thought to be an element of sexual reproduction (now known to be the genes inside egg and sperm cells).[39] The passage bears further sexual connotations: 'short-breathed' and the

---

[32] Francis D. Perkins, 'Koussevitzky presents "1933" by Roy Harris', *New York Herald Tribune*, 3 February 1934. This review is cited in Stehman, *Roy Harris: A Bio-Bibliography*, 379.

[33] Smith, 'Stravinsky's Ballet'.

[34] W. J. Henderson, 'Roy Harris Work Played by Boston Symphony', *New York Sun*, n.d., found in Harris's scrapbook of *Symphony 1933* reviews, Harris Papers, box 42.

[35] Theodore Chanler, 'Forecast and Review – New York – 1934', *Modern Music* 11 (1934): 142–7. Typescript found in Harris Papers, box 42.

[36] For a recent interrogation of how the organic realm and its botanical metaphors fostered Germanic idealist musical ideologies, particularly musical unity and seemingly autonomous goal-directed growth, see Holly Watkins, 'Towards a Post-Humanist Organicism', *Nineteenth-Century Music Review* 14 (2017): 93–114.

[37] Parker, 'Manifold, Abundant, Individual'. Levy also discusses this review in 'The White Hope of American Music', 149.

[38] Byron Adams, '"Thor's Hammer": Sibelius and British Music Critics, 1905–1957', in *Jean Sibelius and His World*, ed. Daniel M. Grimley (Princeton: Princeton University Press, 2011), 125–57, 142–3.

[39] See, for instance, August Weissman, *The Germ-Plasm: A Theory of Hereditary*, trans. W. Newton Parker and Harriet Rönnfeldt (London: W. Scott, 1883); P. Kyle Stanford, 'August Weissman's Theory of the Germ-Plasm and the Problem of Unconceived Alternatives', *History and Philosophy of Life Sciences* 27 (2005): 163–99.

phallic imagery of 'broaden and lengthen'. Needless to say, Harris's American reviewers presupposed the naturalness of Harris's 'right' to inhabit the West; as Slonimsky put it, 'his music is born, not invented'.[40]

Even negative reviews stayed in the same territory. Although in the *New York Times* Olin Downes called the symphony an 'ineptitude', he nonetheless used the qualifying adjective 'American'. The overlap in other reviewers' vocabularies with the language of heroism and masculinity in Downes's more idolatrous writings on Sibelius makes his refusal to champion Harris's symphony particularly noteworthy.[41] As Glenda Dawn Goss has noted, Downes commended Sibelius's 'manly' and 'savage' scores: for instance, the Second Symphony was 'gloriously rude';[42] the Fourth spurred him to write of 'eternal and unconquerable heroism'[43] and 'primeval power'.[44] For Downes, who had seen Harris's score before the New York performance and attended some rehearsals, *Symphony 1933* did not live up to expectations: 'The structure of the piece, its map on paper, and some of its motives, have the creative seed and offer good opportunities for symphonic development. For this writer, the promise of the symphony stops there. ... There is little genuine organic development.'[45] For all Harris's swagger, Downes felt the composer ultimately renegaded on his promise to stride manfully across the plains.

Downes's evaluation notwithstanding, for most of the reviewers the work seemed to represent a certain kind of subjectivity writ large. And that subjectivity was firmly located by the reviewers in the Western landscape of Harris's boyhood.[46] Supposedly born in a log cabin on, of all days, Abraham Lincoln's birthday,[47] Harris had spent his early years in Oklahoma before moving to California while still a child. These two

---

[40] Slonimsky, 'From the West'.

[41] Glenda Dawn Goss, *Jean Sibelius and Olin Downes: Music, Friendship, Criticism* (Boston: Northeastern University Press, 1995).

[42] Ibid., 37, 97. According to Goss, 'Gloriously Rude' was the headline for Downes's *Boston Post* review of the Second Symphony on 7 January 1911.

[43] Olin Downes, 'A New Finnish Symphony', *Boston Post*, 4 August 1912; Goss, *Jean Sibelius and Olin Downes*, 55.

[44] Downes, 'Sibelius Symphony Features', *Boston Post*, 14 November 1914; Goss, *Jean Sibelius and Olin Downes*, 56.

[45] Olin Downes, 'Harris Symphony Has Premiere Here', *New York Times*, 1 February 1934, 9, also referring to the piece as 'an American ineptitude'.

[46] See Levy, 'The White Hope of American Music', especially 144–51.

[47] As Stehman notes, little documentation of Harris's early years remains, meaning that historians have had to rely on Harris's own recollections, which 'proved increasingly unreliable as time passed'. See Stehman, *Roy Harris: A Bio-Bibliography*, 1.

far-flung states together formed a locus for a catch-all notion of the American 'West' crucial to the Harris 'myth'. The westward route from Oklahoma to California had added cultural significance in Harris's day: John Steinbeck was to appropriate it for his protagonists in *The Grapes of Wrath*, which he began writing in 1938, responding to the Oklahoma Dust Bowl of the mid-1930s.[48] Further biographical detailing of Harris's farm-working, truck-driving youth did nothing to dispel the all-American mythology that emerged around the composer in the written media, but everything to strengthen the supposed authenticity of his voice to be able to speak for the American people. Western 'authenticity' was here contrasted with (and explicitly constructed against) East Coast – and therefore European-influenced – superficiality;[49] for instance, the critics downplayed the formative significance of Harris's cosmopolitan Parisian education under Boulanger. According to Slonimsky, in an article introducing the composer to Bostonians in advance of the premiere of *Symphony 1933*, Harris's was a life that 'presents a picture of individualistic endeavor, culminating with success in high places ... When his parents (Scotch-Irish) arrived in 1898 in Lincoln County, Oklahoma, they had an oxcart, some provisions, an ax [*sic*] and a gun. They staked their claims, cut down trees, built the house.'[50] Such implicit – and not so implicit – parallels that were frequently drawn between Harris's apparently rough and ready origins and the mythological figure of the pioneer settler hardly happened by accident and recall the myth-building around Harris's older contemporary Carl Ruggles. Landscape, transcendentalism, and questions of what constitutes authenticity for American identity are similarly thematised in the commentaries on Ruggles's broadly contemporary works such as *Men and Mountains* (1924, revised in 1936) or *Sun-Treader* (1932).[51]

The trope of Harris as pioneer does significant ideological work, then. It invokes liberal discourses of land ownership to legitimise the composer's presence and freedom in Western landscapes while complementing suggestions of his artistic sovereignty. In an article exploring authorship and intellectual property law, Keith Aoki uncovers the robust connection

---

[48] John Steinbeck, *The Grapes of Wrath* (London: Penguin, 2000), originally published in 1939.

[49] For Slonimsky, for example, 'his music ... reflects not the European ready-made manufacture, but a free and somewhat mysterious firmament of America'. Slonimsky, 'From the West'. For further discussion of Slonimsky's article, see Levy, 'The White Hope of American Music', 145–6.

[50] Slonimsky, 'From the West'.

[51] See, for example, the discussion in Deniz Ertan, 'When Men and Mountains Meet: Ruggles, Whitman, and Their Landscapes', *American Music* 27 (2009): 227–53.

between 'property' and 'sovereignty' in Anglo-American law.[52] Aoki argues that the conceptions of authorship, property, and sovereignty that shape liberal ideology are indebted to late eighteenth- and early nineteenth-century Romantic ideologies of the artist and of individual creative thought. What is critical is how these ideologies blurred the distinctions between the categories of authorship and ownership, largely due to both being pervaded by the notion of sovereignty underwriting the model of the Romantic artist. Aoki traces this to Enlightenment discourses, where the emerging idea of a free individual was wedded to the concept of private property – that is, the private civil realm that the sovereign individual inhabited. As he shows, this is the intellectual climate from which Anglo-American conceptions of authorship originate, indicating just how closely embroiled with each other authorship and ownership have historically been. Folding them together becomes a particularly deft ideological sleight of hand; in the reception of *Symphony 1933* something similar is taking place around Harris's status as both composer and settler.[53]

In addition, the reviewers' rhetorics that situate the work and its composer in the West acquire some of their power from appropriating an existing set of rhetorics pertaining specifically to the symphonic genre and its historically associated discourses of masculinity, idealism, organicism, and nation-building. As the value system against which Downes assessed Harris's symphony indicates, metaphors of organicism and of masculinity, entrenched both in symphonic discourse and in discussion of the American landscape, made it easy to sublate the idea of the West within discourses already associated with the genre. Organicism, as Levy has shown, has a dual function in relation to Harris's tonal language, negotiating the oppositions between idealistic Romanticism and 'scientific systematising' – two aspects of modernity that his music assimilates. Levy illustrates this through his attitude towards the tonic's immanent potential – 'the sounding fundamental tone'. Abandoning key signature and conventional scales, Harris's tonic is the generative centre out of which tonality, consonance, and even melody grow as if by pure instinct. Likewise, Harris's idiosyncratic harmonic syntax is centred on the fundamental tone. Harris's harmony was predicated on a system of triad

---

[52] Keith Aoki, '(Intellectual) Property and Sovereignty: Notes Toward a Cultural Geography of Authorship', *Stanford Law Review* 48 (1996): 1293–355, 1297.

[53] Ibid. See also Rosemary J. Coombe, *The Cultural Life of Intellectual Properties: Authorship, Appropriation and the Law* (Durham: Duke University Press, 1998); Coombe, 'Authorial Cartographies: Mapping Proprietary Borders in a Less-Than-Brave New World', *Stanford Law Review* 48 (1996): 1357–66.

relations governed by the relation of a particular chord's upper notes to the partials of the overtone series generated by its fundamental tone. Chords were categorised in terms of their relative 'brightness' or 'darkness' – the extremes, according to Harris's terminology, being 'savage bright' and 'savage dark' – and Harris's tonal colour palate was biographically infused with his tales of watching, and attempting musically to render, the changing light of a sunset. Thus, harnessing together pseudo-physics and intuitive Romanticist impulses, 'bright' chords were those for which the overtone series generated by the fundamental tone was consonant with the upper notes of the chord; 'dark' triads, by contrast, were those where the series was dissonant.[54]

Although the organic imagery used in the reviews signified something idealist in the sense of growth towards the boundless skies, such language equally channelled early twentieth-century biological discourses through its evocation of divisions into irreducible, interchangeable units of 'seed' and 'germ' and their internal, self-propelling growth logics.[55] For instance, at the most detailed motivic level, Harris's treatment of 'organic' motivic units was controlled in a way that plays just as easily into rationalising modernist musical imperatives as it does into transcendental Romantic ones. But there is a spatial implication, too, and the offhand identity that Downes drew up between score and 'map' is revealing. Hence, the contradictory impulses smoothed by organicist metaphors intersect with the oppositional spatial impulses associated with the West and, as explored in greater detail below, the symphonic genre.

American Identity and Self-Determinism in *Symphony 1933*

Harris had a strong hand in manipulating and controlling his self-image, invoking frontiersman spirit to his advantage.[56] His contribution to *Symphony 1933*'s programme note is a good example: in what one reviewer called a 'formidable postulate',[57] Harris marked out the ambitious proportions and philosophical scope for the identity the work sought to project:

---

[54] Levy, 'Roy Harris and the Crisis of Consonance', in *Tonality 1900–1950: Concept and Practice*, ed. Felix Wörner, Ullrich Scheideler, and Philip Ernst Rupprecht (Stuttgart: Franz Steiner Verlag, 2012), 247–60, 248–9.

[55] Adams, 'Thor's Hammer', 142–3.

[56] See Levy, 'The White Hope of American Music', especially 141–2, 150.

[57] Cyrus W. Durgin, 'Music: Symphony Hall Boston Symphony Orchestra', *Daily Boston Globe*, 27 January 1934.

In the first movement I have tried to capture the mood of adventure and physical exuberance; in the second, of the pathos which seems to underlie all human existence; in the third, the mood of a positive will to power and action.[58]

Glossing over the influence of Nietzschean rhetoric, although this identity drew in part on Romantic notions of human universals, the flanking commentary shaped it as distinctly American: Harris's comments followed John N. Burk's introductory discussion of how Harris and his music evoked 'an undeniable air of the West', and how those who had written about its 'vast prairies', 'open space', and 'cowboy origins' participated strongly in America's 'persisting racial self-consciousness and root-seeking'.[59] Mirroring the simultaneously inwardly and outwardly striving impulses that characterised many of his musings on American subjectivity (later in the programme he is quoted as remarking that 'our [American] dignity lies in direct driving force; our deeper feelings are stark and reticent'[60]), Harris here articulates an externalised impulse towards progress – 'the mood of physical adventure' – which contrasts with Romantic introspection. Significant, however, is how in the programme note Romantic universalising discourses about human experience are casually transposed onto American identity – a move that colonises the space of American experience for those who perceive nineteenth-century Western philosophy as their intellectual heritage. Harris's words also confirm the ongoing currency of Romantic ideologies that held the symphonic genre to be the prime musical vehicle for projecting a universalised notion of human subjectivity. We have seen in previous chapters how contemporary theorists like Bekker similarly argued that the symphonic genre functions to collectivise subjective authorial experience. It bridges the gulf between the individual and wider formulations of collective national identity.

Driven musically by self-generative processes that parallel individual self-determinism, the symphony is a genre that takes human subjectivity as its subject matter, and in *Symphony 1933* Harris's symphonic subject, like the pioneer, is active and free-moving. Since few scholars aside from Levy and Harris biographer Dan Stehman have paid *Symphony 1933* much critical or analytical attention, it is instructive to provide a brief overview of the work and Harris's highly ideological tonal and developmental musical principles by way of accompaniment to discussions of its reception

---

[58] 'Boston Symphony Orchestra, Fifty-Third Season, 1933–1934: Programme, with Historical and Descriptive Notes by Philip Hale and John N. Burk' (hereafter Boston Symphony Orchestra Programme), 646.
[59] Ibid., 644.   [60] Ibid., 654.

in relation to space, American identity politics, and the collectivisation of the Harris 'myth'.[61] Despite the energy around the work at the Boston premiere, more recent commentators have been less forgiving about its shortcomings: for instance, Malcolm D. Robertson cites overenthusiastic use of ostinati, excessive repetitions, dependence on motivic devices, and a slackness in the structure – thereby largely confirming the same weaknesses in *Symphony 1933* as were identified by Stehman.[62]

With only three movements, marked Allegro, Andante, and Maestoso, *Symphony 1933* resists conventional nineteenth- and early twentieth-century European symphonic models. Characterised by driving, irregular rhythmic patterns and phrase lengths, the first movement lurches into action with a pounding timpani triplet '3+2' rhythmic motif, shrill woodwind, and forthright brass. Although tripartite, the movement's structural principles depart from traditional sonata form: monist rather than dualist, the first section has neither a secondary theme nor the clear sense of two competing keys that would gesture emphatically towards early classical monothematic sonata form, for instance. Channelling a Romantic sense of solipsism, its core idea grows to create an entire world for itself. As Stehman observed, virtually the whole movement can be derived from the asymmetrical opening timpani rhythmic motif (bar 1), its retrograde, and the initial theme (bars 11–28) (Example 3.1).[63] Indeed, since the opening rhythmic motif, which Stehman labels r1 (Example 3.2), is the generative material for the initial theme, Stehman argues that the entire movement is ultimately powered and unified by r1. As such, this is a clear example of – as discussed earlier in relation to Harris's tonal language – the conflicts present within Harris's organicism. On the one hand, this motivic work evinces a modernist impulse to control at the most detailed motivic level – 'scientific systematising'; on the other, it betrays a seductive Romanticism which promised that the sublime irregularity of Western landscapes could be captured by the large-scale working out of an asymmetrical triplet/duple motif. Writing about the *Symphony 1933*'s third movement, Harris coined a label for such design in relation to his melodic work – 'autogenetic', or self-generative, invoking quasi-biological

---

[61] A useful overview of *Symphony 1933* is to be found in Malcolm D. Robertson, 'Roy Harris's Symphonies: An Introduction (I)', *Tempo* 207 (1998): 9–14. See also Levy's description of the first movement in 'The White Hope of American Music', 146–8. For a more comprehensive analysis of the work, see Stehman, 'The Symphonies of Roy Harris: An Analytical Study of the Linear Materials and of Related Works' (PhD, University of Southern California, 1973).

[62] Stehman, 'Symphonies of Roy Harris', 93; Robertson, 'Roy Harris's Symphonies', 10.

[63] See Stehman, 'Symphonies of Roy Harris', 89.

Example 3.1 Roy Harris, *Symphony 1933*, initial theme, horns and trumpets, bars 11–28. Reproduced from manuscript score (Harris Papers, box 6).

Example 3.2 Harris, *Symphony 1933*, rhythmic motif r1. Reproduced from manuscript score (Harris Papers, box 6).

terminology as well as the self-reliance of the pioneer.[64] Others adopted similar language: in his *Boston Evening Transcript* pre-concert article, Slonimsky presented Harris's melodic line as 'heliotropic', evoking the image of growth towards the sun.[65]

Levy identifies precisely this kind of 'heliotropic' melodic design in the first movement's second theme (see Example 3.3).[66] After the bravado of the first theme (bars 11–28), in this middle section (bars 134–282) Harris finds a more reflective mode. A soaring, lyrical melody in the strings is introduced (bars 174–94), twice varied and restated. As Levy has shown, the same passage also illustrates clearly one of Harris's most important tonal principles, which centres on his treatment of the tonic as an anchor that 'provides solidity while the superimposition of two or more modes allows for interestingly variable scale degrees.'[67] The tonic is a starting point for exploration in tonal space, for multiple meandering directions may be taken and retraced. The movement culminates in a powerful

---

[64] Boston Symphony Orchestra Programme, 648.   [65] Slonimsky, 'From the West'.
[66] Levy, 'The White Hope of American Music', 148.
[67] Levy, 'Roy Harris and the Crisis of Consonance', 249.

Example 3.3 Harris, *Symphony 1933*, first movement, bars 174–94, violins 1 and 2. From example in Beth E. Levy, 'Roy Harris and the Crisis of Consonance', in *Tonality 1900–1950: Concept and Practice*, ed. Felix Wörner, Ullrich Scheideler, and Philip Ernst Rupprecht (Stuttgart: Franz Steiner Verlag, 2012), 247–60, 250, modified with reference to manuscript score (Harris Papers, box 6).

fortissimo bitonal dissonance scored for full orchestra: an E♭ minor triad jars against an arpeggiated D major triad picked out in the upper woodwind and brass.

Harris employs a free rondo form in the sinuous second movement, Andante. It opens and closes in E minor, with A minor as a secondary tonal centre. The principal theme initially appears in the viola part, from bars 22 to 32. Legato passages for solo woodwind intertwine with solo string writing, occasionally punctured by pizzicato strings. Once again loosely situating the symphony and its subjects within rural spaces, in the programme note Harris identified these woodwind passages as 'pastoral'.[68] The finale evokes the same unrelenting motion as the previous movements, but is primarily energised by juxtaposed contrasting gestural material. The structure is derived from a single theme (bars 1–8) – this is the melody Harris specifically referred to as 'autogenetic' – which he develops, varies, and transforms through canon, imitation, and other contrapuntal devices. Harris thus used numerous musical strategies paralleling the self-reliance and exploratory qualities characteristic of the pioneering self-made man to reinforce his own biographical claims to that status.[69]

---

[68] Boston Symphony Orchestra Programme, 646.

[69] See also the closely related discussion in Levy, 'The White Hope of American Music', 148.

Legitimising White Presence in the West

Yet, the vision of selfhood that Harris's symphony affirmed was anything but one with which Americans could commonly identify. Slonimsky's article covering the upcoming Boston premiere alluded to the symbolic and deeply racialised kind of dominant American subjectivity represented by composers such as Harris and Ruggles, using a seemingly irreverent reference to the language of livestock sales: 'Roy Harris of Oklahoma, thirty-five, white, and healthy, is well-equipped to be a musical emissary.'[70] It is worth noting that the dominant narrative of westward progress that privileges this subjectivity runs at a ninety-degree angle to the south to north axis of early twentieth-century African-American migration, and runs in the opposite direction to the nineteenth-century west to east migration of Chinese railroad labourers and miners, while the ethnic cleansing and enforced migrations of Native Americans followed no such linear general trend.[71] As a composer cast as the 'white hope' for American music, Harris saw great importance attached to his '"Scotch-Irish" lineage'.[72]

Whiteness in the 1930s was not, and never had been, something coherent; rather, its boundaries and preconditions had been constructed and enlarged ad hoc, yielding both to political pressures and to rudimentary, provisional, and ultimately fabulous supposedly scientific reasoning. Regardless, its political and social power was vast. As whiteness scholars like Nell Irvin Painter have argued, from the beginnings of whiteness as a category shaped by a supposedly Protestant Anglo-Saxon origin myth, it had many times over expanded to assimilate new waves of immigrants throughout the nineteenth and early twentieth centuries.[73] At the core of US whiteness was the idea that it was the racial condition for liberty, property ownership, and ultimately citizenship.[74] US whiteness, then, was most sharply defined against its other – those Black racial identities initially brought to the United States by the transatlantic slave trade – building an ideology of race that was fundamentally rooted in questions of freedom and enslavement, even if this was infrequently acknowledged.

[70] Slonimsky, 'From the West'. The livestock comparison is Levy's; see Levy, 'The White Hope of American Music', 151.

[71] Brückner and Hsu, *American Literary Geographies*, 16.

[72] Levy illuminates the racial aspects of the Harris 'myth' further; see Levy, 'The White Hope of American Music', especially 151–5.

[73] See Nell Irvin Painter, *The History of White People* (New York; London: W. W. Norton, 2010).

[74] Pierce, *Making the White Man's West*, 14.

By the time of Harris's birth, at the turn of the twentieth century, white identity had become a category that comfortably assimilated his 'Scotch-Irish' background. The Catholic Irish and Germans in particular had been some of the first to cross over the threshold into whiteness, and by 1900 they were well on their way to paid-up membership; later, whiteness came to include further influxes of European immigration like Polish and Russian Jews (with whom the educated New England ideologues driving racial and anthropological theory had an even harder time identifying). 'Scotch Irish' meant Protestant Irish and, being closer to Anglo-Saxon, held an even longer, higher claim to racial legitimacy than that of the 'Catholic Irish'.[75] This explains why the word 'Scotch' is so important in the Harris reception: it sets him apart from the (Catholic) Irish, who, as recently as the mid-nineteenth century had been widely held in contempt, considered drunken, violent, impoverished, feckless, and lazy, as well as being frequently depicted as ape-like.[76] As English poet and critic Matthew Arnold put it in an 1866 essay, 'balance, measure, and patience are just what the Celt has never had'[77] – Celts being at the time categorised as racially inferior.

The emphasis placed on Harris's staunch northern European heritage in the reception of Harris's symphony in early 1934 reveals the pervasiveness of anxieties about whiteness. The economic crisis of the Depression had aggravated race anxieties, having severely obstructed the social gains made by Black Americans during the heyday of the Harlem Renaissance in the 1920s, and had destabilised the hegemony of white working-class American masculinity – the core hardy 'stock' from which American white race ideologues imagined themselves descending. And, broadly put, the focus of American unease about transatlantic white migration had shifted further east to Poland, Hungary, and Russia. In addition, the scale of that migration to the United States troubled many. With mass immigration facilitated by mass transportation technologies that allowed relatively easy passage across the Atlantic, race theorists became concerned that the supposed 'quality' of the 'white race' was degenerating.[78] If

---

[75] See Painter, *History of White People*, 133.

[76] For further discussion, see Painter, *History of White People*, 132–50 (chapter 9, 'The First Alien Wave'); Noel Ignatiev, *How the Irish Became White* (New York: Routledge, 2009); David R. Roediger, 'Irish-American Workers and White Racial Formation in the Antebellum United States', in *The Wages of Whiteness: Race and the Making of the American Working Class*, revised edition (London: Verso, 2007), 133–63.

[77] Matthew Arnold, *Complete Prose Works*, vol. 3, *On the Study of Celtic Literature*, ed. R. H. Super (Ann Arbor: University of Michigan Press, 1960), 291–395. Quoted in Painter, *History of White People*, 145.

[78] See Painter, *History of White People*, 210.

ideologues had once been able to imagine America as an experimental Darwinian utopia – a promised land repopulated with only Europe's fittest – they now imagined their experiment diluted and corrupted. When getting to America was straightforward, weaker specimens could withstand the journey.

So-called empiricists developed extensive, but grossly spurious, edifices to justify white supremacy. White supremacy became the foundation for fictitious sciences, with academics – white, of course – eager to prove empirically their biological superiority.[79] By the 1920s, American eugenics had far-reaching institutions and influential supporters. It sought systematically to maximise the white race's biological potential through Darwinian ideologies that went as far as interventions like state-endorsed compulsory sterilisation of the 'unfit', legitimised by the Supreme Court's infamous *Buck* v. *Bell* ruling. In this light, Slonimsky's use of the language of livestock sales to describe Harris seems even more sinister: 'thirty-five, white, and healthy'. America's eugenics movement elided scientific ideals about biology with technological aesthetic ones about streamlining, motion, and propulsion.[80] The fantasy figure of the 'pioneer' similarly elided white masculine settler identity with that of the industrialist or technological innovator.

White people, then, had never 'belonged' in Western landscapes. This idea relied on a fantasy – a foundational American myth – of America as a quasi-religious promised land; a utopian, prelapsarian, pastoral, and – crucially – empty space of redemption and possibility where Europe's strongest and boldest could start anew. A close reading of the reviews that document the reception of *Symphony 1933* furnishes insight into the strategies by which Harris was symbolically naturalised in Western landscapes in ways that aimed implicitly to legitimise their occupation by white settlers in general. In line with paradigms governing the European Enlightenment project, those naturalisation strategies were rationalist, sanitised, and cerebral, obscuring the brutality of the West's colonisation. The organicist and quasi-biological imagery – phrases like 'germ-idea',[81] 'heliotropic', or 'auto-genetic' – sought to locate the white subjectivity of Harris's pioneering symphony within the natural order, insidiously suggesting that was where

---

[79] See, for example, Painter, *History of White People,* 72–90 (chapter 6, 'Johann Friedrich Blumenbach Names White People "Caucasian"'), 212–27 (chapter 15, 'William Z. Ripley and *The Races of Europe*').

[80] See, for example, Christina Cogdell, 'The Futurama Recontextualized: Norman Bel Geddes's Eugenic "World of Tomorrow"', *American Quarterly* 52 (2000): 193–245.

[81] Slonimsky, 'From the West'.

it rightfully belonged. 'Heliotropic' in particular, suggesting skyward botanical growth, frames the flourishing of white subjectivities as inevitable. It recalls the inevitability of manifest destiny, underscored by unwavering faith in progress. But it also carried the implication that land was something interchangeable, into which settlers could therefore plant roots both literally and metaphorically. A hagiographic 1932 article on Harris by his former composition tutor Arthur Farwell for *The Musical Quarterly* offers a particularly clear example of poetic enfolding of musical and Western spaces, where he describes the composer's 'teachers of melody' as 'the broad horizon, the long undulations or the craggy lines of mountain contours, winding streams, and the gracious curvature of tree branches'.[82]

Perhaps a more important legitimising strategy, however, was the use of language pointing to the rationalising liberal discourses of land ownership that underpinned Harris's role in constructing a certain vision of the West – 'the West that bred Mr Harris and in which he works most eagerly', in Parker's previously quoted review. Far from organic, then, Harris's biographical connections with Western landscapes acted as a conduit for the pervasive and entrenched binding together of labour, property, and sovereignty within the liberal ideology elucidated by Aoki above, predicating individual autonomy on property and the ownership of the products of one's (creative) labour. But this paradigm of autonomy appeared increasingly unsustainable in the 1930s where, as *The Grapes of Wrath* reveals, artisanal models of ownership, labour, and production were imperilled by new processes of industrial farming.

The following quotation from Steinbeck's novel elucidates clearly the same sense of ownership and autonomy insisted upon by the Harris 'myth', as it came into conflict with, and was undermined by, wider contemporary economic imperatives:

Sure, cried the tenant man, but it's our land. We measured it and broke it up. We were born on it, and we got killed on, died on it. . . . That's what makes it ours – being born on it, working it, dying on it. That makes ownership.[83]

The voice of the tenant man weds rationalist measurement and labour to ideas of property ownership, expressed in the emotive rhetoric of belonging and identity. Steinbeck articulated a romanticised relationship between land and the biographical life cycle, which aimed to express just how tightly land and identity – and particularly white male identity, somewhat

---

[82] Arthur Farwell, 'Roy Harris', *Musical Quarterly* 18 (1932): 18–32, 25.
[83] Steinbeck, *Grapes of Wrath*, 35.

perversely given the white man's historically recent occupation of the American landscape – were enmeshed in the cultural consciousness.

Interrogating the pressures to which that close cultural connection between land and identity was exposed around this time, Cotten Seiler has diagnosed a profoundly 'modern' shift in the ideological foundations of individualism around the turn of the century, propelled by Frederick Winslow Taylor's *The Principles of Scientific Management*, published in 1911. There, Taylor elucidated his systematic aim 'to increase productivity by precise delineation, measurement, surveillance, and enforcement of workers' activities',[84] fully alienating workers from their labour and, by extension, creating a mobile, contingent workforce. In a (post-)Taylorist economic context, then, what did it mean to self-determine, when the American economy could no longer sustain the idea that property and labouring the land were fundamental conditions for sovereignty?

American 'individualism', as Seiler has observed, had to be a mutable construct that could accommodate changing cultural and political imperatives and norms moving into the twentieth century, and the Harris reception reflects some of the discourses shaping ideas of 'individualism' as they shifted. The late eighteenth- and nineteenth-century ideology of 'sovereign selfhood anchored by artisanal production' was reforged under a new roughly twentieth-century regime of industrial capitalism, which posited a new kind of individualism subordinated to consumer culture, where the individual was no longer the locus of land ownership and of self-reliant material production.[85] Seiler proposes that, in the early decades of the twentieth century, in politics just as in popular culture, American mobility, an obvious requirement of a capitalist workforce, became the newly central condition of freedom and of the modern, self-determining American condition. The archetypal technology of this kind of self-determinism would be the automobile, and the archetypal figure the lone driver. One American myth – that of the yeoman pioneer – was supplanted by another in a way that masked the rift between shifting political economies.[86] Freedom through property became freedom through mobility.

---

[84] Cotten Seiler, *Republic of Drivers: A Cultural History of Automobility in America* (Chicago: University of Chicago Press, 2008), 26. See Frederick Winslow Taylor, *The Principles of Scientific Management* (New York: Harper, 1913).

[85] Seiler, *Republic of Drivers*, 24.

[86] Ibid., especially 1–16 (introduction, 'Automobility and American Subjectivity'), 17–35 (chapter 1, 'Individualism, Taylorization, and the Crisis of Republican Selfhood').

What is thus striking about the organic and biological imagery in the Harris reception is its mutability. It captures some of the tensions shaping the modern reconfiguration of white masculine subjectivities in this era and in response to the Depression. Encompassing a sense of something simultaneously both permanent and provisional, metaphors like 'heliotropic', weighted towards the universality of the sun in a way that renders the specificity of the ground of relative inconsequence, align with the uprooted, suspended state of the modern subject: that which is rooted can also be uprooted and dislocated. Perhaps even less about roots and more about directed motion, 'heliotropic' evokes little more imagery than the empty sky towards which to grow, a perfect fantasy of unbounded space. Indeed, in the context of a historical imaginary conditioned by westward expansionism, in turn moved by a vision rolling out towards the setting sun, might not words like 'heliotropic' – sunward growth – have evoked images inspired by the technologies of progress: the locomotive heading 'out West', the weightless cruising of the automobile on the open road, or the steamship crossing the Atlantic – all symbolic images for white American mythologies?[87]

Liberalism's Spatial Ideologies and the Symphonic Genre

Liberal discourses underpinned the various strategies implicated in how the sense of American identity constructed through Harris's biography were expanded outwards and collectivised in the national imagination. The vision of the West that emerges from *Symphony 1933*'s reception clearly prioritises liberal values and narratives: for instance, in the recurring allusions to sovereign, autonomous subjectivity ('individualistic endeavor'), and the tacit role played by liberal discourses of land ownership in authenticating Harris's biographical claims to the West. Indeed, the West as an ideological construct is arguably emblematic of Bruckner and Hsu's

---

[87] In addition, Christina Cogdell has made a convincing case for how technological discourses of streamlining tied up with transportation innovations were consonant with eugenicist, evolutionary discourses, strengthening the rhetorics and imagery of twentieth-century white supremacy. See, for instance, Cogdell, 'The Futurama Recontextualized', 193–245. Conversely, while white identity and ideas of technology had become ideologically intertwined, Louis Chude-Sokei reminds us that blackness and technology have long been historically positioned as oppositional: 'much of our understanding of the blacks/technology dyad assumes that the former is opposed to the latter or allowed so little access to the latter that the relationship is rare or adversarial'. Louis Chude-Sokei, *The Sound of Culture: Diaspora and Black Technopoetics* (Middletown: Wesleyan University Press, 2016), 6–7.

previously discussed vision of how landscape is conditioned by liberalism as an endless space that affords free motion. Likewise, the symphony is a genre heavily implicated in liberal ideology. Bekker's vision of the symphony's intended audience can be traced back to the genre's Enlightenment origins, aligning with the infinite scope and reach of the democratic movement. On the one hand the symphony is an idealist, expansionist project; on the other, it directs its lens to the subjective interior, and musically it demands that the composer dissever and unitise according to rationalising structuring principles. That all-encompassing social impulse towards Bekker's *Hörerschaft* makes the symphonic genre very much consonant with the 'infinitely expandable' spatial ideology of liberalism. We saw previously how Rehding has excavated the strong ideological charge to the vast imagined spaces conjured up by the symphonic genre for 1930s German musicologists Schering and Besseler.[88] By contrast, the spaces that *Symphony 1933* projected in the concert hall, its contemporary reception suggested, were those of the American West.

Perhaps, then, the most profound of the strategies that combined to merge Harris's symphonic space with the space of the West are the imbricated ideological tensions that structure both imagined spaces. And, like the symphonic genre, the mythology of the West was just as much an idealising project as it was a rationalising one, caught between two opposing impulses: the transcendental, utopian ideal of the West that drew settlers out there, and the rationalist projects that established and perpetuated colonial claims to the land. Yet, despite the idealism behind expansionist ideologies under the banner of manifest destiny, historically the ideological and legal foundations of American westward expansion owed much to obviously rationalist conceptualisations of space. European ideologies of spatial abstraction, homogeneity, and reproducibility arguably underscored the whole project of federalism after America obtained political sovereignty in the late eighteenth century, and underscored westward expansion. Yvonne Elizabeth Pelletier puts this concisely as '[t]he collective will to see ... all geographies as equally available for transformation'.[89] This is the narrative of which the nostalgic, nineteenth-century Western pioneer figure was the protagonist, after whom Harris,

---

[88] See Alexander Rehding, *Music and Monumentality* (New York: Oxford University Press, 2009), especially 172–80.

[89] Yvonne Elizabeth Pelletier, 'False Promises and Real Estate: Land Speculation and Millennial Maps in Herman Melville's *Confidence-Man*', in *American Literary Geographies: Spatial Practice and Cultural Production, 1500–1900*, ed. Martin Brückner and Hsuan L. Hsu (Newark, DE: University of Delaware Press, 2007), 191–205, 192.

aided by the press, fashioned his public image. In Harris's reception, musical elements like thematic self-determinism ('autogenetic' melody) likewise massaged the same spatial narrative which allowed white Anglo subjectivities to flourish.

Early US federal land ordinances, such as the North West Ordinance of 1787, emphasised the rationalist aspect of the liberal dynamic between sovereign individual and space.[90] As literary scholar Michele Currie Navakas has argued, invoking Martin Brückner's work on cartography, a sense of a 'modern homogenous spatiality' facilitated the creation of a unified nationhood out of the geographical diversity of the North American continent, underwriting the logic of America's political sovereignty.[91] The North West Ordinance, for example, was an agreement about how additional states could be incorporated under the centralised federal authority governing the existing East Coast states. From the ground up, the authorities measured the gained landscape into units of property and rationalised human subjects as rights-bearing owners as a basis for endlessly replicating and extending a hegemonic model of law and governance under a centralised power. The Homestead Act of 1862 provides a later historical example of rationalist legal approaches to landscape that persisted well into the twentieth century. Under this Act, land was handed out to American citizens in identical 160-acre units, with the stipulation that the land be cultivated – that is, possessed and disciplined.[92] As such, westward expansionism is fundamentally embroiled historically in those liberal discourses explored by Aoki, which were indebted to the notion of land as anonymous, interchangeable property, and which blurred the boundaries between property and the sovereignty of the individual. Steinbeck put it trenchantly in a critique of American individualism in *The Grapes of Wrath*: 'the quality of owning freezes you forever into "I", and cuts you off forever from the "we"'.[93]

This suggests some parallels with how *Symphony 1933*'s first movement saw Harris devise an entire symphonic space from one strident, highly

---

[90] For further information see, for example, Peter S. Onuf, *Statehood and Union: A History of the Northwest Ordinance* (Bloomington: Indiana University Press, 1987).

[91] Michele Currie Navakas, 'Island Nation: Mapping Florida, Revising America', *Early American Studies: An Interdisciplinary Journal* 11 (2013): 246; she cites Martin Brückner, *Early American Cartographies* (Chapel Hill: University of North Carolina Press, 2011).

[92] See Karen R. Merrill, *Public Lands and Political Meaning: Ranchers, the Government, and the Property between Them* (Berkeley: University of California Press, 2002); Michael L. Lanza, *Agrarianism and Reconstruction Politics: The Southern Homestead Act* (Baton Rouge: Louisiana State University Press, 1990). See also Paul W. Gates, Free Homesteads for All Americans: The Homestead Act of 1862 (Washington: Civil War Centennial Commission, 1963).

[93] Steinbeck, *Grapes of Wrath*, 158.

abstract initial '3+2' rhythmic motif (r1), expanding it outwards with dynamic, sprawling fervour. In Harris's view, asymmetry was a quality integral to the natural world – the natural world reduced down to its most essential ingredient – and r1 embodied asymmetry in perhaps its most distilled, most rational, musical form, simply setting '3' against '2'. When, as noted earlier, Farwell imagined 'broad horizons', 'mountain contours', 'winding streams, and the gracious curvature of tree branches' as Harris's unlikely composition pedagogues (move over Nadia Boulanger!), he suggested that what unified these elements 'is asymmetry existing with purpose and proportion, unfolded out of the Nature-urge'.[94] The 'purpose and proportion' of r1's asymmetry suggests an effort to render the 'Nature-urge' musically and build a radically organic whole spawned from what was a quasi ur-natural initial material. Indeed, for Farwell Harris's musical structure was a profoundly idealist project: 'He refuses to debase music by conforming to the misshapen and non-musical molds which the world about him extends to him, he must perforce rear its form from out its own inmost self.'[95] And yet the project also feeds into profoundly liberal spatial narratives; the abstract rhythmic motif r1 and its development evince very similar spatial ideologies to those governing, for instance, the North West Ordinance, suggesting that Harris's Romantic sense of the (supposedly) untouched Western landscape is nonetheless something that in one light passes for transcendence, but in another betrays a deep-rooted interchangeability, a lack of specificity. Recall Pelletier and 'the collective will to see … all geographies as equally available for transformation', and how such a *tabula rasa* vision connects with the potential for ownership.

If, then, the ideology behind documents like the North West Ordinance homogenised and anonymised land, it nonetheless still proposed land ownership as a determining factor for individual autonomy. Steinbeck's semifictional account of conditions in the 1930s under industrial agriculture in *The Grapes of Wrath*, however, depicts a landscape even further homogenised into anonymous spaces of mass production, where land was owned by ever fewer, ever richer firms and individuals. This critique of capitalist modernity and of the virtually impossible conditions faced by migrant farmworkers is germane to understanding the desperate situation in the early 1930s as a realist foil to the utopianism of Harris's mythologised West. The Depression hit the white working class hard, threatening to destabilise the male workers – modern pioneers – who formed the bedrock of white American identity – that is, the kind of hard-working, straight-talking, no-frills masculine identity

---

[94] Farwell, 'Roy Harris', 25.   [95] Ibid., 24.

performed at the concert hall by Harris's symphony.[96] It saw the mass dispossession of farmworkers and westward migration, focused anxieties over mechanisation and the labouring jobs it made redundant, and fuelled Fordist fears about the rationalisation of labour more generally. Now expected to move vast distances to locate work, farm labourers lost their connection to the land on which they and their families had been born, had lived, and had died. As such, by 1933 the liberal discourses about the sovereign yeoman subjectivity on which the nineteenth-century American political economy depended rang hollow.

Only one listener is documented as having heard the desolation of the period as the programme underlying Harris's symphony. As his former teacher Farwell wrote to Harris after hearing the radio broadcast of the Boston performance: 'The second movement ... gave a very pathetic impression, even one of despair – I presume reflecting the despair of the year 1933.'[97] With its faultlessly even sense of motion in each part within a small pitch range, lethargic pathos and resigned introspection characterise the Andante, in contrast to the exuberance of the outer movements (See Example 3.4).

Modern Music's reviewer described the movement's melancholy as 'suprapersonal'.[98] Farwell may have hit the mark when he implied that *Symphony 1933* politicised the plight of working Americans – why else put the year in the title? Working Americans were disempowered by the depressing regularity of capitalist industrial spaces, reflected back at the listener in the Andante's metrical regularity. But even so, *Symphony 1933* nonetheless naturalised in the cultural imagination a very specific vision of the West and of what it meant to be an American. Over all others, it privileged the white subjectivities that were mythologised in narratives of manifest destiny and whose narratives of disenfranchisement were most strongly focused by the Depression's ecological and economic crises of landscape.

Conclusion

Despite the democratising social impulse historically associated with the symphonic genre, then, it is perhaps its spatial implications that had the greatest power to absorb and perpetuate the idealised West's inherent

---

[96] See Monica Rico, *Nature's Noblemen: Transatlantic Masculinities and the Nineteenth-Century American West* (New Haven, CT: Yale University Press, 2013).

[97] In the letter's margin, Farwell annotates this comment, 'Not meant the way it first sounds!' Letter from Farwell to Harris, 6 February 1934, Harris Papers, Correspondence (mixed), box 25. Reproduced with kind permission of the Arthur Farwell family.

[98] Chanler, 'Forecast and Review – New York – 1934'.

Example 3.4 Harris, *Symphony 1933*, second movement, Andante, bars 66–72.
Reproduced from manuscript score (Harris Papers, box 6).

contradictions in the myth-making surrounding *Symphony 1933*. Symphonic discourses inherited from the nineteenth century offered existing conceptual furrows transposable onto the contradictory outwardly and inwardly striving impulses structuring both the West and white American subjectivities, buttressing the hold of the imagined West in the cultural imagination. The symphony's immense, even (to invoke Gustav Mahler) world-encompassing musical frame is congruent with the horizonless reach of the West. Yet, it contrasts with the genre's rationalising modernist musical imperatives to control at the most detailed motivic level, congruent in turn with the rationalising projects of dissection into small units that underpinned Westward expansionism, or the homogenous, reproducible spaces of industrial capitalism. The critical elision of Harris's symphony with the landscapes of the West, through organicist rhetorics in particular, suggests that, insofar as it is a modernist project of musical dissection, it is also ideologically allied with colonialist projects to dominate the landscape of the West. And these abstract, homogenous, infinitely expandable liberal spaces were vital correlates for the sense of identity constructed by the Harris 'myth'. Just as the space of the West and the space of the symphony claimed to be infinitely expandable, so too the particular kind of all-American identity projected by Harris feigned boundless inclusivity. The way in which white settlers sought to level Western plains of histories of cultivation and occupation by diverse ethnic groups functions as a spatial analogue here. This was an identity that levelled the diversity of human experience onto one homogenous plane recalling Currie Navakas's 'modern homogenous spatiality', racialised as white.

Over the course of his career, Harris proved particularly committed to the symphony as a central musical apparatus in his project of sonic nationalism. He went on to compose sixteen symphonies, many with explicitly 'American' themes clarified by subtitles such as *Folksong Symphony* (No. 4), *Gettysburg* (No. 6), and *Abraham Lincoln* (No. 10). Exploring ideologies of space has allowed something new to be uncovered about how the symphonic genre functions as a tool of nationalist identity formation.

But in the reception of his first symphony, *Symphony 1933*, we can see how the public constructions of Harris's subjectivity, his symphonic music, and its landscapes together animated a particular kind of American selfhood that had enormous traction in the public imagination. That selfhood is conditioned by a liberal ideology that asserts the abstraction, homogeneity, and reproducibility of space. It was an identity that appeared timeless, but had yet explicitly to reach maturity. It scanned the world beyond the frontier, but also looked inwards in its search for authenticity, caught between the transcendentalist impulse towards the infinite skyline and the rationalist impulse to control, dissect, and limit. Rooted in a collectively imagined past era of nation-forming and struggle, it had its eyes fixed on the horizon, with a keen sense of advancing ahead through both space and time. For Leon Mandel, America is a nation that 'narrates itself as novel, singular, and in forward motion'.[99] The kind of American subjectivity and narrative performed by Harris's symphony, and the profoundly ideological role played by the connection between Harris's biography and idealised notions of the American landscape, come at the cost of the other subjectivities and narratives, both American and otherwise, that it erases and silences.

---

[99] Leon Mandel, *Driven: The American Four-Wheeled Love Affair* (New York: Stein and Day, 1977), 76, quoted in Seiler, *Republic of Drivers*, 8–9.

4 | Aaron Copland's and Carlos Chávez's Pan-American Bounding Line

New York – Mexico City

Mexico was a rich time. Outwardly nothing happened and inwardly all was calm, yet I'm left with the impression of having had an enriching experience. It comes, no doubt, from the nature of the country and the people. Europe now seems conventional to me by comparison. Mexico offers something fresh and pure and wholesome – a quality which is deeply unconventionalized. The source of it I believe is the Indian blood which is so prevalent. I sensed the influence of the Indian background everywhere – even in the landscape. And I must be something of an Indian myself, or how else explain the sympathetic chord it awakens in me.[1]

The final months of the genesis of Aaron Copland's *Short Symphony* straddled the end of 1932 and the beginning of 1933, and they coincided with a five-month trip to Mexico undertaken by the composer and his new lover, violinist Victor Kraft.[2] The New York pair were hosted by Carlos Chávez, then already a powerful figure in Mexico's political and artistic life, and a champion of Copland's music. While in Mexico, Copland attended the first ever orchestral concert featuring only his music,[3] organised and produced by Chávez. He also composed and spent time photographing both the Mexican landscape and his partner's body within it.

A photograph album survives from this trip. In many ways, it is a typical tourist artefact in that it functions partly as a diary and contains plenty of the kind of photographs that attempt to render unfamiliar sights and experiences transportable, clearly taken by both men: photos of Mexico City, of their accommodation, of day trips, of desert and rural landscapes, and photos of the couple at play. Also interleaved between the Mexican land- and cityscapes are often suggestive pictures of Kraft in various states of undress: shirtless on the tennis court, draped over garden furniture,

---

[1] Letter from Aaron Copland to Mary Lescaze, 13 January 1933, Copland Collection, box 258. All archival materials in this chapter created by Copland are reproduced by permission of The Aaron Copland Fund for Music, Inc., successor to Aaron Copland. All excerpts from Carlos Chávez's correspondence in this chapter have been reproduced by permission of Carlanita Music Company, LLC, successor to Carlos Chávez.

[2] See letter to Henry Brandt, 16 November 1932, Copland Collection, box 249.

[3] The programme was as follows: *Two Pieces for String Quartet, Piano Variations, Upon the Hills* and *An Immorality* (for chorus), *Music for the Theatre*.

Figure 4.1 Photos of Victor Kraft from Aaron Copland's 1932–3 Mexico trip album. Copland Collection, box 514.

reclining, topless and provocatively spread-legged across a rowing boat, sunbathing nude, posing naked and athletic in the sunshine like a Classical Greek statue (there are visual parallels with the fetishisation of the second-century-AD Roman emperor Hadrian's boy-lover Antinous, who was typically portrayed in the Classical style of the fifth and fourth centuries BC). Although there are some off-guard photos of Copland, who turned thirty-two during the trip, that suggest Kraft might at times have held the camera – for instance, of the composer sleeping naked on a deckchair – Copland's viewfinder repeatedly returned to the seventeen-year-old's muscular physical form (see Figure 4.1). Away from prying eyes, it seems Mexico offered the foreign couple a more permissive space than New York.

In many of the album's images, we find a curious symmetry: both the Mexican landscape and the flawless, even Hellenic, body of the young Kraft seem to promise Copland a kind of *tabula rasa* – that is, a blank slate – troublingly channelling a sense of an idealised empty universal. The album encompasses a sense of energy: a budding new relationship; empty landscapes; potent, gleaming automobiles; blazing sun; youthful bodies; open deserts; a new world to be explored by the young men. The objectification of both figure and environment into a romanticised, yet highly potent, inertia seems to signal an orientalist fantasy, and arguably it plays out not only in Copland's pictures but also in the symphonic work, *Short Symphony* (1931–3), he composed around this time.

Questions about border-crossing encounter, connection, and friendship within the Americas – as well as the power dynamics they negotiate – are at the core of this chapter's exploration of Copland's *Short Symphony*. Chávez's fingerprints are all over the work and its history. For instance, *Short Symphony* saw its premiere under Chávez's baton in Mexico City in November 1934. He was also the work's dedicatee. And when Copland had difficulty naming the work, Chávez suggested the evocative title, 'the bounding line', which Copland assumed until he settled on the final title *Short Symphony* – 'short', of course, aims to disassociate from the heaviness of symphonic aesthetics and ideology. Given Copland's interpretation of 'bounding' as 'bounce', *Short Symphony*'s classical musical aesthetic cannot help but invoke the motion of dancing bodies. Echoing how Kraft figures in Copland's photographs, the classically inspired idea of the body in *Short Symphony*, animated by a musical language prescient of Copland's later ballet scores, walked a tightrope between (sexualised) objectification and admiring reciprocity – between domination and play. The body, the ultimate locus of colonial power, is a cypher for relations of coloniality. Investigating the work, composed at a moment of particularly intense friendship between Copland and Chávez, and how Copland's symphony channels musical bodies, as well as an aesthetics of presence and liveness, forms a starting point from which to begin to pick apart the often bewildering, or flatly contradictory, relationship between Chávez, Copland, and coloniality.[4]

One way in which scholars have previously sought to understand such a process of border crossing and negotiation is through the lens of Pan-Americanism. Copland's visit to Mexico was characteristic of a particular cultural moment that saw mutual solidarity and idealisation that crossed the border between Mexico and the United States. Carol Hess gives a succinct definition of Pan-Americanism as a seemingly utopian social movement of the 1930s and 1940s that 'reflected north-south psychological

---

[4] Such enquiry raises enormously messy, intractable questions about how colonial networks of power that triangulate Mexico, the United States, and Europe played out then and continue to play out now. See, for instance, Mabel Moraña, Enrique D. Dussel, and Carlos A. Jáuregui, eds., *Coloniality at Large: Latin America and the Postcolonial Debate* (Durham, NC: Duke University Press, 2008); Walter D. Mignolo, *The Darker Side of Western Modernity: Global Futures, Decolonial Options* (Durham, NC: Duke University Press, 2011); Walter D. Mignolo and Catherine E. Walsh, *On Decoloniality: Concepts, Analytics, Praxis* (Durham, NC: Duke University Press, 2018). Also relevant is a growing scholarship on borderlands and frontiers initiated by Gloria Anzaldúa's late 1980s work on identity at the US-Mexican border. See Gloria Anzaldúa, *Borderlands/La Frontera: The New Mestiza* (San Francisco: Aunt Lute Books, 1987); more recently, in musicology, see Alejandro L. Madrid, *Transnational Encounters: Music and Performance at the US-Mexico Border* (New York: Oxford University Press, 2011).

and spiritual bonds, celebrating the identities of the individual American republics while subsuming them within a hemispheric framework'.[5] Pan-Americanism is a contested and historically flexible category, reflecting shifting agendas from perspectives south and north of the US-Mexican border. The contingencies of the historical material considered here mean that my project is chiefly concerned with Pan-Americanism as a US-oriented construct. For all its utopian aspirations, it oiled mechanisms perpetuating geopolitical asymmetries of power. For instance, a central ideological image within that project was the *tabula rasa*.[6] It encapsulated the movement's ideals of freshness and universalism. Yet it also wiped American geographies clear of their histories in ways that served established power structures, privileging the United States. Like the symphonic genre, this vision of Pan-Americanism was a hegemonic apparatus that activated an expansive, utopian sense of community formation to ends that were far from utopian. Engaging critically with Northern conceptions of Pan-Americanism can offer keener insight into the ways in which such border-crossing relationships were shaped, represented, and performed, but without neglecting issues of agency, especially for participants south of the border. Indeed, Leonora Saavedra has rejected the paradigm of Pan-American sameness for understanding the significance of Chávez's music to the US New Music agenda in the 1920s and 1930s. Instead, she suggests Chávez and his music were valued for how he expanded their collective difference vis-à-vis Europe, 'regarding it as an asset by which to extend the margins of their own peripheral position in Western culture'.[7]

In the main, published analysis of *Short Symphony* has given relatively scant notice to its Mexican context.[8] *El Salón México*, which Copland began on the same trip and completed in 1936, far overshadows *Short Symphony*'s

---

[5] Carol A. Hess, *Representing the Good Neighbor: Music, Difference, and the Pan American Dream* (New York: Oxford University Press, 2013), 3.

[6] As Hess summarises it, the *tabula rasa* 'signified all that was pristine, unprecedented, and hopeful in the Americas'. Hess, *Representing the Good Neighbor*, 26.

[7] Leonora Saavedra, 'Carlos Chávez's Polysemic Style: Constructing the National, Seeking the Cosmopolitan', *Journal of the American Musicological Society* 68 (2015): 99–149, 142.

[8] Elizabeth Bergman Crist considers the Mexican context for *Short Symphony* in *Music for the Common Man: Aaron Copland during the Depression and War* (Oxford: Oxford University Press, 2005), although the standpoint is not music-analytic. In an unpublished paper, Leonora Saavedra deals with the music-analytical influence on Copland's *Short Symphony* of his time in Mexico in 1932, as well as the 'ethical' impact of that visit, speculating on how the lively dialogue between conductor and public he witnessed in Mexico may have influenced Copland's increased interest in his audiences in the 1930s. Saavedra, 'Revisiting Copland's Mexico', lecture delivered at 'Cultural Counterpoints: Examining the Musical Interactions between the US and Latin America', Bloomington University, Indiana, October 2011.

Mexican credentials and has perhaps drawn attention away. This chapter unfolds in two main parts. Initially, *Short Symphony*'s classicism is set up as an aesthetic ideal from which we can begin to tease out – but, of course, cannot hope to resolve – questions of mutuality, influence, and failure in the aesthetic project Copland shared with Chávez, visible in their correspondence and symptomatic more broadly of the difficulties within a friendship inflected by unequal cross-border power relations. Then, the focus turns to Chávez's temporary title, 'The Bounding Line'. This moniker directs us to a more thorough understanding of the work's potential relationship with an aesthetic modernism also championed by Chávez, governed by objectivity and self-sufficiency, but also by vitalist ideas of authenticity to the immediate time and place of creation. For discussion of Copland's work specifically, the ideas of presence, spontaneity, physicality, and – importantly – dance, implied by the notion of 'the bounding line', together present just as important an aesthetic polarity as the cerebral qualities of classical abstraction highlighted by previous commentators. In seeking an aesthetic of balance, line, lightness, and freshness that drew on a musical language closely associated with dance, Copland's symphony can be read as idealistically seeking to promote Pan-Americanist values – that is, musically to mediate more sensitively tensions between hegemonies and multiplicities, and to render the body not as an exoticised other but as a site of pleasure and sensual wholeness. Those images of Kraft in the Mexican landscape might stay in mind, then, as the discussion develops. On the one hand, they prompt questions about Northern objectification, domination, and exclusion. Yet on the other, they also seem to suggest a sense of play – of eroticism located not in conquest, but rather in exchange and reciprocity. This complicates the supposed transparency of Copland's objectifying gaze across the borders, without exonerating him, or his symphony, from the colonial charge.

'Well, Here Is the Real Thing': A Classicist Symphony

Copland and Chávez met in New York in 1926 during one of Chávez's several lengthy trips north,[9] and *Short Symphony*'s genesis and first performance are closely tied to the two men's strengthening relationship. After Serge Koussevitzky deemed *Short Symphony* rhythmically too challenging

---

[9] Howard Pollack, 'Aaron Copland, Carlos Chávez, and Silvestre Revueltas', in *Carlos Chávez and His World*, ed. Leonora Saavedra (Princeton: Princeton University Press, 2015), 99–110, 99.

to incorporate into the Boston Symphony Orchestra's season, it was Chávez who, on 23 November 1934, ultimately premiered the work at the newly completed Teatro del Palacio de Bellas Artes in Mexico City with the Orquesta Sinfónica de México (Copland regretted being unable to attend the premiere). The first half of the concert, the final of the season, show-cased Chilean pianist Claudio Arrau. In the second half, Chávez juxtaposed *Short Symphony* with deliberately 'light' Stravinskian neoclassicism (Stravinsky's Suite No. 2 for small orchestra, divided into March, Waltz, Polka, and Galop) and some of Chávez's own latest aesthetic attempts to reconcile North-South difference in excerpts from the *H.P.* suite of his ballet of the same name (premiered – its one and only performance – in Philadelphia in 1932 under Leopold Stokowski). Mexico City's audiences may have been suffering overexposure to Chávez's work: one critic com-plained of being, 'for the umpteenth time', 'forced (without being asked for our opinion, of course)' to listen to the two excerpts.[10] The ballet *H.P.* (for *Horsepower*) thematised the culture clash between the industrial North and rural South, complete with giant dancing fruit, and a solo from a half-man, half-machine hybrid representing Northern mechanisation that opened the production.[11]

Chávez wrote to Copland after the premiere to tell him that *Short Symphony*, finally, was the supreme example of an authentic, of-its-time classicist aesthetic – an aesthetic that happened to chime resolutely with the one he had articulated in his 1927 essay published in the New York music journal *Modern Music* titled 'Technique and Inner Form', where he claimed that 'external form unfolds from the center of a work of art'.[12] Straight after the performance, Chávez enthused to Copland: 'well, here is the real thing: here is our music, my music, the music of my time, of my taste, of my culture, here it is as a simple and natural fact to my own self, as everything belonging to one's self is simple and natural'.[13] He lavished praise on what he saw as the work's definitional historical contribution, arguing that there had been 'very much talk about music in which everything is essential, nothing super-fluous' but that despite such talk, until the 'Little Symphony', as he

---

[10] See Maurice Le Vahr, 'Música y Músicos', *Revista de Revistas: El Semanario Nacional* 24, no. 1281 (2 December 1934): 4 (trans. Lola San Martín Arbide).

[11] Hess, *Representing the Good Neighbor*, especially 50–80.

[12] Carlos Chávez, 'Technique and Inner Form', *Modern Music* 5 (1928): 28–31, 28. This essay developed a previous Spanish-language version published in Mexico in 1924. See Luisa Vilar-Payá, 'Chávez and the Autonomy of the Musical Work: The Piano Music', in *Carlos Chávez and His World*, ed. Leonora Saavedra (Princeton: Princeton University Press, 2015), 112–33, 114.

[13] Letter from Chávez to Copland, 1 December 1934, Copland Collection, box 249.

called it, the music itself had yet to materialise. 'And yet', Chávez wrote, 'the human content, the inner expression is freely emotional. It is precisely that tremendous human impulse that made [the realisation of *Short Symphony*] possible.'[14]

Barely fifteen minutes long and in three movements performed *attacca*, following a balanced fast-slow-fast formal design, *Short Symphony* is terse and lithe. In the same letter Chávez wrote, in a way that seems straightforwardly to echo ideals of part-whole integration, that 'each and every note comes out from the other as the only natural and logical possible one . . . . The work as a whole . . . is an organism, a body in which every piece works by itself 100% but whose musical mutual relation is such, that no one could possibly work and exist without the other.' Notwithstanding the political utility to Chávez of responding so warmly to Copland's work, *Short Symphony* in many ways hits Chávez's classicist mark. *Short Symphony* returns the symphonic genre to the sense of flexibility associated with its classical origins, railing against all the kinds of monumental and sentimental excess that were to be found in a genre Copland was later, in a 1938 lecture series, to describe as 'an overripe art', referring to the impacts of Romanticism on the form.[15] Here, Copland sang from the same song sheet as Chávez, who, as Henry Cowell had it, 'abjures sentimentality and voluptuousness in his music'.[16]

And yet, despite the absence of sentimentality or voluptuous excess, sensual bodily presence is nonetheless key to this symphony's classical poetics, as will be discussed in more depth further on. This is achieved through its immediacy and use of gesture. Such poetics cut against the grain of idealist symphonic models and their associated Austro-Germanic ideologies, bound up with the mind, interiority, and emotion. After all, the eroticised body has always been central to Classical Greek aesthetics, even if it has been selectively forgotten by those with more puritan attitudes to music. Concerns with *symmetria* (commensurability of proportions as the principal foundation of beauty) and balance were prevalent in Classical Greek thought and preoccupied sculptors and other artists working with the human form.

The first movement, which, as the Bellas Artes premiere programme note intimated, conveys the 'character and vivacity of an *Allegro*', is marked

14 Ibid.
15 Copland, 'Symphonic Masterpieces Lecture 7: Mahler, Symphony No. II', lecture series, Copland Collection, box 214, 1938–9.
16 Henry Cowell, 'Carlos Chávez', *Pro Musica Quarterly* 7 (1928): 19–23, 23.

Example 4.1 Aaron Copland, *Short Symphony (No. 2)*, opening nine-note motive in oboes and flutes, reproduced from example in Sandra Müller-Berg, '*Ultramodern* versus *Neoklassizistisch*: Ruth Crawfords *Three Songs* und Aaron Coplands *Short Symphony*', in *Symphonik 1930–1950: Gattungsgeschichtliche und analytische Beiträge*, ed. Wolfgang Osthoff and Giselher Schubert (Mainz: Schott, 2003), 58–83, 72. All examples from Copland's *Short Symphony* are reproduced by permission of Boosey & Hawkes Music Publishers Ltd.

preciso e ritmico and is almost entirely developed from the leaping contours and syncopation of the opening nine-note motive heard in the woodwinds (see Example 4.1): here is, simply put, a 'bounding line' of music.[17]

It has a tripartite ABA′ structure. The US critic Paul Rosenfeld, a close friend of Copland's, described form as the most important 'attribute of intrinsic classicism'.[18] The main theme's asymmetries have larger-scale structural significance throughout the movement. Sandra Müller-Berg has observed the pianistically gestural nature of the motivic material – presumably meaning it suggests hands leaping across a keyboard – which foregrounds the interval of the octave in particular.[19] Copland, like Stravinsky, tended to compose at the piano. Pushing her observations further, in so doing it draws attention to musical bodies, both the real bodies of the performers and bodies summoned 'on stage' into the imagined metaphorical space of the music. Perhaps a stronger theoretical link between specifically classical asymmetry and muscular bodies, however, is the concept in Ancient Greek sculpture of *rhythmos*. *Rhythmos* denotes the sense of a whole movement that can be conveyed by a single composition of a body's pose. Flux is captured in stillness, the moment in a motion that tells the viewer what is going to happen, characterised by asymmetry. The textbook example is Myron's *Diskobolos*, which depicts an athlete in an unsustainable position mid-swing, his arm thrown back, poised about to release the tension in his muscles and propel the discus

---

[17] '11 November 1934, Teatro del Palacio de Bellas Artes, Orquesta Sinfónica de México', programme note, Programs 1934–70, Copland Collection, box 417, 1934 (trans. Sirio Canos Donnay) (hereafter Orquesta Sinfónica de México Programme Note).

[18] Hess, *Representing the Good Neighbor*, 40; she cites Paul Rosenfeld, *By Way of Art* (Freeport, NY: Books for Libraries Press, 1967), 276.

[19] She suggests this sense of 'bounding' – leaping – gave rise to the work's temporary title. Sandra Müller-Berg, '*Ultramodern* versus *Neoklassizistisch*: Ruth Crawfords *Three Songs* und Aaron Coplands *Short Symphony*', in *Symphonik 1930–1950: Gattungsgeschichtliche und analytische Beiträge*, ed. Wolfgang Osthoff and Giselher Schubert (Mainz: Schott, 2003), 58–83, 70.

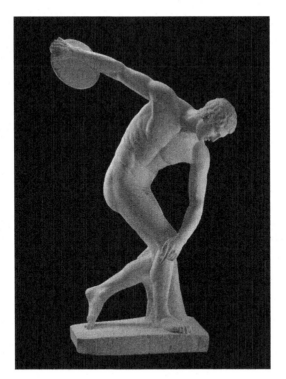

Figure 4.2 Myron's *Diskobolos*. Second-century copy of the lost Greek original (c. 460–450 BC), with an incorrectly restored head set at the wrong angle, British Museum. © The Trustees of the British Museum.

forwards (Figure 4.2).[20] In *Short Symphony*'s first movement, then, metrical irregularities and the main theme's accents and syncopation further emphasise a sense of bodily presence and movement, and suggest links with the neoclassical balletic mode of Stravinsky's *Pulcinella*. Parallels with the suite's movements 3b Allegro, 4 Tarantella, and 8b Finale are perhaps particularly strong. This is music that cannot help but invite the listener to move, to try to find the pulse, to jolt along to the syncopations.

The lyrical second movement also takes a balanced ABA' form (A (bars 1–33) B (bars 34–74) A' (bars 75–96)) and begins with a four-note descending motivic contour heard solo in the alto flute, introduced here for

---

[20] Greek sculpture in this period has a murky aesthetic legacy, of course, particularly as adopted by the Nazis as tools of political discourse to further their ideals of purity and bodily perfection. See, for example, the posters for the Berlin Olympics in 1936 and Leni Riefenstahl's 1938 film *Olympia: Fest der Völker*, in which Myron's *Diskobolos* transforms into a live German athlete in the opening sequence. See, for instance, Michael Squire, *The Art of the Body: Antiquity and Its Legacy* (New York; Oxford: Oxford University Press, 2011), especially 19–23.

Example 4.2 Copland, *Short Symphony (No. 2)*, movement II, bars 1–2.

the first time in the work (Example 4.2). This instrument both timbrally closely approximates the human voice and ambiguously blurs two ancient contexts: we might hear both the pan flute (syrinx) of ancient Greek culture and Mayan and Aztec pan pipes. Indeed, breath is also a form of touch and can be a highly eroticised one.

To cite the programme note's curious description of this passage, 'there is luminosity'; sound now expands to fill, sostenuto, the full parameters of the space.[21] This sustained sense of line contrasts with how, in the first movement, the musical gestures cast pointillist shapes in the air that faded and were replaced just as instantaneously, like fireworks against the night sky or light reflected on water. Yet 'luminosity' suggests that such musical presence is not cumbersome but spacious, light, and airy. The characteristically conjunct vocal motion and vocal timbre of the flute at the movement's outset – the programme uses the verb *decir* (to say) – and the contrapuntal development of this theme and its counter-theme (one bar before figure 19, in the violins) contrast with the jerkier gestural motion of the outer movements, only recalled through sporadic leaps of an octave or so.[22] At times, the movement foreshadows the reflective, twilight mood found in the lyric dance of *Corral Nocturne* in *Rodeo* or *Prairie Night* in *Billy the Kid*: after all, they are both imaginative evocations of the south-west. The movement's affect is of deep tenderness, with its smooth lines and the sense of interplay between isolation and dependence. The Pan-like dotted-rhythm flute theme – summoning the lone shepherd at dusk – accentuates this atmosphere, extending an invitation to a Hellenic dance (see Example 4.3). It recalls the pastoral mode of the second movement of Mozart's Piano Concerto No. 27 K595, where the principal theme is reprised doubled by the flute and violin. The descending scalar fourth also recalls the second bar of Mozart's melody.

---

[21] Orquesta Sinfónica de México Programme Note.

[22] See Jennifer DeLapp, 'Speaking to Whom? Modernism, Middlebrow and Copland's *Short Symphony*', in *Copland Connotations: Studies and Interviews*, ed. Peter Dickenson (Woodbridge: Boydell Press, 2002), 85–102, 87.

Example 4.3 Movement II, solo flute in G with accompaniment, bars 34–8. Copland, *Short Symphony (No. 2)* (New York: Boosey and Hawkes, 1955), 30.

Opening with discrete gestures pirouetting in all directions, it is easy to imagine dancers preparing the stage for a new scene at the beginning of the third movement (see Example 4.4). The original programme note describes 'a sort of brief indecision [before] the last movement appears unexpectedly in a well-paced Allegro.'[23] But it is not indecisive; rather, it is a moment where the music takes a breath, poised in balance. Different complementary components together create 'perfect' tension between motion and rest, before an ostinato is established in the violins at figure 28, which creates a clear sense of impulse. This mode invokes the classical ideal of temporarily suspended motion, as depicted, for instance, in that ideal Ancient Greek manifestation of the human body *Doryphoros* (Spear Bearer) (c.450–440 BC) by Polykleitos, a statue whose *contrapposto* pose, with the weight on the left foot and the other leg slightly bent, as if coming to rest or starting to move, harnesses a perfect sense of equilibrium (Figure 4.3).

---

[23] 'Hay como una breve indecisión y aparece imprevisto el *último movimiento* en bien ritmado Allegro.' Orquesta Sinfónica de México Programme Note.

Example 4.4 Movement III, figure 27 and figure 28. Copland, *Short Symphony (No. 2)*, 37-8.

After the ostinato is established, two main themes are stated, which are then varied and developed, one built on the interval of a fifth, the other on a fourth (the 'perfect' intervals, found respectively one and two bars after

Example 4.4 (Cont.)

figure 28 in flute I and oboe I) (see Example 4.4). A cinematic reference infiltrates the score. The movement climaxes at figure 48 with a quotation from a contemporary film, Eric Charell's 1931 German musical block-buster *Der Kongress Tanzt* (see Example 4.7). Set during the Congress of

Example 4.5 Melody from the chorus of 'Das gibt's nur einmal', bars 1–8.

Das gibt's nur ein - mal, das kommt nicht wie - der. Das ist zu schön, um wahr zu sein.

Figure 4.3 Polykleitus's *Doryphorus*. Roman Hellenistic copy (c.27 BC–AD 68) of the Greek original (c.450–440 BC), Minneapolis Institute of Arts. Credit: The John R. Van Derlip Fund and gift of funds from Bruce B. Dayton, an anonymous donor, Mr and Mrs Kenneth Dayton, Mr and Mrs W. John Driscoll, Mr and Mrs Alfred Harrison, Mr and Mrs John Andrus, Mr and Mrs Judson Dayton, Mr and Mrs Stephen Keating, Mr and Mrs Pierce McNally, Mr and Mrs Donald Dayton, Mr and Mrs Wayne MacFarlane, and many other generous friends of the Institute.

Vienna, the plot centres on an unlikely romance between Czar Alexander I and a local glovemaker played by international film idol Lillian Harvey.[24] The fragment references the *Schlager* hit by Werner Heymann 'Das gibt's nur einmal', originally sung by Harvey (Example 4.5). When the theme first

---

[24] For more on *Der Kongress Tanzt*, in particular the final scene featuring 'Das Gibt's Nur Einmal' and its technical accomplishment, see Carolyn Abbate, 'Offenbach, Kracauer, and Ethical Frivolity', *Opera Quarterly* 33 (2017): 62–86, 68–71.

Example 4.6 Movement III, figure 31 'Das gibt's nur einmal' theme. Copland, *Short Symphony (No. 2)*, 43-4.

Example 4.6 (Cont.)

appears, at figure 31, Copland quotes the first two lines of the song's chorus – 'Das gibt's nur einmal, das kommt nicht wieder' – although, disguising the origins of the quotation, it is rhythmically modified (Example 4.6).[25]

Immediacy – the passage of the fleeting moment – and spontaneity are encoded as an extra-musical allusion, 'Das gibt's nur einmal'. At the same time, a contemporary listener might associate the quotation with the romance of the film's denouement or the dance of the film's title. The movement ends abruptly on an open fifth (although in its published form this chord is repeated twice more; it is likely that Leonard Bernstein persuaded Copland to make this alteration).[26] Nothing is laboured. Brevity is the order of the day.

Neoclassicism has been a major critical centre for previous discussion of *Short Symphony*. Scholars have frequently attributed *Short Symphony*'s balanced form, spare textures, and ostinati to the influence of specifically Stravinskian neoclassicism,[27] referencing *Symphony of Psalms* (1930) and *Symphony in Three Movements* (despite post-dating *Short Symphony* by almost a decade).[28] Frequent changes of time signature, with an emphasis on 5/8 in the opening bars, make *Symphonies of Wind Instruments* another obvious reference point, as does the unusual instrumentation, particularly foregrounding alto flute. Greek antiquity has also been thought a likely inspiration: Sandra Müller-Berg has linked *Short Symphony*'s 'objective, impersonal' thematic emphasis on the octave, fourth, and fifth to ancient Greek music theory (perfect divisions of the octave, another component of *symmetria*) and to the aesthetic proportions of European antiquity, and has proposed that it is thus in the original, supposedly historically unencumbered Greek sense of 'sounding together' that the title *Short Symphony* should be understood.[29]

What unites these interpretations is a search to identify how *Short Symphony* challenges the excesses of the Romantic European symphony,

---

[25] DeLapp, 'Speaking to Whom?', 87; previous commentators have speculated about the potential hidden meaning alluded to by the quotation. Pollack, for instance, hypothesises that the reference reflects 'the work's vitality and humour'. Howard Pollack, *Aaron Copland: The Life and Work of an Uncommon Man* (London: Faber and Faber, 1999), 290; see also Müller-Berg, '*Ultramodern versus Neoklassizistisch*', 81. Equally, though, it could be a reference to the mock-serious motto theme in the finale of Beethoven's String Quartet in F major Op. 135 ('Muß es sein?', 'Es muß sein!').

[26] Pollack, *Aaron Copland: The Life and Work of an Uncommon Man*, 290.

[27] See DeLapp, 'Speaking to Whom?', 87; David Matthews, 'Copland and Stravinsky', *Tempo* 95 (1971): 10–14, 12–13; Ryan Keith Dudenbostel, 'The Bounding Line: Rhythm, Meter, and the Performance of Aaron Copland's *Short Symphony*' (DMus thesis, UCLA, 2014).

[28] DeLapp, 'Speaking to Whom?', 87; Matthews, 'Copland and Stravinsky', 12–13.

[29] Müller-Berg, '*Ultramodern versus Neoklassizistisch*', 80–1.

Example 4.7 Movement III, figure 48 'Das gibt's nur einmal' theme reprised.
Reproduced from Copland, *Short Symphony (No. 2)*, 62-3.

Example 4.7 (Cont.)

and in the main these scholars' answers stress Copland's supposedly abstract classical compositional attitude.[30] But the work's physicality is

---

[30] Others have emphasised the importance of Copland's democratic world-views for reading the work. Howard Pollack and Jennifer DeLapp, for instance, have discussed the work as in different ways symptomatic of Copland's 'democratising' and 'middlebrow' impulses, respectively. For Pollack, those rhythmic and metric difficulties in the work that dissuaded Koussevitzky from holding the

Example 4.7 (Cont.)

work's premiere decentre the authority of the conductor in rehearsal and performance, a function of Copland's egalitarianism. See Howard Pollack, 'Aaron Copland's Short Symphony and the Challenge to Human Supervision and Control in Music', *Journal of New Music Research* 31 (2002): 201–10, 206–9. For DeLapp, *Short Symphony* is symptomatic of Copland's anxieties about the need to bridge contemporary disconnections between composers and the public, channelling the anti-elitism of the Depression, although, like Pollack, her essay downplays Copland's interests in Communism at the time. DeLapp, 'Speaking to Whom?', 85–102.

Example 4.7 (Cont.)

absent from these analyses; none have dealt convincingly with the gestural foregrounding of the body or the work's balletic musical language on a trajectory alongside *El Salón México*, *Rodeo*, and *Billy the Kid*.[31]

---

[31] Matthews, 'Copland and Stravinsky', 12–13.

This rationalist focus overlooks the potential of the music's Hellenism for exploring the body: for talking about dance as weight, movement, and touch, and even alluding to the music's queerness – Hellenism acknowledged as an 'ambiguous signifier' of desire when Hellenism was the *fin de siècle*'s underground language for homosexuality.[32] The second movement, for instance, may then be reheard, beginning with the breath, as an eroticised fantasy of tenderness, or as a slow balletic duet, weightless, in the dusk of the Mexican plains.

In addition, to search no further than Europe for Copland's symphonic models, whether European neoclassicism or specifically European antiquity, is to neglect the trace of Copland's Mexican colleagues like Chávez or Silvestre Revueltas, as Leonora Saavedra, Howard Pollack, and Roberto Kolb-Neuhaus have shown.[33] Chávez, as already noted, supplied the temporary title, 'The Bounding Line', and Copland dedicated the work to Chávez. And as Copland completed the work, he remarked to friends that the third movement 'begins to sound rather Mexican to me'.[34] Saavedra has pursued this remark and attributed it not to any specific 'audible signifiers' of Mexico (e.g. folk materials) but to the influence of Revueltas, with the layers of ostinati Copland uses in the third movement recalling a stylistic trait of the Mexican composer's. The ostinati then culminate in the work's abrupt ending gesture, another nod to Revueltas's compositional style.[35] Gesturing towards the 'idea' of Mexico, *Short Symphony*'s third movement also uses hemiola, encouraging the listener to move with the juddering shifts of metrical emphasis, particularly as they take place in the lower registers. Within Mexico's nationalist art music, hemiola and metrical change were a way of representing the sounds of folk music and dance, like the *son* and the *jarabe*. Rather than referencing specific, culturally locatable rhythmic materials, however, Copland's use of these devices in *Short Symphony* instead only alludes to the pulses of the Mexican dance hall, to be developed more fully in *El Salón México*, and

---

[32] Sarah Waters, '"The Most Famous Fairy in History": Antinous and Homosexual Fantasy', *Journal of the History of Sexuality* 6 (1995): 194–230, 218.

[33] See Saavedra, 'Revisiting Copland's Mexico'; Pollack, 'Aaron Copland, Carlos Chávez, and Silvestre Revueltas'; Roberto Kolb-Neuhaus, 'Silvestre Revueltas's *Colorines* vis-à-vis US Musical Modernism: A Dialogue of the Deaf?', *Latin American Music Review/Revista de Música Latinoamericana* 36 (2015): 194–230. Dudenbostel also points in this direction, suggesting that Copland was influenced by Chávez's classicism in the early 1930s. See Dudenbostel, *The Bounding Line*, 2–4.

[34] Pollack, 'Aaron Copland's Short Symphony', 202.

[35] Saavedra, 'Revisiting Copland's Mexico'.

carried through as an identifiable influence on his ballet scores *Billy the Kid* and *Rodeo*.[36]

It is also worth observing the parallels between *Short Symphony* and Chávez's contemporaneous *Sinfonía de Antígona* (1933), a one-movement reworking of his incidental music for Jean Cocteau's stage play *Antigone*, after Sophocles' tragedy, staged by the Mexican Department of Fine Arts in 1932. Chávez premiered the symphonic rendering on 15 December 1933 at the Palacio de Bellas Artes. In the programme note Chávez insisted that, despite the literary inspiration, it was a 'symphony, not a symphonic poem', stressing the absolute qualities. 'Antigone, her pride and her defiance, her heroism and martyrdom, are expressed not successively but in the entirety of the work. The most elemental musical materials are used to this purpose, for it should not be grandiloquent. Unencumbered and elemental, this music can only be expressed in the force of the laconic.'[37] Parallels are particularly pronounced in both works' spare textures and orchestration. Both prominently use alto flute and a heckelphone, although the heckelphone was also a fairly common instrument in early twentieth-century French orchestras. The sketches for the incidental music are dated July 1932; they were written shortly before Chávez hosted Copland for the first time in Mexico from September.[38]

Short Symphony may channel Hellenism in its affect, then, but Chávez's *Sinfonía de Antígona* goes all in. *Antígona* is an explicit engagement with ancient Greek myth, using only the tonal resources of that Classical context such that it also becomes a modernist project of fidelity. Relying exclusively on the ancient Greek modes, and specifically the Doric mode in its harmonic form and its derivative the Hypodoric, Chávez conjures the sonic atmosphere of the ancient world. Julian Orbón, in one of very few published accounts of the symphony, observes that through this tonal limitation Chávez cultivates an attitude of objectivity, of distance, not dissimilar to the modernist use of a series or tone row.[39] Chávez's symphony thus takes the listener to a fantasised classical Greece. At the same time, Stravinsky and fashionable art deco interwar Paris are ever present: a setting of a Sophocles play by Cocteau recalls Stravinsky's *Oedipus Rex*. This juxtaposition of consciously modernist practice with ancient subject matter and musical materials situates *Antígona* within a category Saavedra

---

[36] Ibid.   [37] 'Mexican Novelty Offered by Iturbi', *New York Times*, 29 June 1934.

[38] Chávez Correspondence, folder 99a.

[39] Julián Orbón, 'Las Sinfonías de Carlos Chávez (II Parte)', *Pauta: Cuadernos de teoría y crítica musical* vol. 6 no. 22 (1987): 81–91, 81–2.

has applied to Chávez's pre-Columbian ballets *Toxiuhmolpia: El fuego nuevo* (The New Fire) (1921) and *Los cuatro soles* (The Four Suns) (1927): since no sources allow the reconstruction of either pre-Columbian music or Classical Greek music (beyond our understanding of Greek modes), both are, as Saavedra puts it, 'modernist works in a primitivist style'.[40] As with *Antígona*, both works explored the use of tonally limited musical resources, with fixed pitch collections for *El fuego nuevo* (initially C major with lowered 6th and 7th degrees, but with further pitches added as the work develops) and a pentatonic pitch collection the basis for *Los cuatro soles*. And all three works, the ballets and the one-movement symphony, looked consciously to cosmopolitan, arch-modernist contexts like Paris, as Chávez hoped to mobilise exoticism for commercial success.[41] *Sinfonía de Antígona* presents the possibility that to be influenced by the idea of Mexico and the country's music was to engage with an ambiguous sense of the ancient classical, frustrating clear distinctions between the pre-Hispanic American and the Classical Greek.

Questions about Copland's engagement with Mexico, and about his symphony's corporeality, then, remain unaccounted for. But in pursuing these, something of an impasse is necessarily reached, and it has to do with the limits of Copland's subject position. Mexico was, for Copland, as he put it in the letter that opens this chapter, an 'enriching experience'; it had a psychologically transformative use-value that 'awakens a sympathetic chord'. In short, Mexico remained the 'other'. Also unavoidable is how specifically Copland's sense of the body shapes *Short Symphony*'s classicist aesthetics. Hence, rather than Aztec or Mayan sculpture, Hellenic marble bodies seem the more appropriate model to understand this symphony's muscular immediacy within an aesthetics of balanced proportion. These Classical Greek aesthetics and their erotic connotations capture that sense of Copland as Northern visitor during his first visit to Mexico to work on *Short Symphony*. Tracing the identifiable musical impact on *Short Symphony* of Copland's Mexican colleagues, then, is important foundational work, but can only take discussion so far. Less tangible questions of influence may hold just as important critical revelations: the legacy of

---

[40] Saavedra, 'Carlos Chávez's Polysemic Style', 126.

[41] Saavedra has called this 'strategic otherness'. Ibid., 101–2. See also Leonora Saavedra, 'Of Selves and Others: Historiography, Ideology, and the Politics of Modern Mexican Music' (PhD thesis, University of Pittsburgh, 2001), 167–72; Leonora Saavedra, 'Carlos Chávez y la construcción de una alteridad estratégica', in *Diálogo de resplandores: Carlos Chávez y Silvestre Revueltas*, ed. Yael Bitrán and Ricardo Miranda (Mexico City: Consejo Nacional para la Cultura y las Artes, 2002), 125–36.

Copland's colonial fantasies of Mexico and his ideals of US-Mexican relations; the aesthetic ideologies of his Mexican colleagues and their mutual posturing in relation to modernism, to Parisian neoclassicism, or to indigenous Aztec and Mayan aesthetics – another kind of classicism, to be explored further on. Together, these might help make some cautious inroads into the question of how, and how far, around the time of his first visit to the country, Copland related to, and attempted to connect with, Mexico.

Short Symphony in Mexico

Copland arrived in Mexico, at Chávez's invitation, in 1932, with roughly two of *Short Symphony*'s three movements under his belt. His correspondence illuminates the work's prior development, first mentioned in a letter to Henry Brant dated 10 September 1931 written from Tangier, Morocco. At Gertrude Stein's suggestion, Copland was visiting Tangier with Paul Bowles, both men seeing the city for the first time. Easy to reach from Europe, and, at least within the International Zone, allowing tourists and expatriates extreme latitude as far as sex, drugs, and tax avoidance were concerned, Tangier was on its way to gaining its post-war status in the eyes of queer Americans as '*the* archetypal city of the Orient' (Tennessee Williams and William Burroughs were among its best-known US literary visitors).[42] Bowles later wrote in his 1952 novel *Let It Come Down*: 'It was one of the charms of the International Zone that you could get anything you wanted if you paid for it. Do anything too – there were no incorruptibles. It was only a question of price.'[43] Bowles thought it 'a dream city' and went on to make it his permanent home from 1947 until his death in 1999; Copland was less enamoured, calling it 'a mad house, a mad house'.[44] The pair rented a place on the hill above the city and got hold of a piano. Copland wrote to the then seventeen-year-old Brandt, 'I'm working on a new orchestral piece and am very pleased with my thematic material. It's probably a symphony.'[45] The next update, also to Brant, followed in 1932,

---

[42] Gregory Woods, *Homintern: How Gay Culture Liberated the Modern World* (New Haven, CT: Yale University Press, 2016), 246.

[43] Paul Bowles, *Let It Come Down* (London: Penguin, 2000), 21, quoted in Woods, *Homintern*, 246.

[44] Iain Finlayson, *Tangier: City of the Dream* (London: Flamingo, 1993), 93, quoted in Woods, *Homintern*, 246.

[45] Letter from Copland to Henry Brandt, 10 September 1931, Copland Collection, box 258.

undated but presumably sometime before Copland travelled to Mexico at the end of August: 'I have 3 separate orchestral movements completed, but unfortunately they don't belong in the same piece!'[46] Copland travelled a great deal during the period between his time in Tangier in 1931 and his sojourn in Mexico from August 1932: he spent time in Berlin, London, New York City, and at Saratoga Springs, NY, where he organised the first of his Yaddo composers conferences at the beginning of May 1932. There, work on other compositions disrupted progress on *Short Symphony*. In June 1932, he wrote to John Kirkpatrick from Yaddo, 'My new work [viz. *Short Symphony*] is being upset by the fact that I've started still a newer [viz. *Statements*] and am working on the two simultaneously.' Two of the symphony's three movements were now 'practically done'.[47]

Copland planned to time his arrival in Mexico to coincide with Chávez's concert exclusively of his works on 2 September 1932 at Mexico City's Palacio de Bellas Artes. A few days before setting off, Copland wrote audaciously to Chávez asking if the planned concert could be moved to 9 September to ensure that Copland could arrive in time, as he aimed to leave New York on 24 August. Since the date could not be altered, the journey to Mexico in high summer,[48] no mean feat at the best of times, was especially gruelling. It took eight days to drive to Laredo, a border city in southern Texas, beyond which the composer took the train to Mexico City. In the letter, he added: 'I am bringing with me a young violinist who is a pupil, companion, secretary, and friend!' That young man was to become Copland's long-term partner, Victor Kraft, or, as he was introduced in that letter, Kraftsov. 'I'm sure you will like him.'[49]

Mexican-US relations were of course the inescapable and troubled cultural backdrop to Copland and Chávez's friendship in the early 1930s. As Saavedra has noted, Copland's relationship with Chávez and Mexico at this point had a grassroots, personal character. This contrasts with Copland's later explicitly political, government-directed tours of South America after 1940 under the banner of Pan-American goodwill.[50] Relations between the two countries followed a turbulent and militarised history, which reached back into the nineteenth century and expressed

---

[46] Letter from Copland to Brandt, probably August 1932, Copland Collection, box 258.

[47] Aaron Copland and Vivian Perlis, *Copland, 1900–1942*, 2nd ed. (New York: St Martin's Press, 1987), 208.

[48] Ibid., 213.

[49] Letter from Copland to Carlos Chávez, 18 September 1932, Chávez Correspondence, JOB 93–4, folder 11.

[50] Saavedra, 'Revisiting Copland's Mexico'. Copland's tours of South America in the 1940s took place in 1941 and 1947.

evolving and expedient US interest in Mexico. In the late 1920s and early 1930s, this, as the *New York Times* famously put it in 1933, was the 'enormous vogue of things Mexican',[51] which saw the US idealisation of Mexican art, architecture, and spiritual ideals as a more wholesome and historically deeper-rooted antidote to the North's industrialisation and supposed spiritual bankruptcy. At the same time, border-crossing cultural projects emerged: Chávez, for instance, was a founding member of the Pan American Association of Composers in 1928 with Henry Cowell and Edgard Varèse, although Chávez's role was largely nominal.[52] What perhaps showed Chávez at his most consciously Pan-American was his 1932 collaborative ballet project *H.P.*, the work on which the suite of the same name, programmed at *Short Symphony*'s premiere, was based. Stokowski directed the production, Catherine Littlefield was the choreographer, and Diego Rivera was responsible for sets and costume.[53]

As Saavedra reminds us, the provisional Pan-Americanism that emerged in the 1920s was often an 'ephemeral result' rather than the conscious starting point of such transnational engagements.[54] Yet, as the 1930s progressed, Pan-Americanism also began to be staged more prominently in the political arena. From 1933, Franklin Delaney Roosevelt's administration prioritised the strengthening of economic and cultural ties between North and South America, rather than US military intervention.[55] In his inaugural address, Roosevelt announced the Good Neighbor Policy, an effort to underline commonalities between the nations making up the Americas: 'In the field of world policy I would dedicate this nation to the policy of the good neighbor – the neighbor who resolutely respects himself and, because he does so, respects the rights of others.'[56] Roosevelt packaged international relations within a rhetoric that invoked citizenly responsibility to the local community. Outside a US frame of reference, however, things looked quite different, and Chávez's take on Pan-Americanism

---

[51] Helen Delpar, 'Carlos Chávez and the Mexican "Vogue", 1925–1940', in *Carlos Chávez and His World*, ed. Leonora Saavedra (Princeton: Princeton University Press, 2015), 204–19, 204.

[52] See Stephanie Stallings, 'Collective Difference: The Pan-American Association of Composers and Pan-American Ideology in Music, 1925–1945' (PhD thesis, Florida State University, 2009).

[53] Christina Taylor Gibson, 'The Reception of Carlos Chávez's *Horsepower*: A Pan-American Communication Failure', *American Music* 30 (2012): 157–93.

[54] Saavedra, 'Carlos Chávez's Polysemic Style', 104.

[55] As recently as 1916, during the Mexican Revolution, the United States and Mexico had come close to war.

[56] Franklin D. Roosevelt, *Addresses and Messages of Franklin D. Roosevelt: Compiled from Official Sources, Intended to Present the Chronological Development of the Foreign Policy of the United States from the Announcement of the Good Neighbor Policy in 1933, Including the War Declarations* (London: His Majesty's Stationary Office, 1943), 5.

reflects this. Stephanie Stallings notes that Chávez favoured the 'more inclusive concept of "Americanism", referring to the entire continent'.[57] He shunned the way national distinctions were enshrined within the US-oriented concept of Pan-Americanism. After all, those distinctions had historically served US imperialist agendas. The 'good neighbor' who respects himself first and foremost, of course, is strongly concerned with his status as an individual, and it is his rights that come first.

Little material documents the months Copland and Kraft spent in Mexico together in 1932, save for Copland's correspondence and that intriguing photo album. We find photographs of Copland, Kraft, and Chávez larking about in a dusty landscape, reclining atop a rock (see Figure 4.4), and an action shot of Chávez jumping in the air. The album shows street scenes in Mexico City, panoramas, Copland at work, a garden (presumably of the house in which Copland and Kraft were staying in their final two months in the country), and a group of composers, including

Figure 4.4 Kraft, Copland, and Chávez, from Copland's 1932–3 Mexico trip album. Copland Collection, box 514. The image of Carlos Chávez is reproduced by permission of Carlanita Music Company, LLC. The image of Aaron Copland is reproduced by permission of The Aaron Copland Fund for Music, Inc.

---

[57] Stephanie N. Stallings, 'The Pan/American Modernisms of Carlos Chávez and Henry Cowell', in *Carlos Chávez and His World*, ed. Leonora Saavedra (Princeton: Princeton University Press, 2015), 28–45, 30.

Revueltas, posing behind the same garden seat over which Kraft had draped himself in the more intimate photograph elsewhere in the album mentioned earlier. Some beach photographs of Copland and Kraft were perhaps taken in Acapulco; on their way back to the US-Mexican border the pair had taken a detour, as 'Victor wanted to experience swimming in the Pacific'.[58]

'My Mexico trip has been all I could have hoped for and more', Copland enthused to Brandt in a letter of November 1932, although in the same breath he casually denigrated both Mexico and Mexicans – 'I can't rave too much about the country itself – nor the populace, for that matter' – a far cry from his retrospective romanticisation to Lescaze in the letter that opened this chapter. In the letter to Brandt, he reported on the progress of the new symphony, explaining that the first two movements were now done and orchestrated. Having spent his first two months in Mexico City, he now had 'a lovely house in the country' providing him with ideal working conditions for tackling the symphony's third movement, although he wasn't optimistic about finishing it before leaving Mexico. 'I'm using an orchestra with no trombones or tuba and only two trumpets. It should be interesting to see what that gives. I still haven't a name for it, and I begin to despair of getting a really satisfactory one.'[59]

While in Mexico Copland also composed two *Elegies for Violin and Viola*, although ultimately he withdrew *Elegies* and used the musical material in his *Statements*. As predicted, when Copland left Mexico in January 1933, the symphony was still incomplete. Copland wrote to Mary Lescaze: 'Whoever told you I had finished a piece was a bit ahead of the facts. It's only almost done. Two movements are orchestrated and *in ink*. But there's that damn last movement. I have the theme and the form but the notes have to be filled in. I wish I had it finished in time to bring it back with me [to New York] and play it to everyone.'[60] Copland was referring to his informal Young Composers' Group that had met every few weeks throughout 1932 and which Lescaze had often attended.[61] Regulars included Arthur Berger, Henry Brant, Israel Citkowitz, Lehman Engel, Vivian Fine, Irwin Heilner, Bernard Herrmann, Jerome Moross, and Elie Stiegmeister. Copland did indeed complete the work not long after arriving back in New York, and an undated telegram from Copland reveals that just

---

[58] Copland and Perlis, *Copland, 1900–1942*, 216.
[59] Letter from Copland to Brandt, 16 November 1932, Copland Collection, box 249.
[60] Letter from Copland to Lescaze, 13 January 1933.
[61] For more details on the Young Composers' Group, see Copland and Perlis, *Copland, 1900–1942*, 192.

such a casual get-together of composers – most likely including the usual suspects from the Young Composers' Group – took place at some point after his return to hear what was probably a piano reduction of *Short Symphony*. 'Last get-together of season ... First public performance of Copland's "Short Symphony"', it read. And then light-heartedly: 'No destructive criticism invited, only the other kind.'[62]

A work which had been troublesome to get down on paper and troublesome to name proved equally troublesome to bring to perform-ance, at least in the United States. Koussevitzky had premiered Copland's first symphony, his *Symphony for Organ and Orchestra*, in 1925 with Nadia Boulanger as soloist. (At the performance in New York, conductor Walter Damrosch had famously exclaimed from the podium: 'If a gifted young man can write a symphony like this at twenty-three, within five years he will be ready to commit murder!')[63] Initially, Copland had expected that Koussevitzky would likewise premiere *Short Symphony*. While discussions were in progress with Koussevitzky, Chávez proposed a performance of Copland's new work in Mexico. In November 1933, a month prior to the Bellas Artes premiere of Chávez's own *Sinfonía de Antígona* on 15 December, and still calling the symphony by its working title 'The Bounding Line', Chávez wrote to Copland: 'Now: The Bounding Line? I am eager to have the score and play it for the concerts of May [1]934.' Evidently, *Sinfonía de Antígona* and *Short Symphony* were on Chávez's mind around the same time. Asking for the score, which he promised to return swiftly after having the parts copied, he enquired after progress with the Koussevitzky performance: 'Is it going to be played this season by Kouss? Let me know all about it.'[64] Koussevitzky's decision not to premiere *Short Symphony*, however, on account of the rhythmic challenges it posed for the orchestra, has been well rehearsed in the literature.[65] But in October 1934, even eighteen months after *Short Symphony*'s completion, Copland still seemed to be expecting Koussevitzky ultimately to premiere the work – after all, the conductor now had his own copy of the score, no longer quite so fresh off the press. Copland wrote Chávez a letter in which his frustrations were close to the surface: 'The performance of the work which Koussevitzky was to have done last season was postponed because of what he told me was the *extreme* difficulty of the work. He expects to do it here this season, but

---

[62] Telegram from Copland to Brant (1933), Copland Collection, box 249.

[63] As recounted in, for instance, Copland and Perlis, *Copland, 1900–1942*, 112.

[64] Letter from Chávez to Copland, 25 November 1933, Copland Collection, box 250.

[65] See, for example, Pollack, 'Aaron Copland's Short Symphony'; DeLapp, 'Speaking to Whom?'.

as yet it has never been played.'[66] Koussevitzky was well known for struggling with changing metres, re-barring Stravinsky's *The Rite of Spring*, for instance. Given that even modest metrical changes could cause the conductor difficulty, however, the use of 'extreme' seems sarcastic. But then, as plans for the Mexican premiere began to take shape, Copland began to seem rattled by the celebrated Russian conductor's reluctance to take on *Short Symphony*, perhaps additionally spooked by a belief that Chávez's orchestra was inferior to one from the United States,[67] writing to Chávez: 'Are you *sure* you can prepare the performance in so short a time? Otherwise perhaps it would be better to wait – as I am afraid that with this work a shaky performance would give an incoherent impression to the public.' Ultimately, though, he was careful not to appear interfering: 'Of course, I leave it absolutely in your hands to do as you like.' Copland then reported on his latest projects, including 'a ten-minute "light piece" called "Salon Mexico" which only needs to be orchestrated'. Although, unsurprising for this time and place, whether or not it was appropriate for Copland to use the musical folk materials of a culture that was not his own went unquestioned, he nonetheless had some anxieties about composing something Mexican as an outsider: 'I am terribly afraid of what *you* will say of the Salon Mexico – perhaps it is not Mexican at all and I would look so foolish. But in America del Norte it may sound Mexican!'[68]

Chávez wrote Copland an – unsurprisingly – glowing report on the concert held in Mexico City as part of the final concert of the 1934 season, and on the success of the rehearsal period: 'I hope you will agree with the way your work was placed between Strawinsky Suite and H.P. The performance was accurate and "souple"; we had 10 rehearsals and it was worked out with the utmost of interest and energy.' Chávez stressed the enthusiasm of the musicians, reporting that they were at first 'sceptical', but, as he was 'amazed to see', 'by the third rehearsal or so ... had a real genuine and growing interest', and concluding that 'this last concert was the best of the entire season'.[69] Corroborating Chávez's account, an article in the Mexico City daily newspaper *Excelsior*

---

[66] Letter from Copland to Chávez, 15 October 1934, Chávez Correspondence, folder 11.

[67] Elsewhere, Copland had styled the country as one 'virtually without composers, without organized orchestras, without even a musical season. No tradition of art music exists there.' Copland, 'Carlos Chávez: Mexican Composer', in *American Composers on American Music: A Symposium*, ed. Henry Cowell (Stanford: Stanford University Press, 1933), 102–6, 103. In his correspondence, Chávez himself often lamented the state of the orchestra in Mexico, and its meagre funds. For instance, 'Our symphony season will start November 7. ... We are terribly poor. The salaries were cut down to half, which will give you an idea.' Letter from Chávez to Copland, 3 August 1930, Copland Collection, box 250.

[68] Letter from Copland to Chávez, 15 October 1934.

[69] Letter from Chávez to Copland, 1 December 1934, Copland Collection, box 250.

advertising the concert assured readers likewise that 'those who have heard [*Short Symphony*] in rehearsal guarantee the public's enthusiasm – from both those who are keen on modern music and those who are not', describing it as 'without a doubt one of the most perfect compositions of the contemporary recent output'.[70] Copland responded positively in turn:

What you said about the 'Short Symphony' naturally made me very happy. Only a week before your performance, I had a conversation with Koussevitzky in which he told me that he regretted it very much that he could not play the 'Short Symphony' as he had promised. 'What's the matter, I said, is it too difficult.' 'No, he said, not too difficult, but just impossible.' This week I will be seeing him again and I will be able to tell him that in Mexico they do the 'impossible'! How I wish I could have heard it. And what a strange feeling it gives me when I think that you have heard a piece of mine which I have not yet heard. I will probably try to get Stokowski to play it, but it is too late for this season, of course.[71]

The performance with Stokowski did not materialise either.[72]

Whether *Short Symphony*'s premiere was as unambiguous a success as Chávez described is a matter of dispute. In a 1941 issue of *Modern Music* seven years after the event, Paul Bowles, the friend with whom Copland had travelled to Tangier, bizarrely reported *Short Symphony*'s premiere first-hand in a way that suggested it was a concert of the season just past. There, Bowles described the world premiere at the Palacio de Bellas Artes as a 'good old-fashioned *succès scandale*', and the critics of the city's major dailies as 'divided'. Into the crucible Bowles added widespread antisemitism:

One [critic] simply announced he considered it shameful that Chávez would stoop to conduct such a piece publicly just because it happened to be dedicated to him. Later I questioned this gentleman as to why he had so heartily hated the piece. 'Copland is a Jew,' he replied, 'and I never review Jewish music. Not even Ravel.'[73]

Finding Copland reduced to his race in Mexico is evidence of situationally shifting levels of power and authority between Copland and Chávez. No matter how robustly the politics of the hegemonic and the subaltern might seem to be

---

[70] 'Es, sin duda, una de las composiciones más perfectas de la producción contemporánea, y quienes la han escuchado en los ensayos aseguran que entusiasmará al público aficionado o no a las manifestaciones del arte moderno.' *Excelsior*, 21 November 1934.

[71] Letter from Copland to Chávez, 31 December 1934, Chávez Correspondence, folder 11.

[72] On 20 September 1935, the *New York Times* announced Stokowski's plans to perform the work. See Delapp, 'Speaking to Whom?', 85.

[73] Paul Bowles, 'Forecast and Review: Letter from Mexico', *Modern Music* 19 (1941): 36–9, 38 Bowles's correspondence places him as travelling in the Caribbean and Central America in November and December 1934. See Jeffrey Miller, ed. *In Touch: The Letters of Paul Bowles* (New York: Farrar, Straus and Girouz, 1994).

configured at a national level (here, hegemonic United States vs subaltern Mexico), those politics and categories do not remain static as they play out within different contexts, for instance, within individual reception. What the city's major dailies actually printed following the concert is of little use in substantiating Bowles's accusation, since no reviews of the premiere itself are to be found there.[74] In the arts periodical *Revista de Revistas*, Maurice Le Vahr reserved judgement, because he did not think Chávez equal to doing a brand-new work justice.[75]

When Bowles published his account in 1941, *Short Symphony* was still awaiting a US premiere. This did not take place until 1944, when it was broadcast over the radio under Stokowski's baton. It would be yet another thirteen years before it was heard in a concert hall. In a bid to get it played in the United States, Copland had decided to re-orchestrate *Short Symphony* as a sextet for clarinet, piano, and string quartet while spending the summer of 1937 in Mexico with Chávez – a revision for which, critically, he re-barred the more difficult metrical shifts, engendering its relatively greater twentieth-century success than *Short Symphony* given its increased user-friendliness. In this form, only as recently as in 1939 the work had been premiered in New York by Juilliard students.[76] A motivation for sensationalising a reasonably obscure performance that had received little coverage, then, would be to drum up publicity for *Short Symphony*. All the more convenient if that performance had taken place south of the border, in an unverifiable context of which a US readership was generally ignorant. Indeed, the alleged antisemitic views of the Mexican critics echoed Nazi ideology, and in 1941

---

[74] Although note that beyond the main two Mexico City dailies, *El Universal* and *Excelsior*, I was unable to obtain access to, for example, *El Nacional*. *El Universal* advertised the concert (the last of the season) with a short paragraph introducing Copland's new work, but did not publish a review. The reviewer for *Excelsior*, after publishing a positive account of the rehearsal, wrote an account of the concert titled 'Concierto Extraordinario de Claudio Arrau', focusing exclusively on the pianist's first half with no mention of *Short Symphony* (or Chávez's *H.P.*). *Excelsior*, 'Concierto Extraordinario de Claudio Arrau', 24 November 1934, 8.

[75] 'La versión de una obra nueva, viniendo de Chávez, no puede suministrar suficientes elementos de juicio para escribir sobre ella. Y, como la opinión estampada en letras de molde tiene sus responsabilidades, nos abstenemos de agregar nada, más acerca del estreno de la "Short Symphony", que, dicen, es la más reciente producción de Aaron Copland.' ('A version of a new work, when coming from Chávez, does not provide us with enough information to review it. And as putting an opinion in print brings with it a certain responsibility, we shall refrain from elaborating any further on the premiere of the "Short Symphony", said to be Aaron Copland's most recent creation.') Le Vahr, 'Música y Músicos', 4 (trans. Lola San Martín Arbide).

[76] See Copland and Perlis, *Copland, 1900–1942*, 212. For more on the Sextet's performance history, see, for instance, Delapp, *Speaking to Whom?*, 86; Daniel E. Mathers, 'Closure in the Sextet and Short Symphony by Aaron Copland: A Study Using Facsimiles and Printed Editions' (MM thesis, Florida State University, 1989).

would have played into contemporary US discomfort about trade agreements between National Socialist Germany and Mexico. Without suggesting that antisemitism was not a strong, or indeed ever-increasing, force in Mexican culture at the time (it certainly was),[77] Bowles's version of events may also have sought to cover up a tepid reception in Mexico City, or the fact that critics had simply devoted their column space elsewhere.

'Our Music': Grassroots Pan-Americanism?

Copland's dalliance with Chávez's proposed title for *Short Symphony* underscores mutual aesthetic influence within their friendship. This influence potentially reached beyond straightforwardly discernible technical musical elements of *Short Symphony* to ideological and spiritual elements. Copland seemed to believe himself to have undergone some sort of psychological shift in the country, apprehending the 'conventional' nature of Europe – or perhaps even identifying Europe as an aesthetic convention.[78] Questions might then productively be posed about how *Short Symphony* was marked by Copland's imaginings and projections concerning his Mexican colleagues and their aesthetic agendas, about Mexico as an exoticised spiritual ideal and the role of indigeneity within that ideal, and about Copland's romanticised version of the Mexico-US relationship. First steps in addressing them can be taken by examining Copland's writings and music criticism dealing with Chávez and Mexico, as well as by investigating the correspondence between Chávez and Copland that indicates overlap within their aesthetic projects. Thus, although *Short Symphony*'s compositional history and temporary title, 'The Bounding Line', signal the value of exploring aesthetic and personal influence across the US-Mexican border, also to be explored are the failures to connect that, while common to all friendships, are especially pronounced and take on specific dimensions across a colonial divide. Ultimately, this points to how, entwined within what it means to connect with another being who is ultimately unknowable, are highly subjective fantasies of both the nature of the other and the nature of the relationship.

Classicism is a fertile territory for exploring such questions of mutuality, influence, and failure – an aesthetic playground on which composers and critics exchanged, developed, and of course frequently misunderstood each

---

[77] See Andreas Eberhard Winckler, 'The Nazis in Mexico: Mexico and the Reich in the Prewar Period, 1936–1939' (PhD thesis, University of Texas at Austin, 1983).

[78] Letter from Copland to Lescaze, 13 January 1933.

other's musical and ideological projects. Classicism is also, or so it emerges, ideologically absorbent. Between the two World Wars modernist composers focused anew on classical aesthetics, and *Short Symphony*, as well as Chávez's coeval symphony, *Sinfonía de Antígona* (1933), are fine examples of how this classicist turn played out in the American symphonic genre. As the work of Carol Oja and others has shown, classicist aesthetics (Oja calls them 'neoclassicist'; Hess 'urclassicist', reflecting how scholars have differently framed them in relation to international trends, to be discussed further shortly) were important in different ways for a nexus of composers working in New York in the 1920s.[79] Many, of course, had studied in France. With respect to Chávez's reception at a number of concerts of musical organisations for up-and-coming composers – for instance, Varèse's Pan American Association of Composers and the Copland-Sessions concerts – key musical commentators like critic Paul Rosenfeld, as well as Copland himself, heralded Chávez as an archetypical classicist, and in different ways positioned his music as a clear indication of the long-anticipated awakening of America's unique, yet universal, musical spirit. The year 1928 was especially eventful for Chávez reception in the United States, and his work, particularly his three *Sonatinas* of 1924 – for piano, cello and piano, and violin and piano – garnered much attention commending their manipulation of classical form and feel, although, as Saavedra notes, for all the attractions of classicism's forms and emotional restraint, Chávez 'never adopted a neoclassicist aesthetic'.[80] All were performed at the first of the Copland-Sessions concerts in April, and two were heard later in the year on the West Coast, premiered by Henry Cowell's New Music Society. In 1928, Rosenfeld characterised Chávez's aesthetic as a clear indication of 'a Pan American revival' in his article 'The Americanism of Carlos Chávez'.[81]

Chávez had only limited agency in so far as these representations went. The concerns of the US reception context shaped Chávez and his music in this anglophone discourse. Its key voices have been analysed by Saavedra, who underlines how they differently styled Chávez with a rhetoric echoing

---

[79] Carol Oja, *Making Music Modern* (Oxford, Oxford University Press, 2000); Hess, *Representing the Good Neighbor*.

[80] Saavedra notes that despite a 'lifelong interest in Classical forms and his attraction to the emotional restraint of classicism', Chávez 'never adopted a neoclassicist aesthetic'. See Saavedra, 'Carlos Chávez's Polysemic Style', 132.

[81] Paul Rosenfeld, 'The Americanism of Carlos Chávez', in *By Way of Art: Criticisms of Music, Literature, Painting, Sculpture, and the Dance* (New York: Coward-McCann, 1928; reprinted Freeport, NY: Books for Libraries Press, 1967), 282–3, quoted in Saavedra, 'Carlos Chávez's Polysemic Style', 141. See also Saavedra's further discussion.

classicism – whether essentially Mexican, like Copland, or a 'universal' modernist, as Cowell did – to mobilise him within their (Pan-)American musical project.[82] Carol Hess has examined the trends in US music reception in the late 1920s surrounding Chávez's musical classicism, aligning it with a wider reception phenomenon gaining currency in the period that she calls 'ur-classicism'. What Hess underlines is how Copland, Rosenfeld, and others tapped into a broad culture, beyond music, of writing about classical aesthetics and their universalising potential, while explicitly divorcing them from eighteenth-century Europe or Classical Greece. Instead, in spheres ranging from architecture to journalism, commentators relocated classical ideals of balance, unity, and harmony within the aesthetics, spirituality, mathematics, and landscape of the pre-Hispanic Americas – for instance, referencing the clean lines of Aztec and Mayan architecture. There was an important organicist aspect to how this classicism was seen as growing out of its local terrain and history. As Hess eloquently summarises it, 'ur-classicism ... created conditions for absolute music that united the usable past of ancient America with the universal whole, all within the "freshness" the tabula rasa promised'.[83] If the Germanic prefix seems incongruous to describe a concept that is about searching for non-European roots, it perhaps fittingly underscores problematic tensions within 'ur-classicism', although Hess does not problematise its central European ideological heritage or the relative legibility of a local equivalent.

Yet, despite styling the Mexican Chávez as the 'ur-classicist' archetype, 'ur-classicism', like the Mexican vogue, was very much a US phenomenon, and it responded to nationalist anxieties about American creative impotence and to how the young generation of US composers and critics sought to position themselves in relation to German Romanticism (which they saw as moribund deadwood) and the clean (Apollonian?) twentieth-century Parisian sound. It thus pitted American classicism against European classicism. Whereas, according to Rosenfeld, neoclassicism relied on resurrecting pre-established moulds and patterns – as Hess paraphrases Rosenfeld, neoclassisicists were 'obsessed with the ossified dictates of the eighteenth century' – American classicism was fresh, vital, and 'authentic', reacting spontaneously to contemporary formal problems.[84] Stravinsky was Rosenfeld's archetypical neoclassicist (Copland and Chávez, it should be noted, took no such exception to the Russian). In identifying and applauding Chávez's classicism, US commentators suggested that, specifically in

---

[82] Saavedra, 'Carlos Chávez's Polysemic Style', especially 133–43.
[83] Hess, *Representing the Good Neighbor*, 48–9. [84] Ibid., 43–4.

the Americas, classical ideals could organically channel vital 'modern' impulses attuned to their context and thereby transcend the artifice and posturing of neoclassicism. 'Ur-classicism' seems to be another way of looking at the same question of American vitalism that preoccupied Roy Harris and his critics in the Chapter 3. When US composers celebrated and promoted Chávez's music, then, it was in ways that imagined him as they wished and moulded him to their personal agendas.

None more so than Copland himself. Copland was particularly keen to proclaim the significance of the aesthetic Chávez was forging, which he saw as uniquely Mexican and a model for finding an autonomous American sound, distinct from Europe. In an article which appeared first in *New Republic* in – again – 1928 and was republished in a somewhat expanded form in Henry Cowell's 1933 volume *American Composers on American Music*, he described Chávez as 'one of the few American musicians about whom we can say that he is more than a reflection of Europe', arguing how Chávez 'had caught the spirit of Mexico – its sunfilled, naïve, Latin soul'.[85] From Copland's point of view, he was commending an enviable development, attributing to Chávez in Mexico exactly what Copland hoped to achieve in the United States – the vitalist fusion of place, time, and musical idea. ('We in the United States who have long desired musical autonomy can best appreciate the full measure of his achievement. We cannot, like Chávez, borrow from a rich, melodic source or lose ourselves in an ancient civilization, but we can be stimulated by his example.')[86]

Without consciously attempting to be 'modern,' his music indubitably succeeds in belonging to our own age. . . . Chávez is essentially of our own day because he uses his composer's gift for the expression of objective beauty of universal significance rather than as mere means of self-expression. . . . [His music] exemplifies the complete overthrow of nineteenth-century Germanic ideals which tyrannized over music for more than a hundred years. It propounds no problems, no metaphysics. Chávez's music is extraordinarily healthy; it is clear and clean-sounding, without shadows or softness.[87]

Copland's comments on Chávez's music celebrated Chávez's rejection of German Romanticism. After thus deploying a rhetoric remarkably redolent

---

[85] Copland, 'Carlos Chávez: Mexican Composer' in *American Composers*, 102–6; see also Copland, 'Carlos Chávez: Mexican Composer', *New Republic*, 54 (1928): 322–3; both are discussed briefly in Hess, *Representing the Good Neighbor*, 40. Saavedra has argued how this major essay by Copland lauding Chávez's aesthetic practice from this time had been decisive in canonising long-term ideas about Chavez's music that locked Chávez within nationalist discourses, overlooking his polysemic musical style in favour of an essentialised Mexican one.

[86] Copland, 'Carlos Chávez: Mexican Composer', *New Republic*, 323.

[87] Copland, 'Carlos Chávez: Mexican Composer', in *American Composers*, 102–3.

of Nietzsche on Georges Bizet in *The Case of Wagner* – 'Bizet's music seems to me perfect. It comes forward lightly, gracefully, stylishly'[88] – Copland concludes: 'Here is absolute music if ever there was any.' The parallels with the North-South sickness-heath dialectic found in Nietzsche's portrait of nineteenth-century European aesthetics are arresting, especially given Nietzsche's attraction to the figure of the dancer as a way out of idealism's moribund intellectual inwardness.[89] As Nietzsche continues, extolling the lithe physicality of Bizet's music: '"All that is good is easy, everything divine runs with light feet": this is the first principle of my aesthetics.'[90] Note also how Nietzsche's assertions about *Carmen* anticipate the same notion of the South as a catalyst for holistic spiritual fulfilment that shaped the Mexican vogue: 'How such a work [*Carmen*] completes one! … I became so forbearing, so happy, so Indian, so *settled* … .'[91] In spite of professed aspirations to cut loose from Europe, then, European aesthetics appears nonetheless to be lurking just outside the frame and cast long shadows. And, as Saavedra has argued, Copland's prominent characterisation of Chavez's music ultimately ossified and racially essentialised its immediate and later twentieth-century reception.[92]

Even if Chávez had never styled himself as a 'neoclassicist', his musical and aesthetic thinking shared common ground with the US American project, similarly strongly buying into a vitalist agenda. In 1927, he published an essay titled 'Technique and Inner Form' in the New York journal *Modern Music*, which was the journal of the League of Composers, Copland's musical home turf. In it, he argued that place, time, idea, and form had to coalesce in order for music to be authentic or vital:

It is only authentic work that has validity or any inherent reason for being. Validity in art might be defined as the result of a vital interest of the author which is transmitted to the person to whom he addresses himself. It is obviously impossible to extract something vital from an already exhausted process. After a unique

---

[88] Friedrich Nietzsche, *The Case of Wagner, Nietzsche Contra Wagner, and Selected Aphorisms*, trans. Anthony M. Ludovici, 3rd edition (Gloucester: Dodo Press, 2008), 1.

[89] See ibid., especially 8–9.   [90] Ibid., 1.   [91] Ibid.

[92] Chávez was not the only Mexican composer whose music suffered essentialised mischaracterisation at Copland's hand, as Kolb-Neuhaus has shown. In a consciously subaltern avant-garde aesthetics Kolb-Neuhaus has described as 'marginal hybridity', Revueltas's music spurned asymmetries between centre and periphery, rejected a 'unitary, synthetic voice', and othered modern Europe by quoting its music as found material. However, for Copland, Revueltas's music evinced another fantasy of Mexican culture and character that contrasted with Chávez the classicist 'intellectual': one of spontaneity. Kolb-Neuhaus, 'Silvestre Revueltas's *Colorines*', 197, 202–3.

creation there remains no margin of vitality; Palestrina exhausted Palestrina, Wagner exhausted Wagner and Debussy exhausted Debussy.[93]

Raw artistic idea and form (or, as Chávez interchangeably calls it, technique) were thus inextricable and depended on the artist's local environment: 'The creative artist is a condenser of the energies in the universe he inherits. . . . [I]t is impossible to conceive of the Greeks expressing their internal sense by carefully borrowing the external forms of the Aztecs or the Egyptians'. Making the point more clearly in relation to music, he bemoaned the 'artificial' instruction in the technique of other composers at composition schools. 'Beethoven, Debussy and Schoenberg are valuable precisely because their work has been evolved by no such inauthentic means', he argued.[94] At a composer roundtable discussion organised by Copland in 1932 at Yaddo, where Copland was at work on *Short Symphony*, a select group of US composers elucidated their own very similar preoccupations about their creative practice – the inadequacy of inherited form to represent the 'mutual psychology' of American composers, severing the blood supply to real, organic creative impulses. For instance, Israel Citkowitz argued that 'form', which he conceived of as responding organically to social and historical conditions, 'becomes mold to later generations'.[95]

Both Copland and Chávez, then, engaged themselves in a project to create a vital 'American' music of the present, with a sound distinct from that of the young European, and specifically French, modernists. They wrote to each other about the shared aspects of their aims. Copland's long-term musical dialogue with Stravinskian modernism is not in dispute. But it seems reasonable to suggest that we read *Short Symphony*'s classicism as being just as much in dialogue with homespun modernist trends in classical aesthetics and reception that reached south of the border – and potentially with how Copland was interpreting Chávez's aesthetic practices. For instance, Copland wrote to Chávez in December 1931: 'I am through with Europe, Carlos, and I believe as you do, that our salvation must come from ourselves and that we must fight the foreign element in America which ignores American music.' He told Chávez of his

---

[93] Chávez, 'Technique and Inner Form', 29.   [94] Ibid., 29–30.

[95] 'First Yaddo Composers' Conference' (transcript of proceedings, Copland Collection, box 357, 2 May 1932). According to the transcript, present were Copland, Marc Blitzstein, Israel Citkowitz, Richard Donovan, Wallingford Riegger, and Robert Russel Bennet. The composers reflected on their creative practice, aiming to find a way of composing that reflected their 'mutual psychology' as Americans. Conversation circled around the problem of using pre-existing forms to carry the 'individuality' of American compositional voices.

anxiousness to see the music of Mexican and South American composers, expressing his hope that Chávez would bring scores with him to New York. 'And I have plans to go there myself in the fall to see how things are.'[96]

Copland sought to turn his attention south for musical models. Reporting in a letter to Chávez on a recent concert, presumably in New York, conducted by Alexander Smallens, at which he had heard a piece of Chávez's performed, Copland was eager to identify musical differences between 'our' works and those of the Europeans, and thus to stress the similarities between his own works and those of Chávez: 'The difference between our works and those of the Europeans was striking. Theirs were so smooth and refined – so very much within a particular tradition, and ours quite jagged and angular.'[97] The trope of describing European music as refined – and the Europeans more generally as over-refined – is typical and well rehearsed. Here, however, for Copland it perhaps ties in to arguments about the superficiality of neoclassicism, rooted, according to Hess, in neoclassicism's 'presumably French characteristics of wit, brevity, and refinement',[98] as opposed to the 'jaggedness' and 'angularity' of what seemed primitivist in American classicism. Not just musically, but also on a spiritual or emotional level, the connectedness of the Americas supposedly operated much more immediately and deeply than the connection bridging 'old' and 'new' worlds – at least in the way Northern participants fantasised the relationship as having a physical effect. As Copland explained in a letter to Chávez after his visit: 'As soon as we crossed the border, I regretted leaving Mexico with a sharp pang. It took me three years in France to get as close a feeling to the country as I was able to get in three months in Mexico. I can thank you for this, for without your many kindnesses, the opportunity for knowing it and loving it so well would never have come.'[99]

Of course, this exchange of letters was as much about solidifying the two men's relationship as it was about aesthetics. Pollack has painted the correspondence as evidence that 'Copland and Chávez strongly identified with each other – perhaps more deeply than with any other musical contemporary, a remarkable phenomenon considering their differences in background

---

[96] Letter from Copland to Chávez, 26 December 1931, Chávez Correspondence, folder 12.

[97] Letter from Copland to Chávez, 7 April 1932 or 1933, Chávez Correspondence, folder 11.

[98] Hess, *Representing the Good Neighbor*, 26.

[99] Letter from Copland to Chávez, 2 January 1934 (1933?), Chávez Correspondence, folder 11.

and temperament'.[100] It was also politically expedient for the two men, given their significance in their respective contexts, to invest in developing a mutual understanding. As Saavedra has noted, from as early as the 1920s the United States and modernism served Chávez as a 'refuge' from stifling musical expectations at home.[101] By the early 1930s, Chávez occupied within Mexico's emerging art music culture a unique position of influence and control of which US composers could only dream, but Chávez himself looked longingly across the border at the advantages of the existing institutions and initiatives that US composers took for granted: concert halls, orchestras, press, a relatively established touring circuit from Europe. Chávez did not want to be a big fish in a small pond. He had his sights set on international success, and the United States was the most obviously proximate market in which to gain a foothold. He saw himself as operating binationally – within Mexico and within the United States – and he stayed up to date with goings-on in New York when he was absent by reading foreign press and writing to expatriate Mexican artists and diplomats.[102]

Like Copland, then, Chávez was concerned with emphasising the commonalities between the two composers' music, but romanticising any spiritual links between Mexico and the United States was probably less of a priority.[103] In a letter dated 1 December 1934, written after he received the score of *Short Symphony*, he complained to Copland:

What I understand by 'modern music' or 'contemporary music' is first *our music*: all the rest belongs to historical periods . . . . Well I think that I don't get any kick out of so called European modern composers because they *actually* belong to already past musical periods, they belong to history: we had this season a lot of Honegger, Hindemith etc stuff here, and let me tell you that they are simply unbearable for me, they are artificial, full of literature, bad literature and [the] worst possible taste, I cannot stand them anymore. They should be shut up forever, so much the better. And to think that it is that stuff that is taken for contemporary music? *No, it is not.*[104]

Just as Copland had, Chávez pitted 'our' modern music against modern European music. His letter evinces the same notions of American vitality in contemporary musical developments as those found in the Harris reception in Chapter 3, contrasted with the pretensions and empty posturing of European music that he perceives as representing out-of-place relics of a bygone age. Critical here is the idea of 'presentism' as vital to any aesthetic

---

[100] Pollack, 'Aaron Copland, Carlos Chávez, and Silvestre Revueltas', 99–110.
[101] Saavedra, 'Carlos Chávez's Polysemic Style', 116.   [102] Ibid., 122.
[103] Hess, *Representing the Good Neighbor*, 7 (using the expression 'sameness-embracing').
[104] Letter from Chávez to Copland, 1 December 1934.

shared between Copland and Chávez (and perhaps also extending to others Chávez saw as engaged with their aesthetic project more broadly), as implied by 'our music'. In a later letter Chávez complained that 'our present is formed up [*sic*] of 95% past and only 5% of present – we must not agree with that'.[105] Elsewhere in the same letter Chávez described European musical taste as 'sweetish, rotten, old'.[106]

These comments contrast explicitly with Copland's observations about Mexico being 'fresh and pure and wholesome' – as Hess has noted, 'freshness' was a key term in the Pan-Americanist rhetorical arsenal.[107] Perhaps it is in this light that *Short Symphony*'s musical quotation in the third movement might be understood. Harvey's lyrics quite literally draw attention to the fleetingness of each moment – 'Das gibt's nur einmal, das kommt nicht wieder' – allowing Copland to weave into the work's structure a vitalist reference to presence, which possibly even suggests the eroticism he shared in Mexico with Kraft. For Copland, in a fairly straightforward act of exoticism, Mexico seemed an energising antidote to rotten old Europe. Recall how Nietzschean comparisons to Bizet infused Copland's writing on Chávez's 'healthy', 'clear and clean-sounding' music of the South, and the marvellous, rejuvenating lightness Nietzsche heard in the music of the South. We might, then, suppose that for Copland, 'The Bounding Line' as a potential title for *Short Symphony* appealed because it captured some of that lightness and ease he associated with the South (like Nietzsche's 'All that is good is easy, everything divine runs with light feet').

'The Bounding Line': Line, Body, Motion

Short Symphony did not remain 'The Bounding Line' for long. In the end, Copland called the work a symphony – albeit a 'short' one, to profit by any work that adjective could do to attenuate the genre's ideological baggage. A 'short' symphony cannot be a nineteenth-century style Germanic symphonic monument of the kind denigrated by Copland as 'overripe'. But the fact that 'The Bounding Line' was adopted by Copland as the title gives a key critical insight into what kind of symphony we are dealing with – that is, how exactly *Short Symphony* functions in ways that both reinforce and challenge values considered 'symphonic'. Copland's indecision over the title suggests this is a 'symphony' ambivalent about its status. In its musical

---

[105] Letter from Chávez to Copland, 18 January 1935, Copland Collection, box 250.   [106] Ibid.
[107] Hess, *Representing the Good Neighbor*, 30.

language of the body and immediacy, it brings an impermanence and a spontaneity that profoundly destabilise what Copland believed was over-wrought Germanic symphonic monumentality or 'metaphysics'. Coupled to this question of symphonic ambivalence, Copland's use of a title proposed by Chávez puts the focus on Chávez's agency in relation to the work in ways that bolster *Short Symphony*'s grass-roots Pan-American credentials. As such, imaginatively reading the work in relation to the temporary title is of value within a project concerned with North-South border-crossing exchange.

But Chávez's title for the work may have been something of an aesthetic mistranslation, a failure of communication. Chávez's temporary title for *Short Symphony* was a critically freighted one, pointing to musings on ideals of form and beauty posed by William Blake and then picked up in the early twentieth century by James Joyce.[108] It hints at a particular literary facet to the expansive and cosmopolitan modernist context for Chávez's aesthetic philosophy of authenticity and structural self-sufficiency in the late 1920s and early 1930s.[109] As Blake wrote, posing 'the bounding line' (outline) as his counterpart to Hogarth's 'line of beauty': 'The great and golden rule of art, as well as of life, is this: That the more distinct, sharp, and wirey the bounding line, the more perfect the work of art; and the less keen and sharp, the greater is the evidence of weak imitation, plagiarism, and bungling.'[110] Blake, in his idiosyncratic artistic philosophy, was committed to line as truth, which was opposed to its 'contrary', colour, representing

---

[108] Joyce mentions 'the bounding line' in his semi-autobiographical *A Portrait of the Artist as a Young Man* (1916). Not only does 'the bounding line' reference a crucial moment in the novel – and in the *Bildungsroman* trajectory of the central character, Joyce's alter ego Stephen Dedalus – a moment that rehearses a core aesthetic treatise concerning artistic autonomy; this part of the novel is also underpinned by anxieties about imperialism and artistic nationalism, which might have resonated particularly with Chávez's interests and compositional concerns at the time. James Joyce, *A Portrait of the Artist as a Young Man*, ed. Seamus Deane (Harmondsworth: Penguin Books, 2000), 230.

[109] Further attention here would complement recent scholarship on Chávez's stylistic development by those like Christina Taylor Gibson, Alejandro Madrid, and Leonora Saavedra, whose work brings Chávez's musical identity into relief. Multiple and complex, Chávez's musical identity negotiated the cosmopolitan modernisms of different individual metropolitan centres, as well as conflicting ideologies within Mexico, including a post-revolutionary nationalism preoccupied with cultivating indigeneity. See Christina Taylor Gibson, 'Chávez, Modern Music, and the New York Scene', in *Carlos Chávez and His World*, ed. Leonora Saavedra (Princeton: Princeton University Press, 2015), 2–27; Alejandro Madrid, *Sounds of the Modern Nation: Music, Culture, and Ideas in Post-Revolutionary Mexico* (Philadelphia: Temple, 2009), chapter 2, 'The Avant-Garde as a Style of Identification: Style and Ideology in Carlos Chávez's Early Music'; Saavedra, 'Carlos Chávez's Polysemic Style'.

[110] William Blake, *The Complete Poetry and Prose of William Blake*, ed. David V. Erdman (Berkeley: University of California Press, 1982), 550.

everything that was fake and falsified – after all, he was an engraver, and line was his domain. Line, for Blake, was where artistic inspiration and imagination resided; it was a source of energy.[111]

Copland and Chávez must surely have discussed what Chávez meant by the proposed title, but whatever it was, Copland claimed he had the most prosaic, down-to-earth reading in mind: a musical line with a bouncy quality. Copland later glossed the significance of the temporary title in his biography, recalling that a friend – their identity no longer remembered – had pointed out that '"bounding" seemed more like "boundary" than the "bounce" I had in mind'.[112] This story probably accounts, too, for the lack of critical attention to the temporary title to date. For Copland, it seems, with thoughts of 'bounce', it was the resonance of 'the bounding line' with bodies in motion – leaping, taut, making contact with one another and the earth, governed by gravity – that had seemed the most fitting associations of Chávez's proposed title.

Blake's bounding line lurks even here, however. Music's illusion of motion was where Copland's close colleague Israel Citkowitz located the implications of Blake's 'bounding line' for music. (Was Citkowitz Copland's 'friend' with whom the title was discussed?) Citkowitz mentioned Blake's 'bounding line' in a 1932 review for *Modern Music*, and he characterised it as the 'free and varied … flow from idea to idea':[113]

If the essence of music is motion, a motion controlled and brought to definite issue, it is interesting to note each new work's version of this essential motion as its characteristic feature, its very physiognomy. This motion, this fundamental shape and direction corresponds in music to [William] Blake's 'bounding line'. 'How do we distinguish the oak from the beech but by the bounding outline?'[114]

In Citkowitz's application of the concept to music, Copland's distinction between 'bounding' as boundary and as bounce blurs. 'Physiognomy' invokes bodies, and classical aesthetics can also be felt in the background, since Blake's bodies were some of the most neoclassical-looking components of his work as a visual artist.

But it is elsewhere within *Modern Music* that aesthetic ideas about music as motion perhaps come closest to illuminating Copland's sense of line, pointing to its Dalcrozian connotations and to the analytical relevance of

---

[111] James Grande, '*Articulate Sounds: Music, Dissent, and Literary Culture, 1789–1840* (forthcoming, British Academy and Oxford University Press), chapter 1, 'Hearing Blake's Visions'.

[112] Copland and Perlis, *Copland, 1900–1942*, 209.

[113] Israel Citkowitz, 'Spring Concerts in New York', *Modern Music* 9 (1932): 168–72, 168.

[114] Ibid.

Dalcrozian eurythmics. Titled 'The Dynamic Line', the essay's author, Marion Bauer, wrote: 'Imagine a piece of music tracing in its course every change of dynamic color, not only the more obvious *pianissimo* to *fortissimo*, but every slight graduation of nuance and accent, *crescendo* and *diminuendo*, attack and release, and you will have a Dynamic Line.' As she continued, offering a brief outline of some principles of Dalcroze's eurythmics: 'The natural tendency is to increase the volume of tone as the pitch goes higher, and to decrease it with a descending passage: every phrase has a climactic point, usually its highest tone; the volume increases to the point and diminishes as it leaves it.'[115] This musical line, then, gives impulse to physical movement – Dalcroze's pedagogical system aimed to synchronise music with motion to create embodied musical and rhythmic learning experiences. We are also not all that far from Blake's sense of line as energy.

A sense of line, the body, and presence materialises particularly strongly at the opening of *Short Symphony*'s second movement. This movement can be read as a prolongation of Dalcroze's principle, which becomes a way of exploring symphonic and timbral weight – monumentality – through the prism of motion. An analogy would be the application of pressure and consequent increasing weight and thickness of the unbroken artist's brush or pen stroke. Copland's initial use of the solo alto flute timbre evokes breathy voice, and its touch on skin, and initiates a sense of line, with a descending four-note contour. Such a conception of line, according to Dalcrozian eurythmics, summons the body to follow its motion. The alto flute motive is answered by further gestures sounding one by one from cello, viola, bassoon, violin, oboe, and clarinet – individual musical bodies in motion entering the stage, falling in and out of synchronisation with one another. The bass line never quite allows the passage to settle harmonically (see Example 4.8). Likewise, Copland's reluctance to stress the downbeat generates a sense of balance and weightless suspension that evokes the feeling of balletic motion. Two bars before figure 19, the gestures coalesce homophonically for the first time in legato contrary motion. The sound world gradually thickens until at the climax of this movement, the *fortissimo* at figure 26, the aural line has accrued a weight that takes on characteristics of the monumental. The line physically overwhelms the listener with the force of its auditory presence and weight (see Example 4.9). If the monument seeks to overpower, Copland's work ultimately aims for balance, however. In line with Dalcroze's philosophies, its peak in volume comes as the orchestra articulates the extremes of register, yet as soon as the

---

[115] Marion Bauer, 'Rediscovering the Dynamic Line', *Modern Music* 6 (1929): 28–31, 28–9.

Example 4.8 Movement II, figure 18. Copland, *Short Symphony (No. 2)*, 27.

Example 4.9 Movement II, figure 25 to end of movement (climax comes at figure 26). Copland, *Short Symphony (No. 2)*, 34–6.

Example 4.9 (Cont.)

Example 4.9 (Cont.)

tide of sound passes over the listener, it suddenly recedes, both in timbral force and in register. Manipulating suggestions of permanence, Copland seems to use the ebb and flow of the Dalcrozian line to dispel the energy of the monumental and sweep it away. The slate is once again wiped clean, ready to begin anew. In this way, Copland balances and tempers symphonic monumentality, rendering it transient. After energy slowly accrues over the course of the movement, its dissipation – to borrow Daniel M. Grimley's term – is 'telescoped' at the very end in a fluid gesture that undermines symphonic monumentality through its ease.[116] Even the idea of voice, foregrounded by the opening alto flute gesture, forms a counterpoint to monument's eternal marble: voice evokes living – and ultimately dying – breath and flesh.

Hearing *Short Symphony* through the temporary title is not, then, just about destabilising symphonic monumentality or exploring Chávez's agency; significantly, and more radically, it is also about re-inserting bodies – pleasurably, messily, or even violently – into the often cerebral-seeming world of objectivising classicism with its mathematical ratios and balanced structures. Let us not forget that those ratios served beauty, and that beauty elicited not just the pure stasis of aesthetic reverie, but desire, much less controlled and contained. Indeed, Copland's adoption of Chávez's title, whether it suggests bodily form or the flow of dance, provides strong grounds for hearing even Hellenic eroticism in *Short Symphony*. Ancient Greek and Roman theories on visuality considered vision 'a tactile process, akin to touching'. Furthermore, these theories suggested that to 'gaze upon an object is to have it physically enter into oneself', and that beautiful objects (e.g. a statue or a picture) could elicit desire in the viewer, which the object itself could not satisfy.[117] In some cases, the beautiful object could even generate overtly erotic feelings, as in the cult statue of the goddess of sex Aphrodite of Knidos by Praxiteles. Arguably, theories of vision by Democritus, Plato, and Aristotle thus gave the beautiful object power over the viewer, in opposition to how power relationships between viewer and object tend to be cast in the twentieth century.[118] This relationship between viewer and viewed was manifest in Classical Greek art through the object's 'glance', with the head position

---

[116] See Daniel M. Grimley, '*Symphony/Antiphony*: Formal Strategies in the Twentieth-Century Symphony', in *The Cambridge Companion to the Symphony*, ed. Julian Horton (Cambridge: Cambridge University Press, 2013), 285–310, 288.

[117] Mark D. Stansbury-O'Donnell, 'Desirability and the Body' in *A Companion to Greek and Roman Sexualities*, ed. Thomas K. Hubbard (Chichester: Wiley-Blackwell, 2014), 33–55, 42.

[118] Ibid.

tilted down and the look cast askance in a way that was inviting and introspective, pulling the viewer into the object's subjective world.[119] A pertinent example is the conscious eroticism of Antinous, Hadrian's boy lover and archetype as eromenos (beloved) for homosexual love across an age gap, whose coy, submissive gaze in typical representations invites the observer in. Antinous is 'sensuous but sulky', in the words of classicist and art historian Caroline Vout (Figure 4.5).[120]

Besides, Hellenism (the study of ancient Greek philosophy, history, and aesthetics first developed in eighteenth-century Germany by Johann

Figure 4.5 Antinous (right) and Hadrian (left). Second-century Roman marble head (Antinous) and bust (Hadrian), British Museum. © The Trustees of the British Museum.

[119] Jaś Elsner, 'Reflections on the "Greek Revolution" in Art: From Changes in Viewing to the Transformation of Subjectivity' in *Rethinking Revolutions through Ancient Greece*, ed. Simon Goldhill and Robin Osborne (Cambridge: Cambridge University Press: 2006), 68–95, 70.
[120] Caroline Vout, 'Antinous, Archaeology, and History', *Journal of Roman Studies* 95 (2005): 80–96, 85.

Joachim Winckelmann) has a long-standing history of codifying homo-sexuality, from its eighteenth-century establishment by the homosexual Winckelmann, to the poetry of Percy Shelley and Lord Byron in the early nineteenth century, and its prominence particularly within *fin-de-siècle* circles in Oxford.[121] Homosexual relationships were a key part of ancient Greek society and education for elite men. It is hard not to consider these kinds of erotics, too, conjured up as they are by the bodies and the classical aesthetics of the work, and forming a kind of corporeality that previous commentators have avoided elucidating in favour of the work's rational components.

Drawing on a musical language closely associated with dance that anticipated Copland's later ballet scores like *Billy the Kid* (1938) and *Rodeo* (1942), the second movement sees the body re-imagined, perhaps not as an exoticised other, but as a site of play and pleasure, and of mutual reciprocity echoing Pan-American ideals. Indeed, Copland had reworked *Short Symphony* into the Sextet immediately before working on *Billy the Kid*. Both ballet scores were set in the disputed borderland territories of the nineteenth century that belonged to Mexico before they were ceded to the United States after the Mexican-American war of 1846 to 1848. In these territories, national histories blurred and ideas of the nation came under threat. The musical language of the ballet scores found an early iteration in *Short Symphony*, whose sense of physicality responded to a core tension within any utopian Pan-American idealism that sought to place the United States and Mexico on an equal footings. It suggests a more fluid means of mediating unresolvable contradictions of hegemony and diversity. It sug-gests an erotics that places reciprocity at the heart of questions of domin-ation and power, and at the heart of the complex dance between autonomy and interdependence. Perhaps Copland's most radical contribution is not to try to resolve those contradictions – between autonomy and inter-dependence, and between the viewer and the viewed – but to attempt to engender a sense of balance and possibility moving forward.

When Chávez called the work 'an organism, a body in which every piece works by itself 100% but whose musical mutual relation is such, that no one could possibly work and exist without the other',[122] perhaps part of what he was referring to was the second movement's musical exploration of the interplay between dependence and independence, with musical gestures

---

[121] See, for instance, Linda C. Dowling, *Hellenism and Homosexuality in Victorian Oxford* (Ithaca: Cornell University Press, 1994).

[122] Letter from Chávez to Copland, 1 December 1934.

moving in and out of synchronisation, for instance. This is a profoundly classical archetype. Yet, heard through a different filter, the work is also suggestive of those political preoccupations about interdependence and autonomy that characterise US-Mexican relations. Ancient Classical aesthetics offer a way of imagining the relationship between the viewer and the viewed as inviting and joyful. Or, at the very least, they offer something more ambivalent than the negativity of unqualified objectification. If Classical Greek theories of vision subvert twentieth-century theories of power and the gaze, suggesting that it was the viewer who was dominated by the beautiful object, not the other way around, then think again of those pictures of Kraft in the Mexican landscape. They suggested the playful eroticism of exchange, rather than domination, and that playfulness complicated the supposed transparency of Copland's objectifying gaze. As in those images, perhaps *Short Symphony*'s encounter across the borders – of viewer and viewed, metaphorically extended to north and south, centre and periphery, and inside and outside – takes on the same ambivalent reciprocity.

'It's Probably a Symphony'[123]

For Copland, the symphony was a genre that brought with it historical responsibility, and a particular aesthetic responsibility vis-à-vis the American context. Conceived as a symphony – an idea Copland had been toying with at least since his letter to Brandt from Morocco – *Short Symphony* thus became an attempt to negate the symphony's weighty critical heritage. And yet, *Short Symphony* was still a symphony, and Copland's Pan-Americanism painfully utopian. *Short Symphony* was caught within coloniality's contours of privilege that benefitted Copland and conditioned his vision of Pan-American cooperation. As such, if Copland's impulse was to connect with Chávez and Mexico as equal partners, it was a pipe dream. If, for instance, the symphony is held up next to Copland's photo album, could the music's sense of immediacy and presence within an overall aesthetic of classical clarity ever avoid aligning with the symbol of the *tabula rasa*, and with it the hubris-infused hope that contained within the work's aesthetic might be the seedlings of not just a US American but a Pan-American sound? Counter-intuitively, then, Copland's 'little symphony', as Chávez affectionately called it, ultimately envisions an expansionism in many ways aligned with that of Harris's 'big

---

[123] Letter from Copland to Brandt, 10 September 1931, Copland Collection, box 258.

symphony from the West'. Copland and Kraft's visit to Mexico even takes on aspects of the eighteenth-century 'Grand Tour', when elite Europeans travelled an established route to experience the Classical foundations of Western civilisation. There is a feeling of searching for a new ancestral home.

Likewise, it is hard for the music's sense of the body to avoid elision with discourses of primitivism, of looking hungrily to Southern bodies for inspiration. Just as he did when writing about Chávez's music, Copland easily lapsed into essentialism when talking about Mexico in more general terms. As he wrote just after leaving the country in 1933 in the much-quoted letter that heads this chapter: 'Mexico offers something fresh and pure and wholesome – a quality which is deeply unconventionalized. The source of it I believe is the Indian blood which is so prevalent.' Kolb-Neuhaus has made a similar point about Copland's exoticist misinterpretation of the provocative hybridism in Revueltas's satirical, ironic music in relation to Mexican indigenism. Such a misreading is surprising given that the two composers had personally socialised a great deal in Mexico; nonetheless, in the end '[Copland's] ears were capable of and interested in recognizing only what they expected and desired' in Revueltas's music – that is, Copland heard only instinctively drawn 'vivid tone pictures' of Mexican culture.[124] Copland's symphonic work and its idealist American modernist aesthetics, then, are troubling, because they both maintain and obscure existing power relations, all the while signalling utopian possibility.

Perhaps more than other chapters, this one signals a beginning. Relative agency and authority subtly shifting as the two composers move between settings and cross borders can be tracked in ways that are far from intuitive. There is clearly more to be learned from careful attention to the relationship between Chávez and Copland – and about Copland's relationship with Revueltas, too. *Short Symphony*, alongside Copland's later *El Salón México* or Chávez's *Sinfonía India* (of 1935–6), points outwards towards a wider and underexplored period of creative and intellectual exchange, in which these composers grapple differently with the question of what it is to be American. Furthermore, building on existing work by those like Saavedra and others, there is still music-analytical work to be done that might support stronger claims about direct musical influence between Copland and Chávez.

Pan-Americanism has been positioned in this chapter not as a historical aesthetic category, but as a frame for understanding the failures of

---

[124] Kolb-Neuhaus, 'Silvestre Revueltas's *Colorines*', 203–4.

hegemonic subject positions, as well as the aesthetic apparatuses that support them within the asymmetries of coloniality. In this respect, Pan-Americanism serves as a point of access for the book's wider project of exploring how the symphonic genre illuminates ideas of space and subjectivity circa 1933. This project is necessarily contingent and preliminary. It confronts the methodological paradox that to direct attention to where power is structurally located, even to deconstruct it, is in many ways to reproduce its authority and force. Nonetheless, the urge remains to keep trying to do this historical and theoretical work better, while remaining vigilant about its limits. When, over the past few years, the US-Mexican border has loomed so large on the global stage, it is clear that the need to address anxieties over failures of transnational connection and questions about the United States' authority to shape representations of Mexico is only intensifying.

5 | Arthur Honegger's 'Modernised *Eroica*'

Paris – Berlin

When, in the Berlin Philharmonie on 27 March 1933, three days before the performance of Pfitzner's Symphony in C♯ minor, the final bars of Arthur Honegger's *Mouvement symphonique n° 3* dissipated into intense quiet, it was a potentially incendiary moment. Honegger's work, after all, had been a commission for the Berlin Philharmonic's fiftieth anniversary – a moment of celebration, but also of stocktaking and reflection: the orchestra had invited Honegger to engage with the symphonic tradition and its associated values at a time of acute political upheaval. Honegger, a foreign composer best known for his Old Testament-themed oratorio *Le Roi David* (1921) and the later critique of capitalist modernity *Cris du monde* (1931), responded with a work that, after the midpoint introduction of a lyrical alto saxophone voice unfamiliar to the symphonic tonal palate, descended into the depths of the orchestra to simply tail away. Quite the opposite of symphonic apotheosis, two pianissimo C♯ quavers were left reverberating into a concert hall still reeling from Bruno Walter's exit only days earlier.

So risky was a performance of the new symphony in this charged setting that conductor Wilhelm Furtwängler, to whom the work was dedicated, had not been able to guarantee that the scheduled performance would go ahead. At home in Paris, Honegger had waited for news, and when the critical telegram arrived, it read: 'Playing as planned, but suggest you don't come.'[1] Honegger's absence might at least dampen the inflammatory potential of his controversial statement on the symphonic genre while political tensions sizzled within and without. For in this work Honegger had dismantled the symphonic ideal, returning something recognisable but deeply estranged. Paring the symphony down to its rawest dialectical building blocks, his critique of the liberal values associated with symphonies was potent and, I suggest in this chapter, musically enacted the liberal subject's ultimate dissolution.

But beyond the curious ending during the Adagio, evaporating to deny the listener any symphonic sense of return and leaving the work

---

[1] Harry Halbreich, *Arthur Honegger*, ed. Reinhard G. Pauly, trans. Roger Nichols (Portland: Amadeus Press, 1999), 131.

deliberately off-kilter, a second feature of *Mouvement symphonique n° 3* stands out as particularly remarkable. The work is titled 'Symphonic Movement' in the singular, but it is clearly bipartite, containing two movements, an Allegro, and an Adagio. This raises the linked questions of which of these is the 'real' movement and what function the other one plays in relation to it. These features alone justify this chapter's critical sociopolitical reading of Honegger's third Symphonic Movement that went, if not unnoticed, then certainly unremarked upon by contemporary critics – unsurprising, perhaps, given the dangerous situation, with control tightening over music journalism. After all, *Mouvement symphonique n° 3* was the final part of a trio of Symphonic Movements written over ten years, following Honegger's well-known machine-music archetype *Pacific 231* (1923) and the bodily vigour of *Rugby* (1928). Honegger's own suggestion that the 'absolute' title was 'sober and unprepossessing' hints at more revealing or even programmatic alternatives he might have considered and discarded.[2] Perhaps he sought provocation by situating readily identifiable musical tropes of modernity within a work that was given the elevated status 'symphonic', and that was an anniversary commission for the German symphony orchestra par excellence. Or perhaps, given the volatile political climate, the decision was not aesthetic, but a bid to deflect attention from the work's programmatic aspects.[3] Either way, it was a decision he was later to regret, and for which by 1954 he believed his 'poor' *Mouvement symphonique n° 3* 'paid dearly'; lacking a juicy title, it generated little interest from subsequent performers or academics.[4]

---

[2] See Willy Tappolet, *Arthur Honegger* (Zurich: Atlantis, 1954), 85.

[3] He had also been frustrated by how his programmatic titles had obliterated all other modes of critical engagement with his work, particularly in the wake of *Pacific 231*'s success, whose reception had been dominated by its supposed 'train music' programme, even though he had insisted that the work aimed in no way to emulate the noise of the locomotive. Egon Voss, '*Pacific 231*: Reine Programmemusik oder doch ein Stück absoluter Musik?', in *Arthur Honegger: Werk und Rezeption*, ed. Peter Jost (Bern: Peter Lang, 2009), 199–212, 210. In irritation, Honegger had attempted to shift its reception discourse to more abstract spheres, for instance in 1925 describing the work as 'a varied chorale, of a wholly classical architecture'. See ibid., 203, citing Alexis Roland-Manuel, 'Opinions d'Arthur Honegger', *Dissonances: Revue musicale indépendante* (1925): 87.

[4] See Tappolet, *Arthur Honegger*, 85. The occasional Honegger scholar has quietly championed the work, however. Geoffrey K. Spratt calls *Mouvement symphonique n° 3* Honegger's 'finest achievement in the field of purely orchestral symphonic music to date'. Geoffrey K. Spratt, *The Music of Arthur Honegger* (Cork: Cork University Press, 1987), 243. In a similar vein, according to Spratt, Honegger's 'curt reaction' to the work's criticism in 1933 'had been to say that it was due to their failure to recognize it as an infinitely better work than the other two', referring to *Pacific 231* and *Rugby*, although Spratt provides no source for this comment (see Spratt, *Music of Arthur Honegger*, 244). Despite Spratt's assessment, thus far the work has received only cursory

I suggest that in *Mouvement symphonique n° 3*, as in *Cris du monde* before it, Honegger critically engaged with some of the ways in which selfhood and self-realisation were threatened by the imperatives and anxieties of modernity. Written during the economic depression and political uncertainty of the early 1930s, his work voices an elegy over the wreckage of liberalist symphonic utopianism. Heard in an unexpectedly charged context after Hitler's rise to power, however, these themes became heightened.

As Furtwängler anticipated, plenty of critics reacted negatively to the work, with conservatives writing off *Mouvement symphonique n° 3* as a superficial French novelty, continuing an extensive tradition of the French symphony being relativised by its German neighbours.[5] These 'hostile' reviews have been taken as representative in the secondary literature.[6] Such reception strains set up Honegger as a figurehead for all things French, international, and new.[7] Symphonic reception, once again, was in large part about asserting identity. The problem posed by assimilating a Swiss symphony that, for contemporary critics, fell straightforwardly into neither the French nor the German compositional traditions underlines how questions of nationalist purity had enough force in symphonic criticism to overpower other issues well before the National Socialists took office. Simply put, then, critics did not engage with potential programmatic readings because matters of national identity consumed their attention.

The picture painted in existing scholarship of a damning premiere tells only part of the story, however. In contrast to the negative reception that lambasted the symphony by emphasising its Frenchness, many other strands of criticism welcomed Honegger's latest concert offering,[8] some

consideration from academics. An exception is Matthieu Carlier, 'La forme dans les trois *Mouvements symphoniques* d'Arthur Honegger' (thesis, Paris-Sorbonne University, 1992). There are some references to *Mouvement symphonique n° 3* as part of a detailed discussion of *Rugby* in Keith Walter's doctoral dissertation, but it is paid no sustained analytical attention. See Keith John Walter, 'Rhythmic and Contrapuntal Structures in the Music of Arthur Honegger' (PhD thesis, Eastman School of Music, University of Rochester, 1997). Both Halbreich and Marcel Delannoy give short analytical treatments of the third Symphonic Movement in their larger life-and-works studies: see Halbreich, *Arthur Honegger*, 356–8; Marcel Delannoy, *Honegger*, ed. Geoffrey K. Spratt (Geneva: Slatkine, 1986), 147–9.

[5] See, for instance, Andrew Deruchie, *The French Symphony at the Fin de Siècle: Style, Culture, and the Symphonic Tradition* (Rochester: University of Rochester Press, 2013).

[6] See Halbreich, *Arthur Honegger*, 131, where the reception is described as 'icy' and 'hostile'; see also Delannoy, *Honegger*, 149–50. Delannoy gives a similarly false impression of the coldness of the Berlin reception. Emphasising these reviews may be politically expedient, having the positive benefit of distancing Honegger from the incumbent regime's politics.

[7] See Ernst Heinrich Schliepe, 'Neuntes Philharmonisches Konzert: Honegger, Schumann, Strauß, und Elly Ney', *Deutsche Allgemeine Zeitung*, 29 March 1933.

[8] Heinrich Strobel, '9. Furtwängler-Konzert', *Berliner Börsen-Courier*, 28 March 1933.

even demonstrating a desire to assimilate the work's abstractions with the weighty critical rhetoric of German aesthetic traditions. More than simply benefitting Honegger scholarship, or rehabilitating another work from 1933 that has dropped out of our historical consciousnesses,[9] collating and evaluating the reviews here for the first time also gives a more accurate picture of the deep ambivalences within the Berlin reception context. Such revisionary activity – especially activity that turns a close eye and ear to the first few weeks of Nazi Germany – is particularly important because it finesses historical narratives of National Socialist persecution. But as critics circled and recircled a terrain that dealt with national identity at the expense of all other questions, perhaps our attention might most fruitfully push at that discourse's limits and turn to the pregnant silences – to what was not said, and why. Honegger's work gives a sense of the kinds of themes with which symphonic discourse could not deal, and the constraints that shaped how listeners heard and wrote about Honegger's symphony in Berlin 1933.

The imaginative reading of the symphony offered in this chapter is based on themes hinted at in the Berlin reception, set in dialogue with broader Weimar-period social commentary. In some ways, then, this is an attempt to reconstruct what critics might have said, had the premiere not been such a misfortune of time and place, had the setting felt less perilous, had journalistic restrictions not been shifting, and had imaginative programmatic associations been less restricted. Nonetheless, it remains a twenty-first century interpretation: to quote Laura Tunbridge, we will never quite be able to listen with 'a period ear'.[10] This chapter begins by examining more closely

---

[9] Furthermore, the oblique status of this work as a 'true symphony', coupled with its perplexing relationship with the two other Symphonic Movements, *Pacific 231* and *Rugby*, means that it has been omitted from studies that have dealt with and traced aesthetic lines of development through some or all of Honegger's named and numbered symphonies. Foremost here is Jean Maillard's study of all five of Honegger's numbered symphonies, in which *Pacific 231* and *Rugby* are mentioned in passing but *Mouvement symphonique n° 3* is not. See Jean Maillard, *Les symphonies d'Arthur Honegger*, ed. Jacques Nahoum (Paris: A. Leduc, 1974). Tappolet devotes separate chapters to the five numbered symphonies and to the three Symphonic Movements in Tappolet, *Arthur Honegger*. For more recent literature see, for instance, Ulrich Konrad, 'Die Sinfonie liturgique von Arthur Honegger und die Tradition der Sinfonie um 1945', *Musik-Konzepte* 135 (2007): 25–44; Ulrich Tadday, '"Ziemlich unabhängig von herkömmlicher Ästhetik": Arthur Honeggers *Symphonie liturgique* und Sinfonie *Deliciae Basilienses* zwischen Innovation und Affirmation', *Musik-Konzepte* 135 (2007): 45–56. The only exception is Sergej Èrazmovič Pavčinskij, *Simfoničeskoe Tvorčestvo A. Oneggera* (Moscow: Sovetskij Kompozitor, 1972). Èrazmovič Pavčinskij is unique in discussing *Mouvement symphonique n° 3* and the numbered symphonies within the same frame, but there is no English translation.

[10] Laura Tunbridge, *Singing in the Age of Anxiety: Lieder Performances in New York and London between the Wars* (Chicago: University of Chicago Press, 2018), 11.

the dismissive strand in the reception. These sources are revealing about the status of the symphonic genre as a specifically Germanic cultural object. Then the focus will shift, to introduce more favourable reception, which reveals grounds for interpreting the work as exploring specifically 'modern' narratives of subjectivity. Given *Mouvement symphonique*'s ambiguous thematic relationship to the machines of *Pacific 231* and the bodies of *Rugby*, I suggest it be heard with reference to some of the themes evinced in Weimar-period criticism of subjectivity, particularly concerned with changing relationships between the body, the machine, and the mass that contemporary thinkers considered characteristically modern. It seems that a key cultural anxiety Honegger explores through his symphony concerns the mass and its assimilationist drive to absorb the individual through the quasi-mathematical abstraction and reification of the body into what Siegfried Kracauer described as 'mass ornaments'.[11] Honegger focused his grim fascination with modernity's dissolution of subjective interiority, as part of a wider debasement of Enlightenment values, through the dialectical prism of the symphonic form.

'Icy' Reception? Nationalist Gatekeeping

'Wilhelm Furtwängler has finally dared to put Arthur Honegger's "Symphonic Movement No. 3" on the programme', wrote Jewish critic and editor of the *Zeitschrift für Musikwissenschaft* Alfred Einstein acerbically at the top of his review in the *Berliner Tageblatt*, foregrounding the conductor's prevarication about performing the work.[12] Einstein himself was soon to be made redundant from the *Berliner Tageblatt*. Cognisant of the dangers of remaining in Germany, he left for London later in 1933, ultimately emigrating to the United States in 1939, following his physicist 'cousin' Albert. According to some accounts, misinformation was circulating about Honegger's racial background – was he Jewish?[13] (He was not). Reviews of the concert appeared on the inside front pages of the Berlin daily papers, flanked by reports on the so-called Nazi defence action (*Abwehraktion*) beginning to take place elsewhere in Germany against

---

[11] Siegfried Kracauer, *The Mass Ornament: Weimar Essays*, trans. and ed. Thomas Y. Levin (Cambridge, MA: Harvard University Press, 1995), 75–86.

[12] 'Wilhelm Furtwängler hat es endlich gewagt, den "Sinfonischen Satz Nr. 3" von Arthur Honegger aufs Programme zu setzen', Alfred Einstein, 'Vorletztes Philharmonisches Konzert', *Berliner Tageblatt*, 28 March 1933.

[13] Spratt, *Music of Arthur Honegger*, 244.

alleged foreign Jewish *Hetzpropaganda*: the newspapers reported SA
guards stationed in front of Jewish businesses in other cities to prevent
trade.[14] Rumour was as powerful as fact in the National Socialist political
machine, and – a calculation Furtwängler must have made – even suspicion
seemed enough to cause chaos. In short, therefore, Furtwängler was right to
be wary about the composer's presence in Berlin: it was hard to predict
quite what was going to cause trouble, or how far such trouble would run.

On 13 March 1933, two weeks before the planned premiere, Furtwängler
wrote to Honegger asking whether he might consider postponing the first
performance of *Mouvement symphonique*, convinced that political strains
would have abated by the start of the following season. Falling in the middle
of the Berlin Philharmonic's spring Beethoven cycle, it was isolated within
a season that was overwhelmingly Teutonic – the figures forming the
programme's bulk were Beethoven, Brahms, Bruckner, Liszt (an honorary
German, of course), Pfitzner, Strauss, and Wagner.[15] National Socialist
cultural policy was already beginning to have its effect, and simply by the
fact of its composer being Swiss(-French?) Honegger's work was already
conspicuous. Given the tumultuous and precarious politics following
Walter's ousting that week, Furtwängler's decision to ask Honegger not
to attend the premiere is perhaps understandable. But besides the question
marks hanging over Honegger's racial background,[16] just as important was
the fact that Honegger's presence would also have drawn press and political
attention to this foreign commission within the programme, spotlighting
its already potentially inflammatory treatment of the orchestra and of
symphonic form. Conversely, without him there, the work could be styled
differently, downplayed as a light opener to Furtwängler's ninth and
penultimate Philharmonic Concert of the season, a programme that otherwise showcased towering figures within the Austro-German canon:
Schumann's Fourth Symphony, Beethoven's Piano Concerto No. 4 (with
Elly Ney as the soloist) and Strauss's *Till Eulenspiegel.*

---

[14] Ernst Heinrich Schliepe, 'Neuntes Philharmonisches Konzert: Honegger, Schumann, Strauß,
und Elly Ney', *Deutsche Allgemeine Zeitung*, 29 March 1933. Above it, in the first column, is an
article reporting 'die nationalsozialistische Abwehraktion gegen die jüdische Hetzpropaganda
im Ausland'. Staatsbibliothek zu Berlin, Preußischer Kulturbesitz. See also Strobel, '9.
Furtwängler-Konzert', 2. The same paragraph as in the *Deutsche Allgemeine Zeitung* leads the
article 'Folgen der Greuelhetze', about the SA guards posted in front of Jewish businesses to
discourage shoppers' entry. Staatsbibliothek zu Berlin, Preußischer Kulturbesitz.
[15] 'Konzerte der Berliner Philharmoniker 1932–1934 (In- und Ausland)', in Peter Muck, *100 Jahre
Berliner Philharmonisches Orchester* (Schneider: Tutzing, 1982), as digitised and revised for the
Berlin Philharmonic Archive, March 2013.
[16] Delannoy, *Honegger*, 149.

In spite of Furtwängler's efforts, for some listeners that juxtaposition immediately foregrounded what they perceived as the incongruity of Honegger's 'French' sound.[17] One of these listeners was Ernst Heinrich Schliepe of the *Deutsche Allgemeine Zeitung*. Calling the title 'grandiose and pretentious', Schliepe was explicit in his rejection of the work along national Franco/German lines: 'We know Honegger sufficiently; he is always introduced as Swiss, although his entire musical and intellectual disposition marks him out as a typical proponent of the new French music.'[18] Schliepe implied that Honegger's alleged Swissness was a coincidence of parentage only, and a category being deployed in the programme to dupe the German public into listening in frustration for absent Germanic depths in his music. Schliepe's diffuse complaints centred on the work's superficiality:

[N]othing further is hidden behind the mystico-pretentious title of this orchestral movement than yet another commonplace piece, no different to any of those we find concocted en masse by the so-called 'international' composers who have nailed their colours to the mast of contemporary music, and who will continue to mix together the familiar ingredients until their public has finally had enough. Our German public has already reached that point.[19]

The supposed lack of substance was linked not only to the work's 'Frenchness', however, but also to its 'internationalism': the categories were clearly blurred in line with indiscriminate senses of foreignness, strongly shaped by 'American' culture, increasingly pervasive in German nationalist ideologies. The review evokes a sense of weariness, of nerves worn out by too much interchangeable, mass-produced material. By emphasising the fatiguing modern condition it engenders, Schliepe resisted any suggestion that this work could be vital or regenerative of the spirit – qualities bound up with 'true' Germanic aesthetics. This review represents the reflexive conditioning of French symphonic discourse at its most insidiously desultory, characterised by non-engagement. Honegger's symphony was denigrated as a mere 'novelty', a word which places it in the highly subordinated category of *Trivialliteratur*: 'The rejection of the

---

[17] See Schliepe, 'Neuntes Philharmonisches Konzert'; Strobel, '9. Furtwängler-Konzert'.

[18] Schliepe, 'Neuntes Philharmonisches Konzert'.

[19] '[H]inter diesem Orchestersatz mit dem mystisch-hochtrabenden Titel verbirgt sich nichts weiter als ein Stück jener Allerweltsmusik, wie sie alle dem Zeitprogramm mit Haut und Haar verschriebenen "internationalen" Komponisten massenhaft gemixt haben und nach den bekannten Ingredienzien weiter mixen werden, bis das Publikum dessen endgültig überdrüssig ist. Unser deutsches Publikum ist so weit.' Ibid.

French novelty was polite, but emphatic.'[20] More damningly still, that 'novelty' was 'French'. Schliepe elevated the discerning German public above it all.

Slightly more nuanced in his appraisal than Schliepe, Heinrich Strobel, writing in the *Berliner Börsen-Courier*, nonetheless had a strong tendency to essentialise on national terms. We saw this in Chapter 2, too, in his writing on Pfitzner – commenting on the Symphony in C♯ minor, he wrote: '[The work] is filled with a deep and authentic Romantic sensibility; it is the expression of a personality in which contemplative, brooding, and sensitive qualities synthesise uniquely.'[21] Strobel had some faint praise for the Honegger premiere, but throughout his review he constructed an antagonism between French surface and German depth which implicitly dismissed any engagement with the work on 'symphonic' terms – that is to say, via harmonic, thematic, and formal development. Although his opening remarks on Honegger's national influences sounded only cursory, they reveal deeply entrenched oppositional geopolitical sentiment: 'The work shows off the best side of the highly able Swissman, in whom German and French elements strive against each other in the most peculiar ways: a rhythmist of vigorous origins, and a colourist of unusual inventiveness.'[22] His world-view did not appear to permit the synthesis of nationalist essentialisms, which instead strive against one another. Strobel thus distanced Honegger from Germanic and specifically symphonic aesthetic traditions by emphasising his proficiency in the fields of rhythmic invention and orchestral colour. Such surface-level musical parameters did not stir the mechanisms of deep organic musical logic. And Strobel extended these discourses to shape the character of the composer himself: although Honegger was admittedly 'highly able', Strobel followed with a backhanded compliment by describing him as 'versatile and not particularly self-critical'.[23] Again, these are tropes bound up with superficiality, in contrast to brooding Germanic spiritual depth. His skilful use of colour became a problem for Honegger elsewhere in the reception, too. The *Berliner Lokal Anzeiger* emphasised it even more negatively as the irritant presence of 'brash colours', alongside 'florid sounds' and 'harmonic

---

[20] 'Die Ablehnung der französischen Novität war höflich, aber deutlich.' Ibid.

[21] Heinrich Strobel, 'Pfitzner dirigiert', *Berliner Börsen-Courier*, 31 March 1933.

[22] 'Das Werk zeigt den hochbegabten Schweizer, in dem deutsche und französische Elemente in der merkwürdigsten Weise gegeneinander streben, von seiner besten Seite: als einen Rhythmiker von starker Ursprünglichkeit, als einen Koloristen von ungewöhnlicher Originalität.' Strobel, '9. Furtwängler-Konzert'.

[23] Ibid. ('wendige und keineswegs besonders selbstkritische').

inconsistency' that 'ruined the taste for listeners', and the subtext, at least in part, was the French influence.[24]

Evidently, some reviews were highly dismissive and consequently afforded historians easy opportunities to report the work's cold reception in Berlin. Although these illuminate acutely nostalgic Germanic anxieties about the corruption of symphonic depth and purity, they nonetheless give only a one-sided, incomplete sense of the response to the work. By contrast, other critics sought overtly to draw continuities through Furtwängler's programme, stressing Honegger's embeddedness in Germanic aesthetic traditions.[25] Despite the way the work sought to relate itself to a self-conscious idea of modernity, making it an easy target for the prejudices of the reviews already seen, the historical allusions in the work, completely missed by commentators like Schliepe, were rich, multilayered, and frequently distinctly Germanic. The following brief cross-section of how some other reviews introduced Honegger's work to their readers – Hans Pringsheim writing in a journal at the more conservative end of the spectrum, *Die Allgemeine Musikzeitung*; and a figure more progressive in outlook, Einstein, in the *Berliner Tageblatt* – uncovers a set of responses that were far from 'icy', and took risks. Einstein and Pringsheim are just two of the several commentators who engaged thoughtfully and seriously with the work on symphonic terms. As Einstein ended his review: 'It is a peculiar and exciting – yet certainly not aggressive – work, that one would gladly hear again.'[26]

Mouvement symphonique n° 3, as the title indicates, is technically a single movement, but, as both Pringsheim and Einstein argued, it can be heard as two symphonic movements coupled together.[27] The first, Allegro marcato, is in sonata form and built from four themes. Roughly equal in length to the first half, the Adagio second movement is dominated by the quasi-vocal timbre of the lyrical solo saxophone, accompanied by *Trauermarsch* gestures in the strings. Pringsheim argued that despite the

---

[24] 'Klangliche Ueberladenheit, grelle Farben, und harmonische Ungereimtheit verderben dem Zuhörer ... den Geschmack.' G[?], 'Klassik, Romantik, Moderne: 9. Furtwängler-Konzert', *Berliner Lokal Anzeiger*, 28 March 1933, 3.

[25] Otto Steinhagen, 'Das Musikleben der Gegenwart: Berlin', *Die Musik* 25 (1933): 619–21, 620. Note also the continuities drawn in the title of G[?], 'Klassik, Romantik, Moderne: 9. Furtwängler-Konzert'.

[26] 'Es ist ein merkwürdiges, erregendes und doch nicht aggressives Werk, das man gern nochmals zu hören bekäme.' Alfred Einstein, 'Vorletztes Philharmonisches Konzert, *Berliner Tageblatt*, 28 March 1933.

[27] Ibid.; Hans Pringsheim, 'Aus dem Berliner Musikleben', *Die Allgemeine Musikzeitung*, 7 April, 1933, 208.

reference to and development of motivic materials from the sonata form of what he designated the principal movement (*Hauptsatz*), the Adagio's completely different, funereal character, its introduction of a new meandering saxophone melody, and its self-generative thematic expansions ('*eigenwüchsigen Ausdehnung*') qualified it as far more than simply an extended accompanying coda.[28]

The final gestures dissipate into nothing, and both Pringsheim and Einstein drew weighty comparisons with Beethoven's *Eroica*, a cornerstone of the Germanic symphonic tradition, with Pringsheim evocatively describing its 'disintegration into nothing' ('*Zerflattern ins Nichts*') as palpably evocative of Beethoven's work.[29] Einstein's emphasis seemed to be even less explicitly on the musical parallels and more on the sociopolitical ones. Enigmatically calling *Mouvement symphonique* 'a modernised *Eroica*', he appeared to point to how Honegger manipulated Beethoven's heroic narrative of individual subjectivity to reflect contemporary sociopolitical anxieties.[30] Perhaps Einstein was suggesting that Honegger's ambiguous two-movement work was modelled on the failure of symphonic realisation found in works like Schubert's 'Unfinished' Symphony. Teasing out this allusion further, perhaps its inability to stretch to three or four movements and failure to achieve a sense of symphonic apotheosis was, then, indicative of the newly contemporary crisis surrounding Enlightenment notions of subjectivity and the role of dialectical thinking in this process.

Pursuing Einstein's insinuation, the rest of this chapter suggests that the 'absolute' title concealed a sociopolitical exploration of a nexus of cultural anxieties about post-Enlightenment rationalism[31] and its destructive

---

28 Pringsheim, 'Aus dem Berliner Musikleben', 208 ('Formal betrachtet sind es eigentlich eher zwei zusammengekoppelte Sinfoniesätze: ein lebhaft bewegter, rhythmisch sehr energischer "Sonatensatz" mit drei Themengruppen und ein Adagio von mehr rhapsodischer Haltung, das man, ungeachtet des Aufklingens motivischen Materials aus dem Hauptsatz, schon wegen der ganz neuen, weit geschwungenen Saxophonmelodie, mit der es anhebt, des völlig anderen, trauermarchartigen Grundcharakters – das Zerflattern ins Nichts ist fühlbar der Eroica nachempfunden – und nicht zuletzt der eigenwüchsigen Ausdehnung beim besten Willen nicht mehr als zugehörige "Coda" empfinden kann.')

29 See ibid.

30 Einstein, 'Vorletztes Philharmonisches Konzert', 4 ('und zwar einer modernisierten Eroica').

31 Observed by contemporary cultural theorists like Kracauer, Theodor Adorno, and Max Horkheimer, anxieties about rationalism – a cultural impulse inherently bound up with the intellectual revolutions of the Enlightenment – were acute in Weimar Germany. Rationalism was considered a destructive cultural force whose increasing and pervasive effects commentators highlighted as impacting upon many spheres: the military, the capitalist economy, the body, the industrialisation of the workplace and dissection of labour, the culture industry. See, for instance, Max Horkheimer and Theodor W. Adorno, *Dialectic of*

effects on selfhood. It then returns to look at the positive strands of the reception in slightly more detail, asking why, in the main, they failed to engage with the sociopolitical reading. Symphonies are fundamentally bound up with liberal Enlightenment values – in particular, it is worth noting that Beethoven explicitly dedicated his Third Symphony to democratic ideals. Typical of Beethoven's heroic style,[32] as Scott Burnham has shown, is the symphonic narrative of subjective 'becoming'. Yet Honegger's '*Zerflattern ins Nichts*' cuts it off midway, re-inscribing the *Eroica* narrative in light of the crises of the early 1930s. After all, the individual's demise forms the subject matter of the *Eroica*'s second movement. My argument here builds on an interpretative direction taken by Geoffrey Spratt. Speculating about *Mouvement symphonique n° 3*'s politics, Spratt foregrounds Honegger's comments about what he aimed to thematise in his oratorio *Cris du monde*, as reflected upon in *I Am a Composer*: 'Some saw a communist work in it, others a reactionary hymn. Actually, in it I gave expression to the revolt of the individual against the crowd that crushes him – a timely subject.'[33] The Symphonic Movement seems to be about modern selfhood and about exploring the distractions and restrictions against which it struggles – technology, mechanisation, the military – and in relation to which it ultimately fails to achieve authentic self-realisation. It reifies spaces of subjective interiority as a balm for the incessant pressures of modern, mechanised life. In the end, though, Honegger's stance on these issues remained ambiguous: throughout the work, he seemed simultaneously enthralled and appalled by the impulses he articulated. Of course, these issues were incisive, as Honegger composed the work in the mood of political turmoil that pervaded 1932, but they had only become more provocative since the National Socialists came to power in January 1933.

Body, Mass, Machine: Allegro marcato

Cris du monde had a political message about authentic self-realisation. It shows manifold modern pressures denying the individual the mental and emotional space to achieve true knowledge of the self. The project was inspired by John Keats's 'Hymn to Solitude', and Honegger asked his close

---

Enlightenment, trans. John Cumming (London: Allen Lane, 1973); Thomas W. Levin, 'Introduction', in Kracauer, *Mass Ornament*, 1–30.

[32] See Scott G. Burnham, *Beethoven Hero* (Princeton: Princeton University Press, 1995).

[33] Spratt, *Music of Arthur Honegger*, 244, citing Tappolet, *Arthur Honegger*, 108.

friend René Bizet to write the text. *Cris du monde* is in three parts. The first portrays the 'Voices of Morning' and the commotion of the city awaking: the sounds of factories, cries of harried workers, calls to arms, calls of suffering. In the second, we hear the voices of the mountains, the sea, open spaces, and distant lands offering humankind a space of respite and solace. Finally, the third – 'Voices of Night' – returns us to the frenzy of modernity. Workers leave the factories; cinemas, trains, trams, and wirelesses clamour for attention; and the remorseless cycle begins once more as night transitions to day.[34] Harry Halbreich summarised the oratorio's message as 'a prophetic warning about matters that then had no name ... quality of life, the environment, pollution, enlistment, mass culture ... in short, everything that contributes to the destruction of the soul and the death of the individual'.[35] Bizet's libretto was animated by contrasts. Spratt summarises it thus: 'a perfect opposition of the need for solitude with the whole ethos of the modern world; a philosophical argument which is full of vivid contrasts, driven by a thrusting force of immense power and consistent energy but totally unified through its large-scale block structure'.[36]

Evidently, in the very late 1920s and early 1930s Honegger had been worrying – at least artistically – about selfhood in modernity. In 1932, however, as an explicit commission for Berlin, it seems *Mouvement symphonique* presented Honegger with the opportunity to particularise those anxieties to the German political context, and to focus them through the lens of symphonic discourses, particularly the genre's dialectical form. I suggest that in *Mouvement symphonique n° 3*, developing preoccupations from his work on *Cris du monde*, Honegger sought to explore the contradictions that shaped notions of subjectivity in modernity, and sonata principles offered a way of refining the musical architecture he had developed to mirror the block structure of Bizet's text. The symphony also provided a more 'abstract' form for investigating the crisis of modernity – a crisis, indeed, that some contemporary cultural theorists rooted in a surplus of rationality and in impulses towards false abstraction that were destructive tendencies for 'authentic' selfhood.[37] The work, then, seems to allow an analysis of several impulses that act to cripple self-determinism to play out: the militarisation, the politicisation, and the

---

[34] For a more detailed introduction to *Cris du monde*, see Spratt, *Music of Arthur Honegger*, 201–22.

[35] Halbreich, *Arthur Honegger*, 417. cited in Deborah Mawer, '"Dancing on the Edge of the Volcano": French Music in the 1930s', in *French Music since Berlioz*, ed. Richard Langham Smith and Caroline Potter (Aldershot: Ashgate, 2006), 249–80, 249.

[36] See Spratt, *Music of Arthur Honegger*, 202.   [37] See Levin, 'Introduction', especially 16–19.

industrial and mechanical rationalisation of the individual. All of this is to suggest that Honegger's Symphonic Movement investigates the individual's absorption into the collective. As will be argued in the next section, however, the Adagio second part then gestured towards a spiritual antidote to 'the death of the individual' put forward in the first.

Channelling the mood of 'Voices of Morning', the Allegro is chaotic, and brings to mind Weill's comment about the musical content of his Symphony No. 2: 'the opposite of pastoral'. Yet, a more abstract form of *Cris du monde* requires a different critical framework for reading how it explores these issues of modernity. Without a concrete programme, I suggest that holding up the Allegro alongside some of the themes in Kracauer's *The Mass Ornament* illuminates some cultural anxieties about the shifting relationships between body, machine, and mass that seem to inform Honegger's work, because it deals with a cultural phenomenon about mass shapes and abstract patterns relevant to the genre. Kracauer pointed to the dissolution and dissection of individual dancers within the kinds of mass spectacles performed in stadiums across the world, whereby they became mere anonymous components of 'girl clusters, whose movements are demonstrations of mathematics', no longer of human erotic or spiritual impulses.[38] The Allegro also invites this comparison hermeneutically. For example, organised mass bodily motion is referenced from the outset by the march tempo marked simultaneously 12/8 and 4/4. In addition, the movement is interwoven with 'modern dance' rhythms, as Hugo Leichtentritt's programme note put it.[39] Evoking a military band, the instrumentation, too, references the ordered mass, with heavy brass and woodwind, including saxophone; indeed, this suggests a parallel with the march section in the third movement of Weill's symphony. But Leichtentritt's relatively dry commentary on the Allegro in the programme note did not acknowledge any extra-musical preoccupations beyond the dance rhythms. Instead, he focused on the manipulations of sonata form, the thematic developments, and descriptions of the instrumentation.[40] Kracauer's text, then, provides a theoretical entry point that mediates the presumed abstraction of absolute music and the physical concerns of the local environment, offering a perspective on how 'abstract mass effects'

---

[38] Kracauer, *Mass Ornament*, 76.

[39] Berlin Philharmonic Archive, P 1933 27.3, concert programme, 3–5 (hereafter Leichtentritt Concert Programme). Leichtentritt was also forced to leave Germany in 1933 and was invited by Harvard University to emigrate to the United States.

[40] Ibid.

obscured more immediate, tangible concerns about the body, and about selfhood and its absorption within the collective.

The sublation of the individual within mass motion and mass formations, a sense of modern mechanised industry and its effect on the individual, and the powerlessness of the individual in the face of mass hysteria all appear critical concerns of the Allegro. The first two bars articulate a C♯ minor ascending scale of accented triplet quavers (see Example 5.1).[41] As the layers and registers increase, tension mounts, and there is almost a feeling of something with regularly spaced gears and cogs winding up into action. The passage establishes the tonal domain, but also the march idiom and its associations of human regimentation. Alluding perhaps to the metronomic beating of a snare drum, with sharp, biting ricochets, the march idiom also reminds us of the state's violent militarisation of the body. Even on a visual level, the dual time signature articulates a highly rationalised temporal space.

The fact that the work is linked to both *Rugby* and *Pacific 231* strengthens the reading that it mediates body and machine – the mechanical train and the muscular, sweating bodies of the sportsmen – and the tonal area of C♯ worked as a hinge throughout the trio of Symphonic Movements. *Mouvement symphonique n° 3*'s C♯ minor tonality builds coherence with the C♯ tonal centre of *Pacific 231*, which ends in C♯ minor and whose development section is a forty-two-note cantus firmus grounded on C♯. Sometimes, however, it is foregrounded in a way that was more oblique. Although unison C♯s are the first notes sounded in *Rugby*'s introduction, the main key of *Rugby* is D major; here, Honegger emphasises the leading note to describe 'the tension of anticipation' before the sports match begins.[42] Halbreich observes that C♯ was one of Honegger's favourite keys.[43] As noted in discussion of Pfitzner's symphony in Chapter 2, the other major canonical referents for C♯ minor are Beethoven's String Quartet Op. 131 and Mahler's Symphony No. 5, and the same affective connotations of fraught brightness as observed in relation to Pfitzner's work can be detected in *Mouvement symphonique n° 3*'s atmosphere. It generates an unease in relationship to the subject matter.

Characterised by dotted rhythms and wide leaps, the main theme is then heard at bar 3 in the first violins (Example 5.1) – for Marcel Delannoy, pent-up and potently 'aggressive, tense like a muscle'[44] – against a countertheme in the trumpets. This instrumentation exacerbates the sense of militarism; indeed, the supposed main theme has to fight to be heard

---

[41] Similarly, Halbreich describes it as 'two measures of violent scales'. Halbreich, *Arthur Honegger*, 357.
[42] Ibid., 355.   [43] Ibid., 351.   [44] Delannoy, *Honegger*, 148.

Example 5.1 Allegro marcato, bars 1–10. Arthur Honegger, *Mouvement symphonique n° 3 pour orchestre* (Paris: Éditions Maurice Senart, 1933), 1–3. All examples from Honegger's *Mouvement symphonique n° 3* are reproduced by kind permission of Hal Leonard Europe BV (Italy).

Example 5.1 (Cont.)

against it. Consistent with Spratt's reading of the work as a whole, a sense of struggle thus characterises even the initial statement of the first theme. The grotesque militarism becomes even more apparent at figure 1, with the introduction of whirling horns, fanfare-esque semiquaver triplet trumpet

Example 5.1 (Cont.)

interjections, and parodic overuse of violently shrill, trilling woodwinds (and piccolo in particular) at extremes of register – all effects that stress the mechanistic aspects of the instruments themselves and generate a sense of inhuman presence.

Figure 2 introduces the driving second theme, heard in the basses, which intensifies over seven bars (Example 5.2). The layered escalation through the registers creates a relatively crude sense of something advancing. This is interrupted by jarring motion in the strings, accompanied by an elongated, soaring sostenuto melody in the woodwinds at figure 3, perhaps a moment of subjective freedom from the cacophony. Figure 6 brings in a new theme in 3/4, identified as the exposition's fourth motive in the Berlin programme note, initially heard in the horns and supported by the strings digging into each of the beats of the new tempo with repeated down-bow gestures. The development section that follows principally works with this theme. A sense of growing hysteria builds to a climactic restatement of the opening theme at figure 10, with the theme now appropriated by unison trumpets, the same instrument that had almost drowned out its initial rendition at bar 3.

After a pounding two-bar bass drum lead-in accentuated by down-beat cymbal crashes, the Allegro's recapitulation culminates at figure 16 in a *sempre forte* tutti which then crescendos to *fortissimo*. A fragment of the main theme is insistently, even obsessively, repeated in the upper strings until it loses any sense of meaning (see Example 5.3). Instead, it becomes automated, like a political slogan at fever pitch. The increasingly frenzied repetition and the chromatically ascending register of its apex is almost unbearable. Finally, four flutter-tongued glissandi upwards on irregular beats in the trombones ratchet up the accumulated tension. There are some clear comparisons to be drawn between the very end of Weill's Symphony No. 2 and the end of the Allegro, not least the grotesque use of trombones. Again, as in the march in Weill's third movement, Honegger creates a musical analogue for the synchronism of militarised bodies, or bodies participating in any kind of co-ordinated mass spectacle, at once alluring, terrifying, and ridiculous. That first musical theme is wrenched apart – obliterated, even – within the furore of the unthinking mass, assimilating the individual with the collective.

Yet, a reader would guess none of this from glancing over the programme note. Describing it – in a bid, perhaps, to focus attention on the politically more neutral quality of the sound rather than its potentially inflammatory programmatic associations – as a 'shimmering climax' ('*diesem glanzvollen Höhepunkt*'), Leichtentritt steers well clear of any extra-musical signifying territory, concentrating instead on the passage's impressive technical work: 'This third main section climaxes in a tutti-episode in which the main theme no. 1 unfolds through the whole orchestra, artfully led in octave canon in the

Example 5.2 Allegro marcato, figure 2, first eight bars, second theme. Honegger, *Mouvement symphonique n° 3*, 6–8.

Example 5.2 (Cont.)

Example 5.3 Allegro marcato, figure 16 to end of movement, reduced score showing string parts and trombones, omitting woodwinds, percussion, and other brass. Honegger, *Mouvement symphonique n° 3*, 46–9.

violins and basses.'[45] Arguably more significant, however, seems to be the way in which it crystallises an accretion of energy through the Allegro, which ultimately moves beyond musical argument to become meaningless noise. Indeed, this recapitulation seems utterly unhinged, the final effect being of perilously balancing over a cliff edge, with potential energy in such surfeit that the whole enterprise might come crashing down at any moment.

The Allegro musically creates a seeming objectivity, a brash and ordered sound-world which provides a dialectical antithesis to the Adagio's more subjective mode. Despite the largely condescending tone of the rest of his *Berliner Börsen-Courier* review, Strobel conceded that 'a rhythmic strength and a musical energy is operating here that one doesn't encounter in contemporary music all too frequently'. He also observed that 'the sharp edges to the sound-world in the first part may alienate some listeners', unintentionally striking upon a critical point about register: the Allegro seeks to distance its audience, who witness, but are not necessarily subject to, its musical onslaught.[46] The Allegro establishes a space of alienation, aligning Honegger's symphony with the alienating registers explored in Weill's Second Symphony, and differentiating it from Pfitzner's more romantically immersive exploration of the interplay between subjective and collective space.

Subjective Interiority in the Adagio

If those upward glissandi left the symphony at a point of maximal fervour and tension, then the beginning of the perplexing Adagio hermeneutically signals something quite different. The music dissolves into 'a kind of symphonic fantasy' dominated by the entrance of the solo saxophone, whose character Leichtentritt, in the original programme, described as 'noble' and 'broadly sweeping', commenting, like some critics, that the accompanying figures take on the character of a funeral march.[47]

---

[45] 'Dieser dritte Hauptteil gipfelt in einer Tutti-Episode das Hauptthema Nr. 1 in größter Klangentfaltung des ganzen Orchesters kunstvoll geführt im Kanon der Oktave, in Geigen und Bässen.' Leichtentritt Concert Programme, 5.

[46] 'Hier eine rhythmische Kraft und eine musikalische Energie wirkt, die man in der zeitgenössischen Musik nicht allzu häufig antrifft. . . . Die klanglichen Schärfen des bewegten Teils mögen manches Ohr befremden.' Strobel, '9. Furtwängler-Konzert', 2.

[47] 'Eine Art symphonischer Fantasie über die verschiedenen Motive des ganzen Stückes, voll gewählter Reize der Klangfarbenmischung, reich an Feinheiten der Kontrapunktik. Den Anfang des Adagio beherrscht das Saxophon in einem noblen, breit ausladenden Solo, weiterhin abgelöst von den Violinen. Die Begleitrhythmen nehmen hier den Charakter eines Trauermarsches an.' Leichtentritt Concert Programme, 5.

Adopting a more poetic register that contrasts with his stricter formal description of the Allegro – a mode of writing congruous with the Adagio's fantasy atmosphere – Leichtentritt continued: 'At the end only a shadow of this rhythm remains. All stressed parts of the bar become pauses; only the unstressed parts of the bar reverberate, as if fading away into the dusk.'[48]

Indeed, interpretations of the Adagio vary wildly in the secondary literature. Delannoy has argued that it provides an aesthetic counterweight to the tension of the first movement.[49] This reading seems unconvincing, however: the dissipation of energy at the saxophone entry is too abrupt for it persuasively to perform this function. Insofar as the two parts have radically different characters, I argue that their relationship is dialectically antagonistic, not harmoniously balanced. The ending has proved especially vexing. For Delannoy, throughout the narrative of the work, 'it is the saxophone's song that sweetly triumphs'.[50] For Halbreich, by contrast, the ending to this 'vast epilogue' – meaning the coda, from bar 327 – represents 'a veritable death agony of sound, prefiguring the "conclusion muffled as though in terror" of Honegger's Fifth Symphony'.[51] Delannoy hints at the idea that the Adagio represents an arena exploring subjective interiority, but asserts that this area of the work ultimately wins out over the Allegro; Halbreich's nihilist reading seems closer to the mark.

The sensory assault of the Allegro evoked a brash outwardness, objective, massive, mechanical, and ultimately dehumanising. By contrast, the Adagio turns inwards to invoke internal space, retreating to a restorative world to counteract those rationalist tendencies – referencing the oppositional symphonic tendency towards a universalised sense of interiority. Narratives about the subject, of course, are a mainstay of Germanic symphonic criticism, within which Beethoven's music generated a particularly influential 'mythology of selfhood';[52] the Berlin critics alluded to this with their *Eroica* references.

The words of Leichtentritt, Delannoy, and Halbreich above illustrate how previous Honegger scholars and critics have gestured towards the notion that the Adagio represents a subjectively dominated realm. But

---

[48] 'Am Schluss bleibt nur noch ein Schatten dieser Rhythmen übrig, Pausen auf allen betonten Taktteilen, so daß nur die unbetonten Taktteile nachschlagen, wie wesenlos im Dämmerlicht verschwindend.' Ibid.

[49] Delannoy, *Honegger*, 148.   [50] Ibid., 149.   [51] Halbreich, *Arthur Honegger*, 357–8.

[52] Holly Watkins, *Metaphors of Depth in German Musical Thought: From E. T. A. Hoffmann to Arnold Schoenberg* (Cambridge: Cambridge University Press, 2011), 3, citing Burnham, *Beethoven Hero*, 118.

I further suggest that the musical and hermeneutic space of the Adagio presents a core problem, because it is not formally acknowledged in the title of the work: after all, Honegger describes it as a Symphonic Movement, not multiple Movements. As already seen, the contemporary reviewers who analysed the formal structure – Pringsheim and Einstein – were unsatisfied with the status of the Adagio as an ancillary coda, suggesting instead that it represented something closer to a symphonic second movement in its own right. Seeming to fall somewhere between the two, the Adagio becomes an ambiguous para-generic space of the kind identified by Hepokoski and Darcy, and fulfils a corresponding function.[53]

This prompts the question of why the Adagio is not formally acknowledged in the title of the work, and what the failure to articulate the nature of its identity and function as musical space does to alter that nature? For one, it echoes modernity's increasing renunciation of the subjective realm, marginalising the space and everything that is articulated within it. But perhaps more significant is its critical function. A space that is not acknowledged gains a certain freedom. That freedom allows it to act as a space of commentary and critique in a way that permits it to reflect upon, transcend, and transform the space of the Allegro. Important here is how the passage musically invokes historical generic spaces that had just this interiorised reflective function, standing outside narrative time. And the failure to acknowledge the second movement in the title ultimately raises the potentially destabilising question of which movement is the real symphony.

The hermeneutic role played by the saxophone is vital to a reading of the Adagio as an exploration of subjective interiority, and to understanding its role as a critical space that reflects on the Allegro. The timbral world at the opening of the Adagio is one closely evocative of the human voice, using only middle registers: violas, bassoons, saxophone, and cellos. These warm and welcoming timbres invite the listener in. Halbreich observes that Honegger seldom uses saxophone in his purely orchestral works, although it frequently appears in his stage works and oratorio, perhaps heightening the allusion to voice.[54] In comparison to the Allegro's impersonal timbral attack and sheen, the Adagio's scale is more human, potentially even suggesting a chamber space – to draw another parallel with the manipulation of space in Pfitzner's C# minor symphony. There is something

---

[53] James Hepokoski and Warren Darcy, *Elements of Sonata Theory: Norms, Types, and Deformations in the Late-Eighteenth-Century Sonata* (New York: Oxford University Press, 2006), 282.

[54] Halbreich, *Arthur Honegger*, 357.

fantastical about the relaxed tone of the saxophone, in particular – perhaps because of its otherworldly generic foreignness within the symphony.

At figure 17, the downward-plunging arc of the first bar-and-a-half of the saxophone solo thus literally begins by receding inwards (Example 5.4).

Example 5.4 Adagio, figures 17 to 18. Honegger, *Mouvement symphonique n° 3*, 50.

Example 5.4 (Cont.)

Lowering the listener down into a new kind of musical or generic space, contrasting with the ascending motion of the introduction to the Allegro, it articulates a microcosm of the fourteen-bar melodic line's broader two-octave melodic descent. Given the quality of the Adagio as a symphonic 'fantasy', perhaps that space represents the intimate sphere of individual consciousness. The conjunct, yearning motions within that overall melodic arc, typical of the interweaving melodic lines that characterise the whole Adagio, likewise signify such subjective space, recalling the subjective striving located by contemporary reviewers in similar melodic lines in the first movement of Pfitzner's work (see Chapter 2).[55] Honegger's harmonic language is dependent on suspensions and on sparse, but closely harmonised, chords that again connote voice. The generally static harmonic motion generates a reflective stability. Nonetheless, the accompanying rhythmic echoes of Wagner's 'Siegfrieds Tod' in *Götterdämmerung* serve as a reminder that this is a *Trauermarsch*, a death march for that subjective realm.

The way Honegger tended to connect the saxophone with church music is significant. The scoring of solo woodwind over strings heard at the beginning of the Adagio is evocative of Bach's cantatas, and the reflective mode of the arias in particular, which had the function of presenting a moment of pause for internal reflection. Indeed, the use of obbligato woodwinds signalled the arrival and function of this generic mode: the saxophone then becomes a modern analogue for the plaintive cries of the oboe d'amore. Honegger was tapping into a deep-rooted historicism, invoking an interiority linked to spirituality, a balm for the harsh drives of modernity expounded in the Allegro. The Adagio in the *Easter Oratorio* seems a particular point of reference, strengthened by the counterpoint with the bassoon, the other solo woodwind it uses. Yet the saxophone also codifies subjectivity and self-expression by referencing jazz, a shorthand for the US American democratic values idealised by German *Individualismus*. Canonic referents are blended with the contemporary in a multilayered tapestry of historical allusion, with the aim of foregrounding, through voice, an alternative image of the human body to that painted in the Allegro. In the Adagio, the human body becomes something singular, sacred, and in need of protection against the mass and against industrial and military forces.

The ending of the Adagio likewise supports this reading. If, as quasi-coda, the Adagio presents a para-generic space offering commentary on

---

[55] Hans Sachße, 'Hans Pfitzner: Symphonie in cis-moll', *Zeitschrift für Musik* 6 (1933): 559–61, 560.

what has gone before, then perhaps, to quote Pringsheim, the 'Zerflattern ins Nichts' of the closing bars – the way the music completely dissipates into nothing – focuses the frantic, overpowering dynamism of the Allegro through a new lens, spotlighting its effect on the subject (see Example 5.5). Whereas the first subject of the Allegro found itself competing for an unimpeded voice from its very first statement at bar 3, before ultimately being drowned out and losing its identity within the militaristic cacophony at figure 16, the Adagio shifts the focus emphatically to give that which is lost in the narrative of the Allegro – individual subjective space – prolonged attention. Once the Allegro's public, monumental symphonic space is inverted to spotlight the subjective perspective within, Honegger is able to re-narrate the Allegro in a fantasy mode. He then foregrounds the concurrent erosion of subjective space that underpins the Allegro's symphonic bombast, and leaves the symphony's subjective narrative unsatisfyingly incomplete, ineffectually fading away into nothing. Fragments of motivic themes from the Allegro are interspersed throughout the Adagio, underlining that the two musical spaces are entwined and mutually illuminate one another. For instance, the first bar of the violin 1 main theme at bar 3 of the Allegro marcarto (see Example 5.1) surfaces again at the beginning of the Adagio as an accompanying gesture in the cellos beginning two bars after figure 17, and then in the double basses two bars before figure 18 (see Example 5.4). These are the most discernible quotations, but more dream-like transformations and fragmentations, as if the symphonic theme is only half remembered, come in the other accompanying lines (bassoons and violas), with frequent dotted rhythms, triplets, and octave (or – now – two octave) leap descents characteristic of that theme. The taut, aggressive, high-pitched symphonic material is loosened, relaxed out over a much broader, deeper pitch space. Indeed, this reading helps address the problem of how the two spaces are formally connected; as we saw, contemporary commentators had difficulty formally accounting for the degree and quality of thematic referentiality between the two parts, which left the Adagio positioned clearly as neither coda nor second movement.[56]

Perhaps the most curious feature of this work is how the music simply evaporates into nothing at the close of the Adagio (see Example 5.5). According to this reading, that ending thus signals the dissipation of the subjective realm and the dissolution of the individual in response to the kind of incessant onslaught of political hyperbole, militaristic collectivity, and frenetic mechanistics manifested in the Allegro – reflecting the crisis of

[56] See, for instance, Pringsheim, 'Aus dem Berliner Musikleben', 208.

Example 5.5 Adagio, figure 20 to end. Honegger, *Mouvement symphonique n° 3*, 57–60.

Example 5.5 (Cont.)

the 'mass ornament'. And although these themes were pressing when Honegger was composing the work in 1932, their urgency only intensified in the context of the National Socialist takeover, as did their political sensitivity. The point Honegger makes by permitting this para-generic, fantasy space of liberal musical play and subjective exploration to evaporate into the silence of the concert hall is deeply troubling. Honegger could not have predicted just how chilling that space would turn out to be on the evening of 31 March, marked by Walter's ousting and the threats of violence there the previous week. In that context, his saxophone solo mourns not only modernity's erosion of subjectivity but the complete breakdown of liberal symphonic values.

Embedding *Mouvement Symphonique N° 3* in Symphonic Discourses

Fascist Germany, then, raised the stakes for hearing the work, increasing the definition and immediacy of the political and social themes with which *Mouvement symphonique* was occupied. Yet, at the Berlin performance, Leichtentritt's programme notes and the concert reviews barely engaged with the extra-musical associations Honegger voiced, instead locating the work in relation to safer questions of symphonic formalism and thematic development. Einstein's and Pringsheim's veiled parallels with the *Eroica*'s second movement, alluding perhaps to its subject matter of death in battle – an extreme form of state annihilation of the individual – were the closest anyone came to acknowledging any suggestions that the music gestured to the preoccupations of modernity. Could the *Eroica* reference have been a coded allusion to the death knell sounding over democracy in the concert hall? If so, it was certainly guarded, easily dismissed as a canonising assimilationist gesture from a peripheralised symphonic nation, France. Name-dropping from the heights of Germanic symphonic aesthetic traditions carried relatively little risk.

No comparable extra-musical parallels surfaced in the vast majority of the reviews, however. Indeed, in the *Berliner Börsen-Courier*, Strobel stated explicitly that this was a work in which Honegger sought to free himself from the programmatic associations that had determined the worldwide success of *Pacific 231* and *Rugby*.[57] For the most part, reviewers engaged much more explicitly with the work's formal elements, and not only

---

[57] Strobel, '9. Furtwängler-Konzert'.

because to do so deflected the question of the work's politics. Many agendas seemed more actively positive: such engagement demonstrated a willingness to situate the work within broad Germanic historical-aesthetic arcs that implicitly elevated it in ways that overlap with the *Eroica* comparisons. This was perhaps most pronounced in Otto Steinhagen's review. In the context of a programme which, he argued, highlighted the close relationship between classical, Romantic, late-Romantic, and contemporary music, he noted how 'the Swissman Honegger, representing the most recent developments, returns to closed sonata form', indicating how deeply steeped '*der Schweizer*' (stressing his Germanic, not French affiliations) was in the richness of this musical history and how fundamentally his work was tethered to earlier traditions.[58] Rather than new music's stylistic rupture, Steinhagen emphasised Honegger's formal continuity with Schumann and Strauss – certainly not pinnacles of the German symphonic canon, but central German musical figures nonetheless.

We heard from Steinhagen in Chapter 2, where he was quoted extolling the metaphysics of Pfitzner's symphony, focusing in particular on the clarity of its intellectual rigour, as opposed to any sentimental excess, and its supposed capacity to yield the 'world of the Self' to the listener. By early 1933, *Die Musik*'s academic credibility was deteriorating and it was fast becoming a mere mouthpiece for official propaganda: the June issue opened with an article by Goebbels.[59] As noted in Chapter 2, *Gleichschaltung* (co-ordination) of the press – the process of centralising, unifying, and standardising print publications – began in the very early weeks of the Nazi administration, although Goebbels' decrees affecting aesthetic criticism came later – first, the *Schriftleitergesetz* of October 1933, controlling who could write aesthetic criticism, and, in 1936, a decree specifically about art criticism (legally termed *Kunstbetrachtung*), controlling what journalists could write. Steinhagen was enamoured of the concert as a whole; carving a place for Honegger's Symphonic Movement within the world of Germanic musical values, the vocabulary in which he couched Honegger's work was not noticeably different from that which grounded

[58] 'Klassisches, Romantisches, Spätromantisches und Gegenwärtiges standen in engster und erkenntnisreicher Beziehung . . . . Der Schweizer Honegger [kehrt] als Vertreter der jüngster Entwicklung wieder zur geschlossenen Sonatenform zurück.' Steinhagen, 'Das Musikleben der Gegenwart', 620.

[59] See Michael Meyer, *The Politics of Music in the Third Reich* (New York: Peter Lang, 1993), 34; see also Fabian R. Lovisa, *Musikkritik im Nationalsozialismus: Die Rolle deutschsprachiger Musikzeitschriften, 1920–1945* (Laaber: Laaber-Verlag, 1993), 21–39.

Pfitzner's symphony within Germanic idealist music aesthetics a few days later. First describing it as bringing 'something unfamiliar, austere, and melodically somewhat inaccessible', he then commended the 'clear and genuine musical vision', suggesting that 'the strength of the logical tectonics and the art of the thematic structure alone should enthral even non-partisan listeners'.[60] Steinhagen drew attention to elements of the work with which he imagined listeners would have difficulty. Yet he framed them positively, as an austere sound-world that challenged the listener to achieve new heights – although he admittedly stopped far short of the promises of Enlightenment he attached to the sense of confrontation in Pfitzner's work. As in his review of the Pfitzner concert, where he had seemed very invested in separating the interiority of the mind from the emotional excesses of the body, he commended musical aspects that are logical, intellectual, or non-sensual, suggesting the moral elevation of immanence and internal mechanism over external manifestation.

A closer look at Pringsheim's review in *Die Allgemeine Musikzeitung*, a relatively conservative journal, shows that it was not only with the *Eroica* reference that he located Honegger's work in Germanic musical discourses. He gestured towards symphonic organicism and intellectualism as he outlined the work's main attributes: 'a certain strength and vitality to the thematic invention, tremendous rhythmic energy, and an elaborately worked-through structure'.[61] These are all nationalistically loaded qualities integral to the Germanic symphony, encapsulating a prominent tension between the rigour and inner purity of academic counterpoint and the vigour of organicist development. Pringsheim draws particularly on qualities of strength, depth, and purity prominent in the discourses surrounding Pfitzner's symphony. But, unsurprisingly given the journal's political and aesthetic sympathies, he also identifies weaknesses in Honegger's musical language, typical of aggressive tendencies in new music, criticising 'the seemingly indissoluble attachment of the composer to the brutal conceptualisations and violations of sound in so-called "new music"'.[62]

---

[60] 'Honeggers hier uraufgeführte Arbeit "Mouvement Symphonique Nr. 3" bringt Ungewohntes, klanglich Herbes, melodisch noch nicht leicht Eingehendes. Aber allein die Kraft der logischen Tektonik, die Kunst der Thematischen Gefüges, musikalisch echt herausgeworfen aus einer klargeschauten Vision müssen den Nichtvoreingenommenen unbedingt packen.' Steinhagen, 'Das Musikleben der Gegenwart', 620.

[61] Pringsheim, 'Aus dem Berliner Musikleben', 208 ('eine gewisse Kraft und Vitalität der thematischen Erfindung, gewaltige rhythmische Energien und kunstvoll durchgearbeitete Aufbau').

[62] Ibid. (die anscheinend unlösliche Verbundenheit des Tondichters mit den brutalen Klangvorstellungen und Klangvergewaltigungen der sogenannten 'Neuen Musik').

So why did Leichtentritt and the reviewers hear – or at least write about – the symphony in the ways that they did? The limitations of the reception as a whole are indicative of a broader theoretical question about the failure to self-determine within developing fascist contexts. Perhaps some critics did not recognise the potential sociopolitical reading; those who did perhaps did not dare express it in print. As politics intensified, the press became more restricted. Critical, then, becomes what is left unsaid. Given the strong nationalist critical tendencies to reject Honegger's work, the mere willingness of many writers to embrace Honegger's symphony within nationalist aesthetic traditions may become politically resistant. Or it may be symptomatic of other impulses entirely. These contexts are exceptionally difficult to unpick – and the question of motivation is especially contentious – but in laying out the criticism more carefully, some groundwork has been done here to help begin to complicate this concert.

Yet, whatever the reason for avoiding *Mouvement symphonique n° 3*'s explicit militarism, its machine allusions, the Adagio's potential status as a modern lament, or, indeed, the programmatic questions raised by the movement's predecessors *Pacific 231* and *Rugby*, reviewers fell back on nationalistically loaded discussion of the 'pure' music, to which the work lent itself easily. The Berlin reception of *Mouvement symphonique n° 3* shows how flexibly German commentators were willing to apply German idealist aesthetic categories as an assimilatory gesture, but equally the ease with which they could close ranks around anything they wanted to label alien. Thus, in contrast to discussion about the symphony as a Germanic cultural export in the intervening chapters, this chapter has considered what happens when that cultural export is re-imported. As a work that shows an outsider looking in at the German symphonic tradition, as well as providing a focus on how German critics attempted to assimilate the world outside the Reich, Honegger's symphony facilitates a shuttling between national perspectives. Examining Honegger's symphony has investigated a trajectory in which the symphonic genre folds back on itself to become a mutable site of cultural transaction within Germany.

'Fading Away into the Dusk'

Like the stance Pfitzner articulated in his symphony heard a few days later, Honegger's position in relation to the themes his symphony explored seems to have been genuinely ambivalent. *Mouvement symphonique n° 3* offers a commentary on absolute music, and, through that commentary, it investigates the ability of the individual to self-determine in spite of industrial modernity's constant onslaught of pressures and distractions. Yet, Honegger's attitude appears at once repelled and enraptured by the destructive modern tendencies he expounds: the military, the industrial machine, and the mass. Rather than thinking about it as deflective, then, *Mouvement symphonique*'s unambiguously 'absolute' title may furnish the key to reading its situation in Berlin in 1933 and its political ambivalence. Delannoy claims that Honegger defended the topic of the work, in contrast to *Pacific 231* or *Rugby*, as 'music itself',[63] an incredibly loaded concept in the German context for which Honegger was writing. To invoke 'absolute' music was to recruit a whole host of discourses and ideologies that for many people would have seemed very immediate in the political and economic climate of the early 1930s – ideas of nationalist purity and liberalist ideals about individual autonomy – but, as with a trick of the light, look away and they just as easily recede behind the abstractions of the 'pure' music.

Perhaps, then, for Honegger the symphonic genre was a sophisticated plane on which simultaneously to engage with and disengage from modernity – but also more specifically Germany, politics, and nationalism – in the same way as the reviewers had. Given that Berlin's elite symphony orchestra, the Berlin Philharmonic, had commissioned the work, Honegger was privileged in the knowledge that his reflections on the German symphonic tradition and the contemporary political situation would be given a potentially influential platform in the heart of the capital. But the commission turned out to be a poisoned chalice, and the capability simultaneously to engage and disengage, rather than reflecting a mealy-mouthed lack of commitment, was instead evidently a vital survival tactic in the dangerous political climate of 1933. In finding himself unable to commit to the work's status, however, paradoxically Honegger himself enacted that same anxiety about authenticity and self-determinism. Clearly these anxieties were keen in 1933, as the freedoms of citizens in Germany were becoming increasingly limited and controlled.

Indeed, Berlin 1933 has emerged from the way reviewers engaged – or were not at liberty to engage – with the work as a key context in which notions surrounding liberal subjectivity were disintegrating at an especially alarming rate. Writing the work in October 1932, Honegger may have been responding to concerns outside Germany about Hitler's party and their effective censorship of cultural and self-expression based on reports by

---

[63] Delannoy, *Honegger*, 148.

those travelling in and out of the country. The cultural proximity of Honegger's Swiss-German background might have predisposed him to be particularly invested in what was going on. Those anxieties are encapsulated in an article by Hans Heinsheimer for the American journal *Modern Music*, in which he referred to the 'increasing political terrorism of the Hitlerites' and how they were 'transforming the picture at the expense of modern music'.[64] In January 1933, he reported that 'the aim of the National Socialists was to push us back to the Middle Ages. ... What has resulted from the tremendous supremacy of a party which has so active and definite a culture program? Their politico-cultural demands are radical. They include not only strong anti-Semitism, but just as much anti-Slav and anti-French feeling; they set up the German superman against the "inferior foreigner".'[65]

Thinking more theoretically about agency, the two-movement form of *Mouvement symphonique* seems to impart a negative dialectical form of musical argument that illuminates the idea of modern subjectivity and its embroilment with the German symphonic tradition. Formally, then, Honegger supplies a meta-commentary on the kinds of tensions embedded within the Germanic symphonic tradition, and with them the ultimately destructive tendencies that contemporary theorists like Theodor Adorno and Max Horkheimer considered entrenched within Enlightenment liberal values.[66] At a structural level, he does this by presenting a thesis (the Allegro) and then a space that seems to antagonise and reflect on that thesis (the Adagio); he makes the incomplete dialectic audible. Likewise, picking up on a theme raised in Chapter 2 on Pfitzner's symphony, perhaps Honegger sheds light on aspects of how absolute music seemed to contain the seeds of the inherently collusive imperatives that paved the way for totalitarian values. Reinhold Brinkmann asks whether 'first traces of [the] totalitarian imbalance at the expense of subjectivity might not already be present in the forced revolutionary form and message' of Beethoven's most canonical symphonic works.[67] In the Allegro, Honegger exposes pent-up aggression, crass hyperbole, and even potential undertones of militarism as embedded within the symphonic tradition, and within its rigid sonata form in particular.

Honegger's Adagio then follows as a lament over the ruins of symphonic utopianism, displaying liberalism and the symphonic project in tatters. Walter Benjamin wrote about the 'ruins of the bourgeoisie', invoking

---

[64] Hans Heinsheimer, 'Nightmare in Germany', *Modern Music* 10 (1933): 115–17, 115.

[65] Ibid., 115–16.   [66] Horkheimer and Adorno, *Dialectic of Enlightenment*.

[67] See Reinhold Brinkmann, 'The Distorted Sublime: Music and National Socialist Ideology – A Sketch', in *Music and Nazism: Art under Tyranny, 1933–1945*, ed. Michael H. Kater and Albrecht Riethmüller (Laaber: Laaber-Verlag, 2003), 43–63, 48.

Honoré de Balzac. 'With the destabilisation of the market economy', he argued, 'we begin to recognise the monuments of the bourgeoisie as ruins before they have crumbled.'[68] Prescient of Vaughan Williams's later epilogue to his Symphony No. 6, which contemporary commentators suggested evoked a post-nuclear wasteland,[69] Honegger leaves us with a post-apocalyptic vision of spiritual corruption and debasement, where the only escape is to turn inwards. Whether, for Honegger, the situation remains salvageable is unclear. He seems to hint at the possibility of a space for spiritual redemption, but equally, in a nihilist gesture, he then dissolves away that space into nothing. To return to the observations Leichtentritt made in his programme note, Honegger ultimately destabilises the rhythms and metric structures that characterised the Adagio, 'as if fading away into the dusk'.[70] If the symphony is one of the Enlightenment's, and liberalism's, archetypal musical genres, then this work gestures towards the wasteland dystopia beyond the point at which faith in those ideals was tenable. *Mouvement symphonique n° 3* offers a glimpse of the ruins of the sovereign palace built on the foundations of the Enlightenment project, a sense of waking to our own destruction, and a despairing threnody for the future. Its eschatology is simultaneously horrifying and compelling.

That 'fading away' makes it a symphony of its time and place, harnessing a cultural moment during which narratives of subjective self-realisation or symphonic apotheosis perhaps seemed impossible to sustain. In failing to achieve a symphonic finale, Honegger's subjective narrative in the symphony becomes simultaneously closer and further away from genuine self-realisation. And as such this work is highly attuned to the cultural and philosophical concerns about selfhood acute in 1933.

---

[68] Benjamin, *The Arcades Project*, trans. Howard Eiland and Kevin McLaughlin (Cambridge, MA: Belknap Press, 1999), 13.

[69] See, for example, Michael Kennedy, *The Works of Ralph Vaughan Williams* (London: Oxford University Press, 1964), 301.

[70] Leichtentritt Concert Programme, 5.

6 | The Right Kind of Symphonist: Florence Price and Kurt Weill

New York and Chicago 1933–4 – London 2020

When Bruno Walter showcased Weill's Symphony No. 2 with the New York Philharmonic at Carnegie Hall on 13 and 14 December 1934, two months after the Concertgebouw premiere, whether the concert work would fare any better across the Atlantic than it had in Amsterdam was likely a pressing concern. The first conspicuous implication of the negative Amsterdam reception was Walter's decision to revise the title, steering away from the celebrated Austro-German symphonic canon. In New York, therefore, rather than 'Symphonische Fantasie: Symphonie No. 1', Weill's symphony was performed under the title *Three Night Scenes: A Symphonic Fantasy*, apparently proposed by Walter on account of the work's 'nocturnal, uncanny, mysterious atmosphere',[1] and presumably in an attempt to respond more sensitively to a set of expectations made clear by the Amsterdam reception about Weill's theatrical background. And yet, despite such window dressing, those who looked harder would find Weill's symphonic ambitions still explicit in the programme note, which launched him as a 'symphonic composer of serious intentions'.[2] Critics were vexed; one voiced a concern that the new title was assumed 'somewhat rashly'.[3] In New York, Weill's hopes of being taken seriously as a symphonist were unravelling before even the possibility, presented by Walter's 'gateway title',[4] had the chance to pique listeners' interests. Yet precisely this uncertainty and prevarication about the work's status and Weill's aspirations emphasise how ideologically freighted the genre was, and how fraught the stakes were for a US audience. It seems that here, in particular, the work could not bear the burden of the title 'symphony'.

Or perhaps it wasn't the work; it was rather Weill who, in New York, could not bear the burden of the status of 'symphonist'. As much as following Weill's symphony to New York is revealing about anxieties around the

---

[1] Programme of the Philharmonic Society of New York, Carnegie Hall, 13–14 December 1934, with programme note by Lawrence Gilman, Weill-Lenya, series 50B (hereafter New York Philharmonic Concert Programme).

[2] Ibid.

[3] Pitts Sanborn, 'Concerts in New York', *Christian Science Monitor*, 22 December 1934, 10.

[4] For a discussion of 'gateway titles', see James Hepokoski, 'Beethoven Reception: The Symphonic Tradition', in *The Cambridge History of Nineteenth-Century Music*, ed. Jim Samson (Cambridge: Cambridge University Press, 2002), 424–59, 445.

symphonic genre in the United States specifically, which bore echoes of similar questioning over the nature of a 'true' symphony in Amsterdam, the more important question here is about Weill himself. And this is what underlining the symphonic genre as an international, rather than national, phenomenon – that is, as this book has done, traversing a constellation of transnational works in this synchronous historical moment – highlights above all else. Following Weill's symphony to New York raises, once again, questions about the right kind of symphonic composer, which mask even more profound questions about what kinds of people – composers, listeners – counted as cultural and political agents; about the cultural mechanisms by which the limits of those groups have been determined; and about how these groups and their policing mechanisms varied in different places. Although the nineteenth-century symphony's Germanic liberalist-idealist ideological legacies concerning selfhood and space play out differently in different contexts, we now return to the matter of how they nonetheless always have a powerful role in the question of determining who it is, ultimately, that is valued – that is, whose voice gets to be heard.

This final chapter considers two quite different symphonic events in parallel: first, Weill performed in 1934, and then, fast-forwarding to almost a century later, Florence Price in 2020. The chapter begins by asking how we should read Weill's New York reception and the concerns it raises in light of where the book has been, and then considers some twentieth- and twenty-first century legacies of the works from 1933 explored along the way. And if the book ends there, with questions about legacies and by suggesting that the symphony is one of many cultural mechanisms complicit in shaping our thoughts on who possesses cultural and political agency, then what, we go on to ask, might the mainstream Price revival of the late 2010s tell us about how these dynamics still play out today?

Weill, New York, 1934

A letter from Walter to Weill reveals that Walter had never been convinced by Symphony No. 2's generic claims. Although he agreed the form was symphonic, the conductor believed that the 'remarkable popular tone, half ironic, half tragic, which constituted the charm of the work' was inappropriate in something described as a symphony.[5] Indeed, Walter had first

---

[5] Ronald Taylor, *Kurt Weill: Composer in a Divided World* (London: Simon & Schuster, 1991), 203 ('Symphonisch ist gewiss die Form, aber keineswegs symphonisch ist ebenso gewiss die

advised against calling it a symphony the very first time he had met Weill to look over the score in Italy in 1934, suggesting instead a variant on the New York title;[6] evidently, his convictions only strengthened after the hostility in Amsterdam. Despite ultimately accepting this re-invention in New York, Weill's insistence in the Concertgebouw programme note that the work was conceived without a programme, as well as his commitment to the title 'symphony' in Amsterdam in spite of Walter's reservations, suggests his unease over introducing a programmatic frame, no matter how vague. This echoes the stance Honegger took regarding his *Mouvement symphonique n° 3*, underlining the disparity in status both composers felt between 'programmatic' and 'absolute' music, and how this was reflected in the level of respect they commanded in the public eye.

Weill's symphony did not create the same stir as it had achieved in Amsterdam. Despite a brief Broadway run, *Die Dreigroschenoper* did not have the same cultural capital in the United States as in the Netherlands. While Weill had been presented in Amsterdam as a composer known for his 'juicy, fluent, and successful music',[7] his introduction in the *Christian Science Monitor* read simply: 'one of the German modernists whose compositions have been little heard in this country'.[8] If American listeners were familiar with anything by him, then it was most likely his radio cantata *Der Lindberghflug*, a performance of which by the Philadelphia Orchestra was broadcast in the United States in 1931; conceivably also *Royal Palace*, *Die Dreigroschenoper*, and *Mahagonny*.[9] Consequently, there are far fewer reviews of the concert on record – and they were even less sympathetic, and quicker to stereotype.[10] And since the work was accompanied by such contradictory messages about the its status and Weill's objectives, in the New York reception the genre discourses are especially complex and

---

Orchesterbehandlung wie Clarinetten solo mit folgender Trompeten Melodie, "Bolero" Rhythmus der Streicher, schliesslich auch die "Begleitung" des Posaunen Solos im 2ten Satz und andere ähnliche Dinge. Schliesslich ist ja gerade der Reiz des Werkes der sonderbare ironische tragisch populär Ton, den Sie mit dem Wort Symphonie irgendwie schamhaft verleugnen.'), original German text cited in Christian Kuhnt, '"Das Gegenteil von Pastorale": Anmerkungen zu Kurt Weills 2. Sinfonie', in *Exilmusik: Komposition während der NS-Zeit*, ed. Friedrich Geiger and Thomas Schäfer (Hamburg: Von Bockel, 1999), 315–32, 319.

[6] Letter from Weill to Maurice Abravanel, August 1934, Weill-Lenya, series 30, 15/6 ('he suggests not to call it a "Symphony" but rather e.g. "3 Scenes for Orchestra" or something like that, since the music is so dramatic') (trans. Weill-Lenya Research Center).

[7] 'Concertgebouw', *N. Rott. GT* (Rotterdam Gazette?), 12 October 1934 (trans. Josephine Kahn).

[8] Sanborn, 'Concerts in New York'.   [9] New York Philharmonic Concert Programme.

[10] Kowalke has also summarised these reviews from the New York performance and concludes that, as in Amsterdam, with limited knowledge of Weill's output the American newspapers showed no awareness of Weill's 'aesthetic or musical goals'. Kim H. Kowalke, *Kurt Weill in Europe* (Michigan: Ann Arbor, 1979), 87.

difficult to untangle. Critics were unsure whether it was a symphony or a series of light orchestral vignettes. The programming didn't give any strong clues either, positioned as it was immediately before the concert's interval, after Handel's Concerto in D major for Orchestra and Organ (featuring Zoltan Kurthy) and Mozart's 'Haffner' Symphony in D major. The key of Weill's work was anomalous – the second half of the concert clearly restored D major, with soloist Bronislaw Huberman performing Beethoven's Concerto for Violin (see Figure 6.1).

New York critics were not kind to Weill. In the *New York Times*, Olin Downes proposed an acerbic alternative title for Weill's work: 'Three Night Club Pieces in the Outworn and Thin-Blooded Modern German Style'. Positioning Weill as archetypal of the latest – and seemingly lamentable – developments in contemporary German music, and paying no heed to Weill's exile status in France, Downes injected a venom into the criticism not seen in Amsterdam. 'The Weill pieces ... are disappointing', he wrote, 'the more disappointing because Kurt Weill has long been reckoned one of the smartest young men of modern Germany'. Downes's charges against the work for the most part closely echoed those in the Netherlands, especially those concerned with the expectations of a symphony. He pointed out 'the complete banality and lack of originality of the musical material' and 'the prolixity and dullness and absolute lack of distinction in the development'. He described the vigorous culmination of these 'dreary, dull and witless' pieces as mere 'speed and noise' – deploying signifiers of urban modernity. His review rounded off with the damning remarks: 'The music heard last night simply serves to show how easy it is to write satirical measures, especially if you have stage, action, and dialogue to help you, compared with the difficulty of writing real music.'[11] That muscular and suggestive phrase 'real music' reveals a lot about how Downes constructed musical value, and symphonic value in particular. Slickly obfuscating multiple extra-musical discourses, it parallels the assertion in the Amsterdam reception that 'the nature of Weill's music is just not suitable for absolute music'.[12]

One of these extra-musical discourses was Downes's views about the relationship between ethnicity and symphonic character, as evinced, for example, in his Sibelius reception, where he celebrated rugged and heroic Norse masculinity.[13] Indeed, whereas in the Amsterdam reception racial

[11] Olin Downes, 'Walter Presents Novelty by Weill', *New York Times*, 14 December 1934, 28.

[12] See 'Weill en Prokofieff – Symphonie in Songs – Prokofieff's derde pianoconcert', *Maast.* (Maastricht newspaper?), 12 October 1934 (trans. Josephine Kahn).

[13] See Glenda Dawn Goss, *Jean Sibelius and Olin Downes: Music, Friendship, Criticism* (Boston: Northeastern University Press, 1995), especially 37.

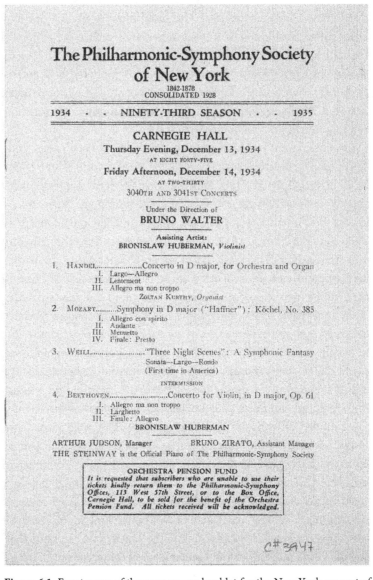

Figure 6.1 Front cover of the programme booklet for the New York concert of Weill's *Symphonic Fantasy*. Reproduced with the permission of the New York Philharmonic Shelby White & Leon Levy Digital Archives.

discourses had been heavily codified, in some of the New York reception they were much more explicit. 'Kurt Weill, like the Rock of Ages, never changes' were the opening words of Lazare Saminsky's review in *Modern Music*, making it clear that the reviewer knew little of Weill's music beyond the typecasting of his biggest commercial successes. The 'Rock of Ages' refers to a Hannukah hymn – note that these racialised criticisms come in spite of (or perhaps, indeed, because of) Saminsky's own Jewish faith, his upbringing in Russia, and his prolific academic interest in Jewish music.

As Saminsky's review continues, it becomes clear race is part of a twisted knot of issues; this is more than Weill being essentialised as inherently Jewish and thus 'rootless', therefore presenting a challenge to the close links between the symphony and ideas of nationhood.[14] Unlike Downes, Saminsky's geographical centre of reference was Paris, not Berlin. 'His orchestral *Night Scenes* ... proved to be a protracted and tearful midinette [Parisian shopgirl] elegy, reeking of shrewd obviousness', he wrote, adding that the work was 'well mounted and equipped with everything helpful to a commercial career'.[15] Parisian commercialism becomes emblematic of the triviality of European mass culture as a whole; the question of Weill's relationship to the French musical tradition was beside the point. In 1930s America, antisemitism was raw, but the New York reception shows that we can only unpick the discourses ensnared within the supposed banality and limitations of Weill's symphony – commerce, nationalism, race – inasmuch as we again acknowledge that they belong together, wrapped up with one another.

Ultimately, the problem with Weill's orchestral work for the New York critics was perhaps less a direct question of race and more one of two closely related issues: scope and sincerity. Overwhelmingly, critics found its vision myopic – for Downes, 'dreary, dull, and witless' – in contrast to America's hopes for ambitiously outward-looking, organic, and expansionist 'real' symphonic voices. Insofar as Saminsky's nexus of complaints centred on Weill's commercial reputation, then, they played into the same juxtaposition explored in relation to Harris's *Symphony 1933*. The supposedly insincere, inauthentic drives of big-city East Coast American and European commercial and ethnically mixed cosmopolitanism were pitted against the authentic, rural American vitality and virility of the West. But we need not review those rhetorics from Chapter 3; Saminsky's Weill review directly followed that of a new Harris choral poem, and he provided plenty more. 'A breath of significance is always present in any work of Roy Harris', wrote Saminsky. 'His gift of great scope and vitality never fails to captivate.' Like other critics and commentators who racialised Harris's 'homespun'[16] music as explicitly white 'Scotch-Irish', Saminsky also

---

[14] Constructions of Jewish composers as 'rootless' and thus contrary to American values are discussed in Rachel Mundy, 'The "League of Jewish Composers" and American Music', *Musical Quarterly* 96 (2013): 50–99.

[15] Lazare Saminsky, 'New Malipiero, New Harris and Weill', *Modern Music* 12 (1935): 89–90, 90.

[16] Ibid.

stressed this dimension in Harris's music: 'Virility of impetus and a tense racial note make his diction clear and winning.'[17] Such racial discourses were harnessed within musical commentary to legitimise the authenticity of Harris's musical voice and his right to speak for the American people through his music. Maybe this aspect of the Harris reception illuminates something of what Weill might have been hinting at in relation to the stakes for the symphonic genre through his comment in the Concertgebouw programme note that 'an appropriate title would be a word that expressed the opposite of "pastoral"',[18] given that landscape and white racial identities were constructed in parallel within symphonic discourse not only in the United States but in Germany too, as Weill must have been aware. Bruckner reception, for instance, increasingly fostered *Blut und Boden* ideologies.[19]

Rather than attacking a generalised sense of European sophistry, other reviews were differently underscored by preoccupations about America's place on the world stage. For Pitts Sanborn, Weill's so-called symphonic fantasy sounded 'in large part like a latter-day Berliner's idea of Broadway, with, of course, a tentative grasping at the "jazz spirit"'.[20] Building on a new-found, if fragile, sense of American cultural confidence about its place within the international music scene that had blossomed through the 1920s[21] – including, for instance, the inclusion of the United States in the International Society for Contemporary Music (ISCM) in 1923 – Sanborn oriented Weill's *Night Scenes* in relation to American musical traditions, also reminding readers of Weill's interest in the United States demonstrated in *Mahagonny*. Yet, his largely negative reactions to the work perhaps also evince a prevalent unease over European enthusiasms for jazz among the white American cultural establishment.[22] In the racially charged atmosphere of 1930s America,

---

[17] Ibid.

[18] Kurt Weill, programme note in Programme of the Subscription Concert (Bruno Walter/Concertgebouw Orchestra), 11 October 1934.

[19] See Bryan Gilliam, 'The Annexation of Anton Bruckner: Nazi Revisionism and the Politics of Appropriation', *Musical Quarterly* 78 (1994): 584–604.

[20] Sanborn, 'Concerts in New York'.

[21] Carol J. Oja, *Making Music Modern: New York in the 1920s* (New York: Oxford University Press, 2000), 3.

[22] As Oja has shown, visiting European modernists tended to value African-American music above anything the American concert hall had to offer, and had no qualms about lecturing white Americans on its superiority. Ibid., 295–6. Beth E. Levy describes the 'sometimes violent' debates between American composers and music commentators about the 'proper relationship' between jazz and American composition in the 1920s and 1930s, and it was not uncommon for prominent voices explicitly to discourage other American composers from engaging with jazz in order to cultivate an 'authentic' so-called Anglo-Saxon Americanism. Levy, 'The White Hope of American Music', 151–3.

with so many white American composers invested in finding alternative sources of material to jazz for re-invigorating American music, yet another European modernist 'grasping at the jazz spirit' perhaps appeared to Sanborn as yet another snub to white American art music.[23]

Injured by such unrelenting negativity, Weill summarised the press reactions at both the Amsterdam and New York concerts to Maurice Abravanel in January 1935:

It was a great success with the audience – catastrophic press ('banal', 'disjointed', 'empty', 'Beethoven in the beer garden', etc.) . . . Not one friendly word. Apparently this piece has unleashed against me in the most determined manner those factions that have always been latent up to now.[24]

But was Weill right to collapse the Amsterdam and New York symphonic criticism together in this way? Both sets of reception reflected the fact that symphonic discourse oscillated between two planes: between local concerns and the seemingly universalised ones of which the symphony was emblematic. When the same issues are raised against the foil of symphonic discourse in different contexts – for instance, Weill's Jewishness, (the lack of) organicism, commercialism, and the kind of community or audience the symphonic genre might build – those issues begin to look international or even universal. What this book has aimed to show, however, is how vital it is to keep sight of the fact that these were locally inflected issues with localised stakes in the different contexts we have visited: in short, we need to be aware that those universals were constantly re-formulated in response to quite different stimuli and preoccupations. At the same time, this is not to dissolve these big ideas completely. They are still required as centres to orient the comparisons, and they are historically justifiable, rooted as they are in late eighteenth- and nineteenth-century debates and ideologies linked to the genre. In order, then, to examine such an ideologically saturated cultural construction as the symphony, it is necessary to be equipped to switch with care between these multiple registers and scales – the seemingly 'universal' and the specific; global political concerns and their localised ramifications; the concept's historical freighting and the contemporary issues that collide against it. And this will remain important as, further on, the role of the genre today comes into focus.

---

[23] Sanborn, 'Concerts in New York'.

[24] Letter from Weill to Abravanel, 21 January 1935, Weill-Lenya, series 30, 15/6. This translation is found in Kim H. Kowalke and Lys Symonnette, trans. and eds., *Speak Low (When You Speak Love): The Letters of Kurt Weill and Lotte Lenya* (London: Hamish Hamilton, 1996), 145.

Legacies

In spite of its reception, Weill's faith in his work was unwavering, as, seemingly, was Walter's. As his letter to Abravanel of January 1935 continued: 'it takes a hell of a lot of self-confidence and a capacity for resistance to keep on living with this kind of dreck. . . . The symphony sounds excellent, and Walter was beside himself because of my ability to orchestrate only what's essential while being able to retain a full and beautiful sound.'[25] Although there was a short period after the New York performance in which Weill seemed unsure what next to do with the work – and he had his sights set elsewhere, on breaking into the Parisian theatre scene – some plans seem finally to have crystallised, perhaps with the intervention of the Princesse de Polignac.[26] Weill's symphony was performed again in Paris on 25 April 1935 under the title *Fantaisie symphonique*, a radio broadcast with the Orchestre national under musical director Désiré-Emile Inghelbrecht. This time the press were admiring, picking up on Mendelssohnian influences, and 'the delicacy of Haydn and Mozart'.[27] Two months later, on 24 June, it finally received its promised performance in Polignac's salon on Avenue Henri-Martin, programmed with works by Beethoven and Chabrier.[28] Still championing the symphony, Walter himself gave the work another chance, performing it once more in Vienna on 18 April 1937, with Toscanini in attendance and to an unusually positive reception from the Viennese public,[29] but that was to be the work's final outing before Weill's death in 1950.

---

[25] Letter from Weill to Abravanel, 21 January 1935. The translation is a modified version of that attached to original at Weill-Lenya Research Center ('es gehört schon eine gehörige Portion Selbstvertrauen und Widerstandskraft dazu, diesen ganzen Dreck noch länger mitzumachen. . . .. Die Symphonie klingt hervorragend, Walter war ganz ausser sich über meine Fähigkeit, nur das notwendigste zu instrumentieren und doch einen vollen, schönen Klang zu erreichen.').

[26] He wrote to Jascha Horenstein in January 1935: 'Despite that, or perhaps for that reason [his success in breaking into the Parisian theatre scene], I can't decide whether to do anything with the symphony. At any rate, it's now up to the Princesse de Polignac to make me her suggestions.' Weill-Lenya, David Drew Collection, letter from Weill to Jascha Horenstein, 5 January 1935.

[27] P.B., 'Concerts Divers', *Le Ménestrel*, 3 May 1935, 152; Darius Milhaud, 'La Scène: Une première audition à l'Orchestre national de la radiodiffusion', *Le Jour*, 28 April 1935, 6, Weill-Lenya, series 50B.

[28] As recorded in 'Le Monde et la ville', *Le Figaro*, 19 June 1935, cited in Sylvia Kahan, *Music's Modern Muse: A Life of Winnaretta Singer, Princesse de Polignac* (Rochester: University of Rochester Press, 2003), 328.

[29] 'In last Sunday's *Times* there was a report from Vienna that [Bruno] Walter performed my symphony there. . . . The article says the audience reacted more positively to the work than to any other modern one.' Letter from Weill to Lenya, 8 May 1937, in Kowalke and Symonnette,

The symphony's poor initial reception on such prestigious global platforms as Carnegie Hall and the Concertgebouw must have contributed to the fact that Weill never wrote another symphony. Had political events unfolded differently, and had the work been received by the same Berlin critics who reviewed Honegger's symphony, for instance – critics willing to find the points of connection with the Germanic symphonic tradition, to highlight the Mozartian influences, or to probe the meaning of 'the opposite of pastoral' – quite a different symphonic career might have ensued. That seemingly neither Weill's nor Walter's faith in the quality of the symphony were diminished by the mixed reception is telling. But other creative opportunities began to emerge instead. As a work that forged connections for Weill in Paris and travelled there with him, there is symmetry in the observation that in September 1935 – ten months after the Carnegie Hall performance – Weill once again followed a path mapped out by his symphony, emigrating permanently to New York with Lenya.

The twentieth-century silence of Weill's symphony was long; it was not resurrected until after British musicologist and music critic David Drew had published the score in 1966. For many years Weill was not seen as a composer worthy of study in his own right: the earliest resurgence of post-war Weill interest was ancillary to a growing literature around Brecht in the 1950s and 1960s. Although other factors were at play, National Socialist suppression of Weill's music, alongside derisive European attitudes to his later American output, prevented Weill from regaining a foothold in twentieth-century history. Discourses about superficiality and inauthenticity, with their racial undertones, have been pernicious in framing Weill's whole career. For instance, the pervasive construction of the 'Two Weills' has compromised academic engagement with his output.[30] Canonised as a subtitle in Drew's 1980 *New Grove* article, it portrayed his emigration to the United States and work on Broadway as

---

Speak Low, 238. Kowalke and Symonnette, however, point out that this was not exactly how the *New York Times* reported the concert, citing the original review as follows: 'The Viennese received the Weill novelty with a good deal more equanimity and good-will than they usually extend to things of the sort. But all told, it hardly seemed to me one of Walter's better days.' H. F. P., 'Toscanini Visits Vienna', *New York Times*, 2 May 1937, cited in Kowalke and Symonnette, *Speak Low*, 239. Original review in Weill-Lenya, series 50B.

[30] David Drew, 'Kurt Weill', in *The New Grove Dictionary of Music and Musicians*, ed. Stanley Sadie, 20 vols. (London: Macmillan, 1980), vol. 20, 300–10. Tamara Levitz has critiqued the article and its 2001 revision, accusing it of evincing a commitment to colonialist intellectual positions and charging Drew with the articulation of Weill's life and *oeuvre* through a purely modernist agenda characteristic of the 1980s. See Tamara Levitz, 'Putting Kurt Weill in His Historical Place: The *New Grove* Articles', *Kurt Weill Newsletter* 20 (2002): 4–9.

an irreconcilable stylistic rift – and a betrayal of his early modernist promise. Yet, the seeds of the idea were already present in Weill's lifetime, as shown in Adorno's uncompromising obituary, which informed readers that 'the profile of this composer … can hardly be encompassed by the [unified] concept of a composer at all'.[31] Weill historiography hardly set him up as the kind of coherent subject associated with authentic symphonies.

But, eventually, ideas of coherence loosened their grip on the cultural imagination, and interest in the work has exploded since the year 2000, which marked the centenary of Weill's birth (1900) and fiftieth anniversary of his death. Celebrations were directed in part by the Kurt Weill Foundation for Music (KWF). Indeed, the Weill-Lenya Research Center, the archive of materials bequeathed to the KWF, has documented a significantly greater number of post-millennial performances of the work than throughout all preceding years combined.[32] As the product of a figure thus repeatedly painted in ways that resist notions of unity, it is little wonder that Weill's single mature symphonic work has received such scant twentieth-century attention. Kim H. Kowalke's groundbreaking 1979 analytic study *Kurt Weill in Europe* demonstrated the first signs of an impulse to change the field and overhaul attitudes to Weill, however.[33] And since the founding of the KWF in 1983, Weill scholarship has increased in volume and ambition, gradually breaking down some of the elitist, imperialist, and racist musicological positions that have inflected discourse on Weill and accounted for his critical neglect – for instance, by valuing his German over his American output. The post-modern critical and aesthetic turns of the 1990s and 2000s, moreover, provided versatile critical vocabularies for how Weill navigated popular and high-art forms in his symphony.

This brings us to the question of the impact of National Socialist history on the legacies, historiography, and indeed absences of aesthetic works from the period around 1933. Biographical narratives of exile, like Weill's,

---

[31] Theodor W. Adorno, 'Kurt Weill', *Frankfurter Rundschau*, 15 April 1950, reprinted in Adorno, *Gesammelte Schriften* (Frankfurt am Main: Suhrkamp, 1984), 544–7, found in Kowalke, 'Kurt Weill, Modernism, and Popular Culture: "Offentlichkeit als Stil"', *Modernism/Modernity* 2 (1995): 27–69, 29. As Kowalke indicates, the original reads: 'Die Figur des Komponisten, der in Amerika starb, wird vom Begriff des Komponisten kaum recht getroffen.'

[32] Its list is not exhaustive, but the Weill-Lenya Research Center has documented twenty-eight performances of the work before 2000, and 117 from 2000 to September 2022 (the term 'performance' here includes multiple performances, if given by the same conductor at the same venue). See finding aid to Weill-Lenya, series 50B. See also Weill-Lenya, Performance Calendar Archive, 2015–19; www.kwf.org/events/ (accessed 8 September 2022).

[33] Kowalke, *Kurt Weill in Europe*.

foreground only one set of ways in which the rise of the National Socialists explicitly impacted upon the symphonic genre in this period. It would be easy to characterise National Socialism as an uncontrollable tide rolling over the era, dragging works like Weill's, Honegger's, and Pfitzner's into its undertow. But its legacy is much more complex in terms of how and why it has caused these omissions from the repertory, and it furthermore continues to shape academic engagement with works from this period in manifold subtle ways. It is a context difficult to gain critical purchase upon, apart from in the most polarising sense; it is also a context that sent shockwaves across the world, with new diasporas and a perception of ethical rupture, and whose horror has an almost magnetic pull for Western academics, stealing attention from 1930s histories centred elsewhere on the globe.

For Honegger, Berlin 1933 represented barren critical ground for the acceptance of his symphonic message. Coupled with Nazi rumour-mongering, this proved the launch pad for *Mouvement symphonique*'s virtually complete disregard throughout the twentieth-century. Indeed, such Nazi constructions as *entartete Kunst* (degenerate art) have had more pervasive influence beyond National Socialist Germany on the twentieth century reception of both Weill's and Honegger's symphonies than contemporary scholarship might like to admit, and it is worth remembering that National Socialist Germany was a formative context for the disciplinary development of *Musikwissenschaft*.[34] Whereas the rehabilitation of Weill's music towards the end of the twentieth century and beyond has been supported by the carefully cultivated financial resources available to an institution like the KWF, Honegger's music, by contrast, has yet to enjoy anything remotely resembling that level of attention.[35]

Just as decisive for this period's absence from symphonic surveys, however, has been a reluctance to engage with symphonies like Pfitzner's that demonstrate some alignment with the fascist project – perhaps because adequate critical frameworks for dealing with political complicity and resistance are still lacking. As much as symphonic discourse historically took its bearings from notions of racial purity, the Pfitzner reception has shown how complex and counter-intuitive the relationship between symphonic discourse and ethnicity could be, even within the context of a highly

---

[34] See Pamela M. Potter, *Most German of the Arts: Musicology and Society from the Weimar Republic to the End of Hitler's Reich* (New Haven, CT: Yale University Press, 1998).
[35] See Ulrich Mosch, '(Kein) Platz in der Geschichte? Das Honegger-Bild in der Musikgeschichtsschreibung', in *Arthur Honegger: Werk und Rezeption*, ed. Peter Jost (Bern: Peter Lang, 2009), 15–35.

racialised state like National Socialist Germany. It is only by revisiting works by ambivalent figures like Pfitzner, and finding ways of grappling with often uncomfortable histories, that we can understand more fully what went on in this pivotal year and the kinds of persistent historical absences its events and its historiography have created.

We are far from being the first generation to have the impression of living in uncertain times, but uncertain they nonetheless are. Much about contemporary society and politics suggests the urgent need to understand better what happened in 1933, with a particular focus on those nationalist apparatuses complicit in the fascist political transition in Germany. Today, we are witnessing a rise of right-wing popularism in Europe and the United States, alongside a generalised mistrust of out-of-touch intellectual elites (increasingly conditioned by misinformation spread through siloed echo-chamber social media communities); increasing nationalist isolationism in response to a vast refugee crisis in Europe; and the changing political dynamics precipitated by a global health crisis, not to mention devastating ecological crises. The early 1930s is a period that underlines our political inertia and ethical inadequacies and reflects them back at us. And thus, keeping the question of persistent historical absences and ethical inadequacies in mind, it is with discomfort, but also with hope, that the role of the 1930s symphony in the present day might come under scrutiny.

Price, London, 2020

On 12 October 2020, the Chineke! Orchestra, the first majority Black and ethnically diverse orchestra in Europe,[36] appeared at the Royal Festival Hall, London, to perform Price's Symphony in E minor under the eerie conditions of lockdown. On YouTube, no applause accompanies American conductor Roderick Cox taking to the podium in the virtually empty auditorium in a live-streamed concert titled 'Black Landscapes'.[37] Alongside Price's symphony, the concert featured a work by twentieth-century pianist, conductor, and composer Avril Coleridge-Taylor, daughter of Samuel Coleridge-Taylor,

---

[36] The Chineke! Foundation was established in 2015 by Chi-chi Nwanoku 'to provide outstanding career opportunities to established and up-and-coming Black and ethnically diverse classical musicians in the UK and Europe'. Alongside the Chineke! Orchestra, the Foundation also runs the Chineke! Junior Orchestra, comprising players aged between eleven and twenty-two. See www.chineke.org/our-mission (accessed 7 December 2021).

[37] The concert was available for fourteen days after the initial screening and the performance of Price's symphony could subsequently be watched on YouTube. www.youtube.com/watch?v=ht4H_eKjb0w (accessed 7 December 2021).

Sussex Landscape, and Beethoven's Piano Concerto No. 3, with Dutch pianist Nicolas van Poucke as the soloist. Cox gives the downbeat, and a lilting half-beat later the bassoons enter quietly with their syncopated pentatonic motif, cutting through shimmering strings. This is the four-bar prelude to the work, readying the listener for the riches of the sound-world to come. One of only six critics allowed in the hall, Fiona Maddocks wrote in *The Observer*: 'The music is distinctive, emotional, bursting with melody; not experimental, but expressive and confident. Dvořák's New World symphony meets Gershwin (who attended the first performance), but Price's own musical personality holds sway. . . . Chineke! embraced its episodic charms with elegance, making a convincing case.'[38]

In BBC Four's *Black Classical Music: The Forgotten History*, first broadcast in September 2020, comedian and broadcaster Lenny Henry and classical music presenter Suzy Klein watched back a performance of Price's symphony by the same orchestra on a laptop screen. After the symphony's opening, Henry remarked: 'That's beautiful . . . pastoral . . . heart-filling, romantic, and it just makes me . . . it just makes my heart sort-of go bof-bof [he mimed a giant heart beating] – bigger'. Klein replied: 'She, I think, deserves her due alongside the top-rate symphonists of her age because I think, you watch something like that and you just see the way she controls the orchestra, it's like a painter with a palette.' Bowing to the computer, arms outstretched, she said, 'We love you Florence Price.' This was a long-overdue gesture of deference that, in its self-mockery, seemed to acknowledge its insufficiency. 'We love you Florence', echoed Henry, in a jokingly masculine fan voice, a toned-down version of what might be heard yelled across a British football pitch. They both paused, looking reverent, and a little awkward, seemingly at a loss. For two Brits, in this moment it appeared only levity could cover the depths of the unease.[39]

As I write in the winter of 2021, the symphony from 1933 for which public appetite feels most widespread is Price's. That is to say, the one we are hearing is the one that, following its premiere in Chicago 1933, disappeared into virtual obscurity for the best part of a century. But such mainstream appetite for Price's symphony – kept from national circulation in Price's lifetime and beyond by white institutional gatekeepers like

---

[38] Fiona Maddocks, 'Chineke! Orchestra Review: Broadening Horizons', *The Observer*, 3 October 2020, www.theguardian.com/music/2020/oct/03/chineke-orchestra-review-broadening-horizons (accessed 7 December 2021).

[39] *Black Classical Music: The Forgotten History*, first broadcast 27 September 2020, BBC Four, Douglas Road Productions.

conductor Koussevitzky or music publishers like Schirmer,[40] among others – is very new indeed. It still matters that we pay attention to the symphonic genre, then, because just as with Weill in New York or Amsterdam, dynamics of symphonic belonging continue to play out in politicised ways. Price's symphony and its twentieth-century history, like Weill's, raise questions about who the right kind of symphonic composer might be, and how that category is shaped. In the wake of #MeToo and Black Lives Matter, the symphony is to be found embroiled, still, in the question of who it is that counts, who is bestowed with cultural and political agency. What to make of this phenomenon – that is, the sudden celebrity of Price and her music after the indignity of nearly a century of obscurity, and the role of the symphonic genre within it – is the problem framing the concluding section of this book.

Mainstream interest in Price has surged since 2018 following the commercial release and prominent reviews of her two violin concertos performed by Er-Gene Kahng and the Janáček Philharmonic.[41] Both had been thought lost until their discovery when a large repository of works was unearthed in Price's former summer home near St. Anne, Illinois, in 2009 – a key catalyst for fresh and intensified attention to Price. Kahng's release prompted concerts of Price's works by noteworthy orchestras;[42] the Fort Smith Symphony in her native Arkansas recorded two of her four symphonies for Naxos.[43] Biographical articles have appeared in highbrow US publications like the *New York Times* and *The New Yorker*.[44] In the United Kingdom, Price's Symphony in E minor was premiered in London in 2017,

---

[40] Shadle has shown how Schirmer published only a tiny proportion of her music during her lifetime. If music is not published, then it is easily lost, lacking a key set of institutional records. Douglas Shadle, 'Plus Ça Change: Florence B. Price in the #BlackLivesMatter Era', *NewMusicBox*, 20 February 2019, https://nmbx.newmusicusa.org/plus-ca-change-florence-b-price-in-the-blacklivesmatter-era/ (accessed 3 February 2021).

[41] Florence Price, *Violin Concertos*, Er-Gene Kahng (violin) and the Janáček Philharmonic, conducted by Ryan Cockerham, recorded 2–4 May 2017 (Albany TROY1706, 2018) [CD].

[42] In their 2018–9 seasons, the New Jersey Symphony, North Carolina Symphony, and Minnesota Orchestra performed Price's music. See Shadle, 'Plus Ça Change'.

[43] Florence Price, *Symphonies Nos. 1 & 4*, Fort Smith Symphony, conducted by John Jeter, recorded 13–14 May 2018 (Naxos American Classics 8559827, 2019) [CD].

[44] See Michaela Baranello, 'Welcoming a Black Female Composer into the Canon. Finally', *New York Times*, 9 February 2018, www.nytimes.com/2018/02/09/arts/music/florence-price-arkansas-symphony-concerto.html (accessed 3 February 2021); Alex Ross, 'The Rediscovery of Florence Price: How an African-American Composer's Works Were Saved from Destruction', *The New Yorker*, 29 January 2018, www.newyorker.com/magazine/2018/02/05/the-rediscovery-of-florence-price (accessed 3 February 2021); see also Ross, 'Black Scholars Confront White Supremacy in Classical Music', *The New Yorker*, 14 September 2020, www.newyorker.com/magazine/2020/09/21/black-scholars-confront-white-supremacy-in-classical-music (accessed 3 February 2021). In the United Kingdom, see Andrew Farach-Colton, 'Florence Price: Out of the

and her music was performed on *BBC Proms Extra* in 2018; meanwhile BBC Radio 3 has featured Price twice on *Composer of the Week* since early March 2020. This is in part thanks to the championing of composer, conductor, and educator Shirley Thompson since 2017 within the joint AHRC/Radio 3 Forgotten Women Composers Project.[45] More recently, scholar and pianist Samantha Ege has crafted recital programmes and lecture recitals that situate Price within her Black intellectual milieu.[46]

And yet, in many ways, there is nothing at all sudden about this revival. It is the result of concerted and painstaking slow-burn efforts of scholars, performers, and composers since the 1970s, many hailing from those Black and local communities where Price's music has never been 'forgotten': Rae Linda Brown, Barbara Garvey Jackson, Wayne Shirley, Douglas Shadle, A. Kori Hill, Ege, and Thompson, to name but a very few.[47] 'Obscurity' is

Shadows', *Gramophone*, 18 January 2022, www.gramophone.co.uk/features/article/florence-price
-out-of-the-shadows (accessed 25 January 2022).

[45] The Forgotten Women Composers project was timed to coincide with the 100-year anniversary of women in the United Kingdom getting the vote, and it searched out unheard work by women composers. Alongside working with the musical groups to which BBC Radio 3 has access, the project also involved liaising with publishers that might take the music on. By broadcasting newly edited music, the project aimed to develop the BBC's library of recordings, and a concert at LSO St Luke's, London, on International Women's Day, 8 March 2018, was a focal point. See https://webarchive.nationalarchives.gov.uk/ukgwa/20220204133857/http://ahrc.ukri.org/ documents/publications/forgotten-female-composers/ (accessed 17 August 2022).

[46] See, for instance, 'Fantaisie Nègre: The Piano Music of Florence Price', Samantha Ege, piano, 24 November 2021, Barbican Centre, London, where she performed music by Bonds, Price, and Vítězslava Kaprálová. See also 'Samantha Ege: Trailer', 11 November 2021, www.youtube.com/ watch?v=5u_LFAvLZMI&t=12s.

[47] See, for instance, Barbara Garvey Jackson, 'Florence Price, Composer', *Black Perspective in Music* 5 (1977): 30–43; Rae Linda Brown, 'Selected Orchestral Music of Florence B. Price (1888–1953) in the Context of Her Life and Work' (PhD thesis, Yale University, 1987); Florence Price, *Symphonies Nos. 1 and 3*, ed. Rae Linda Brown and Wayne Shirley (Middleton, WI: A-R Editions, 2008); *The Caged Bird: The Life and Music of Florence B. Price*, film produced by James Greeson (University of Arkansas Press, 2015) [DVD]; Douglas W. Shadle, *Orchestrating the Nation: The Nineteenth-Century American Symphonic Enterprise* (New York: Oxford University Press, 2016); Marquese Carter, 'The Poet and Her Song: Analyzing the Art Songs of Florence B. Price', (DMus thesis., Indiana University, 2018); Samantha Ege, 'The Aesthetics of Florence Price: Negotiating the Dissonances of a New World Nationalism' (PhD thesis, University of York, 2020); Samantha Ege, 'Composing a Symphonist: Florence Price and the Hand of Black Women's Fellowship', *Women and Music: A Journal of Gender and Culture* 24 (2020): 7–27; Rae Linda Brown, *The Heart of a Woman: The Life and Music of Florence B. Price* (Urbana: University of Illinois Press, 2020); Samantha Ege, 'Chicago, the "City We Love to Call Home!": Intersectionality, Narrativity, and Locale in the Music of Florence Beatrice Price and Theodora Sturkow Ryder', *American Music* 39 (2021): 1–40; A. Kori Hill, 'Creating a Nationalist Modernism: New Negro Aesthetics in the Concertos of Florence B. Price' (PhD thesis, University of North Carolina at Chapel Hill, forthcoming). Pianist and composer Karen Walwyn is currently engaged in a four-volume recording project of Price's music for solo piano and some chamber works, alongside which she runs an online platform dedicated to promoting

a relative term, determined by those who hold power. The trope of 'redis-covery', as Hill points out, is a deeply damaging one for Black artists, because it disguises a process that is active: 'Certain histories and cultural memories are not considered "relevant" to the mainstream until they prove useful.'[48] And so it is warranted to view this surge of interest in Price and in her symphonic music from predominantly white institutions with a degree of cynicism, particularly within the United Kingdom, where historically the interest in twentieth-century American music has been smaller than in the United States.[49] Enthusiasm that is this abrupt cannot help feeling precari-ous. It prompts fears about whether its longevity can be trusted, as well as questions about how identity categories of race, class, and gender are manipulated at different times to serve political interests and movements. These fears relate to the capriciousness of a top-down model of policing the category of symphonist, where the people who hold and confer institution-ally accredited knowledge decide who it is that counts, who it is that is bestowed with cultural and political agency.

The sheer quality and quantity of Price's music, as well as considered, Black-led long-term plans for sustained future engagement with it (for instance, the International Florence Price Festival founded in 2020), brings confidence that broad public appetite to hear her work will continue beyond her introduction to new mainstream audiences.[50] But it is import-ant to question and weigh up who exactly Price's current presence and the proliferation of her music, specifically her symphonies, serve at different times and in different settings. Questions might rightly be posed about when they better serve racial justice – and the vital importance of promin-ent Black female historical role models should not be underestimated – and

Price research and contemporary performance, including posting user-submitted video performances, programmes, and research materials. See: https://florenceprice.com (accessed 7 December 2021). These efforts also include the initial work done by Jackson and Mary Dengler Hudgins during the years 1974 and 1975 to establish the Florence Price collection at the archives of the University of Arkansas.

[48] A. Kori Hill, 'To Be Rediscovered When You Were Never Forgotten: Florence Price and the "Rediscovered" Composer (Tropes of Black Composers, Part One)', Harry T. Burleigh Society Blog (29 November 2018), www.burleighsociety.com/blog/2018-11-29/florence-price-part-one (accessed 15 December 2020).

[49] Shadle makes a similar point in a recent online piece; see Shadle, 'Plus Ça Change'.

[50] See www.pricefest.org (accessed 7 December 2021). See also Walwyn's research platform, https://florenceprice.com (accessed 7 December 2021). Ege's recording projects for piano include *Fantasie Nègre: The Piano Music of Florence Price* (Lorelt LNT144, 2021) [CD]; *Black Renaissance Women* (Lorelt LNT145, 2022) [CD]. See also forthcoming academic volumes set to cement Price's institutional status; for example, Samantha Ege and A. Kori Hill, eds., *The Cambridge Companion to Florence B. Price* (Cambridge University Press); Samantha Ege and Douglas W. Shadle, *Price: Master Musician Series* (Oxford University Press).

when they tip over to benefit what Teju Cole has described as the White Saviour Industrial Complex, which makes liberal society feel better while papering over, or, worse, actively perpetuating, structural inequalities.[51] And when, of course, they might ambivalently do both, or no answer can be found; and when Price's music thus exists in an ambivalent space of both/and, and how contemporary listeners, musicians, and musicologists live with that tension. Progress in terms of representation is crucial progress, of course: if all intentions had first to be pure before Black artists could find their way onto concert programmes and radio broadcasts, it would simply never happen – assuming there even is such a thing as a pure intention.[52] But it is nonetheless hard to avoid observing how Price's treasure trove of music has apparently arrived at a convenient moment, allowing orchestras and broadcasters to showcase their supposedly relevant, socially progressive credentials against the energy growing globally around the Black Lives Matter movement, following the public murder of George Floyd by a white police officer in May 2020. If orchestras, broadcasters, and musicologists – myself included – are to avoid exploiting Black artists and female labour for their own gain, then it is necessary to acknowledge, and be sensitive to, a long history of precisely this exploitation. Brown's critical editions of Price's two (at the time) known symphonies were published in 2008, a year before the summer house discovery; there was no rush to perform them in the intervening decade.[53] Recent mainstream advocacy of Price has no necessary bearing on whether institutions are also doing anything active in pursuit of structural change, like building strong pipelines, making early years interventions in schools and nurseries, or appointing racially diverse figures at a senior level.

In the early 1930s, Price's symphony was a political agent within a very different vision of racial community building, connecting with the political

---

[51] Shadle, in 'Plus Ça Change', has noted how the resurgence of interest in Price suggests Teju Cole's reading of the White Saviour Industrial Complex, which sees all problems as solvable with enough enthusiasm applied. Shadle, 'Plus a change'. See also Teju Cole, 'The White Industrial Saviour Complex', *The Atlantic*, 21 March 2012, www.theatlantic.com/international/archive/2012/03/the-white-savior-industrial-complex/254843/ (accessed 3 February 2021).

[52] Relatedly, on 2 March 2021, BBC Radio 3 and the AHRC announced the seven researchers to be funded within a new scheme, launched in autumn 2020, which 'aims to expand the breadth and diversity of what is accepted as belonging to the classical music canon and uncover more about the lives and work of composers who have not had the public recognition that their work deserves'. According to the website, research programmes were selected with the input of a diverse expert advisory panel. See 'BBC Radio 3 and the Arts And Humanities Research Council Celebrate Classical Composers from Diverse Ethnic Backgrounds', 2 March 2021, www.bbc.com/mediacentre/2021/bbc-radio-3-arts-and-humanities-research-council (accessed 7 December 2021).

[53] Price, *Symphonies Nos. 1 and 3*.

and aesthetic ideals widely associated with the Harlem Renaissance, but that also underpinned the additional and lesser-known localised Black Renaissances taking place in Northern American cities like Philadelphia and Chicago, where Price's career was centred. To listen to Price's Symphony in E minor today is therefore to open up a historical window. It is to invite into view a long history of the symphony's imbrication in determining who it is that supposedly counts, who it is that is afforded political and creative agency, and how people created agency for themselves in wholly adverse conditions. Examining the symphonic genre in relation to the ideals of America's Black Renaissances and their anxieties around race and respectability gestures towards perennial problems with integrating Black symphonists into classical music's mainstream today that in some ways have changed little. These problems are to a certain extent shared by any symphonists for whom the Germanic nineteenth-century heritage of the genre does not straightforwardly seem their birthright. The whole problem is precisely contained in that term 'integration', and its cousins 'diversity' and 'inclusivity', and what the term itself implies about the need for radical change and self-reflection within the centre ground doing the integrating. But nor, however, should the prognosis be entirely pessimistic. Looking back into the 1930s, we find a template for how the category 'symphonist' might be shaped that is at odds with the tropes discussed thus far of (re-)discovery by a mainstream and that differs, furthermore, from the kind of policing of the genre faced by Weill. As Ege has shown, Price's identity as a symphonist was formed through the fellowship of the Black women in Chicago who together elevated Price and her music. It was the labour of these women that fostered the conditions allowing her to move into symphonic composition and, indeed, to have her symphony performed.[54] I suggest, moreover, in historical circumstances that placed all kinds of impossible limits on Black and female agency, Price's symphony puts forward a very different aesthetic model of symphonic selfhood – a kind of selfhood that cannot be expansive, universal, Germanic, but one nonetheless that acts and makes considered choices as it moves through the world.

Like her symphonic contemporaries William Dawson and William Grant Still, Price sought to elevate Black music and folk idioms using the elite musical language of the time. Unlike her colleagues Dawson and Still, however, Price did not give her Symphony in E minor a title that made her engagement with a Black musical heritage explicit. Her early subtitle, *Negro Symphony*, was removed from the score. Brown has suggested that it recalled

---

[54] Ege, 'Composing a Symphonist'.

the subtitle of Dvořák's 'From the New World' Symphony, with which Price's symphony was in close musical dialogue.[55] (Dvořák's symphony had in turn been inspired by Black vernacular music. Several contacts in Dvořák's immediate circles may have familiarised him with this repertoire, but primary among them was African-American composer and baritone Harry T. Burleigh, then a vocal student, who would sing him spirituals.)[56] These symphonies by Price, Still, and Dawson spoke to the anxieties of middle-class, educated Black people about race and respectability; about demonstrating civilisation. They aligned with the project of racial uplift. Uplift, broadly signifying liberation, is an expansive and multivalent concept. A strong current within it in the early twentieth century, however, was the politics of class differentiation, centring on the bourgeois values of 'self-help, racial solidarity, temperance, thrift, chastity, social purity, patriarchal authority, and the accumulation of wealth'.[57] As historian Kevin K. Gaines puts it, 'Black opinion leaders deemed the promotion of bourgeois morality, patriarchal authority, and a culture of self-improvement, both among Blacks and outward, to the white world, as necessary to their recognition, enfranchisement, and survival as a class'.[58] Ralph Ellison's investigation into 1920s and 1930s Black selfhood and agency in *Invisible Man* (1947) begins by setting out the following theory, which he ultimately exposes as flawed: 'You [white people] have yours, and you got it yourself, and we [African Americans] have to lift ourselves up the same way.'[59] Even here, the character, tellingly, speaks for the ears of a white listener, thus self-presenting towards whiteness. To do this, one must first see oneself through white eyes, a phenomenon encapsulated in W. E. B. Du Bois's theory of double consciousness.[60] This was the core tension within uplift ideologies, which were always compromised. Gaines has observed that uplift ideology's 'orientation towards self-help implicitly faulted African Americans for their lowly status, echoing judgemental dominant characterizations of the "Negro Problem"', rather than looking more broadly at systemic inequalities.[61]

---

[55] Brown, 'Lifting the Veil', xliii; Price, *Symphonies Nos. 1 and 3*, xv–lii.

[56] See Douglas W. Shadle, *Antonín Dvořák's New World Symphony* (Oxford: Oxford University Press, 2021), especially 97–8.

[57] Kevin K. Gaines, *Uplifting the Race: Black Leadership, Politics, and Culture in the Twentieth Century* (Durham, NC: University of North Carolina Press, 1996), 2. See also Lawrence Schenbeck, *Racial Uplift and American Music, 1878–1943* (Jackson: University of Mississippi Press, 2012).

[58] Gaines, *Uplifting the Race*, 2.

[59] Ralph Ellison, *Invisible Man* (Milton Keynes: Penguin Random House, 2016), 44.

[60] W. E. B. Du Bois, *The Souls of Black Folks*, ed. David W. Blight and Robert Gooding-Williams (Boston, MA: Bedford Books, 1997), 38.

[61] Gaines, *Uplifting the Race*, 4.

To write a symphony as an African American in 1933 was in part to respond to, and to meet the bourgeois expectations set by, white society. Price's symphony excelled within the expectations of the form, as contemporary reviews attest.[62] But the smothering dominance of whiteness, a constructed social category conferring power, as discussed in Chapter 3, meant that even this grassroots Black cultural and political endeavour was compromised. In *Invisible Man*, Ellison frames the inescapable paradox of acquiescence by introducing violent language of resistance in a refrain – the dying words of the protagonist's grandfather – with whose meaning the narrator wrestles throughout the book as he tries to understand whether and how to live by it:

[O]ur life is a war and I have been a traitor all my born days, a spy in the enemy's country . . . . Live with your head in the lion's mouth. I want you to overcome 'em [white people] with yeses, undermine 'em with grins, agree 'em to death and destruction, let 'em swoller you till they vomit or bust wide open.[63]

Such a paradox does not prevent symphonies like Price's from being politically resistant, however. Her music asserted the rights of Black people and culture to exist within an aesthetic arena from which both were barred. In addition to asserting aesthetic rights – about the right to compose abstract music without pushback, for instance,[64] or about claiming back folk materials from composers like Gershwin – it was also about privileged physical spaces, like concert halls or conservatoires, from which African Americans were frequently excluded. The paradox was that these acts of resistance, asserting aesthetic or physical presence, necessarily took place within an aesthetic and political space whose totality had already been articulated by white Americans. The frustration was the challenge – the seeming impossibility – of resisting/existing (for it emerged that they were often the same thing) in a way that fundamentally rejected the totalising, white-determined universe that existed outside it. '[A]gree 'em to death and destruction', as Ellison put it. Acquiesce so hard that it destroys the system: when agency was so limited, simple existence had to become a form

---

[62] See: 'Woman's Symphony Heard at Fair', *Afro-American*, 1 July 1933, 8; E. S., '"Friends" Series to Close', *Musical Leader* 64 (25): 22 June 1933, 9; E. H. B. 'Second and Third Weeks of Symphony Concerts at Auditorium', *Music News* 25 (25): 7 July 1933; Eugene Stinson, 'Music Views', *Chicago Daily News*, 16 June 1933, 41.

[63] Ellison, *Invisible Man*, 16.

[64] See Kira Thurman, 'Singing against the Grain: Playing Beethoven in the #BlackLivesMatter Era', *The Point*, 29 September 2018, https://thepointmag.com/examined-life/singing-against-grain-playing-beethoven-blacklivesmatter-era/ (accessed 7 December 2021).

of resistance, because it became the sole space in which action could be taken.

But Price was not an 'invisible man' and experienced none of the benefits conferred by masculinity. Most of all, Price's symphony asserted the complexities and the contradictions of Black female American subjectivities, which Alisha Lola Jones calls the 'thickest intersections of identity' in the United States:[65] what it meant to self-determine in a world that forced Black women to dissemble, to live inauthentically, where doors were closed on so many fronts with Jim Crow laws, racial barriers to entering feminist or suffragist movements, and barriers to the male-dominated New Negro Movement. Price's decision not to title her symphony in a way that made plain its engagement with a Black musical heritage, for instance, worked to her disadvantage in terms of the work's reception, as it met neither the expectations of the white community nor those of prominent Black intellectuals. Indeed, when in 1936 Harlem Renaissance philosopher Alain Locke deemed Price's symphony 'universal music', this was meant to signify his disappointment over a work that, in his opinion, did not make strong enough use of an abundant musical racial heritage. Locke played a key role in elevating and promoting the music of Price's male colleagues, Still and Dawson. For Locke, music that took 'the path of racialism', as he argued Still's and Dawson's did, was more politically productive.[66] But, as Brown has noted, Locke's misogyny is well documented, and even if Price did not use blues progressions or folk-song quotations, as Brown observes, Locke seems wilfully to have ignored the multiple other, less literal elements of African-American musical traditions – stratification of voices, pentatonicism, polyrhythm, call and response motives – suffused throughout the score.[67] In addition, Price bases the symphony's third movement on a Juba dance, with its syncopations. Locke's comments speak to a long history of how the right to abstraction has been policed, rarely straightforwardly afforded to either Black or to female composers and performers.[68] As first elucidated in Chapter 1, in the course of the nineteenth century symphonic reception and criticism had increasingly leaned towards ideals

[65] Alisha Lola Jones, 'Lift Every Voice: Marian Anderson, Florence B. Price and the Sound of Black Sisterhood', *NPR Music*, 30 August 2019, https://text.npr.org/748757267 (accessed 7 December 2021).

[66] Alain LeRoy Locke, *The Negro and His Music* (Port Washington, NY: Kennikat Press, 1968), 115. See also Rae Linda Brown, 'Florence B. Price's "Negro Symphony"', in *Temples for Tomorrow: Looking Back at the Harlem Renaissance*, ed. Geneviève Fabre and Michel Feith (Bloomington: Indiana University Press, 2001), 84–98, especially 94–7.

[67] See Rae Linda Brown, *Heart of a Woman*, 136.

[68] See Thurman, 'Singing against the Grain'.

of 'absolute' musical autonomy, which were curiously entwined with a general sense of metaphysical struggle, causing the links between the idea of the autonomous musical work and the privileged subject positions that tended to compose them – and were doing the metaphysical struggling – to become tacit. When the claim followed that these autonomous aesthetics were universal, the danger was that, in addition, the sort of personhood they veiled (male, of European extraction) attained a pervasive sense of universality. Thus, accepting the right of someone like Price to compose abstract music, a person doubly othered by race and gender, came to require mental gymnastics, even on the part of Locke.

Nonetheless, in the face of those many barriers, Price succeeded both in writing a symphony and then in having it performed by a major orchestra. But although Price may have been the first woman of colour to have a symphony publicly performed, she was not the exception that the conventional historiography of her symphonic first might suggest. Samantha Ege's article on Price's Symphony in E minor, 'Composing a Symphonist' breaks down the narratives of exceptionalism that have crystallised around Price. Ege has excavated the intellectual environment in Chicago that made it possible for Price to write a symphony, integrating Price within the network of Black women who paved the way for her symphonic achievements – women like Nora Douglas Holt (who studied with Boulanger in Paris in 1931), Estella Conway Bonds (Bonds' salon was a central feature of Black Chicago society), and Maude Roberts George, whose lives and roles interlaced across three major institutions: the Black *Chicago Defender* newspaper, the National Association of Negro Musicians (NANM), and a number of private homes. Black women, she shows, worked together, lifting one another up and thereby fostering the preconditions for Price's symphonic agency – which was something quite different to the expansive, universal, Germanic symphonic agency long associated with the genre.[69] Ege thus indicates the significance of community, of networks and fellowship, of advocacy and social activism, and of collective agency in navigating spaces marked as white and male.[70] Charting Price's Chicago from the ground up, she maps out the places where those communities were built and identifies the individuals who built them, focusing in particular on the domestic sphere as a site of knowledge exchange and collective action at a time when such knowledge

---

[69] Ege, 'Composing a Symphonist'.

[70] As Ege writes, 'Black Chicagoans . . . engaged in geographically grounded, intellectually vitalized, and artistically inspired methods of self-actualisation and collective uplift'. Ibid., 8.

was passed between Black women at kitchen tables and in living rooms.[71] She emphasises the importance of feminist biography – with, as Susan Ware has it, its 'close attention to connections between subjects' personal and professional lives'[72] – to thinking through the material realities of what makes a symphony and a symphonist: what exactly it was that was needed in terms of support and friendship for Price to make such a move from her pre-1927 piano pieces and songs into orchestral music and thus a much more public setting. As Ege observes, 'the scale of Price's works grew in tandem with the opportunities that she encountered'.[73] Scholarship on symphonies has perhaps been an area particularly guilty of severing the link between aesthetic object and composer biography, leaving a false sense of Price as an exceptional Black woman, a historical anomaly and radical outlier, who had little to do with Black experience more broadly. Ege's work reveals something quite different, and likewise suggests a new historiographical register for engaging with the symphonic genre. A symphony scholarship that has looked predominantly at aesthetics, individuals, and firsts has been detrimental to understanding Price and her milieu, and has occluded Black history.

The success of her symphony may not have opened the kinds of doors for Price that were so well oiled for a composer like Roy Harris, but Ege explores how it opened doors and positively impacted her career and her well-being, nonetheless. Newly separated from her abusive husband, the lawyer Thomas J. Price, she had been in a precarious financial situation while writing the work. Price and her two daughters had been taken in by Estella Bonds and her daughter Margaret, living at their home on Wabash Avenue – 'one-part hostel, one-part soup kitchen and one-part music school'[74] – so the $750 she won in the Wanamaker contests for the symphony and her Sonata in E minor for piano was a significant financial boon.[75] The professional recognition she gained, as well as the psychological safety net provided by her time living with the Bonds, were enough to allow her to step out from the shadow of her former husband and forge an independent identity without him. Since her move to Chicago from Little Rock, Arkansas, in 1927, she had been known first and foremost as

---

[71] Ege, 'Composing a Symphonist'. Underlining the significance of domestic spaces for collective organising in Black women's intellectual communities, she cites Tammy L. Kernodle. 'A Woman's Place: The Importance of Mary Lou Williams' Harlem Apartment', *NPR*, 12 September 2019, https://text.npr.org/758070439 (accessed 7 December 2021).

[72] Susan Ware, 'Writing Women's Lives: One Historian's Perspective', *Journal of Interdisciplinary History* 40 (2010): 413–35, 417.

[73] Ege, 'Composing a Symphonist', 8.   [74] Kernodle, 'A Woman's Place'.

[75] See Ege, 'Composing a Symphonist', 21.

Mrs Thomas J. Price, and their divorce had only been finalised in 1931. Through the time she spent living with the Bonds, and their deepening friendship, Price gained professional contacts and was firmly integrated within the network of prominent Black musicians and Black society who passed through Bonds's salon, which was frequented by the likes of Roland Hayes and Lillian Evanti.[76] Margaret Bonds's reminiscences show the scale and warmth of the practical support she gained from this community as the Wanamaker contest approached, with 'every brown-skinned musician in Chicago who could write a note' on hand copying orchestral parts in the Bonds's kitchen to 'help Florence meet her deadline'.[77] Ultimately, as Ege writes, 'it was through the fellowship of Black women, nurturing and networking across the art world before, during, and after her Chicago arrival, that Price found herself in a position to embrace what lay beyond the horizon'.[78]

The premiere of Price's symphony, under Frederick Stock conducting the Chicago Symphony Orchestra, made a brief appearance earlier as the prelude to Chapter 3. Through it, I sought to re-frame how we understand the kinds of institutional opportunities available to a composer like Harris: such mechanisms ran smoothly for some, but faltered for others. Exclusion by those like Koussevitzky, of course, perpetuated and exacerbated existing racial fault lines shaping what it was to be an American in the Depression-era cultural imagination (white, male, and working class). Now revisiting that premiere in the vast Chicago Auditorium, it is worth noting similar dynamics of nationalist identity formation at play, as Shadle has observed in relation to the framing of the concert: the previous evening had been given over to 'American' music in a concert that included Gershwin, while the title of the concert featuring Price was 'The Negro in Music'[79] – the implication being that Black musicians were not American. A further indignity in the programming was the fact that the night began with an overture by known white supremacist John Powell, during which, as the *Chicago Defender* critic noted, 'much of the audience shuffled

---

[76] Ibid., 17.

[77] Ibid., 21, citing Margaret Bonds, 'A Reminiscence', in *International Library of Negro Life and History: The Negro in Music and Art*, ed. Lindsay Patterson (New York: Publishers Company, 1967), 192. See also Brown, 'Lifting the Veil', xl.

[78] Ege, 'Composing a Symphonist', 26.

[79] See Shadle, 'Plus Ça Change'. However, it was not billed as such on the series programme; it was the only evening of the four left without a title. The others were 'Ballet' and 'Pop Concert'. The Ballet night featured the first Chicago performance of William Grant Still's *La Guiablesse* with text and choreography by Ruth Page. See 'Chicago Symphony Orchestra: A Century of Progress Series', concert programme, Rosenthal Archives of the Chicago Symphony Orchestra, Chicago.

uncomfortably'.[80] Additionally, although significant financial underwriting for the concert came from Maude Roberts George in her role as president of the Chicago Music Association (CMA), the first chapter of NANM, this was not mentioned in the programme. Only the name of the white organisation Chicago Friends of Music, sponsor of the series, was emblazoned across the cover. Yet it was the CMA that in fact took on the financial risk.[81]

And this brings us back to the question of why the symphony matters. Clearly, in 1933, Chicago's concert halls were challenging for Price to access. Symphonic spaces like concert halls were politically contested sites, policed strongly from the top down, performed in by all-white, all-male orchestras, and the same goes for who got to write symphonies. Nonetheless, the significance of the optics of that performance were unassailable: to attend that concert was to witness an all-white and male orchestra performing work by a Black woman.[82] And as Ege's article shows so clearly, 'the symphony' – as aesthetic object, public performance, moment of racial vindication – was also a place where Black women, who were among that society's most disenfranchised people, were able to assert their agency through sustained collective action, seek out professional recognition, and increase their autonomy. When the idea of the symphony was at stake, so too was the kind of personhood that counted. The genre becomes not only a place where mechanisms of exclusion become audible and visible, shaping what a society was not – as for Weill, as for Price – but also a space where vital grassroots collective action comes into view to tell forgotten histories and to point to new possibilities of how we may conceive of symphonic agency and self-actualisation. Price and her symphonic story show another way in which the romantic, introspective, and isolated idea of nineteenth-century symphonic subjectivity failed the symphonists of 1933.

Further Legacies

When legacies are put under the spotlight, a similar set of dynamics can be seen playing out in Weill's symphonic re-habilitation of the 1990s and 2000s and in Price's of the late 2010s, albeit for very different reasons. As

---

[80] 'This is Progress', *Chicago Defender*, 24 June 1933, cited in Shadle, *Antonín Dvořák's New World Symphony*, 137.

[81] See Ege, 'Composing a Symphonist', 25, citing Barbara Wright-Pryor, 'Maude Roberts George ... President of CMA of which Price was a member, underwrote the cost of the June 15, 1933 concert', *Africlassical*, 7 April 2014, https://africlassical.blogspot.com/2014/04/barbara-wright-pryor-maude-roberts.html.

[82] Ege, 'Composing a Symphonist', 24.

musicologists, as musicians, and as citizens, we should ask ourselves difficult questions about this. What these symphonic re-habilitations may
reveal is the provisional status with which cultural and political agency is
bestowed on others by those who occupy the centre ground, and how
supposedly universal, expansive discourses of selfhood – the liberal-
idealist legacies of nineteenth-century thought – are mobilised to obscure
the qualified nature of such integration. In talking about the re-habilitation
of Price, there is a risk of falling into discourses of white benevolence –
a tokenistic 'welcoming into the fold' – her presence being qualified by the
rules and conditions imposed by white, patriarchal society. It may be no
coincidence that Price, today seen as a respected upper-middle-class composer, fulfils many of the expectations associated with symphonic subjectivities, even if she does not meet those historical ones of gender and race,
as she herself acknowledged – 'I have two handicaps' – in her immortalised
letter to Koussevitzky. Issues relating to racial uplift and respectability
politics, themes so pressing in 1930s New York and Chicago, still feel
troublingly close to the surface. Recall how in 2020 the statue of Black
Lives Matter activist Jen Reid was substituted for that of Edward Colston in
the British city of Bristol, only to be removed within a day: the statue's
radical construction did not conform to Bristol's regulations and proced-
ures and so was not granted permission to remain.[83] From Weill's to Price's
symphonic re-habilitations, what comes into view is a neo-liberal cultural
and political centre ground that remains adept at manipulating the boundaries of its identity categories – race, gender, sexuality, class – for the
political purposes of the moment. And this in turn should prompt consideration of who (still) gets to bestow agency. Price's symphony raises
questions beyond the scope of this book – and, perhaps, even beyond
what my subject position allows me to address – about how the choices,
compromises, advocacy, and community that characterise Black and
female selfhood and creativity in the 1930s refract some of the painful
questions foregrounded by the Black Lives Matter movement – for
instance, about assimilation and about what it means to be considered
permanent.

And yet, there may also be grounds for optimism. To listen to Price's
symphony today is also to throw out a line to a long history of resilience:
of people finding ways of working with and against and circumventing

---

[83] See Archie Bland, 'Black Lives Matter Sculpture of Jen Reid Removed from Colston Plinth', *The
Guardian*, 16 July 2020, www.theguardian.com/world/2020/jul/16/black-lives-matter-
sculpture-of-jen-reid-removed-colston–bristol (accessed 3 February 2021).

top-down determinations. In 2004, Shirley Thompson, who is of mixed Jamaican and British heritage, became the first European woman to write and conduct a symphony in forty years, with her *New Nation Rising: A 21st Century Symphony*. As she put it in an interview in 2020, when reflecting on the musical education that enabled her to become a composer: 'I'm very grateful to my professors that they did say to me, you know, do take this forward, because you do need the support of a community around you to feel empowered.'[84] Symphonies like Price's and Thompson's point to an alternative vision of what it is to be in the world, underscoring how success is not the result of reified genius made manifest, but of talent finding the right conditions, bolstered by fellowship and by advocates. If symphonies are a way of learning about selfhood, then might works like Price's provide a way, musically, of recognising and learning about selves who deal with systemic adversity and who create within expressive confines? Ege's research – a detailed material history of Price's network and context that lays bare their mapping across local urban geographies – points in that direction. Like literature, might symphonies provide a space for imaginative exploration of subject positions other than one's own – for instance, subjectivities that have different limitations on their agency – as a way of developing empathy and understanding? Even more radically, might they be blueprints for an alternative way of being and of living collectively? Future work might, for instance, engage with Price's musical subjectivities alongside theories of agency from Black literary criticism.[85] Price and her symphony suggest, perhaps, that something may be possible through grassroots activism beyond the same old tokenistic welcoming into the fold and the same old manipulation of identity categories – both those of race/class/gender and those of whom we think of as a composer – to benefit those people whose identities are so rarely challenged and who do not experience their own identities as an existential threat. But the risk here, once again – the perennial problem for the othered composer – is of over-freighting Price's work, burdening her with the institutional needs of progressive scholarship or with political needs that were not hers, and thus setting her up to fail. I do not have answers, but

---

[84] *Black Classical Music*, BBC Four.

[85] See, for instance, Saidiya V. Hartman, *Scenes of Subjugation: Terror, Slavery, and Self-Making in Nineteenth-Century America* (New York: Oxford University Press, 1997). Literary critical work that might suggest a model for an approach to musical subjectivities includes, for instance, Brent Hayes Edwards, *Epistrophies: Jazz and the Literary Imagination* (Cambridge, MA: Harvard University Press, 2017).

I hope what we are witnessing is the beginning of sustained grappling with these issues from many quarters over many years.

Amid this theoretical talk of subjectivity and identity categories, it should not be forgotten that, for symphonic composers like Price, in the musical and cultural/social environments of 1933 the symphonic genre still held intrinsic appeal as a compositional challenge in its own right. The aim of this volume has been to provide an aesthetic snapshot of various composers' engagements with the symphony in a discrete slice of time. The result is an image vividly saturated and richly diverse. Price, Weill, Honegger, Copland, Chávez, Harris, and Pfitzner were all intrigued by the prospect of wrestling with the specific musical issues the form posed: how to reconcile diverse musical forces; how to tackle the requirements of tone and its tricky balance of popularism and academicism; and how to manipulate vast orchestral forces and sound's tangibility or plasticity in the sense of the German word *plastisch*, navigating the problems raised by symphonic monumentalism. If these composers explored and integrated other disciplinary paradigms like ballet, the dance hall, and the musical language of the theatre within the form, or transgressed different orders of 'absolute' music by engaging discursively with chamber musics, it is significant that they chose the symphony as the platform from which to do so. Broadly speaking, the works suggest the need for further discussion about the place of this creative form in a modernist context, and about how composers sought to create meaning symphonically or to re-invigorate the symphony as a site for meaningful communication in the twentieth century.

Attention to the legacies of Price's and Weill's symphonies, of course, also tells us about how closely symphonies have always been, and remain, embroiled in questions of selfhood. Symphonies, and what people said and wrote about them, are conduits for other anxieties: relating to race, economics, class, masculinity, mass culture, and a nexus of issues surrounding space, transportation, and expansionism, and 1933 represented a particularly precarious moment for the genre. The symphonies explored in this book spotlight a genre characterised by uncertainty, ideological saturation, and prevarication. Likewise, symphonies and the discourse surrounding them focused local concerns that often seemed really to be about people's sense of their collective place and significance in a changing global-political setting. Channelling a 'long' intellectual history – and one that was peculiarly Germanic, invested with Romantic idealism and Hegelian dialectics – it was a lens for imagining other nations and identities, and reflexively for modelling the self through those identities. Symphonic community building and spatial expansionism associated with Enlightenment thought took on different ideological colourings in fascist Germany and in the post-colonial Americas, refracting strikingly twentieth-century concerns and dilemmas about reformulations of the relationships between space and subjectivity. An imaginative means of reconciling past with present, forging nostalgic fantasies, and projecting outwards into a collective future, symphonic discourse was nonetheless just as profoundly shaped by the unsounded voices of those it marginalised or failed. This book reveals a symphonic history marked as much by exclusion as by any inclusive notions of communality.

As with the reception of Weill's symphony in 1933, the contemporary re-emergence of Price's symphony shows how today discourse around the 1930s symphony still offers a glimpse into people's sense of their place in the world. In 1933, it was a means for people to define who they were, but equally, and often more revealingly, who they were not. Today, it remains a means for us to define who we are and, perhaps more revealingly, a place for us to contest how we as a society would like to be seen. Symphonies still matter today because often, as these two closing case studies show – Weill in New York in 1934, Price in 2020 – they light up the margins, the blurry border zones of who is allowed to belong. And in so doing, they can expose the supposedly invisible subjectivities of the mainstream that get to wield power unobserved, cloaked in the mantles of so-called common sense, the status quo, or the like. But if we let them, they could also model a new, differently dynamic landscape of selfhood.

Select Bibliography

For concision, this bibliography does not include scores, archival materials, websites, or audiovisual recordings and other multimedia cited in the footnotes.

Abbate, Carolyn. 'Offenbach, Kracauer, and Ethical Frivolity'. *Opera Quarterly* 33 (2017): 62–86.

——— *Unsung Voices: Opera and Musical Narrative in the Nineteenth-Century*. Princeton: Princeton University Press, 1991.

Absher, Amy. *The Black Musician and the White City: Race and Music in Chicago, 1900-1967*. Ann Arbor: University of Michigan Press, 2014.

Adams, Byron. '"Thor's Hammer": Sibelius and British Music Critics, 1905–1957'. In *Jean Sibelius and His World*, edited by Daniel M. Grimley, 125–57. Princeton: Princeton University Press, 2011.

Adorno, Theodor W. *Gesammelte Schriften*. Frankfurt am Main: Suhrkamp, 1984.

——— *Introduction to the Sociology of Music*. Translated by E. B. Ashton [Ernst Basch]. New York: Continuum, 1989.

——— *Mahler: A Musical Physiognomy*. Translated by Edmund Jephcott. Chicago: University of Chicago Press, 1992.

Adorno, Theodor W. and Max Horkheimer. *Dialectic of Enlightenment*. Translated by John Cumming. London: Allen Lane, 1973.

Agawu, Kofi. 'How We Got Out of Analysis, and How to Get Back in Again'. *Music Analysis* 23 (2004): 267–86.

André, Naomi. *Black Opera: History, Power, Engagement*. Urbana: University of Illinois Press, 2018.

——— *Voicing Gender: Castrati, Travesti, and the Second Woman in Early Nineteenth-Century Italian Opera*. Bloomington: Indiana University Press, 2006.

Antheil, George. 'Opera: A Way Out'. *Modern Music* 11 (1934): 89–94.

Anzaldúa, Gloria. *Borderlands/La Frontera: The New Mestiza*. San Francisco: Aunt Lute Books, 1987.

Aoki, Keith. '(Intellectual) Property and Sovereignty: Notes Toward a Cultural Geography of Authorship'. *Stanford Law Review* 48 (1996): 1293–355.

Applegate, Celia. 'How German Is It? Nationalism and the Idea of Serious Music in the Early Nineteenth Century'. *19th-Century Music* 21 (1998): 274–96.

Attali, Jacques. *Noise: The Political Economy of Music*. Translated by Brian Massumi. Minneapolis: University of Minnesota Press, 2006.

Attfield, Nicholas. 'Symphonic Aspirations: German Music and Politics, 1900–1945 (review)'. *Music and Letters* 90 (2009): 296–8.

Bailey, Robert. 'Musical Language and Formal Design in Weill's Symphonies'. In *A Stranger Here Myself: Kurt Weill-Studien*, edited by Kim H. Kowalke and Horst Edler, 207–15. Hindelsheim: Georg Olms Verlag, 1993.

Ballantine, Christopher. *Twentieth Century Symphony*. London: Dobson, 1983.

Bauer, Marion. 'Rediscovering the Dynamic Line'. *Modern Music* 6 (1929): 28–31.

Bauman, Thomas. 'Mahler in a New Key: Genre and the "Resurrection" Finale'. *Journal of Musicology* 23 (2006): 468–85.

Beausang, Ita. *Ina Boyle (1889–1967): A Composer's Life, with an Essay on the Music by Séamas de Barra*. Cork: Cork University Press, 2018.

Bekker, Paul. *Beethoven*. 2nd ed. Berlin: Schuster & Loeffler, 1912.

Die Sinfonie von Beethoven bis Mahler. Berlin: Schuster & Loeffler, 1918.

Benjamin, Walter. *The Arcades Project*. Translated by Howard Eiland and Kevin McLaughlin. Cambridge, MA: Belknap Press, 1999.

'Critique of Violence'. In *Selected Writings*, edited by Marcus Bullock and Michael W. Jennings, 236–52. Vol. 1, *1913-1928*. Cambridge, MA: Belknap Press, 1996.

Besseler, Heinrich. 'Musik und Raum'. In *Musik und Bild: Festschrift Max Seiffert*, edited by Besseler, 151–60. Kassel: Bärenreiter, 1938.

Bhabha, Homi. 'Of Mimicry and Man: The Ambivalence of Colonial Discourse'. *October* 28 (1984): 125–33.

Biddle, Ian. 'The Gendered Eye: Music Analysis and the Scientific Outlook in German Early Romantic Music Theory'. In *Music Theory and Natural Order from the Renaissance to the Early Twentieth Century*, edited by Suzanne Clark and Alexander Rehding, 183–96. Cambridge: Cambridge University Press, 2001.

Blackmer, Corinne E. and Patricia Juliana Smith, eds. *En Travesti: Women, Gender Subversion, Opera*. New York: Columbia University Press, 1995.

Blake, William. *The Complete Poetry and Prose of William Blake*. Edited by David V. Erdman. Berkeley: University of California Press, 1982.

Bohlman, Philip V. 'Musicology as a Political Act'. *Journal of Musicology* 11 (1993), 411–36.

Bonds, Mark Evan. *Music as Thought: Listening to the Symphony in the Age of Beethoven*. Princeton: Princeton University Press, 2006.

Borrel, Eugène. *La symphonie*. Paris: Larousse, 1954.

Bourin, Odile, Pierrette Germain-David, Catherine Massip, and Raffi Ourgandjian, eds. *Elsa Barraine, une compositrice au XXème siècle*. Sampzon: Éditions Delatour, 2010.

Bowles, Paul. 'Forecast and Review: Letter from Mexico'. *Modern Music* 19 (1941): 36–9.

Let It Come Down. London: Penguin, 2000.

Brinkmann, Reinhold. 'The Compressed Symphony: On the Historical Content of Schoenberg's Op. 9'. Translated by Irene Zedlacher. In *Schoenberg and His World*, edited by Walter Frisch, 141–61. Princeton: Princeton University Press, 2012.

'The Distorted Sublime: Music and National Socialist Ideology – A Sketch'. In *Music and Nazism: Art under Tyranny, 1933–1945*, edited by Michael H. Kater and Albrecht Riethmüller, 43–63. Laaber: Laaber-Verlag, 2003.

Brown, A. Peter. *The Symphonic Repertoire*. 5 vols. Bloomington: Indiana University Press, 2002.

Brown, Rae Linda. 'Florence B. Price's "Negro Symphony"'. In *Temples for Tomorrow: Looking Back at the Harlem Renaissance*, edited by Geneviève Fabre and Michel Feith, 84–98. Bloomington: Indiana University Press, 2001.

The Heart of a Woman: The Life and Music of Florence B. Price. Urbana: University of Illinois Press, 2020.

'Lifting the Veil: The Symphonies of Florence B. Price'. In *Florence Price: Symphonies Nos. 1 and 3*, edited by Rae Linda Brown and Wayne Shirley, xv–lii. Middleton: AR Editions, 2008.

'Selected Orchestral Music of Florence B. Price (1888–1953) in the Context of Her Life and Work'. PhD thesis, Yale University, 1987.

Brückner, Martin and Hsuan L. Hsu, eds. *American Literary Geographies: Spatial Practice and Cultural Production, 1500–1900*. Newark, DE: University of Delaware Press, 2007.

Early American Cartographies. Chapel Hill: University of North Carolina Press, 2011.

Brüstle, Christa. 'Elizabeth Maconchy and Bela Bartók: "Ultra-Modernity" in British Music'. In *Elizabeth Maconchy: Music as Impassioned Argument*, edited by Christa Brüstle and Danielle Sofer, 124–49. Vienna: Universal Edition, 2018.

Brüstle, Christa and Danielle Sofer, eds. *Elizabeth Maconchy: Music as Impassioned Argument*. Vienna: Universal Edition, 2018.

Burnham, Scott G. *Beethoven Hero*. Princeton: Princeton University Press, 1995.

Busch, Sabine. *Hans Pfitzner und der Nationalsozialismus*. Stuttgart: J. B. Metzler, 2001.

Canarina, John. 'The American Symphony'. In *A Guide to the Symphony*, edited by Robert Layton, 402–24. Oxford: Oxford University Press, 1995.

Carlier, Matthieu. 'La forme dans les trois *Mouvements symphoniques* d'Arthur Honegger'. Thesis, Paris-Sorbonne University, 1992.

Carter, Marquese. 'The Poet and Her Song: Analyzing the Art Songs of Florence B. Price'. DMus thesis, Indiana University, 2018.

Chávez, Carlos. 'Technique and Inner Form'. *Modern Music* 5 (1928): 28–31.

Chude-Sokei, Louis. *The Sound of Culture: Diaspora and Black Technopoetics*. Middletown: Wesleyan University Press, 2016.

Citkowitz, Israel. 'Spring Concerts in New York'. *Modern Music* 9 (1932): 168–72.

Clague, Mark. 'The Industrial Evolution of the Arts: Chicago's Auditorium Building (1889–) as Cultural Machine'. *Opera Quarterly* 22 (2006): 477–511.

Clement, Catherine. *Opera, or the Undoing of Women*. Translated by Betsy Wing. Minneapolis: University of Minnesota Press, 1988.

Cogdell, Christina. 'The Futurama Recontextualized: Norman Bel Geddes's Eugenic "World of Tomorrow"'. *American Quarterly* 52 (2000): 193–245.

Cohen, Deborah and Maura O'Connor. *Comparison and History: Europe in Cross-National Perspective*. New York: Routledge, 2004.

Cook, Nicholas and Mark Everist, eds. *Rethinking Music*. Oxford: Oxford University Press, 1999.

Coombe, Rosemary J. 'Authorial Cartographies: Mapping Proprietary Borders in a Less-Than-Brave New World'. *Stanford Law Review* 48 (1996): 1357–66.

The Cultural Life of Intellectual Properties: Authorship, Appropriation, and the Law. Durham, NC: Duke University Press, 1998.

Copland, Aaron. 'Carlos Chávez: Mexican Composer'. *New Republic* 54 (1928): 322–3.

'Carlos Chávez: Mexican Composer'. In *American Composers on American Music: A Symposium*, edited by Henry Cowell, 102–6. Stanford: Stanford University Press, 1933.

Copland, Aaron and Vivian Perlis. *Copland, 1900–1942*. New York: St Martin's Press, 1984.

Covach, John. 'Popular Music, Unpopular Musicology'. In *Rethinking Music*, edited by Nicholas Cook and Mark Everist, 452–70. Oxford: Oxford University Press, 1999.

Cowell, Henry. 'Carlos Chávez'. *Pro Musica Quarterly* 7 (1928): 19–23.

Cox, David. 'The Symphony in France'. In *A Guide to the Symphony*, edited by Robert Layton, 193–220. Oxford: Oxford University Press, 1995.

Crary, Jonathan. *Suspension of Perception: Attention, Spectacle, and Modern Culture*. Cambridge, MA: MIT Press, 1999.

Crist, Elizabeth Bergman. *Music for the Common Man: Aaron Copland during the Depression and War*. Oxford: Oxford University Press, 2005.

Cusick, Suzanne. 'Gender, Musicology, and Feminism'. In *Rethinking Music*, edited by Nicholas Cook and Mark Everist, 471–98. Oxford: Oxford University Press, 1999.

Cuyler, Louise. *The Symphony*. New York: Harcourt Brace Jovanovich, 1973.

Daniels, Stephen. *Fields of Vision: Landscape Imagery and National Identity in England and the United States*. Cambridge: Polity Press, 1993.

Day, Timothy. *A Century of Recorded Music: Listening to Musical History*. New Haven: Yale University Press, 2000.

Delannoy, Marcel. *Honegger*. Edited by Geoffrey K. Spratt. Geneva: Slatkine, 1986.

DeLapp, Jennifer. 'Speaking to Whom? Modernism, Middlebrow and Copland's Short Symphony'. In *Copland Connotations: Studies and Interviews*, edited by Peter Dickenson, 85–102. Woodbridge: Boydell Press, 2002.

Delpar, Helen. 'Carlos Chávez and the Mexican "Vogue", 1925–40'. In *Carlos Chávez and His World*, edited by Leonora Saavedra, 204–19. Princeton: Princeton University Press, 2015.

The Enormous Vogue of Things Mexican: Cultural Relations between the United States and Mexico, 1920–1935. Tuscaloosa: University of Alabama Press, 1992.

Denning Michael. *The Cultural Front: The Laboring of American Culture in the Twentieth Century.* London: Verso, 2010.

Deruchie, Andrew. *The French Symphony at the Fin de Siècle: Style, Culture, and the Symphonic Tradition.* Rochester: University of Rochester Press, 2013.

Doherty, Thomas Patrick. *Pre-Code Hollywood: Sex, Immorality, and Insurrection in American Cinema, 1930–1934.* New York: Columbia University Press, 1999.

Dolan, Emily I. *The Orchestral Revolution: Haydn and the Technologies of Timbre.* Cambridge: Cambridge University Press, 2013.

Dowling, Linda C. *Hellenism and Homosexuality in Victorian Oxford.* Ithaca: Cornell University Press, 1994.

Drew, David. 'Kurt Weill'. In *The New Grove Dictionary of Music and Musicians*, edited by Stanley Sadie, 300–10. Vol. 20. London: Macmillan, 1980.

Du Bois, W. E. B. *The Souls of Black Folks.* Edited by David W. Blight and Robert Gooding-Williams. Boston: Bedford Books, 1997.

Dudenbostel, Ryan Keith. *The Bounding Line: Rhythm, Meter, and the Performance of Aaron Copland's* Short Symphony. DMus thesis, UCLA, 2014.

Ege, Samantha. 'The Aesthetics of Florence Price: Negotiating the Dissonances of a New World Nationalism'. PhD thesis, University of York, 2020.

'Chicago, the "City We Love to Call Home!": Intersectionality, Narrativity, and Locale in the Music of Florence Beatrice Price and Theodora Sturkow Ryder'. *American Music* 39 (2021): 1–40.

'Composing a Symphonist: Florence Price and the Hand of Black Women's Fellowship'. *Women and Music: A Journal of Gender and Culture* 24 (2020): 7–27.

Eidsheim, Nina Sun. 'Marian Anderson and "Sonic Blackness" in American Opera'. *American Quarterly* 63 (2011): 641–71.

Ellison, Ralph. *Invisible Man.* Milton Keynes: Penguin Random House, 2016.

Elsner, Jaś. 'Reflections on the "Greek Revolution" in Art: From Changes in Viewing to the Transformation of Subjectivity'. In *Rethinking Revolutions through Ancient Greece*, edited by Simon Goldhill and Robin Osborne, 68–95. Cambridge: Cambridge University Press, 2006.

Èrazmovič Pavčinskij, Sergej. *Simfoničeskoe tvorčestvo A. Oneggera.* Moskva: Sovetskij Kompozitor, 1972.

Erlmann, Veit. *Reason and Resonance: A History of Modern Aurality.* New York: Zone Books, 2010.

Ertan, Deniz. 'When Men and Mountains Meet: Ruggles, Whitman, and Their Landscapes'. *American Music* 27 (2009): 227–53.

Fabre, Geneviève and Michel Feith, eds. *Temples for Tomorrow: Looking Back at the Harlem Renaissance.* Bloomington: Indiana University Press, 2001.

Fanning, David. 'Symphonik 1930–1950: Gattungsgeschichtliche und analytische Beiträge' (book review). *Music and Letters* 85 (2004): 498–9.

'The Symphony in the Soviet Union'. In *A Guide to the Symphony*, edited by Robert Layton, 292–326. Oxford: Oxford University Press, 1995.

'The Symphony since Mahler: National and International Trends'. In *The Cambridge Companion to the Symphony*, edited by Julian Horton, 96–129. Cambridge: Cambridge University Press, 2013.

Farrah, Scott David. 'Signifyin(g): A Semiotic Analysis of Symphonic Works by William Grant Still, William Levi Dawson, and Florence B. Price'. PhD thesis, Florida State University, 2007.

Farwell, Arthur. 'Roy Harris'. *Musical Quarterly* 18 (1932): 18–32.

Fernández-Armesto, Felipe. *1492: The Year Our World Began*. London: Bloomsbury, 2010.

Finlayson, Iain. *Tangier: City of the Dream*. London: Flamingo, 1993.

Fischer, Jens Malte. 'The Very German Fate of a Composer: Hans Pfitzner'. In *Music and Nazism: Art under Tyranny, 1933–1945*, edited by Michael H. Kater and Albrecht Riethmüller, 75–89. Laaber: Laaber-Verlag, 2003.

Flinn, Caryl. *Strains of Utopia: Gender, Nostalgia, and Hollywood Film Music*. Princeton: Princeton University Press, 1992.

Floyd, Samuel A., ed. *Black Music in the Harlem Renaissance: A Collection of Essays*. New York: Greenwood, 1990.

Forkert, Annika. 'Beauty among Beasts? Maconchy, Walton, Tippett, and Britten'. In *Elizabeth Maconchy: Music as Impassioned Argument*, edited by Christa Brüstle and Danielle Sofer, 63–85. Vienna: Universal Edition, 2018.

Franklin, Peter. *Seeing through Music: Gender and Modernism in Classic Hollywood Film Scores*. Oxford: Oxford University Press, 2011.

Gaines, Kevin K. *Uplifting the Race: Black Leadership, Politics, and Culture in the Twentieth Century*. Durham, NC: University of North Carolina Press, 1996.

Gates, Paul W. *Free Homesteads for All Americans: The Homestead Act of 1862*. Washington: Civil War Centennial Commission, 1963.

Gervink, Manuel. *Die Symphonie in Deutschland und Österreich in der Zeit zwischen den beiden Weltkriegen*. Regensburg: Bosse, 1984.

Gilliam, Bryan. 'The Annexation of Anton Bruckner: Nazi Revisionism and the Politics of Appropriation'. *Musical Quarterly* 78 (1994): 584–604.

Gorbman, Claudia. *Unheard Melodies: Narrative Film Music*. Bloomington: Indiana University Press, 1987.

Goss, Glenda Dawn. *Jean Sibelius and Olin Downes: Music, Friendship, Criticism*. Boston: Northeastern University Press, 1995.

Grimley, Daniel M. *Grieg: Music, Landscape, and Norwegian Identity*. Woodbridge: Boydell, 2006.

'Landscape and Distance: Vaughan Williams and the Modernist Pastoral'. In *Music and British Modernism, 1890–1930*, edited by Matthew Riley and Paul Rodmell, 147–74. Aldershot: Ashgate, 2010.

'*Symphony/Antiphony*: Formal Strategies in the Twentieth-Century Symphony'. In *The Cambridge Companion to the Symphony*, edited by Julian Horton, 285–310. Cambridge: Cambridge University Press, 2013.

Gumbrecht, Hans Ulrich. *In 1926: Living at the Edge of Time*. Cambridge, MA: Harvard University Press, 1997.

Habermas, Jürgen. *The Structural Transformation of the Public Sphere: An Inquiry into a Category of Bourgeois Society*. Translated by Thomas Burger and Frederick Lawrence. Cambridge, MA: MIT Press, 1989.

Halbreich, Harry, *Arthur Honegger*. Edited by Reinhard G. Pauly. Translated by Roger Nichols. Portland: Amadeus Press, 1999.

Hartman, Saidiya V. *Scenes of Subjugation: Terror, Slavery, and Self-Making in Nineteenth-Century America*. New York: Oxford University Press, 1997.

Edwards, Brent Hayes. *Epistrophies: Jazz and the Literary Imagination*. Cambridge, MA: Harvard University Press, 2017.

Hecimovich, Gregg A. '"With Pale Blake I Write Tintingface": The Bounding Line of James Joyce's Aesthetic'. *James Joyce Quarterly* 36 (1999): 889–904.

Heiber, Helmut, ed. *Goebbels Reden 1932–1945*. Düsseldorf: Gondrom, 1991.

Heidegger, Martin. *Being and Time*. Translated by John Macquarrie and Edward Robinson. Oxford: Blackwell, 1967.

Heinsheimer, Hans. 'Nightmare in Germany'. *Modern Music* 10 (1933): 115–17.

Heldt, Guido. 'Erste Symphonien: Britten, Walton und Tippett'. In *Symphonik 1930–1950: Gattungsgeschichtliche und analytische Beiträge*, edited by Wolfgang Osthoff and Giselher Schubert, 84–108. Mainz: Schott, 2003.

Hepokoski, James. 'Back and Forth from Egmont: Beethoven, Mozart, and the Nonresolving Recapitulation'. *19th-Century Music* 25 (2001–2): 127–54.

'Beethoven Reception: The Symphonic Tradition'. In *The Cambridge History of Nineteenth-Century Music*, edited by Jim Samson, 424–59. Cambridge: Cambridge University Press, 2002.

'Beyond the Sonata Principle'. *Journal of the American Musicological Society* 55 (2002): 91–154.

'Masculine. Feminine. Are Current Readings of Sonata Form in Terms of a "Masculine" and "Feminine" Dichotomy Exaggerated? James Hepokoski Argues for a More Subtle Approach to the Politics of Musical Form'. *Musical Times* 135 (1994): 494–9.

Hepokoski, James and Warren Darcy. *Elements of Sonata Theory: Norms, Types, and Deformations in the Late-Eighteenth-Century Sonata*. New York: Oxford University Press, 2006.

Hess, Carol A. *Representing the Good Neighbor: Music, Difference, and the Pan American Dream*. New York: Oxford University Press, 2013.

Hill, Ralph. *The Symphony*. Harmondsworth: Penguin Books, 1949.

Hinton, Stephen. *The Idea of Gebrauchsmusik: A Study of Musical Aesthetics in the Weimar Republic (1919–1933), with Particular Reference to the Works of Paul Hindemith*. New York: Garland, 1989.

Weill's Musical Theater: Stages of Reform. Berkeley: University of California Press, 2012.

Hoffmann, E. T. A. *E. T. A. Hoffmann's Musical Writings:* Kreisleriana, The Poet and the Composer, *Music Criticism*. Edited by David Charlton and Martyn Clarke. Cambridge: Cambridge University Press, 1989.

Holden, Raymond. *Richard Strauss: A Musical Life*. New Haven, CT: Yale University Press, 2011.

Horton, Julian, ed. *The Cambridge Companion to the Symphony*. Cambridge: Cambridge University Press, 2013.

Ignatiev, Noel. *How the Irish Became White*. New York: Routledge, 2009.

Illies, Florian. *1913: Der Sommer des Jahrhunderts*. Frankfurt am Main: S. Fischer, 2012.

1913: The Year before the Storm. Translated by Shaun Whiteside and Jamie Lee Searle. Brooklyn: Melville House, 2013.

Ingraham, Mary, Joseph So, and Roy Moodley, eds. *Opera in a Multicultural World: Coloniality, Culture, Performance*. New York: Routledge, 2016.

Jackson, Barbara Garvey. 'Florence Price, Composer'. *Black Perspective in Music* 5 (1977): 30–43.

Jackson, Kevin. *Constellations of Genius: 1922: Modernism Year One*. London: Hutchinson, 2012.

Jarman, Douglas. *Kurt Weill: An Illustrated Biography*. London: Orbis, 1982.

Johnson, Julian. *Mahler's Voices: Expression and Irony in the Songs and Symphonies*. New York: Oxford University Press, 2009.

Webern and the Transformation of Nature. Cambridge: Cambridge University Press, 1999.

Johnson, Stephen. 'After Mahler: The Central European Symphony in the Twentieth Century'. In *A Guide to the Symphony*, edited by Robert Layton, 382–401. Oxford: Oxford University Press, 1995.

Joyce, James. *A Portrait of the Artist as a Young Man*. Edited by Seamus Deane. Harmondsworth: Penguin Books, 2000.

Jürgens, Birgit. *'Deutsche Musik': Das Verhältnis von Ästhetik und Politik bei Hans Pfitzner*. Hildesheim: George Olms Verlag, 2009.

Kahan, Sylvia. *Music's Modern Muse: A Life of Winnaretta Singer, Princesse de Polignac*. Rochester: University of Rochester Press, 2003.

Kalinak, Kathryn. *Settling the Score: Music and the Classical Hollywood Film*. Madison: University of Wisconsin Press, 1992.

Kallis, Aristotle A., ed. *The Fascism Reader*. London: Routledge, 2003.

Kater, Michael H. *Composers of the Nazi Era: Eight Portraits*. New York: Oxford University Press, 2000.

Kater, Michael H. and Albrecht Riethmüller, eds. *Music and Nazism: Art under Tyranny, 1933–1945*. Laaber: Laaber-Verlag, 2003.

Kennedy, Michael. *Richard Strauss: Man, Musician, Enigma*. Cambridge: Cambridge University Press, 1999.

The Works of Ralph Vaughan Williams. London: Oxford University Press, 1964.

Koestenbaum, Wayne. *The Queen's Throat: Opera, Homosexuality, and the Mystery of Desire*. London: Penguin, 1994.

Kolb-Neuhaus, Roberto. 'Silvestre Revuelta's *Colorines* vis-à-vis US Musical Modernism: A Dialogue of the Deaf?'. *Latin American Music Review/ Revista de Música Latinoamericana* 36 (2015): 194–230.

Konrad, Ulrich. 'Die *Sinfonie liturgique* von Arthur Honegger und die Tradition der Sinfonie um 1945'. *Musik-Konzepte* 135 (2007): 25–44.

Korstvedt, Benjamin M. 'Reading Music Criticism beyond the Fin-de-Siècle Vienna Paradigm'. *Musical Quarterly* 94 (2011): 156–210.

Kowalke, Kim H. *Kurt Weill in Europe*. Michigan: Ann Arbor, 1979.

    'Kurt Weill, Modernism, and Popular Culture: "Öffentlichkeit als Stil"', *Modernism/Modernity* 2 (1995): 27–69.

Kowalke, Kim H. and Lys Symonnette, trans. and eds. *Speak Low (When You Speak Love): The Letters of Kurt Weill and Lotte Lenya*. London: Hamish Hamilton, 1996.

Kracauer, Siegfried. *The Mass Ornament: Weimar Essays*. Translated and edited by Thomas Y. Levin. Cambridge, MA: Harvard University Press, 1995.

Kramer, Lawrence. *Classical Music and Postmodern Knowledge*. Berkeley: University of California Press, 1995.

Krones, Hartmut. *Die österreichische Symphonie im 20. Jahrhundert*. Vienna: Böhlau, 2005.

    'Die österreichische Symphonik in den 1930er und 1940er Jahren'. In *Symphonik 1930–1950: Gattungsgeschichtliche und analytische Beiträge*, edited by Wolfgang Osthoff and Giselher Schubert, 28–40. Mainz: Schott, 2003.

Kuhnt, Christian. '"Das Gegenteil von Pastorale": Anmerkungen zu Kurt Weills 2. Sinfonie'. In *Exilmusik: Komposition während der NS-Zeit*, edited by Friedrich Geiger and Thomas Schäfer, 315–32. Hamburg: Von Bockel, 1999.

Kurth, Ernst. *Selected Writings*. Translated and edited by Lee A. Rothfarb. Cambridge: Cambridge University Press, 1991.

Kutschke, Beate and Barley Norton, eds. *Music and Protest in 1968*. Cambridge: Cambridge University Press, 2013.

Kyle Stanford, P. 'August Weissman's Theory of the Germ-Plasm and the Problem of Unconceived Alternatives'. *History and Philosophy of Life Sciences* 27 (2005): 163–99.

Lanza, Michael L. *Agrarianism and Reconstruction Politics: The Southern Homestead Act*. Baton Rouge: Louisiana State University Press, 1990.

Latour, Bruno. *Reassembling the Social: An Introduction to Actor-Network Theory*. Oxford: Oxford University Press, 2005.

Layton, Robert, ed. *A Guide to the Symphony*. Oxford: Oxford University Press, 1995.

Le Vahr, Maurice. 'Música y Músicos'. *Revista de Revistas: El Semanario Nacional* 24, no. 1281 (2 December 1934): 4.

Levi, Erik. *Mozart and the Nazis: How the Third Reich Abused a Cultural Icon*. New Haven, CT: Yale University Press, 2010.

Music in the Third Reich. Basingstoke: Macmillan, 1994.

Levitz, Tamara. *Modernist Mysteries: Perséphone*. New York: Oxford University Press, 2012.

'Putting Kurt Weill in His Historical Place: The *New Grove* Articles'. *Kurt Weill Newsletter* 20 (2002): 4–9.

Levy, Beth E. *Frontier Figures: American Music and the Mythology of the American West*. Berkeley: University of California Press, 2012.

'Frontier Figures: American Music and the Mythology of the American West, 1895–1945'. PhD thesis, University of California, Berkeley, 2002.

'Roy Harris and the Crisis of Consonance'. In *Tonality 1900–1950: Concept and Practice*, edited by Felix Wörner, Ullrich Scheideler, and Philip Ernst Rupprecht, 247–60. Stuttgart: Franz Steiner Verlag, 2012.

'"The White Hope of American Music"; or, How Roy Harris Became Western'. *American Music* 19 (2001): 131–67.

Locke, Alain LeRoy. *The Negro and His Music*. Port Washington, NY: Kennikat Press, 1968.

Locke, Ralph P. *Musical Exoticism: Images and Reflections*. Cambridge: Cambridge University Press, 2009.

Lookingbill, Brad D. *Dustbowl, USA: Depression America and the Ecological Imagination, 1929–1941*. Athens, OH: Ohio University Press, 2001.

Lovisa, Fabian R. *Musikkritik im Nationalsozialismus: Die Rolle deutschsprachiger Musikzeitschriften 1920–1945*. Laaber: Laaber-Verlag, 1993.

Lütteken, Laurenz. *Sinfonie als Bekenntnis: Zürcher Festspiel-Symposium 2010*. Kassel: Baerenreiter, 2011.

MacDonald, Hugh. *Music in 1853*. Woodbridge: Boydell Press, 2012.

Maconchy, Elizabeth. *Ina Boyle: An Appreciation with a Select List of Her Music*. Dublin: Dolmen Press, 1974.

Madrid, Alejandro. *Sounds of the Modern Nation: Music, Culture, and Ideas in Post-Revolutionary Mexico*. Philadelphia: Temple, 2009.

Transnational Encounters: Music and Performance at the US-Mexico Border. New York: Oxford University Press, 2011.

Maillard, Jean. *Les symphonies d'Arthur Honegger*. Edited by Jacques Nahoum. Paris: A. Leduc, 1974.

Mandel, Leon. *Driven: The American Four-Wheeled Love Affair*. New York: Stein and Day, 1977.

Mannheim, Karl. 'Ideology and Utopia'. In *The Weimar Republic Sourcebook*, edited by Anton Kaes, Martin Jay, and Edward Dimendberg, 297–300. Berkeley: University of California Press, 1994. Originally published as *Ideologie und Utopie*. Bonn: Cohen, 1929.

Marx, Leo. *The Machine in the Garden: Technology and the Pastoral Ideal in America*. Oxford: Oxford University Press, 2000.

Mathers, Daniel E. 'Closure in the Sextet and Short Symphony by Aaron Copland: A Study Using Facsimiles and Printed Editions'. MM thesis, Florida State University, 1989.

Matthews, David. 'Copland and Stravinsky'. *Tempo* 95 (1971): 10–14.

Mawer, Deborah. '"Dancing on the Edge of the Volcano": French Music in the 1930s'. In *French Music since Berlioz*, edited by Richard Langham Smith and Caroline Potter, 249–80. Aldershot: Ashgate, 2006.

May, Elaine Tyler, *Homeward Bound: American Families in the Cold War*. New York: Basic Books, 1988.

McClary, Susan. 'Constructions of Subjectivity in Schubert's Music'. In *Queering the Pitch: The New Gay and Lesbian Musicology*, edited by Philip Brett, Elizabeth Wood, and Gary C. Thomas, 205–33. Routledge: New York, 2006.

———. *Feminine Endings: Music, Gender, and Sexuality*. Minneapolis: University of Minnesota Press, 2002.

———. 'The World According to Taruskin' (review-article). *Music and Letters* 87 (2006): 408–15.

McMahon, Jennifer L. and B. Steve Csaki. *The Philosophy of the Western*. Lexington: University Press of Kentucky, 2010.

McPhee, Colin. 'Forecast and Review'. *Modern Music* 13 (1936): 41–6.

Mercier, Richard. *The Songs of Hans Pfitzner: A Guide and Study*. Westport: Greenwood Press, 1998.

Merrill, Karen R. *Public Lands and Political Meaning: Ranchers, the Government, and the Property between Them*. Berkeley: University of California Press, 2002.

Meyer, Felix, Carol J. Oja, Wolfgang Rathert, and Anne C. Shreffler, eds. *Crosscurrents: American and European Music in Interaction, 1900–2000*. Woodbridge: Boydell Press, 2014.

Meyer, Michael. *The Politics of Music in the Third Reich*. New York: Peter Lang, 1993.

Micznik, Vera. 'Music and Narrative Revisited: Degrees of Narrativity in Beethoven and Mahler'. *Journal of the Royal Musical Association* 126 (2001): 193–249.

Mignolo, Walter D. *The Darker Side of Western Modernity: Global Futures, Decolonial Options*. Durham, NC: Duke University Press, 2011.

Mignolo, Walter D. and Catherine E. Walsh, *On Decoloniality: Concepts, Analytics, Praxis*. Durham, NC: Duke University Press, 2018.

Miller, Jeffrey, ed. *In Touch: The Letters of Paul Bowles*. New York: Farrar, Straus and Girouz, 1994.

Moos, Dan. *Outside America: Race, Ethnicity, and the Role of the American West in National Belonging*. Hanover, NH: University Press of New England, 2005.

Moraña, Mabel, Enrique D. Dussel, and Carlos A. Jáuregui, eds. *Coloniality at Large: Latin America and the Postcolonial Debate*. Durham, NC: Duke University Press, 2008.

Morgan, Robert P. 'The Concept of Unity and Musical Analysis'. *Music Analysis* 22 (2003): 7–50.

Mosch, Ulrich. '(Kein) Platz in der Geschichte? Das Honegger-Bild in der Musikgeschichtsschreibung'. In *Arthur Honegger: Werk und Rezeption*, edited by Peter Jost, 15–35. Bern: Peter Lang, 2009.

Müller, Sven Oliver. 'Political Pleasures with Old Emotions? Performances of the Berlin Philharmonic in the Second World War'. *International Review of the Aesthetics and Sociology of Music* 43 (2012): 35–52.

Müller-Berg, Sandra. 'Ultramodern versus neoklassizistisch: Ruth Crawfords *Three Songs* und Aaron Coplands *Short Symphony*'. In *Symphonik 1930–1950: Gattungsgeschichtliche und analytische Beiträge*, edited by Wolfgang Osthoff and Giselher Schubert, 58–83. Mainz: Schott, 2003.

Mundy, Rachel. 'The "League of Jewish Composers" and American Music'. *Musical Quarterly* 96 (2013): 50–99.

Navakas, Michele Currie. 'Island Nation: Mapping Florida, Revising America'. *Early American Studies: An Interdisciplinary Journal* 11 (2013): 243–71.

Nietzsche, Friedrich. *The Case of Wagner, Nietzsche Contra Wagner, and Selected Aphorisms*. Translated by Anthony M. Ludovici. 3rd edition. Gloucester Dodo Press, 2008.

Notley, Margaret. *Lateness and Brahms: Music and Culture in the Twilight of Viennese Liberalism*. Oxford: Oxford University Press, 2007.

——— '"Volksconcerte" in Vienna and Late Nineteenth-Century Ideology of the Symphony'. *Journal of the American Musicological Society* 50 (1997): 421–53.

Ohta, Misako. 'Kurt Weill und Gustav Mahler: Der Komponist Weill als Nachfolger Mahlers'. *Gakushūin Daigaku kenkyū ronshū* 2 (1998): 39–58.

Oja, Carol J. *Making Music Modern: New York in the 1920s*. New York: Oxford University Press, 2000.

Onuf, Peter S. *Statehood and Union: A History of the Northwest Ordinance*. Bloomington: Indiana University Press, 1987.

Orbón, Julián. 'Las Sinfonías de Carlos Chávez (II Parte)'. *Pauta: Cuadernos de teoría y crítica musical* 6 no. 22 (1987): 81–91.

Osthoff, Wolfgang and Giselher Schubert, eds. *Symphonik 1930–1950: Gattungsgeschichtliche und analytische Beiträge*. Mainz: Schott, 2003.

Painter, Karen. *Symphonic Aspirations: German Music and Politics, 1900–1945*. Cambridge, MA: Harvard University Press, 2007.

Painter, Nell Irvin. *The History of White People*. New York; London: W. W. Norton, 2010.

Palm-Beulich, Helga-Maria. *Süddeutsche Komponisten im 20. Jahrhundert: Verzeichnis zeitgenössischer symphonischer Werke*. Munich: Bayerischer Musikrat, 1992.

Pederson, Sanna. 'A. B. Marx, Berlin Concert Life, and German National Identity'. *19th-Century Music* 18 (1994): 87–108.

Pelletier, Yvonne Elizabeth. 'False Promises and Real Estate: Land Speculation and Millennial Maps in Herman Melville's *Confidence-Man*'. In *American Literary Geographies: Spatial Practice and Cultural Production, 1500–1900*, edited by Martin Brückner and Hsuan L. Hsu, 191–205. Newark, DE: University of Delaware Press, 2007.

Pergher, Roberta and Guilia Albanese. 'Historians, Fascism, and Italian Society: Mapping the Limits of Consent'. In *In the Society of Fascists: Acclamation, Acquiescence, and Agency in Mussolini's Italy*, edited by Roberta Pergher and Guilia Albanese, 1–28. New York: Palgrave Macmillan, 2012.

Pfitzner, Hans Erich. *Die neue Aesthetik der musikalischen Impotenz*. Munich: Verlag der Süddeutschen Monatshefte, 1920.

Briefe. Edited by Bernhard Adamy. Tutzing: Hans Schneider, 1991.

Piekut, Benjamin. 'Actor-Networks in Music History: Clarifications and Critiques'. *Twentieth-Century Music* 11 (2014): 191–215.

Experimentalism Otherwise: The New York Avant-Garde and Its Limits. Berkeley: University of California Press, 2011.

Pierce, Jason E. *Making the White Man's West: Whiteness and the Creation of the American West*, Boulder: University Press of Colorado, 2016.

Pistorius, Juliana M. 'Inhabiting Whiteness: The Eoan Group *La Traviata*, 1956'. *Cambridge Opera Journal* 31 (2019): 63–84.

Pollack, Howard. 'Aaron Copland, Carlos Chávez, and Silvestre Revueltas'. In *Carlos Chávez and His World*, edited by Leonora Saavedra, 99–110. Princeton: Princeton University Press, 2015.

Aaron Copland: The Life and Work of an Uncommon Man. London: Faber and Faber, 1999.

'Aaron Copland's Short Symphony and the Challenge to Human Supervision and Control in Music'. *Journal of New Music Research* 31 (2002): 201–10.

Postgate, Raymond. *Story of a Year: 1848*. London: J. Cape, 1955.

Potter, Pamela M. *Most German of the Arts: Musicology and Society from the Weimar Republic to the End of Hitler's Reich*. New Haven, CT: Yale University Press, 1998.

'Richard Strauss and the National Socialists: The Debate and Its Relevance'. In *Richard Strauss: New Perspectives on the Composer and His Work*, edited by Bryan Gilliam, 93–113. Durham, CT: Duke University Press, 1992.

Prendergast, Roy M. *Film Music, a Neglected Art: A Critical Study of Music in Films*. New York: W. W. Norton, 1977.

Rauchhaupt, Ursula von, *The Symphony*. London: Thames and Hudson, 1973.

Rehding, Alexander, *Music and Monumentality: Commemoration and Wonderment in Nineteenth-Century Germany*. Oxford: Oxford University Press, 2009.

Rico, Monica. *Nature's Noblemen: Transatlantic Masculinities and the Nineteenth-Century American West*. New Haven, CT: Yale University Press, 2013.

Robertson, Malcolm D. 'Roy Harris's Symphonies: An Introduction (I)', *Tempo* 207 (1998): 9–14.

Roediger, David R. *The Wages of Whiteness: Race and the Making of the American Working Class*. Revised edition. London: Verso, 2007.

Roosevelt, Franklin D. *Addresses and Messages of Franklin D. Roosevelt: Compiled from Official Sources, Intended to Present the Chronological Development of the Foreign Policy of the United States from the Announcement of the Good Neighbor Policy in 1933, Including the War Declarations*. London: His Majesty's Stationary Office, 1943.

Rosenfeld, Paul. *By Way of Art: Criticisms of Music, Literature, Painting, Sculpture, and the Dance*. New York: Coward-McCann, 1928; reprinted Freeport, NY: Books for Libraries Press, 1967.

Rotosky, Fritz. 'Was ist Kultur'. *Neue Literatur* (July 1933): 380.

Ryding, Erik S. and Rebecca Pechefsky. *Bruno Walter: A World Elsewhere*. New Haven, CT: Yale University Press, 2001.

Saavedra, Leonora. 'Carlos Chávez y la Construcción de una Alteridad Estratégica'. In *Diálogo de Resplandores: Carlos Chávez y Silvestre Revueltas*, edited by Yael Bitrán and Ricardo Miranda, 125–36. Mexico City: Consejo Nacional para la Cultura y las Artes, 2002.

'Carlos Chávez's Polysemic Style: Constructing the National, Seeking the Cosmopolitan'. *Journal of the American Musicological Society* 68 (2015): 99–149.

'Preface'. In *Carlos Chávez and His World*, edited by Leonora Saavedra, ix–xv. Princeton: Princeton University Press, 2015.

Saavedra, Leonora, ed. *Carlos Chávez and His World*. Princeton: Princeton University Press, 2015.

Samson, Jim, 'Analysis in Context'. In *Rethinking Music*, edited by Nicholas Cook and Mark Everist, 35–54. Oxford: Oxford University Press, 1999.

'Nations and Nationalism'. In *The Cambridge History of Nineteenth-Century Music*, edited by Jim Samson, 568–600. Cambridge: Cambridge University Press, 2001.

Sanders, Ronald. *The Days Grow Short: The Life and Music of Kurt Weill*. New York: Limelight Editions, 1985.

Schaarwächter, Jürgen. *Die britische Sinfonie 1914–1945*. Cologne: Dohr, 1995.

Schebera, Jürgen. 'Amsterdam, 11. Oktober 1934: Einiges zur Uraufführung von Weills *Sinfonie Nr. 2*'. In *Kurt Weill-Studien*, edited by Nils Grosch, Joachim Lucchesi, and Jürgen Schebera, 109–18. Stuttgart: M & P, Verlag für Wissenschaft und Forschung, 1996.

Kurt Weill: An Illustrated Life. Translated by Caroline Murphy. New Haven, CT: Yale University Press, 1995.

Schenbeck, Lawrence. *Racial Uplift and American Music, 1878–1943*. Jackson: University of Mississippi Press, 2012.

Schering, Arnold. 'Über den Begriff des Monumentalen in der Musik'. In *Von großen Meistern in der Musik*, 7–44. Leipzig: Breitkopf und Härtel, 1935.

Schoenberg, Arnold. *The Musical Idea and the Logic, Technique, and Art of Its Presentation.* Translated and edited by Patricia Carpenter and Severine Neff. New York: Columbia University Press, 1995.

Scruton, Roger. *The Aesthetics of Music.* Oxford: Oxford University Press, 1999.

Seiler, Cotton. *Republic of Drivers: A Cultural History of Automobility in America.* Chicago: University of Chicago Press, 2008.

Shadle, Douglas W. *Antonín Dvořák's New World Symphony.* Oxford: Oxford University Press, 2021.

    Orchestrating the Nation: The Nineteenth-Century American Symphonic Enterprise. New York: Oxford University Press, 2016.

Shapiro, James. *A Year in the Life of William Shakespeare: 1599.* London: Faber and Faber, 2005.

Simpson, Robert, ed. *The Symphony: Elgar to the Present Day.* Aylesbury: Penguin Books, 1967.

    The Symphony: Haydn to Dvořák. Aylesbury: Penguin Books, 1966.

Slonimsky, Nicolas. 'Roy Harris'. *Musical Quarterly* 33 (1947): 17–37.

Small, Christopher. *Musicking: The Meanings of Performing and Listening.* Hanover, NH: University Press of New England, 1998.

Solie, Ruth A. 'What Do Feminists Want? A Reply to Pieter van den Toorn'. *Journal of Musicology* 9 (1991): 399–410.

Spratt, Geoffrey K. *The Music of Arthur Honegger.* Cork: Cork University Press, 1987.

Squire, Michael. *The Art of the Body: Antiquity and Its Legacy.* New York: Oxford University Press, 2011.

Stallings, Stephanie N. 'The Pan/American Modernisms of Carlos Chávez and Henry Cowell'. In *Carlos Chávez and His World*, edited by Leonora Saavedra, 28–45. Princeton: Princeton University Press, 2015.

Stargardt-Wolff, Edith. *Wegbereiter grosser Musiker.* Berlin: Bote & G. Bock, 1954.

Stansbury-O'Donnell, Mark D. 'Desirability and the Body'. In *A Companion to Greek and Roman Sexualities*, edited by Thomas K. Hubbard, 33–55. Chichester: Wiley-Blackwell, 2014.

Steblin, Rita. *A History of Key Characteristics in the Eighteenth and Early Nineteenth Centuries.* Rochester: University of Rochester Press, 1996.

Stedman, Preston. *The Symphony.* Englewood Cliffs, NJ: Prentice-Hall, 1979.

Stehman, Dan. *Roy Harris: A Bio-Bibliography.* New York: Greenwood Press, 1991.

    'The Symphonies of Roy Harris: An Analytical Study of the Linear Materials and of Related Works'. PhD thesis, University of Southern California, 1973.

Steinbeck, John. *The Grapes of Wrath.* London: Penguin, 2000.

Steinbeck, Wolfram and Christoph von Blumröder. *Die Sinfonie im 19. und 20. Jahrhundert.* Laaber: Laaber-Verlag, 2002.

Steinberg, Michael. *The Symphony: A Listener's Guide.* New York: Oxford University Press, 1995.

Sterling, Bryan B. *Forgotten Eagle: Wiley Post, America's Heroic Aviation Pioneer.* New York: Carrol and Graf, 2001.

Stewart, Jacqueline. *Migrating to the Movies: Cinema and Black Urban Modernity*. Berkeley: University of California Press, 2005.

Still, Judith Anne. *William Grant Still: A Bio-Bibliography*. Westport, CT: Greenwood, 1996.

Stuckenschmidt, H. H. *Twentieth Century Composers*. Vol. 2, *Germany and Central Europe*. London: Weidenfeld and Nicolson, 1970.

Subotnik, Rose Rosengard. *Developing Variations: Style and Ideology in Western Music*. Minneapolis: University of Minnesota Press, 1991.

Tadday, Ulrich. '"Ziemlich unabhängig von herkömmlicher Ästhetik": Arthur Honeggers *Symphonie Liturgique* und Sinfonie *Deliciae Basilienses* zwischen Innovation und Affirmation'. *Musik-Konzepte* 135 (2007): 45–56.

Talbot, Michael. *The Finale in Western Instrumental Music*. Oxford: Oxford University Press, 2001.

Tappolet, Willy. *Arthur Honegger*. Zurich: Atlantis, 1954.

    Arthur Honegger. Translated by Claude Tappolet. Neuchâtel: Editions de la Baconière, 1957.

Taruskin, Richard. *The Oxford History of Western Music*. Vol. 3, *The Nineteenth Century*. Oxford: Oxford University Press, 2005.

    The Oxford History of Western Music. Vol. 4, *The Early Twentieth Century*. Oxford: Oxford University Press, 2005.

Tawa, Nicholas E. *The Great American Symphony: Music, the Depression, and War*. Bloomington: Indiana University Press, 2009.

Taylor, Ronald. *Kurt Weill: Composer in a Divided World*. London: Simon & Schuster, 1991.

Vaget, Hans Rudolf. '"Der gute, alte Antisemitismus": Hans Pfitzner, Bruno Walter und der Holocaust'. In *Bruckner-Probleme: Internationales Kolloquium 7.–9. Oktober 1996 in Berlin*, edited by Albrecht Riethmüller, 215–32. Stuttgart: Franz Steiner, 1999.

Van den Toorn, Pieter. 'Politics, Feminism, and Contemporary Music Theory'. *Journal of Musicology* 9 (1991): 275–99.

Van Nuys, Frank. *Americanizing the West: Race, Immigrants, and Citizenship, 1890–1930*. Lawrence: University Press of Kansas, 2002.

Vilar-Payá, Luisa. 'Chávez and the Autonomy of the Musical Work: The Piano Music'. In *Carlos Chávez and His World*, edited by Leonora Saavedra, 112–33. Princeton: Princeton University Press, 2015.

Vogel, Peter. *Hans Pfitzner: Streichquartett Cis-Moll Op. 36*. Munich: Fink Verlag, 1991.

Von Glahn, Denise, *Music and the Skillful Listener: American Women Compose the Natural World*. Bloomington: Indiana University Press, 2013.

    The Sounds of Place: Music and the American Cultural Landscape. Boston: Northeastern University Press, 2003.

Voss, Egon. '*Pacific 231*: Reine Programmemusik oder doch ein Stück absoluter Musik?'. In *Arthur Honegger: Werk und Rezeption*, edited by Peter Jost, 199–212. Bern: Peter Lang, 2009.

Vout, Caroline. 'Antinous, Archaeology, and History'. *Journal of Roman Studies* 95 (2005): 80–96.

Walter, Keith John. 'Rhythmic and Contrapuntal Structures in the Music of Arthur Honegger'. PhD thesis, Eastman School of Music, University of Rochester, 1997.

Walter, Michael. *Richard Strauss und seine Zeit*. Laaber: Laaber-Verlag, 2000.

Wamlek-Junk, Elisabeth. *Hans Pfitzner und Wien: Sein Briefwechsel mit Victor Junk und andere Dokumente*. Tutzing: Hans Schneider, 1986.

Waters, Sarah. '"The Most Famous Fairy in History": Antinous and Homosexual Fantasy'. *Journal of the History of Sexuality* 6 (1995): 194–230.

Watkins, Holly. *Metaphors of Depth in German Musical Thought: From E. T. A. Hoffmann to Arnold Schoenberg*. Cambridge: Cambridge University Press, 2011.

Weingartner, Felix. *Die Sinfonie nach Beethoven*. 4th edition. Leipzig: Breitkopf & Härtel, 1926.

Weissman, August. *The Germ-Plasm: A Theory of Hereditary*. Translated by W. Newton Parker and Harriet Rönnfeldt. London: W. Scott, 1883.

Whittall, Arnold. 'Autonomy/Heteronomy: The Contexts of Musicology'. In *Rethinking Music*, edited by Nicholas Cook and Mark Everist, 73–101. Oxford: Oxford University Press, 1999.

———. *Music since the First World War*. London: Dent, 1977.

———. *Musical Composition in the Twentieth Century*. Oxford: Oxford University Press, 1999.

Williamson, John. *The Music of Hans Pfitzner*. Oxford: Clarendon Press, 1992.

Winckler, Andreas Eberhard. 'The Nazis in Mexico: Mexico and the Reich in the Prewar Period, 1936–1939'. PhD thesis, University of Texas at Austin, 1983.

Witter, Daniel. *The Settler's Guide to the Entry of Public Lands in Colorado*. Denver: News Printing Company, 1882.

Woods, Gregory. *Homintern: How Gay Culture Liberated the Modern World*. New Haven, CT: Yale University Press, 2016.

Wulf, Joseph. *Musik im Dritten Reich: Eine Dokumentation*. Gütersloh: Rowohlt, 1966.

Zehrer, Hans. 'The Revolution of the Intelligentsia'. In *The Weimar Republic Sourcebook*, edited by Anton Kaes, Martin Jay, and Edward Dimendberg, 295–97. Berkeley: University of California Press, 1994. Originally published as 'Die Revolution der Intelligenz'. *Die Tat* 21 (1929): 486–507.

Index

Page numbers for illustrations are in *italics*.

253

Printed by Printforce, United Kingdom